V
DRE

MW00569575

"A dazzling piece of cultural reportage."
—Peter Gzowski, CBC Radio "Morningside"

"[Kingwell's] ability to analyze thorny issues with lucidity and wit makes *Dreams of Millennium* highly readable and stimulating...[a] clear-eyed overview of our culture, supplied by a man of refreshing independence of mind."
—Philip Marchand, *The Toronto Star*

"[O]ne of the most impressive features of Kingwell's 'report from a culture on the brink' is the combination of charm and shrewdness with which he conducts this guided tour...an engaging grabbag of evidence about mounting cultural anxiety as we approach the year 2000."
—Stan Persky, *The Globe and Mail*

"*Dreams of Millennium* excels at describing what seems to me to be the defining sensation of the 1990s, that of depletion, exhaustion, an emptying out of meaning...What this brilliant book shows us is the ways we are trying to deal with the world we've created, which seems more and more to be unfolding in a mirror held up to a television set."
—*The Vancouver Sun*

"*Dreams of Millennium* is a fascinating and provocative attempt to survey the various forms of apocalyptic thought that are gathering force as the 20th century nears its conclusion."
—*The Georgia Straight* (Vancouver)

"Few writers in Canada are better at rendering complex issues in such vivid, simple writing."
—*Quill & Quire*

"A writer like Kingwell is worth his weight in gold."
—*Books in Canada*

"... spiked with unsettling insights on nearly every page."
—*Publishers Weekly*

PENGUIN BOOKS

DREAMS OF MILLENNIUM

Mark Kingwell is associate professor of philosophy at the University of Toronto. He is a contributing editor to *Saturday Night*, *Shift* and *Descant*, and a columnist for *Adbusters*. Kingwell holds a Ph.D. from Yale University and has published two other books, *A Civil Tongue* (Penn State Press, 1995) and the national bestseller *Better Living: In Search of Happiness from Plato to Prozac* (Viking, 1998), which was chosen as one of *The Globe and Mail*'s top ten books of 1998 and which won that year's Drummer General's Award for Non-Fiction. *Books in Canada* has declared: "A writer like Kingwell is worth his weight in gold."

DREAMS
OF MILLENNIUM
REPORT FROM A CULTURE ON THE BRINK
MARK KINGWELL

Penguin Books

PENGUIN BOOKS

Published by the Penguin Group

Penguin Books Canada Ltd, 10 Alcorn Avenue, Toronto, Ontario, Canada
M4V 3B2

Penguin Books Ltd, 27 Wrights Lane, London W8 5TZ, England

Penguin Putnam Inc., 375 Hudson Street, New York, New York 10014, U.S.A.

Penguin Books Australia Ltd, Ringwood, Victoria, Australia

Penguin Books (NZ) Ltd, cnr Rosedale and Airborne Roads, Albany,
Auckland 1310, New Zealand

Penguin Books Ltd, Registered Offices: Harmondsworth, Middlesex, England

First published in Viking by Penguin Books Canada Limited, 1996

Published in Penguin Books, 1999

1 2 3 4 5 6 7 8 9 10

Manufactured in Canada.

Canadian Cataloguing in Publication Data

Kingwell, Mark Gerald
Dreams of millennium: report from a culture on the brink

ISBN 0-14-028308-0

1. Popular culture. 2. Civilization, Modern—1950- 3. Social change.
I. Title.

HM101.K55 1999   306'.09'049   C98-932918-6

Visit Penguin Canada's web site at **www.penguin.ca**

For Steve
and Sean

Even now, the idea of that Annus Mirabilis,
the Year of Grace 2000, begins to affect us.
We feel that if we could live to witness its advent,
we should witness an immense event.
We should almost expect something to happen
in the Cosmos, so that we might read
the great date written in the skies.

The Spectator (London), 1892

Table of Contents

Who Dreams of the Millennium? xiii

Preface xxxv

Let the End Begin 1

ONE: *Shards of Apocalypse* 17

TWO: *The Prophet Zone* 57

THREE: *To Have and Have Not* 95

FOUR: *The Virtual Future* 137

FIVE: *Our Bodies, Our Selves* 181

SIX: *The Truth Is Out There* 229

SEVEN: *The Best Lack All Conviction* . . 275

EIGHT: *Faith No More* 327

Acknowledgments 352

Notes 354

Index 367

Who Dreams of the
Millennium?

We are already in the anticipated void of the Year 2000, in its
shadow, as if it were an approaching asteroid. Just as any electoral
deadline freezes political life a year ahead of time, so does the
shadow of the millennium, which creates an empty vortex that
swallows the entire century.

Jean Baudrillard, *In the Shadow of the Millennium*

THERE'S EVERY
reason in the world that the millennium should not matter
to us. So how come it does?

In early 1997, thirty-nine disciples of Heaven's Gate cult
leader Marshall Herff Applewhite, otherwise known as
"Do," uploaded their alien spirits into the flying saucer hidden in the tail of the Hale-Bopp comet, leaving their fleshly
"containers" behind. When the news broke, I got a call from
a *San Diego Union* reporter. He wanted to know if this kind
of thing is common in periods of millennial expectation. Of
course it is, I said. Just look at the historical record of
cultists and wackos who have immolated themselves in
search of higher planes of communion at every century's
end since the 1490s. Notice how the Web-savvy talk of disposable "meat cages" and "network consciousness" is just a
techno-spiritual twist on a Gnostic distrust of the body that
goes back at least as far as Plato's *Phaedo*. Observe how the
comet functions now as alien camouflage rather than as
God's harbinger . . .

He interrupted me to say that he had just surfed to a

Heaven's Gate spoof website, set up within twenty-four hours of the news of the largest mass suicide on American soil. It mocked the group's "Star Trek" holo-theology, theorized a link between the cult leader's code-name and Homer Simpson's famous "Doh!" exclamation of blockhead frustration, and depicted Applewhite's grizzled head in the trademark mad-staring-eyes moment that cult leaders invariably have—an image of shining mental unbalance. I had already noticed that even the otherwise staid "Jim Lehrer News Hour" chose to use this image in its coverage of the cult deaths, and it soon after showed up on the cover of one supermarket tabloid next to a picture of actor Patrick Stewart, famous for playing Captain Jean-Luc Picard on "Star Trek: The Next Generation", whom the paper claimed he resembled, suggesting that they might, in fact, be the same person. (He doesn't, and they aren't.)

Sitting there, on the phone, I had one of those abrupt feedback-loop moments, when the relentless self-involvement of our mediated culture seems suddenly to have caught me and my meat cage in its fast-shrinking circle. It only got worse a few days later when the grisly details of those now almost forgotten Rancho Santa Fe suicides, the castrations and barbiturate-assisted suffocations, gave way to the divergent craziness of the Oklahoma City bombing trial. Could anybody blame me if, for an instant, I felt like a denizen of one of Chris Carter's television shows, "The X-Files" or "Millennium," lurching from alien invasion nuts to anti-government nuts, the total body count rising all the while? Surely it was only a matter of time before some Yeats-quoting serial killer flashed onto the cultural radar screen and closed the circle for good, maybe taking Chris Carter hostage along the way, and imprisoned us all in a dark end-time world indistinguishable from the inside of a television.

Cause for anxiety in itself, maybe. But the question we must ask, as we finally approach the turn to 2000, is this:

what does the millennium, that arbitrary calendrical event, have to do with any of it?

If you listen to some people—though not me, despite many accusations and at least one radio-drama parody in which a Professor of Deep Understanding explains away everything by saying it's a product of "millennial anxiety"— the millennium means everything. Cultural and political madness is indeed a standard feature of periods of apocalyptic expectation, from the earliest moments of the Christian world, where converts expected Christ's return at any moment, to the medieval and early-modern eras, in which the disenfranchised or merely credulous performed their own arcane calculations and tried to hasten His coming through violence, both self- and other-directed. By the end of the fifteenth Common Era century, the standard pattern of apocalyptic anxiety was set: hope and dread in nearly equal measure, extreme obsession with the body, a penchant for conspiracy theories, the deep desire for great leaders, ambivalence about technology, and inordinate attention to signs and portents of all kinds. In times like these, history teaches us, all bets are off and anything goes. *Strange Days*, to borrow the title of Kathryn Bigelow's 1995 apocalyptic thriller—and who can doubt that they are very strange indeed, with (to take but one example) more than 1,500 cults active in the United States right now that believe the world is about to end?

Now we might believe that these people are simply fringe crazies, but such a reaction might actually underestimate the cultural power of anxiety, paranoia and fear. Consider a rather fanciful example. Wes Craven's 1997 film *Scream*, together with its self-consciously inferior sequel *Scream 2*, constructs an artful and ironic pastiche of horror-movie clichés, including jokes making arch reference to Craven's own slasher movies and to the well-known conventions of the genre: the phone call from inside the house, the unexpectedly resurrected villain, the stranded busty girl. Inside the conceit of a movie about a small town where some gruesome murders just happen to be taking place whenever people watch scary movies on video, writer Kevin Williamson creates a witty, and indeed very scary, post-modern fable in which people speak entirely in therapeutic psychobabble or in references to movies, preferably scary ones. The town is filled with people who are slightly off-centre versions of characters we seem to have met before: the goofy cop, the feisty and beautiful teenage heroine, her ambiguously attractive boyfriend, the doomed authoritarian high-school principal. (This last is played by Henry Winkler, formerly "The Fonz" on "Happy Days," and his death is particularly gratifying to viewers of a certain age.)

The weirdest guy in town is naturally Randy, the video-store clerk, who extends a recent cinematic run of crazy and/or dangerous video-store clerks whose patron saint in real life is, of course, ultra-violent film director Quentin Tarantino, who acquired his allusive and encyclopedic knowledge of movies while working as a video clerk in Manhattan Beach, California. Unlike the other kids, Randy knows and understands the well-preserved conventions of the horror movie, and during a drunken slasher-video session with the other teens, Randy explains "The Rules". In a horror movie you never have sex, because sex is a sin, and sin equals death, so sex equals death: anyone who has sex will die. You never drink or do drugs because, again calling on the sin principle, drink and drugs are sins, and sin equals death, so drink and drugs equal death: anyone who gets drunk or stoned will die. And you never, *ever* say "I'll be right back"—because you won't. "If this were a scary movie," Randy says at one point, "I'd be the prime suspect." "What's your motive?" a friend asks him. "It's the millennium," Randy replies. "Motives are incidental." You get the message. These are the last days: we're all psycho-killers now.

Yet, if you listen to other people, the millennium has nothing to do with any of the cultural craziness we see around us. Umberto Eco, speaking recently at a conference on the Year 1000, offered this *pronunciamento* when asked to say what, if anything, was typical of the end of the millennium: "Something which is typical is the insistence of journalists and TV to discover that there is something typical of the end of the millennium—the mass-media reaction, which is an artificial one. You are *producing* the expectation. The rest of the people don't care."

Don't they? I'm not so sure, especially when people call me in the middle of the night to relate tales of alien abduction, send me their detailed predictions of how the cycles of life and death will turn in the next few years, sometimes in thick, hand-written tomes, or tell me, as one man did in a Nashville bar not long ago, that fully 80 percent of the portents outlined in the *Book of Revelation* have already fallen into place. (I didn't stay long enough to hear all the details of this claim, but I do remember that the much-pierced apocalyptic shock-rocker Marilyn Manson had something to do with it.) Another man sent a scribbled three-page fax that set out a combination of Latin etymology and sine-wave fluctuations to prove that a massive magnetic upheaval was due in the polar icecap. Yet another, writing from Winnipeg, warned me of a conspiracy afoot within what he called "Dictatorship Kanada," involving the government mind-control agenda behind fluorodated drinking water.

In fact Eco's reaction is itself typical, especially among a certain well-educated class of intellectual skeptics. The impatient waving off of millennial anxiety ignores the complicated ways in which our culture works, folding real-world concerns and events—environmental threats, say, or political issues of divergent haves and have-nots in a world ruled by information—into old tales of destruction and transformation. It is true that the millennial overlay on these issues can sometimes serve to obscure what we might actually do about them, because apocalyptic expectation, both bright and dark, has an enervating effect, letting people off the hook either in a quietism of happy expectation or in a paralysis of mounting fear. "The millennium revises all historical requirements to the point of erasing the very marks of history," Baudrillard argues, in a point as applicable to recent political rhetoric as it is to the restless, attic-rummaging nostalgia of contemporary popular music and fashion. "We dig in the archives. We settle old accounts. We revive memories—including the memory of the Year 2000 in anticipation, as if it had already taken place. We launder and purify, desperately trying to end the century with a politically correct balance sheet. This is by and large a question of historical purification. The entire twentieth century is on trial. And this is new. None of the previous centuries did that. What they did was history. What we are doing is history's trial."

This tendency—this powerful novelty in our way of carrying on, of trying to make sense—is something that we must recognize as true about ourselves and our times. Our propensity to annihilate history is often remarked; we seem to shorten the available span of collective memory by a decade or so every few months, so that formerly proximate events, like the Second World War, fade into the distance. At the same time, the twentieth century has been one of successive and self-consciously declared endings: the end of war, the end of poverty, the end of ideology, the end of history, the end of communism, the end of truth, even the end of philosophy—though this discipline, as I have reason to know, has made a practice of declaring its own end from the earliest times. The millennium is itself another of these illusory but influential endings, but one with a peculiar claim on our imaginations: it is the end of the world, the end of time. Or at least the end of time as we know it.

Things *have* changed as we approach this ending, though I would never suggest that the Year 2000 has been directly causal in making us what I suppose we must continue to call post-modern. Most of us now accept without fuss the idea that truth is embedded in language, or that culture is not a reflection of God's will. Such changes in attitude, together with others like them that loosen the bonds of an age-old metaphysical imprisonment, have been both necessary and liberating. The cultural deadline of the millennium does not cause these changes, as I said, but it does somehow heighten them, make them feel more pressing—as it does, likewise, with other changes and endings that are less positive in effect. The essential task now, in analysing our varied and sometimes confused cultural experience, is to fight the temptation to declare endings left and right in a frenzy of end-time reckoning, to annihilate without regard for what might be preserved. We must resist declarations that, instead of the helpful recognition of contingency, foster a cultural nihilism—or simply the indifferent cynicism of the cash nexus, where everything has a price but nothing has a value. Indeed, I believe such a combination of resistance and recognition is the only attitude worth cultivating as we try to move forward along a trajectory of political change and, I hope, justice.

We cannot acquire that perspective, however, unless we first confront the millennial narratives that cling to our various crises—unless we confront the idea of the millennium itself, and its strangely influential, world-swallowing properties. As a cultural construction, the millennium *obtrudes*. It stands in the way of our future-creating projects as something to get through, a threshold that has to be crossed. And we must see the threshold before we can cross it. That is what this book is about.

Busting hype is our great preoccupation in these waning days of the century—next only, perhaps, to generating hype—and the debunkers have come along in their numbers to take the wind out of the Year 2000. By now their litany of deflation is familiar: the Judeo-Christian calendar is arbitrary and socially constructed; apocalypse is a merely western preoccupation, and theologically suspect in any case; historically there is nothing thicker on the ground than predictions of the world's end or the Messiah's return, all of them unfounded or mad or political. All true. Plans to commemorate the occasion, meanwhile, have taken on a depressing tawdriness. A giant domed theme park at Greenwich. Massive fireworks displays. Bonfires on Fijian headlands. *This* is all we can come up with?

Numerous magazine spreads and newspaper features are now taking on the world-weary tone they love so much in articles dedicated to showing that the millennium is nothing more than a cynical marketing opportunity, and probably a shaky one at that. Indeed, in this age of ceaseless and sometimes thoughtless marketing, nothing has gone stale faster than brand names that appeal to the once-energetic tropes of Millennium or 2000 or Twenty-First Century. The only mildly successful campaign thus far has been based on an adventitious joke, perhaps a little like the millennium itself: M&Ms, plain and peanut, are now being touted as "the official candy of the millennium" because MM, in the grandiose Roman numerals reserved for movie dates and Superbowls, equals 2000. With even the Great Champagne Shortage now thought by many to be just a marketing scam by wily French winemakers, who can blame us for throwing up our hands in disgust? No wonder one of my friends has taken to saying, over and over, his voice rising, "It's just a date, it's just a date, it's just a date," while a restless and able media critic I know is urging people to "Boycott the Millennium."

What these articles and attitudes really do, however, is reinforce the rather childish opposition, the unhelpful binary function, of Everything and Nothing. The millennium does not explain everything, because anything that explains everything is meaningless. But it doesn't follow from that conclusion that the millennium means nothing. Traditionally, as I argue in this book, cultures in the grip of millennial anxiety tend to collapse into a dichotomy of fear and hope, often oscillating rapidly from one to the other. Our own culture preserves this feature while adding a new one, a habit of thought no doubt rooted in the mediated nature of our experience and in our subjection to a relentless barrage of consumer imperatives—maybe, too, in the massive volume of binary code we all use. I mean the sharp dichotomy we tend to draw between the "one" of meaning and the "zero" of marketing. This thinking says, if the millennium is even 1 percent hype, then it's all hype. If it's not the revelation described by the early Christians, then it's just a scam. If it's not "real" like cats and sofas and bicycles are real, then it's nothing at all.

From this deflationary point of view, it seems that all that's left of the millennium is the notorious Y2K computer crisis. By now we've all heard plenty—maybe too much—about this projected calamity, in which elevators will allegedly free-fall, power grids fail, and bank accounts collapse because mainframe computers programmed in the 1940s and beyond were not equipped to process the change from 99 to 00 in their dating mechanisms—an oversight that could cause the computers to believe that 2000 is now 1900 or simply some other, randomly generated year. Should that happen, computers would no longer be able to function, and so the systems that depend on them—electrical power, air traffic control, telephones, banks, actuarial records—would crash. The problem begins at home, with 93 percent of the personal computers manufactured before

1997 in danger of Y2K crashes, but it is much more serious at the level of the big mainframes, some with deeply embedded sedimentary layers of code going back decades, that control utilities, banks and traffic control systems. Some 700 billion lines of code worldwide need to be rewritten in order to fix the problem completely, a task that, even if it were feasible (and it is not, most people now agree), would cost something on the order of $600 billion (U.S.). Indeed, the problem is even worse than it first appeared: computer experts estimate that, because of various combinations of affected numbers, there are some fifteen or twenty dates on which the default-to-zero problem could afflict computers, and some of these dates won't crop up until we are several years into the new millennium. There is now a chance, pegged at 40 percent or even greater, that a U.S. company has already experienced a Y2K-related computer problem. The big crunch comes on January 1, 2000, but the complexity of our computer systems means there is plenty of potential drama to keep us occupied for years to come.

Mainstream messages concerning the impending crisis now range from the calming good cheer of various company memos and flyers that have recently crossed my desk, often printed on heavy coloured paper and illustrated with chipper cartoon characters busily changing nines to zeros, to the more frankly apocalyptic emergency military plans and evacuation procedures being contemplated by federal and municipal governments. The U.S. Federal Reserve plans to print $50 billion in new currency in order to cover potential runs on cash supplies. Canadian computer experts have reported to Parliament with a don't-worry message, all jauntily claiming they will be on a transatlantic airplane come New Year's Eve. Meanwhile, some airline companies, notably British Airways, were planning to cancel many if not all of their December 31 flights, not because they are convinced that air-traffic control systems will certainly fail, but because anxiety about the problem offers an unparalleled marketing opportunity: to become the airline that cares enough not to take a chance with its customers' safety.

Away from the mainstream, there are now numerous websites devoted to advice about the storage of fresh water, the stealthy stockpiling of canned goods, and the acquisition of portable generators, surplus gasoline, and even automatic weapons and ammunition. These sites sport foreboding designations—remnant.org, trapped.com—and, under a veneer of sprightly common sense ("buying a portable power source is a sensible precaution in any home"), send out their message of doom. Some 100,000 Americans have already left urban centres, or plan to do so soon, in order to seek safer environs for the chaos they foresee. The Christian fundamentalist Jerry Falwell recently instructed his flock to stockpile "toilet paper, paper towels, personal products, toothpaste, soap, matches and lighters, candles, kerosene lamps, coffee and tea, sugar and ammunition." (I guess he assumed his congregation already had the guns.) "Not only will these be scarce after grocery stores have been emptied," Falwell continued, "but they could be used as possible bartering items in place of currency." The operative vision is not just of electronic-systems meltdown, in other words; it now embraces the standard-issue nightmare of civic breakdown, complete with widespread looting, fights over non-perishable provisions, gun-toting vigilantes, and the imposition of martial law. It even reinscribes the old saved-or-damned ravages of the *Book of Revelation* into techno-language: "Y2K could be God's way of sweeping the multitudes into the Kingdom of Christ," Falwell thundered. I think the creators of freeze-dried food have a lot to answer for when it comes to our workaday late-century anxieties.

Say what you like about Y2K, though, it at least has the

merit of closing the hype circle in a neat way. And it does so
in a manner that makes it a perfect illustration of millennial
anxiety as I analyse it in the pages that follow. We see here
three prominent themes of the traditional dark millennial
vision vividly depicted, and we observe how they swirl
through imagination to take on a particularly compelling
form of cultural reality.

There is, first, the pervasive and mounting fear of technology as the source of the evils to come. This is the same
sort of fear that caused people in earlier eras to demonize
powered threshers and steam-driven weaving machines. It is
really a phobia, an irrational fear, because it is a fear of qualities that lie within ourselves: the mysterious combination
of ingenuity and will that allows us to create something as
sophisticated as a computer network, with all its wondrous
abilities to regulate and distribute something equally mysterious, such as electricity or telephone access, matched with
the undeniable fact that most of those who use such networks have virtually no idea how they work. Indeed, never
mind electronic technology, with its black-box microchips
and millions of lines of indecipherable software code—
many of us don't even know how mechanical things work. I
could repair my bicycle in a pinch, maybe a car if it had a
circa-1979, Detroit-built V6 engine like the ones we worked
on back in high school shop class; but I couldn't fix the furnace in my house or rewire the light fixtures in my kitchen.
Could you?

More precisely, then, we should note the massive dependence on information technology that we have freely created and accepted over the decades of the current century, a
dependence that leaves us helpless should that technology
fail. We come face to face, here, not only with the brittle-
ness of our complex infrastructure but also with our own
inadequacy as individuals strung along within all those
wires. The real fear is not of what might happen to us; it is,

rather, of what has already happened to us. We are all cyborgs now, irrevocably committed to the half-human, half-machine realities of our world. This is new. We all accept, however unwillingly, that our consciousness is mysteriously dependent for its existence upon the messy carbon-based flesh of these bipedal bodies. What we now confront is the doubly unsettling realization that our "bodies" are composed not simply of the DNA-patterned flesh but also of the steel, plastic, and silicon—and the churning software, the coursing electric impulses—that those bodies need to survive. If consciousness, the fragile sense of the mind's I, is what matters to us, then we must see that our fear of computer chaos is really a fear of the Frankensteins we have become.

The situation is ripe, second, for the peculiar feature of many periods of anxious expectation, the self-fulfilling prophecy. Scholars of apocalypticism have long noted the strange power of prophecies to make themselves come true, from the predictions of assassinations that have often led biddable minions to take up arms, to the claims by powerful cult leaders that the forces of law would resist the aims of the cult. Like these other forms of self-fulfilment, Y2K has its tenuous but essential hold on events in the empirical world—the computers do exist, the problem is not a fiction—but now exhibits a tendency to spin off its effects into the realm of the febrile imagination. All it will take for a major bank's computer system to fail, for example, is for some modest percentage of its depositors—say 25 percent— to attempt to withdraw all their savings as cash in the six weeks or so leading up to January 1, 2000. And when *Wired* magazine profiled a high-ranking computer expert who has decided to go off-grid and begin stockpiling food and weapons, we were confronted with a familiar late-century image in a slightly new guise: the nerd as survivalist, the "great geek migration," as *The New York Times* has dubbed it.

More than half of U.S. executives polled said they did not believe the problems could be solved in time, and 11 percent reported themselves in possession of woodstoves and portable generators as precautions. All irony aside, these defections into fear by knowledgeable insiders, however low-key they remain, only pour fuel on the fire of our anxiety. Fear is sometimes our worst enemy, and we often act to our own detriment not despite warnings but because of them.

So there is, third, the sheer senselessness of the potential crisis, a senselessness that should finally put in their place the ongoing arguments about the reality of millennial anxiety. Arguments that Y2K is the first "real" form of millennial anxiety—as opposed, presumably, to the kinds of cultural anxiety I detail here, from UFO abduction fears to an ongoing crisis in leadership—are wrongheaded. The Y2K bug is no more real than any of them, but also no less. We should rather say that it conforms to type, taking some undeniable feature of the world and making it a focus for a whole complex of fears and hopes: about personal comfort, about the fragility of social order, about the terrifying cold we must endure when heating grids, and civic rules, break down. If Y2K does prove apocalyptic—nobody seems to know for sure, which is usually the way with prophecies—what's ironic is that it's going to be precisely as a result of the very arbitrariness of the date-driven switch from nines to zeros. Score one for the calendar's power after all. You say the millennium's turn doesn't concern you? Boy, have I got news for you . . .

This last feature of our currently dominant millennial anxiety has also finally silenced all those wonky kill-joys who continued, through the latter 1990s, to insist that the new millennium does not begin until January 1, 2001. As always, this is true as far as linear mathematics goes, but, as I argue throughout this book, the millennium is not beholden to mathematics or logic. It is all about the power of the human imagination, and the date with imaginative power is 2000, when the odometer of time reels over into its new epoch.

In fact, you might even say that the millennium is not really a date at all, though we need to date to make it stick. It is, rather, a psychological space, a way of thinking: an intimation of mortality, an opportunity for assessment, a locus of fear, a chance for hope. It is time itself put into question.

Living in time has its costs, and writing books is perhaps more than most things, the kind of future-dependent project that Martin Heidegger had in mind when he limned the existential curves of modern life: the hopeful and anxious casting forward of myself into the murky territory of the not-yet. I began work on this book in 1995, though my interest in its topics extends back to at least 1989. I had come to believe that a cluster of personal obsessions, cultural markers of various kinds that I was following with an amateur's keen interest, could be usefully grouped under the umbrella of millennial anxiety. Those obsessions are what fill the pages that follow. I did, and do, resolutely believe that the millennium's impact is tenuous and subtle, both limited and hazy. But there is often more to our culture than meets the eye. The title of the book was not idly chosen: I wanted to suggest something of the dreamlike quality of cultural experience at our late stage in the century, the oneiric weirdness of displacement and condensation and latent content that Freud, in his masterpiece *The Interpretation of Dreams*, analysed so brilliantly—if also tendentiously. As with the dream, so with a dreamy culture.

Consider, as an example of this, the recent spate of apocalyptic techno-thriller movies. Some of these were known to me when writing the book, to be sure, for the trend of big-budget end-of-the-world movies had already begun in the early 1990s. Others—*Armageddon, Deep Impact*, and their ilk—are of more recent vintage. What goes on in these films, culturally speaking? Well, the manifest content is naturally that of globe-destroying disaster. *We're all afraid of the end of the world!* But there is also ideological content to be mined here: the triumph of renegade individualism over governmental inefficiency, say; or American jingoism and technological superiority in the face of external threats. More deeply still, though, there is latent content in the very fact of these movies: the observation, as the novelist J. G. Ballard once put it, of technology so advanced as to be able to depict the dramatic destruction of advanced technology. (Think, for example, of the *Terminator* movies, especially James Cameron's frightful sequel—not to mention his equally frightful, in a different sense, monster hit *Titanic*.) We are drawn to these movies not simply as an apocalyptic avoidance ritual—though there is surely that: we are warding off disaster by viewing its depiction, very much in the manner of medieval peasants at a morality play. At a different level we are drawn to them because they allow us to indulge unspeakable desires—say, for personal violence in the face of crumbling civic order. This might even be a kind of utopian wish fulfilment, conjoining elite privilege with the images of post-apocalyptic survival. As the critic Fredric Jameson once noted, such films offer for consumption not a nightmare vision so much as a bright one: the astonishing technological success that makes for depiction of the nightmare vision, a "technological bonus" in mass-media consumption, works to confirm the desires, and of course to reinforce the social position, of the viewers, people with money and leisure.

As a method of cultural reportage, analysis of this kind has its risks as well as its rewards. It depends on suggestiveness rather than proof, and therefore asks for an open-minded reader. There are also many other influences and tendencies at play in my writing about culture, of course: I am not a Freudian and this book does not defend any explicit theory of cultural analysis. Nevertheless there is much to be learned in reading the wisps of the morning after in our experience. The critic Marjorie Garber, in her 1998 book *Symptoms of Culture*, explained her decision to adopt the Freud of *Interpretation of Dreams* as a model for examining such cultural material as pro football, Great Books courses, and Jell-O: "I do not propose to diagnose culture as if it were an illness of which we could be cured, but to read culture as if it were structured like a dream, a network of representations that encodes wishes and fears, projections and identifications, all of whose elements are overdetermined and contingent." In Garber's hands, this strategy has more hits than misses, more glowing insights than strained connections; but there is always likely to be a mixture of both. If we are not careful and rigorous critics, "overdetermined" can sometimes begin to mean arbitrary, and "contingent" becomes another word for slippery.

I do not pretend that I avoided these pitfalls completely in this book. I nevertheless hope there is enough insight here to outweigh the inevitable weaknesses. For this new edition, I have consciously not done what I might have, namely gone through the book page by page in search of claims that no longer seemed valid or statistics that cry out for updating. Apart from being a prospect almost too painful to contemplate, there seemed little point. Some aspects of the book, such as its discussion of the Internet, for example, were, like computers themselves, already obsolete by the time the product was unwrapped. I could have substantially rewritten Chapter Four, "The Virtual Future," for this edition, but the central problem would remain.

Other topics have also shifted somewhat with the sands of fashion. Our culture moves fast, arguably faster than ever before, and it has overtaken some of my obsessions with new ones of its own. Y2K is a case in point. Still, I am pleased that some discussions that might have dated in the few short years, such as my treatment of TV's "The X-Files," have instead weathered rather well. And the basics of the analysis are, I think, as relevant as ever, even if the particulars they address alter their shapes as time goes on. I have corrected all factual errors that came to my attention, of course (such as mistaking the monarch Baldwin IX for my fanciful invention, Baldwin XI, who never actually lived); and some small alterations, made for the hardcover U.S. edition of the book, which was published in 1997, have likewise been made here. Otherwise the text is as when I first wrote it.

Which brings me to the second reason I decided to write the book in the first place. The midpoint of the final decade of the century struck me as an appropriate time to begin the sort of cultural reckoning I have attempted here. As the subtitle (also carefully chosen) indicates, this book is a report; it was never intended primarily as a philosophical argument about the validity of millennial anxiety, still less as a collection of guru-delivered predictions about the shape of things to come. I certainly never meant for it to have the status of prophecy or futurism, and was rather alarmed when it was assessed in those terms. I was aiming, instead, for that careful attention to the present which alone can illuminate the future. Perhaps I should not have been surprised, given my own appreciation of the deep roots of millennial anxiety, that the book was taken up in some quarters as a form of cultural fortune-telling. As all writers sooner or later discover, an author cannot control how people read his work. And eccentric interpretations of *Dreams of Millennium* have not been without their interest. My favourite review, from a Catholic newspaper, offered the deliciously back-handed view that "it would be unwise to dismiss Kingwell's perspectives merely as more vitriolic bile being spewed by another faithless infidel." I have also received some very strange invitations over the phone, made friends with a number of endearing and engaging oddballs, and my mail is a treasure trove of exhortations to conversion, world-explaining masterworks, poems, and the charming correspondence of a cloistered Redemptoristine nun.

Interest in the millennium as a topic shows no sign of diminishing. If anything, we seem to be gripped even more firmly by the weirdly unreal-but-real power of the arbitrary line in the sand of time. I think my only regret—and it is one that I am in the process of remedying with new research and writing projects—is that I did not put my political cards on the table as obviously as I might have done in this book. This has led to certain misunderstandings. For example: though I treat them here mostly as symptoms of anxiety, I do not consider environmental degradation or gross disparities in wealth mere surface phenomena or cultural narratives. They support such narratives, yes, and their relationship to structures of cultural belief is not simple or irrelevant, but I harbour no doubts that they matter more, a lot more, than "The X-Files." Furthermore, my championing of hope at the end of the book is meant neither as idle utopianism nor as a cop-out from political responsibility, but rather as a kind of personal call to account. To be any good, a book has to keep its limitations in mind: you can't say everything at once. This book is a cultural report, not a political tract. Yet I fancy that anyone interested in my political convictions will be able to tease them out from what is here.

One concrete thing to mention before leaving this theme has do to do with the idea of "Jubilee". At the time I first drafted *Dreams of Millennium* in 1995, the Roman Catholic Church had not yet released its papal encyclical on the subject of the millennium. When it did, later in 1996, the document changed the terms of debate for many people. Pope John Paul II has called for the millennium to be a Jubilee Year, a period of remission from the penal consequences of sin, something normally observed every twenty-five years. The potential for a millennial Jubilee is striking to me, even though (as this book relates) I no longer keep faith with the Catholic Church of my upbringing. Jubilee is a kind of conscious act of forgiveness, a deliberate transcendence of the normal economy of blame and praise. As a metaphor for appropriate observance of this strange deadline, I find it extraordinary and powerful. Already some politically minded believers are arguing that the notion of Jubilee should be extended beyond the traditional ambit of personal sin to embrace other forms of forgiveness: the erasure of Third World debt, for example, a risky but possibly just measure that regulatory agencies in world finance have frequently contemplated yet always rejected as untenable. I do not have the future-spying telescope that would allow us to see the consequences of writing down those gargantuan debts; I'm not sure anyone does, even the most acute economist at the World Bank or the International Monetary Fund. But just imagine, for a moment, if the millennium were the impetus for that kind of epoch-making material change. It is not impossible.

Closer to home, the theme of Jubilee has implications just as strong, though narrower in scope. People complain that they cannot imagine what would count as an appropriate celebration for this mother of all New Year's Eves. These days I am asked at least once a week what I plan to be doing come December 31, 1999, and I always find myself at a loss to answer with what I take to be the desired vividness. Sometimes I talk vaguely of a trip to London or New York; other times I project a quiet retreat to visit good friends in a nearby town. Above all I suspect, as I say at the end of *Dreams of Millennium*, that I will once more fail to find that mythic, Fred-and-Ginger-style formal ball which, in my overheated cinematic imagination, I never cease to long for. But whatever I end up doing—drinking martinis or making hot chocolate, tripping the light fantastic or just getting under the covers—I trust I will have the courage to look inward, and spend a few moments forming the resolution to make my corner of the world a more just and peaceful place. A personal Jubilee, if you like.

So why resist all the resistance to the millennium? Why persist in thinking that it means anything at all? Surely, you might still want to say, the intelligent attitude is to see the millennium for the hype-fest it is, and simply ignore it.

Well, in closing, here is my reason, and I don't suggest it is for everyone. If you are determined that the millennium means absolutely nothing to you, then fine, I have no quarrel. What I have discovered in thinking and writing about the subject over the past four years, however, is the complex web of desires and fears, many of them unconscious, that cling to transitional dates, those periods of imagined change that stand outside the regular course of time. These are what anthropologists call *liminal spaces*, interstices in the normal flow that must be passed through before the ordinary way of things can be resumed.

It doesn't matter if the transitional date is arbitrary, because it functions despite all the conscious arguments against it. A transitional date organizes and measures cultural beliefs and expectations; it carves out time by drawing lines in the social mind. It reminds us that we are future-producing creatures, dimly aware of our mortality and yet constantly throwing our plans and projects (and our genes and ideas and mortgages) into the unknown not-yet-here. It becomes, finally, a focus for dreams, those "psychological structures, full of significance," as Freud called them in his revolutionary book, whose publication was purposely delayed so it could bear the liminal date of 1900. Dreams express our wishes, anxieties, and hopes. They tell strange stories and flow in odd ways. When we wake they seem to slip away, leaving only wispy traces behind. The traditional dreams of millennium—which speak of transcendence, transformation, violence, apocalypse, and utopia—are among the most powerful dreams we know. We have lately added some new variations, concerning aliens and technology and the ecosystem, but these dreams are real if anything is. They are cultural and psychological forces to be reckoned with, never merely the "undigested bit of beef" that Scrooge preferred to see in Marley's appearance. Dreams teach us our needs; they also remember our failures. They speak the hidden language of the soul.

This may sound altogether too dreamy for the debunkers, perhaps for you as well. But I want to say this: not everything is hype, and not every idea or celebration is reducible to an exercise in product placement. The millennium is not meaningless simply because a lot of silly guff is being promoted in its name. Critical intelligence is a rare enough commodity in this overheated world to risk suggesting that we need less of it. I'm not doing that. Yet we should be careful that our laudable hype-alert doesn't become just one more quick-time parlour game, one more piece of self-congratulatory sophistication which we consume as surely as the material and cultural products that furnish every corner of our world. If we did allow that to happen, we would miss what I think is still, despite everything, a sterling opportunity, one that obviously doesn't come around very often, to reflect on what it means to be who we are: human, mortal, anxious, happy, confused, and much else besides.

Beware the millennium hype, by all means. But don't ever let that skepticism overcome your capacity to dream.

M.K.
Toronto
January 1999

Preface

$\mathbf{S}$OME TIME AGO,
a friend of mine, who heard that I was considering a book
on the millennium, sent me a copy of the London-based
Independent newspaper which featured a series of articles on
"How to Survive the 21st Century." For the most part the
articles made predictable (if depressing) reading, but one on
cultural matters especially caught my eye. "In the short
term," its author advised, "writers and artists should resist
the urge to produce works on millennial themes. There are
already several thousand in the pipeline."

As you can see, I ignored the warning and decided to
write a book anyway. Still, I suppose a bevy of potential
rivals does create a novel form of anxiety about the millennium, at least for writers, and it might be useful to put some
distance between me and the competition with a few pre-
liminary words about what this book is *not*.

It is not a work of prognostication or futurism. I make no
bold predictions here, plot no trajectories of development or
disaster. I don't know whether we'll be working twenty-hour
weeks in 2025, whether a black woman will be president of
the United States, or whether the supply of arable land will
slip below subsistence levels. Contrary to what some people
would have you believe, nobody knows these things.

Nor is this book a meditation on how to meet your guardian angel, perform a miracle, or reach new levels of spiritual fulfilment in a third-millennium world. I hope there is some insight in what follows, but I doubt that reading this book will lead to communion with otherworldly forces. I feel compelled to say up front that it has not been dictated to me by spirits, downloaded by extra-terrestrials, or recovered from a government conspiracy's database. If you find this book in the New Age section of your bookstore, please move it somewhere else.

Nor am I interested, finally, in spreading news of encroaching barbarism, God-sent doom, or Islamic hordes that will roll over the enlightened West. This is not a jeremiad or a prophecy of apocalypse. I paint no dark pictures of the decline of civilization, outline no threats to the Enlightenment project of truth and rationality. I am not a biblical literalist and I don't think the world is going to end anytime soon. Christ is not coming; you need not repent or die.

What interests me, instead, is the strong hold that the dialectics of gloom and hope have on us in the declining days of the century. This book is a reflection on an anxious culture—on its obsessions and dark patches, but also on its prospects and strangely deep pleasures.

A word about dates. While it is strictly true that the new millennium does not begin until January 1, 2001—the year 2000 being the last year of the second millennium, not the first year of the third—I think most people who insist on this strictness are, among other things, going to miss some pretty fabulous parties on New Year's Eve, 1999. Take my advice: follow the fun. And let's just agree up front that, for all practical purposes, the new millennium starts at midnight, January 1, 2000.

M.K.
Toronto
January 1, 1996

Let the End Begin

Meanwhile the millennium was to hand, the polar ice-cap
was melting, the ozone layer depleting. There were sexual
plagues, floods, droughts, severe famines, earthquakes, outbursts
of boils and mass gatherings of locusts. To a nice upstanding
fellow like myself…these were troubling days.

Malcolm Bradbury, *Doctor Criminale*

IN 1970,
when I was seven years old, my father took me to the newly
opened McLaughlin Planetarium in Toronto to see a star
show. I don't know why exactly, but this seemed to me an
ambition that bordered on folly. The Planetarium, that
weird domed building, was to my young mind a thoroughly
forbidding place.

Still, like many children, I regarded my father as something of a conjurer in those days and believed he could
make things happen by simple acts of will. On the same day
as the planned visit to the Planetarium, for example, eating
hot dogs in a downtown deli, he had calmly predicted that
there would be used chewing gum stuck to the underside of
our table. Incredulous, I crawled down to have a look for
myself. By God, there they were: a dozen wads of ossified
gum, multicoloured and various of size, all welded with an
air of permanence to the pressboard.

Surely, to the man who could pull that off, getting me
into the Planetarium should have been nothing. But no, I
had been right about the hubris of the plan. It seemed that I
was too young, or too small—I forget which—to sit in the
big reclining chairs and total darkness of the Planetarium
star show. My father haggled with some energy, which was

1

unusual for him, but there was no budging the officious ushers. They sent us on our way. I can still remember the thwarted longing I felt and the stiff blow of disappointment at my father's apparent impotence.

In our gloom, we walked up to the expansive intersection of University and Bloor, and my father, looking east along the street, was suddenly inspired with a back-up plan. He saw that we just had time to make the matinee of Stanley Kubrick's *2001: A Space Odyssey*, playing at the University Theatre, the old-fashioned movie palace on the north side of Bloor. He didn't stop to consider that I was probably too young to appreciate the film. After all, it was about space and stars, and it was, more to the point, available. It would have to do. In we rushed, along the grubby red carpet leading from the street to the auditorium, through the concession stand's distinctive popcorn reek, and into that big dark room.

And in no time at all, it seemed, I was rigid with terror. Memory of the film's opening sequence, spread across that massive screen, can still make me shudder. I see those howling man-like primates, posturing wildly beneath the black alien slab, snatching up the first human tool—a club—to bash in the head of another ape. And then the club, tossed into the air, transforming into a sleek spaceship. Pouring from the cinema's state-of-the-art speakers, trumpets punching out the notes, was Richard Strauss's great *fin-de-siècle* ode *Also sprach Zarathustra*, which has come to be known as the "2001 Theme." (What a sly move that was, I thought much, much later—to mingle Strauss's triumphant paean to human arrogance, a work inspired by Friedrich Nietzsche's book of the same name, the tale of the original *Übermensch*, with this brutal scene of murderous proto-humans.)

The fear that gripped me at the very first moment never stopped; for the whole two hours and more of *2001* I was entirely stricken. I think my father had no idea of this—at least I hope he didn't. After all, this was my big treat in the city; I could hardly admit that I was on the verge of peeing myself. And in fact I would not have missed it for the world, this window on the world to come. I didn't know anything about Aristotle in those days, but I was proving him right about the strange pleasures of catharsis. I have no idea if I really needed to purge myself of troubling emotions at seven years old, but I do know that being scared half to death was a real kick.

The images of *2001* lodge in my memory for other reasons, too. In our era the film has become a touchstone of anxiety about the shape the future will take. The danger of "instrumental reason"—that part of human intelligence dedicated to control of the world—is a recurrent theme in science fiction, but the contrast of *2001* to then-dominant images of the future was sharp. I can still remember, for example, the upbeat sci-fi magazines of the 1950s that littered our basement, and the nerdy science films they showed us in grade school, with their "big science" perkiness and slavish devotion to the goals of what used to be called the military-industrial complex. Technology would set us free! We would live in domed cities. People would fly through the air. Robots would do the housework, build houses, police cities—all the while, we confidently imagined, following the benign guidelines laid down in Isaac Asimov's Three Laws of Robotics. (The first law states that "A robot may not injure a human being or, through inaction, allow a human being to come to harm"; the second law commands robot self-preservation; the third law establishes the priority of the first law over the second.)

Each age must produce for its own consumption a vision of what the future will hold. So, far from the helpful perkiness of those 1950s robots, *2001*'s artificial intelligence, the computer known as HAL 9000 goes inwardly berserk and, just like any twisted human, acts out his psychopathologies in homicidal violence. As a meditation on species arrogance and on misplaced faith in technology, *2001* has had few equals. It also opened up new vistas for critical reflection at a time when the tools of human reason had, after decades of blithe confidence, begun to seem more menacing than comforting. The internal logic of technological progress, we were made to see, is violence.

During my lifetime, computer technology has come to dominate North American life, a fact that raises the spectre of HAL 9000 anew as we approach 2001 and focuses our attention on some age-old questions. What future is in store for us? Is it even possible to think about "the future" as a coherent thing, susceptible to human imagination? Can our technology help us deal with an uncertain future? Or are the dangers greater than the benefits? What real-world HALs will initially ease our lives, only to complicate, even threaten, them later? The received wisdom, in my grade school anyway, was that HAL was an IBM product (notice the alphabetical correlation: H–I, A–B, L–M). What secret Big Blue agenda was he acting out? In short: what journeys will we embark on, only to find ourselves, like Odysseus himself, beset by unimagined dangers and traps? What resources of guile and courage, if any, will we be able to bring to them?

Seeing the way in which these questions now dominate our collective imagination, I know that I was not alone in feeling unreasoning fear at the sight of those scrabbling monkeys, at the sound of HAL asking in that flat, threatening voice, "What are you doing, Dave?" The trumpet's overture in *Zarathustra* sounds reveille to a culture on the brink. Along the way from that day in 1970 to this, the date 2001 has acquired an almost mantric quality—it resonates throughout the culture of the 1990s, the unspoken endgame of our present confusion. Increasingly, as we pass the midpoint of the final decade of the second millennium, this submerged theme comes bubbling up through the cracks in our popular culture, through the fissures in our economy, through the breaches in our ecosphere.

It turns out that the hazardous journey is not the one into the calendar's millennium, the simple change from 19 to 20—for that is coming closer, like it or not, with each tick of the clock or flicker of the digital diode. The dangerous journey, the odyssey that will test all our reserves of will and courage, is the journey into the heart of our millennial anxiety—the journey into ourselves.

The University Theatre is no longer standing in Toronto. Boarded up for many years, the Bloor Street landmark was finally torn down in 1994, leaving only a shell of its front standing, artfully supported by new steel girders. (In 1995 the Planetarium followed suit, closing its doors for lack of government funding.) You can now walk through the theatre's lovely art deco façade into a Yorkville parking lot, and it makes an effective piece of urban street art—a kind of Magritte painting *in situ*. It also has, to my eye, a strange post-apocalyptic aura; it is a stylized version of what has become a central icon of our time, the bombed-out building. The cinema, the palace of dreams, has become an image in one of the darkest visions we know.

The contrast is strangely apt. Our end-of-millennium culture displays a necessary chiaroscuro quality, light flowing into shadow. There has been, it seems, a gradual decay of the brightest early dreams, those cartoonish images of the 1950s and '60s, into the cinematic explosions and screeching metal that now pass for insight about life in the twenty-first century. Indeed, both sides of this opposition may be seen as expressions of anxiety about the future: at the end of time, hope and despair go hand in hand. If this basic dialectic of bright and brutal is always a feature of anxiety about the future—and it is—we can nevertheless see that conflict between the two visions has recently become more marked. An outpouring of cultural anxiety about the coming millennium has begun.

Consider some of the more accessible evidence. *Sports Illustrated* now runs a feature called "This Week's Sign That The Apocalypse Is Upon Us," a wry commentary on the baffling backwaters of American culture. The urban lifestyle magazine *Toronto Life*, preparing its readers in the best way it knew how, pointed out for future reference that "millennium" has two "n"s. Something called *The Millennium Planner* began appearing in bookstores late in 1994, retailing for a hefty $39.95. It contains a lavishly illustrated softcover book of predictions, including (predictably) those of tabloid psychic Jeanne Dixon and Nostradamus, and a "personal time capsule," which was really a form to be filled out in various ways (three resolutions for the new millennium; predictions concerning money, love, family, home, health) and then set aside for the big day. Better, though, is "The Millennium Planner Contest," which offers $20,000 in travel vouchers for essays predicting what life will be like in 2000. Browsing through the book and its assorted paraphernalia, I briefly considered writing an essay that said, "Just like now, only worse all around." But I figured that probably wouldn't win: too many people would submit it.

There's more. Psychics now apparently control late-night television, where their ads are as competitive and bitter as those between rival long-distance companies. New Agers eager for the imminent Age of Aquarius, and disappointed by the Harmonic Convergence of 1987, are viewing the coming millennium with great anticipation. Some of them foresee a universal spiritual event, a triumphant mingling of human consciousness, in the calendar's turning. Others are haunted by a prediction that extends back to the lost civilization of Atlantis (according to Graham Hancock's 1995 best-seller *Fingerprints of the Gods*, it lies under what is now Antarctica) that the world will be destroyed by fire on December 23, 2012.

Meanwhile, we have been invaded. From television's "The X Files" to a spate of 1996 aliens-among-us movies—*The Arrival, Phenomenon,* the brainlessly jingoistic *Independence Day*—we are everywhere confronted with images of what Carl Jung once called "technological angels": the flying saucers that are by turns our doom and our salvation. In almost identical July, 1996, cover stories, *Time* and *Newsweek* both reported that 48 percent of Americans now believe UFOs are real, and that there is a government plot to deny their existence. In 1995 three New Yorkers were arrested for plotting to kill government officials they believed were responsible for the cover-up.

Even more dangerous forms of millennial craziness have recently swept across Japan, resulting in subway nerve-gas attacks by the "doomsday cult" Aum Shinri Kyo and pushing its leader, Shoko Asahara, a self-styled end-time prophet, onto our television screens. In the wake of that incident, miniature gas masks became a hot fashion accessory in Tokyo's trendy Harajuku district, and a new rice dish called "Armageddon" was suddenly in great demand. When Asahara went on trial in April, 1996, he was described as "the most hated man in Japan," a pudgy Antichrist.

This extraordinary rise in anxiety is not restricted to the fringes of the culture. According to the *Fortean Times,* a London-based magazine dedicated to the bizarre, the times are getting slowly but surely stranger. While it is presumably difficult to quantify such things, 1993, for example, was 3.5 percent weirder than the previous year. The *Times's* "strangeness index," which measures thirty-four components of oddness including crop circles, spontaneous human combustion, and unexplained mass deaths, recorded a record level of 3,520 in 1993 compared to 3,400 in 1992.

Millenarianism, a belief in the literal Apocalypse, is

now, for many North American Christians, a stronger temptation than ever. As always, they find fuel for the end-time fire in the biblical scriptures of Daniel, Zachariah, Revelation, and Thessalonians. But they can also find it in the garish newspapers available at their supermarket check-outs. *The Weekly World News*, long recognized as the most outrageous of the supermarket tabloids, blared in May of 1995—after "My Wacky Hubby Eats Roaches" and "Hospital Food Made My Boobs Go Bust!"—that "a panel of the world's foremost Bible experts" had concluded, from study of the Dead Sea Scrolls and various biblical texts, that the world would definitely end on December 31, 1999. "Our intention isn't to alarm anyone," Dr. Mark Farine, a member of the panel, told the *WWN*. "We merely wish to point out that time is running short for mankind and the world we have inhabited for the past 100,000 years." Dr. Farine went on: "We also concluded that God will pass judgment on everyone who has ever lived on the day the world ends. We have strong reason to believe that God will call a halt to His 'human experiment.'" According to Ted Daniels, editor of the *Millennial Prophecy Report*, in January 1995 there were already some 350 U.S. organizations or groups predicting that 2000 will bring "some form of Armageddon."

We prepare for Armageddon in our different ways, and for some the prospect of the millennium is still leavened with joy. Richard Kieninger, of Adelphi, Texas, plans to launch a fleet of airships to watch dawn break on the new age. The Great Pyramid of Cheops, which archaeologists once speculated held the secret of calendar measurement in its precise dimensions, has been reserved for an exclusive party of three thousand called The Millennium Society—a group founded by some Yale undergraduates, Class of '79, when they were riding high in the Wall Street of the 1980s. There has been a run on vintage champagne to launch these parties into the Third Age. The luxury liner *Queen Elizabeth II*, assuming it is still seaworthy, will launch from New York harbour on December 21, 1999, for a voyage into the new millennium. Fashion shoots of appropriate millennium partywear have already appeared in glossy fashion magazines, and on July 22, 1996, *The New York Times* offically declared New York City "Millennium Central"—"the place to be on New Year's Eve 1999, not to mention the next thousand years."

To be sure, none of this is new. Almost every century since the 1100s has, at least in the West, brought increased anxiety, expressed as both dread and desire, at its close. Warring decadence and puritanism, obsessive devotion to our bodies, plagues, spiritual confusion—these have been found in the Rhine Valley of the 1190s, Florence of the 1490s, and Paris of the 1890s. The generally accepted signs of apocalypse, articulated from the earliest days of the Christian era, are all too familiar: they include, says historian Norman Cohn, "bad rulers, civil discord, war, drought, famine, plague, comets, sudden deaths of prominent persons and an increase in general sinfulness." Indeed, Cohn adds, so pervasive are these features of human life that "there was never any difficulty in finding them" to support millennial movements. We live, as Susan Sontag once put it, in "an era of permanent apocalypse."

And so, for those inclined to look for it, there is plenty of evidence to support the view that the world is coming to an end. We worry about explosions and riots in our cities. Crumbling traditions, social hostility, environmental collapse. Cynicism, lawlessness, disorder. Natural disasters like floods, earthquakes, and hurricanes. Not to mention the fact that there will be nothing left in pension funds when many of us hit retirement age. According to Third Millennium, a New York City research firm, among American adults under thirty-five, the ratio of those who believe in UFOs to those who believe that Social Security will exist when they retire is five to three.

- _ -

Other centuries since the passing of the first Christian millennium have closed with a decade of gradually escalating dread, but for us the situation is compounded. "What the last decade is to a century the last century is to a millennium," the editors of *The Atlantic Monthly* pointed out—in 1891. The implication is clear: the cultural upheavals of the nineteenth-century *fin de siècle* will be nothing compared to what we can expect in the next few years. *The Atlantic*, by the way, is now doing its part to intensify the anxieties that afflict us. Magazine aficionados will have noticed by now that the Boston-based publication seems, in the mid-1990s, to have cornered the market on cover stories of apocalyptic dimension: "The Coming Anarchy" (February 1994, environmental collapse); "Must It Be the West Versus the Rest?" (December 1994, the collapse of democracy); "The Crisis of Public Order" (July 1995, growing urban anarchy).

These reports gave 1995 a particular millennial poignancy. During what *Newsweek* called "the fiftieth anniversary of almost everything," we were forced to come to terms with the late-century implications of the world constructed in 1945. The whole tired century, with its world wars and famines and genocides—this century of Holocaust and Cold War, of the End of History and the New World Order, of the New Age—could all too easily be read as a prolonged overture to final destruction.

I was born in 1963. It was the year John F. Kennedy delivered his *"Ich bin ein Berliner"* speech in what was then West Germany. It was also the year he was assassinated in Dallas. In 1963 Martin Luther King, Jr., gave his most famous oration, the "I have a dream" speech, in Washington, D.C. The Beatles appeared on "The Ed

Sullivan Show." Zip codes were introduced by the United States Postal Service. Betty Friedan published *The Feminine Mystique*. Michael Jordan, arguably the most famous human alive today, was born. McDonald's sold its billionth hamburger. Marshall McLuhan, an obscure English professor at the college I would later attend, was putting the finishing touches on his ground-breaking book *Understanding Media*, a book so far ahead of its time that it still seemed fresh in a 1994 reissue.

Millennial anxiety was already abroad in the 1960s, at least among those inclined to project current events into the future. "The world of the year 2000 has already arrived," the sociologist Daniel Bell wrote in 1968, "for in the decisions we make now, in the way we design our environment and thus sketch the lines of constraints, the future is committed." The conservative commentator Irving Kristol spoke for many, at least in his middle-aged generation, when he wrote in 1969 that the counter-culture was actually a millenarian sect, bent on destroying the world in search of a utopian future. Less seriously, an anonymous essayist in a 1963 issue of *The New Yorker* found cause for concern in this conundrum: how would we *say* the new dates on the other side of the millennial line? "Two thousand? Twenty hundred? Twenty oh-oh? Twenty nought nought? Twenty cipher cipher? Twenty flat?" *The New Yorker* preferred "twenty oh-oh"—"a nervous name for what is sure to be a nervous year."

In February and March of 1963, the philosopher Hannah Arendt was publishing, also in *The New Yorker*, her correspondence from the 1961 trial of Austrian Nazi Adolph Eichmann. The subtitle of Arendt's subsequent book about the trial, *Eichmann in Jerusalem*, is well known: *A Report on the Banality of Evil*, she called it. The phrase "banality of evil" has been much discussed, but I am more struck at the moment by that use of the word "report."

When Arendt was criticized for her suggestion that the Jews were in some way complicit in the Holocaust, guilty too for failing to see evil in its new guise, Arendt angrily defended herself by saying that there was no speculation in her report; it was the result of dispassionate observation, not philosophical speculation. "[T]here are no 'ideas' in this Report," she wrote to her close friend Mary McCarthy, "there are only facts with a few conclusions."

The comment is a bit disingenuous. Arendt might have felt comfortable taking refuge in the objectivity of her reporting, but we live in a more cynical age. In a cultural landscape razed by media manipulation and the video-arcade carnage of Gulf War coverage, we invest reporting with no special status. Still, the idea of the report remains a powerful one. It carries a sense of dispassionate observation, of detached description. I have borrowed the term for this book's subtitle, not because I am pretending to objectivity or even neutrality—you would not find that kind of report very interesting to read, and I would not find it much fun to write—but simply because we badly need some clear-eyed reflection on our accelerated culture.

If this is a report more personal than otherwise, more pop culture than high-brow, that is no more than the first lesson of "brink culture." Today we cannot escape the influence of the popular, and we can find no authoritative standpoint from which judgments can be delivered with finality. This cultural and epistemological vertigo can be frightening, certainly, but it can also be pretty exciting—even liberating. Fear, as I learned so many years ago in the darkness of the movie theatre, brings its own rush of pleasure.

A brink is a precipice, a cliff's edge. And "brinksmanship" is, in the parlance of those arms negotiators who controlled our destiny through the early 1980s, a willingness to take it to the edge—to play a little fast and loose, to dare for the sake of success. For many of us, the language of brinksmanship is a haunting reminder of the nuclear arms race and the prospect, which, in common with a number of my friends, I regarded as very real, that the world would end before we reached our thirtieth birthdays. It is hard, thank God, to recapture the sense of nuclear anxiety that ran through the years of the SALT and START talks, when my friends and I were in university.

The threat of nuclear destruction, that literal apoca-lypse, has receded in our imaginations, replaced by a less focused, less specific anxiety. We have traded one threat for a panoply of them. We now find ourselves afflicted by what existential philosophers call angst: the non-specific worry, the pervasive anxiety of the ill-at-ease. What we find on the edge of 2000 is that anxiety is often in the process of detaching from real objects and becoming, as it were, free-floating. It needs no objective correlative to be a powerful cultural force. Millennial anxiety thus verges on becoming a self-fulfilling prophecy.

These days, I find myself turning again and again to another science-fiction film that has had an unexpectedly large impact on my thoughts: Fred McLeod Wilcox's 1956 masterpiece *Forbidden Planet*. I first saw it in 1983, this time in the dingy rep cinema of my college neighbourhood. Walter Pidgeon plays a Prospero-like character called Dr. Morbius who is, with his beautiful daughter (a demure but sexy Anne Francis), the last remaining member of a group of Earth colonists on a distant planet. Leslie Nielsen, in the kind of straight-faced leading-man role he now only paro-dies, plays the captain of a spaceship sent out from Earth to visit the long-silent colonists. The mysteries Nielsen and his officers must solve are these: What destroyed all the other colonists? And why are Morbius and his daughter (who turns out to be an android) the only ones still alive?

The answer is resonant. It seems that a piece of alien technology from the planet's previous occupants, a kind of massive subterranean supercomputer, has translated the colonists' subconscious thoughts and desires into reality—including, unfortunately, their darkest, most murderous thoughts, the ones they (and we) usually prefer to keep hidden. The colonists have been destroyed, in short, by their very own "monsters from the id." The violence that normally lies buried within the human psyche has been externalized via technology. The only reason Morbius is still alive is that, with his powerful personality made more powerful by the computer, he simply proved stronger (or perhaps more twisted) than the others. In the film's climax, his personal monster from the id just about manages to destroy the visiting spaceship too, as Nielsen and the crew attempt a hasty escape.

It is unlikely, to say the least, that anyone today would have the nerve to make a popular science-fiction movie that combined Shakespearean and Freudian themes, especially with no nudity, dismemberment, or major explosions. But that is not the most striking thing about *Forbidden Planet*. I keep coming back to its central conceit: the idea that technology gives us the power to facilitate our own inner violence, to make our dreams dangerously real. We have the power to destroy ourselves, the film suggests, only when our own unconscious wishes and fears are sent into the world. When, indeed, they *become* the world—a tissue of irrational fears, a screen onto which we project our various phobias and desires. "The first world we find outside is, in part, a repository for the terror inside us, an elsewhere for those desires and objects that bring unpleasure," the psychoanalyst Adam Phillips writes in his book *On Kissing, Tickling, and Being Bored* (1993). "And that world we make outside is the world we need to get away from. It is the place, or one of the places, where we put the objects and desires we wish did not belong to us. To be at home in the world we need to keep it inhospitable."

The cultural world is very much a construction of our dreams, those that express wishes but also those that give shape to our deepest terrors—visions of utopia but also of apocalypse. And our technology, which is not literally alien but is surely sometimes alienating, plays an instrumental part in making those dreams actual. Nobody invented the apocalyptic facts of our end-of-millennium culture—free-falling economies, drastic overpopulation, wars and famines—but our projections of imagination onto these events (phantasies, in Freudian usage) express at least as much about the state of the world as they do about our desires and wishes for that world.

The calendar with which we measure the millennium is, to be sure, an arbitrary cultural creation; it reflects no metaphysical truths. Yet even arbitrary things can gain power over the wayward human imagination. We could as much challenge the power of 2000 as we could, in other contexts, deny the significance of such equally arbitrary calendar events as December 25 or July 4.

The dreams of millennium I describe in this book are, in their way, monsters from the id. They are the dark things we wish did not belong to us. They are the real-world expressions of anxiety, of the commingled hopes and dreads that mark our dreaming hours. They are also, paradoxically, what we must confront in order to be at home in the world. We can do nothing else than begin here, with the dreams that hold us in their grip.

So let the end begin.

ONE

Shards of Apocalypse

> Even the Old Testament expected the Apocalypse "shortly"…
> But I am trying to ignore the world situation. I am hoping it
> will go away. Not the world. The situation.
>
> Martin Amis, *London Fields*

IN THE AIRPORT'S
airless shopping concourse, the news is all bad. Death and
disease jostle for shelf space with the glossy fashion-mag
covers, the poreless youngsters and their sulky looks of hidden
secrets. "Killer Virus," says *Newsweek*. "The Latest
Killer Virus," echoes *The New Yorker*. "Disease Strikes
Back," *The Economist* suggests, "Beyond the Ebola Scare:
What Else Is Out There?" Over on the shelves of thick
books, a brick-like tome shoulders in next to Richard
Preston's *The Hot Zone* and sets out the bad-news answer.
"As the millennium approaches…the skills needed to
describe and recognize perturbations in the Homo sapiens
microecology are disappearing with the passing of the generations,"
Laurie Garrett says in *The Coming Plague: Newly
Emerging Diseases in a World Out of Balance*, "leaving
humanity lulled into a complacency born of proud discoveries
and medical triumphs, unprepared for the coming
plague."

Garrett's book describes, in gruesome detail, all the rivals
to Ebola in the Grossest Possible Viral Death sweepstakes:
Marburg virus, Lassa fever, hantavirus, seal plague. Even old
spectres like cholera are making a comeback in the thickly
populous cities of India, Pakistan, Sri Lanka, and Central

17

America. Garrett sounds hauntingly like a millenarian prophet from the Middle Ages. Complacency, she suggests, is killing us. *Trust no more, fools, in your man-made technology. God's wrath—in the form of invisible microbes that feed on your bodies like bugs on a branch—is hard upon ye. Repent now, wicked ones, or die a horrible death!*

What *else* is out there? It isn't enough, apparently, that in sixty-four U.S. cities AIDS is the leading cause of death for adults between twenty-five and forty-four. It isn't sufficiently frightening that unstoppable hemorrhagic fevers, with no known cures or treatment, come rolling out of the African rainforest to devastate towns and spread like bushfire into major cities. That the fevers are highly contagious and impossible to stop. That they attack the host by liquefying its internal organs, turning the inside of the human body into a mush of destroyed tissue that seeps out through every orifice, blood streaming from the ears and eyes, pouring from the nose and mouth, until the dying host all but explodes, like an overfed tick.

The author of *The Hot Zone*, which details an outbreak of Ebola in a Virginia monkey laboratory, returns to his subject in an issue of *The New Yorker* that I find as I surf the airport newsagent's shelf. A new strain of Ebola has spread through Kikwit, a poor city in Zaire with a population of half a million, Richard Preston reports; officials are rigid with panic that it will spread along the highway to the capital, Kinshasa, about 250 miles distant. "We live in a kind of biological Internet," Preston writes, "in which viruses travel like messages, moving at high speed from node to node, moving from city to city.... In the past couple of decades, [Ebola] has been popping into the human species in different places and in different strains. It keeps touching the human biological Internet. Probing it, so to speak."

This makes the virus sound like an evil attacker, the devilish alien within. Strange to personify a biological force that looks, under a microscope, like a tiny piece of coiled string. But of course we do it, because often we find it difficult to combat an enemy that we do not first demonize. To see Ebola as something just as natural, as biologically pure, as yeast would suck all the meaning—all the fear—out of it. "Tapping into health paranoia is guaranteed to scare the audience silly," the critic Terrence Rafferty writes in a review of the 1995 biohazard thriller *Outbreak*, "and film-makers will undoubtedly use fear of disease the way they once used the threat of nuclear catastrophe, which enhanced ordinary race-against-the-clock suspense with the possibility of apocalypse." In fact, the virus is even scarier because *it grows inside our bodies*. It actually combines two strains of paranoia, the Apocalyptic Disaster and the Enemy Within. Microbial fear is therefore supercharged; it is atomic disaster plus the Red Scare, as if the hand that pushed the button also belonged to an infiltrating Communist agent or body-snatcher.

No surprise, then, that virus-themed television shows and films have proliferated in the wake of the Ebola outbreak. Here, after all, was a scare that was for the moment less real than AIDS (it happened mostly in isolated African villages) and significantly less charged politically (it did not require a sex act for transmission and did not exhibit higher incidence among any "deviant" group). In the first half of 1995 it seemed entirely possible, if you watched television or visited newsstands, to imagine that disease could "strike back" anywhere, that you could become infected simply by standing around a public place—like, say, an airport.

As I stroll along the requisite mile or so of airless airport corridors, I think about the airline maps of interconnecting flight-routes at the back of thick in-flight magazines, those elegantly curving red lines arcing from New York to London, Paris to Madrid, Miami to Florence. At a given moment, I wonder, how many of us are actually *in the air*, suspended along those red curves like packet-switched e-mail messages shooting through the notional ether of the Internet? And how many miles have we all logged in the brief decades of air travel? We simply go everywhere these days, most of the time without a second thought. I cannot calculate how many miles I have travelled in my life: I give up when I realize that I have probably racked up more than four thousand in the last few months alone. What's the total for a routinely travelled middle-class professional? Fifty thousand? A hundred? Five hundred?

The viruses travel as fast as we do, these days, and as effi-ciently. They log their frequent-flyer miles. They bust out of the African rainforests on the backs of monkeys, of humans, or just pass breezily from lung to lung. We pack them in our overnight bags, in our overstuffed leatherette valises, in our Louis-Vuitton matched sets and American Tourister gar-ment totes. We pack them, finally, in our most basic bags, our purely personal luggage, the constant carry-on—our bodies. Worldwide web, oh yes. Global village, certainly.

By the time I reach the departure lounge, I am starting to feel a little woozy. I find myself recalling a passage from an Iris Murdoch novel. "I settled myself in the departure lounge in the far corner," the narrator says. "Outside the enormous window lighted aircraft passed by slowly on their way to the runway. In the warm lounge half-audible voices gave sing-song instructions through loudspeakers to tense people who seemed to understand them. It was like a wait-ing-room for the Last Judgment.... The end-of-the-world atmosphere was beginning to be oppressive, and I could not determine whether a distant roaring noise was made by aeroplanes or by my own blood." Maybe it's the recycled air. Maybe it's the screaming children, who seem to proliferate in departure lounges. These children know all about panic, I figure. They know about the crude physical fear the rest of us manage to suppress, more or less, when our massive machines strain into the air. The children know that we really should be sprinting up and down the lounge in a mad panic at the prospect of hurtling ourselves through space, at a speed of five hundred miles an hour, in a machine that weighs hundreds of tons.

But we ignore their message, or at least block it out as best we can. We trust in our technology. We shuffle into our planes like zombies, the departure-lounge undead. We load down the metal beast with our personal belongings, straining against weight restrictions with densely packed carry-on bags. We follow the safety instructions, the belt buckling and life-jacket activating and air-mask pulling, as though it's an elaborate and really rather boring game of Simon Says. We all know that this is pointless. If this behemoth is going down over the North Atlantic, we are all instant sharkfeed. But I stare calmly ahead like the rest. I locate the nearest emergency exit. I acknowledge, without bothering to look, that there is a life jacket under my seat. I am a rational person. I know that flying is safer than taking a shower. At least, that's what I think somebody once told me.

Seven hours later I am deposited neatly and rudely into another lounge, an arrival lounge this time, at Gatwick. It is indistinguishable from the lounge I left, except that everyone seems to be smoking, lighting up their Senior Service or Silk Cuts with trembling hands and sucking on the sticks like they were love lollipops. I am logy and sandy-eyed, suffering from that peculiarly modern ailment, jet lag. Yes, like everyone else, I have displayed the oh so banal modern trait of temporal arrogance. I have travelled faster than the earth itself can spin, hopping time zones with confident abandon, and now I am paying the price. One symptom is that I have no sensation of having flown. Rather, I feel as though I entered a constricted but immobile space in Toronto, settled into the metal roll of recycled air for one movie, two meals, and numerous sorties in an armrest war with my next-seat neighbour, and now here I am in London, looking for the millennium.

— _ —

"Never before in the history of the world had such a mass of human beings moved and suffered together," the chronicler wrote. "It was the beginning of the rout of civilization, of the massacre of mankind." What was it? The Crusades? The Black Plague? The Great War? Hitler's murder of the Jews? Or perhaps some imagined event. A nuclear war? Environmental destruction? The comet's crash, when worlds collide?

No. It was the invasion of Earth by Martians. The chronicler was H. G. Wells, whose novel *The War of the Worlds* caused its share of panic when published in the millennial ferment of 1898—and another panic half a century later when near-namesake Orson Welles broadcast the tale on American radio. In the radio drama the invasion forces touched down in Paterson, New Jersey, where Welles was manning the microphone. In Wells's novel the invasion ground zero was London, where six million people would die at the hands of the passionless mechanical Martians before a routine Earth virus laid them low. Not even something as riveting as Ebola; it was the common cold the Martians couldn't handle.

Wells's famous book is merely the best remembered of more than fifty book-length Martian tales that surfaced in the years before the turn of the present century, most of them inspired by the 1887 discovery, by the Italian astronomer Giovanni Schiaparelli, that channels scored and crisscrossed the surface of the Red Planet. This suggestion of intelligent life created a potent cocktail when mixed with more routine *fin-de-siècle* anxiety. Unsurprisingly, the Martian books embraced both dystopian and utopian visions, with Mars standing in, as always in speculative fiction, for both our secret hopes and our secret fears. Nor was Wells alone in imagining the Martians as a super-efficient invasion force. Heavier-than-air flight, itself an achievement of the century's turn—and the source of a spate of UFO sightings through the 1890s—made space travel seem not just possible but likely.

A product of his time and place, Wells figured the Martians would choose London as their point of arrival. Who can blame him? London was the largest city in the world in the 1880s, Britain arguably the most powerful nation and the centre of a massive empire on which, famously, the sun never set. Similarly, in the 1951 film *The Day the Earth Stood Still*, Klaatu, a handsome and compassionate alien (played with great aplomb by Michael Rennie) chose Washington, D.C., as the place to land and deliver his warning about atomic foolishness.

Today, nobody is likely to pick London as the forward point of an invasion force, but its millennial mood remains. Walking the streets of London, one no longer feels power or even post-imperial bitterness. Instead, and despite the hot crush of people in Piccadilly and Trafalgar Square, you sense only emptiness—the clapped-out despair of a nation that has slid from prominence to marginality in a couple of generations. It is easy to imagine that they take it out on you by being perhaps the most expensive city on the planet, charging what seems like a week's wages for a sandwich and offering rides in taxicabs whose meters tick over so fast their LEDs are a blur of luminous red.

London is, I find, one place where the imminent millennium is, in a manner characteristic of our age, being taken very seriously. There is, for example, a government-appointed Millennium Commission. In the words of Peter Brooke, the secretary of state for National Heritage, it has been set up to support "exceptionally distinctive proposals that are 'of the millennium.'" But that resounding phrase turns out to have little concrete meaning for the civil servants, journalists, and variously prominent members of the commission. "The commission has been told to approve projects which are 'of the millennium,' but members admitted last week to being unable to define the phrase," Marianne Macdonald wrote in London's *Independent on Sunday* newspaper on September 18, 1994, "and on Friday, the [new] Secretary of State for National Heritage said he had no plans to clarify it."

The phrase "of the millennium" is, as Conor Cruise O'Brien pointed out in his 1994 book *On the Eve of the Millennium*, virtually meaningless, no more than an empty stamp of semantic approval. Still, the commission's vapidity is a sign of the times. Empty-headed as it certainly appears, it says something about the flailing about for meaning that has become characteristic of the West. We simply don't know how to celebrate a momentous date like 2000. We strike a commission, of course; perhaps it will, per convention, write a report. It will certainly fund some projects with money granted by well-meaning politicians. "One of the best proposals so far," Macdonald wrote in her article, "must be the architect David Marks's idea for a Ferris wheel on the site of the Jubilee Gardens standing 200 feet above Big Ben." Well, okay. But what does that say about the momentous event of turning onto the terrain of 2000? Very little. Or rather, it says: we haven't got a clue what we're doing here.

London has known its share of millennial uncertainty, though in earlier times it was most decidedly Christian in outlook. In 1665 a Great Plague, reminiscent of the fourteenth-century Black Death, spread through the unhygienic inner-city precincts of London, killing thousands. The next year a massive fire, probably started in the densely overpopulated slums that were slung across the River Thames on London's wide bridges, reduced large portions of the city to ash and charcoal. These portents, coming as they did in or near a prophetically loaded year (the thousand years of oracular prophecy, plus 666, the sign of the Devil revealed by John), shook London to its foundations. The city was already reeling from the vicious bloodshed of the Civil War in the 1640s, Charles I's execution by Cromwell in 1649, and the bickering of the Commonwealth. The Restoration had touched off a celebratory mood and a new flowering of art and pleasure-seeking, true; but surely here was the punishment for it? The English Parliament began the largest witch hunt since the Middle Ages, tracking down atheists and heretics with unceasing vigour, tossing them into fetid jails where they were starved and tortured.

This religious intolerance prompted the philosopher John Locke to publish, in 1690, what has become one of the great documents in the liberal tradition, his *Letter Concerning Toleration*. The *Letter* suggests that, given the inevitable human uncertainty about the true route to Heaven, the only reasonable (and peaceful) course was to tolerate a plurality of views on salvation. In his moderation and common sense Locke was ahead of his time, which was not ripe for reasonableness. And he had cause to know it: he wrote the *Letter*, and his other great works of political and empirical philosophy, anonymously from Holland, where he had fled in 1683. After the Glorious Revolution installed William and Mary on the throne of England in 1689, Locke returned to England, chastened by the experience of exile and presumably wiser for having considered political events from a distance. What he discovered was a country still in deep conflict with itself.

In the years leading up to century's end, Locke, like all Britons, witnessed an outpouring of aggressively pious millenarian zeal, or "Religious Enthusiasm," that was matched only by the efforts of the religious and political authorities to stamp it out. Many of the targets of this effort to bind the country to a common religion are well known: the Puritans, the Quakers, even the Muggletonians or the "Diggers," who, at mid-century, had followed the prophet Gerrard Winstanley in pursuing an anti-technological millennium near Lobham, in Surrey. Less well known, but more colourful, were the so-called Ranters, devotees of a form of superior spirituality that passed from the more typical asceticism to a new sensuality. The Ranters nicely illustrate one of the great millennial dialectics, that between self-denial and decadence. Calling themselves "high attainers" or "high professors," the Ranters commonly worked themselves into ecstasies of erotic love and argued, as itinerant devotees of the Free Spirit heresy had in the fourteenth century, that God's love freed them from human strictures on behaviour. The medieval "beghards" (male) and "beguines" (female) who followed this millennial path were given to quoting St. Paul. "All things," they liked to say, "are pure to the pure." Anticipating the world's end at any time, they reacted not with self-abnegation but with a riotous physical expression.

The root of the Free Spirit heresy was actually a mystical form of self-deification. The Ranters picked up the thread, with some minor philosophical adjustments, and by the mid-1600s boasted some thousands of converts in London alone. They would gather in pubs or homes and work themselves into frenzies of singing and psalm-saying, addressing each other loudly as "fellow-creature," and culminate the sessions in orgiastic communal sex. For this, to nobody's surprise, they were often tossed in jail. As early as June 14, 1650, the Rump of the Long Parliament expressed its concern and appointed a committee "to consider of a Way for Suppression of the obscene, licentious and impious Practices, used by Persons, under Pretence of Liberty, Religion, or otherwise." A week later the committee reported on "the several abominable Practices of a Sect called Ranters," and a bill was prepared "for suppressing and punishing these abominable Opinions and Practices." It passed into law the following November. The Ranters were forced to develop secret forms of address to avoid detection, but they still frequently ended up behind bars.

The Ranters were often associated by hostile observers with the Quakers, for both believed in "inward salvation." But there the similarities end. George Fox, one of the first Quakers, reports in a letter meeting some Ranters while in prison in Coventry, in 1649: "When I came into the jail," he wrote, "where the prisoners were, a great power of darkness struck at me, and I sat still, having my spirit gathered into the love of God. At last these prisoners began to rant, and vapour, and blaspheme, at which my soul was greatly grieved. They said they were God; but that we could not bear such things.... Then seeing they said they were God, I asked them, if they knew whether it would rain tomorrow? They said they could not tell. I told them, God could tell.... After I had reproved them for their blasphemous expressions, I went away; for I perceived they were Ranters."

Fox was not alone in turning his thoughts to the weather. One of the most vigorous public debates of the day, which gradually took on an apocalyptic tenor as the century closed, concerned the predictions outlined in Thomas Burnet's treatise *The Sacred Theory of the Earth,* which (as its subtitle indicated) contained *An Account of the Origin of the Earth and of All the General Changes Which It Hath Already Undergone or Is to Undergo, till the Consummation of All Things.* The book, first published in Latin in 1681, proved so influential—and its thesis of environmental disaster so compelling—that it was translated into the common tongue in 1684 on the order of the King. A second volume, *On the Conflagration of the World and the Future State of Things,* appeared in 1689. Burnet, an Anglican clergyman, wrote vividly on a theme all too familiar in our own time. His theory was that the Flood had created the imperfect world we live in, full of droughts and deluges, and that this imperfection could only finally be resolved in a millennial transformation of the flawed earthly orb into a new Paradise. He notes, with admirable restraint, that the subject should be of interest to everyone, and he apologizes for his own fervour in pursuing it. "For to see a World perishing in Flames, Rocks melting, the Earth trembling, and a Host of Angels in the Clouds," he says, "one must be very much a Stoick, to be a cold and unconcern'd Spectator of all this."

Burnet was attacked for both his renegade theology and his environmental predictions, but a new feature of the millennial myth was now securely in place. The floods, storms, and famines are only the beginning, harbingers of a much bigger environmental apocalypse waiting, as always, just around the corner. And we thought these anxieties were unique to us, the oil-burning, emission-pumping, gas-guzzling, ozone-depleting people of the warming late-millennium globe. The difference, of course, is that few of us nowadays derive solace from the thought of a world purified by God's fire and flood.

In London today, the sun hangs low in the sky. The pavement shimmers with the heat of it. The radiation flows down, unimpeded by atmospheric block or screen, to scorch and burn the unprotected surface. There are still plenty of ranters about, and they are ranting about a lot of things, from the insistent demands of their personal demons to their poverty and my role in alleviating it. They all seem committed to the imminent end of the world. But there is no forward-looking aspect to the dreams of millennium in London's concrete fields. I listen to their messages, read their placards of woe—tales of unemployment, hungry children, neglect, and misfortune—but there is no sense, here, that despair is ever joined by hope. I find that not one of these contemporary ranters speaks to me of salvation or the purity of God's spirit. Their messages are only of death.

It was not always thus. In the seventeenth century, true to its biblical sources, millennial feeling had two distinct aspects: the bad and the good were always in view, so that for every enthusiast of the coming Kingdom on Earth there was a more sombre soul to warn about the devastation that must pave the way. But, perhaps characteristically, followers of the millennial prophecy have for the most part been content to gloss over the violence in favour of the bright dream of God's Second Coming, to see the dark as essential prerequisite for the light to come. Enthusiastic followers of what theologians call "chiliastic eschatology"—literally, a theory of the end based on the figure 1,000—have been found throughout the history of the Christian era, often despite the best efforts of Church authorities. The belief in a Millennium or Second Coming at the end of time as we know it, followed by a final divine Judgment of the quick and the dead, has proved too attractive to be entirely suppressed.

The earliest Judeo-Christian apocalyptic warnings are those found in the "Apocalyptic Dream" sequence of the Book of Daniel, chapter eight. Written around 165 B.C., during a Maccabaean revolt against the tyranny of Antiochus Epiphanus, the original Antichrist, this text gives us the image of the four beasts of the apocalypse and predicts the fall of Babylon if idolatry is not forsaken. Slightly later, around A.D. 93, was John's Book of Revelation, which rounds out the familiar imagery of fiery end-times and describes the destruction of Rome, a general metaphor for the secular world.

The common threads in all millennial texts are familiar to most of us: the promise of rewards for the just, punishment for the sinful, the culminating battle between good and evil. Their central conceit, and a key reason they have been so popular throughout history, is that they describe the material conditions of an oppressed people in such a way that the spiritual significance of the oppression is foremost.

The Jews and Christians, in other words, predict the end of this benighted world, and the beginning of the next one, as a way of coping with their very real slavery. In these tales there is always, then, a chosen people who are beset by some complex of misfortunes, usually combining the political and the natural.

The political element of chiliastic writing is extremely important: apocalyptic texts often function as manifestos for the downtrodden, the tyrannized, the put-upon. They tap into social unrest in the most powerful way imaginable, by telling a tale of salvation. There is always the announcement of a coming saviour, some kind of super-being who will free the chosen people from their torment, conquer the evil of the world, and establish a harmonious new regime: the Kingdom of Heaven on Earth, God's Paradise regained.

Strictly speaking, the Millennium, in this Judeo-Christian tradition, refers not to the thousand years—or two thousand years—of the pre-apocalypse; it refers to the thousand years of peace that will be established by the coming of the saviour. "Apocalypse," like "revelation," literally means an unveiling, a drawing away of what was covered; it is simply the word given to the expression of this prophecy. But with the portents of the Millennium, darkness begins to creep into the tale. The apocalyptic texts all agree that there will be numerous indicators that the world as we know it is coming to an end: plagues and floods, famines and wars, high-level assassinations. Leaders will not appear trustworthy, and there will be many false prophets, including the plausible but evil ideologue known as the Antichrist. It will be a time when, as Yeats noted in "The Second Coming," "the best lack all conviction." Finally there will be open conflict between the forces of good and the armies of evil: the People of Gog and Magog united under Satan. When the fighting is done, and the chosen people have been purified, the saviour will come to herald the dawning of the New Age.

This dream of salvation is such powerful mythic material that it is perhaps not surprising that saviours have been spotted from the earliest cultural memories of the West, where chiliasm is a stronger force than other forms of eschatology. These harbingers of salvation have not usually been content to be recognized spontaneously by others. Typically, they ramble around announcing their status to anyone and everyone. And that has led to some serious bloodshed, not to mention religious movements of varying degrees of size and craziness. From this historical perspective, Jesus is just one contender among many, maybe not even a consensus choice for the title. The Jews demurred; so did the Muslims. Despite the best efforts of Christians down through the ages, using every means from Bible-thumping to head-thumping, lots of people still refuse to recognize Jesus' claim to be the Son of God. In this, they show admirable historical caution. Pretenders to the saviour's crown are pretty thick on the ground, from Jesus' day to our own.

From the earliest days of the Judeo-Christian world, people have expected the Millennium at any moment. In A.D. 156, Montanus of Phrygia declared himself to be the Holy Ghost, the completion of the Holy Trinity. One imagines that Montanus chose that prong of the Trinity because the memory of the Son of God was too recent for His identity to be challenged overtly. The Montanist creed immediately attracted followers, aided by the political and social unrest of the day, notably the vicious persecution of early Christians by Jewish and Roman authorities, an activity that can be readily expected to foment millennial fever. The philosopher Tertullian was a follower of Montanus for a time, and he, along with the other Montanists, took up arms to hurry along the apocalypse by challenging the authority of Rome. Inevitably, they were put down, thus establishing a long-standing pattern of violent suppression of millennial outbreaks—a pattern that traces a path all the way from Phrygia to Waco, Texas.

In the next few centuries, despite the best efforts of theologians and Church authorities—Origen and Augustine, the best minds of the early Church, both condemned chiliasm and argued that the Kingdom was an inward spiritual destination, not a worldly one—millenarians proliferated through the Christian world. "This idea had such enormous attractions," the historian Norman Cohn says in his book *The Pursuit of the Millennium* (1970), "that no official condemnation could prevent it from recurring again and again in the minds of the underprivileged, the oppressed, the disoriented and the unbalanced." Indeed, the idea's influence grew almost in direct relation to the waxing power, and with it the corruption, of the established Roman Church. Down to our own day, with the ravings of splinter Christian sects in pamphlets handed out on the street, millennial prophecy often identifies the Church itself as the Whore of Babylon and the Pope as the Antichrist.

Legend has it that the year 1000 of the Christian calendar was marked by a widespread outpouring of apocalyptic fever. Pope Sylvester II, known to be a dabbler in black arts like mathematics and chronology, is supposed to have marked the occasion with his collection of precise clocks, which were calibrated to the sun's rising and setting, and caused all the bells of Christendom to peal out. Even as the bells were ringing, it was said, people in the streets were gripped in a "panic terror" of devastating proportions: houses set ablaze, mass suicides, inexplicable perversions of nature visiting themselves on the populace. A Royal Charter written at the time begins with a reference to "the wanton fortune of this deceiving world, not lovely with the milk-white radiance of unfading lilies, but odious with the gall-steeped bitterness of lamentable corruption, raging with venomous wide-stretched jaws."

William Robertson, the great eighteenth-century

Scottish historian, peer of Hume and Gibbon, wrote that "A general consternation seized mankind; many relinquished their possessions, and abandoning their friends and families, hurried with precipitation to the Holy Land, where they imagined that Christ would quickly appear to judge the world." His countryman Charles Mackay, writing with fine late-Enlightenment disdain of *Extraordinary Popular Delusions and the Madness of Crowds* (1852), noted that "In the year 999, the number of pilgrims proceeding eastward, to await the coming of the Lord in that city [Jerusalem], was so great that they were compared to a desolating army.... Buildings of every sort were suffered to fall into ruins. It was thought useless to repair them, when the end of the world was so near.... Knights, citizens, and serfs travelled eastward in company, taking with them their wives and children, singing psalms as they went, and looking with fearful eyes upon the sky, which they expected each minute to open, to let the Son of God descend in his glory."

Across the Channel in France, the historian Jules Michelet was making similar comments, though tinged with more worldliness and melancholy. "It was universal belief in the Middle Ages that the world would end with the year 1000 from the Nativity," Michelet wrote in a section on "The Year 1000" in his *History of France*. "This world saw nothing in itself but chaos; it longed for order and hoped to find it in death. Besides, in those times of miracles and legends, where everything appeared in bizarre colours, as if through dark stained glass, people could wonder whether this visible reality were anything other than a dream.... It could well be that what we call life was really death, and that by ending, the world...began to live and ceased to die."

Unsettling and poignant, these reports suggest disturbing parallels between our own day and the barbarism and credulity of the Middle Ages. The only trouble is, there was in fact no great outpouring of millennial anxiety concentrated on the year 1000. These faintly shocked, certainly superior Enlightenment commentaries on medieval naiveté are the products of a great piece of historical myth-making. The reports of "panic terror" on the eve of 1000 are now widely regarded as false; moreover, contemporary historians argue, they *had* to be false. The Christian calendar had no wide authority in what we now call A.D. 999. Nor was there even an accepted New Year's Day. Indeed, the Arabic zero had not yet been welcomed into the mathematics of the West, and disagreement reigned over the beginning of the day and the week. Therefore the simultaneous pealing of bells described so vividly by subsequent historians could not have happened; neither Sylvester, nor anyone else in Europe, had the technological ability to tell time with precision. It wasn't until the 1290s, when Pope Boniface VIII ordered a Jubilee year for all Christendom, that the centuries began to take on the shape they now have for us. And it was not until the 1690s, according to some historians, that people began to see themselves as products of a given century, each with a peculiar character all its own.

According to Hillel Schwartz, author of *Century's End* (1990), the construction of century's end as a significant time—complete with the predictable but pointless debates about when the new century really begins—is an even more recent phenomenon, the product of the eighteenth century and later. "At century's end," he writes, "we are inevitably host to an oxymoronic time: the best and the worst, the most desperate and the most exultant; the most constrained and the most chaotic.... In a sense, of course, the century's end is a trick, a little razzle-dazzle with nines and zeros...a trick that works because we are time-minded enough to prospect for ends, numerate but visionary enough to be impressed by imaginary numbers, punctual enough to attend to a common calendar of years."

In fact, the real flowering of millennial nuttiness came

only in the half century following the 1000 milestone, and it was usually unrelated to specific calculations. The Second Coming has been variously predicted for, among other years, 666, 1033, 1260, 1284, 1492, 1496, 1524, 1588, 1656, 1666, 1789, and 1844. In fact, the real growth of millennial fever had more to do with rapid social and technological change, swift population growth, and industrialization, than with data-crunching mathematics.

The lack of a common calendar did not stop people from indulging their anxiety about the end-times, though. In the 1100s, for example, the freelance prophet Tanchelm declared himself the Messiah and gathered a large army from the unsettled peasantry of the Rhine Valley. His enthusiastic followers drank his bath water as a form of holy eucharist. At around the same time, a French pretender called Eudes de l'Etoile said *he* was the Son of God and put together a private army.

Both of them were outdone by Pope Urban II, who, without making any claims about his own divinity, drew together the largest army in the history of the Christian world, the First Crusade, in 1095. This followed ten years of floods, droughts, famines, and, from 1089 on, plagues that ravaged most of central and southern Europe. The official crusade, to liberate the Holy Land, was paralleled by the so-called People's Crusade, a ragtag assortment of indigent, diseased, and disaffected peasants who followed the charismatic lead of Peter the Hermit, a crazed former monk who argued that the poor were the true Chosen People of God and that the Millennium was about to dawn. He exhorted his constituents to a "militant pilgrimage" to the Holy Land, where they would engage in "a collective *imitatio Christi*." Most of them died along the way, but not before managing to sack villages, rape young women, and kill as many Jews as they could lay their hands on. Those who made it to Jerusalem then killed all the Muslims they could lay their hands on, and captured the city for the forces of Christian good. "As usual," the historian Norman Cohn wrote of this action, "the route to the Millennium led through massacre and terror."

The idea of the *imitatio Christi*—the imitation of Christ—plays a central role in millennial madness through the middle centuries of the Christian era. In an extreme form it leads to the delusion of identification with the Messiah, a culturally specific form of madness that is still very popular on the streets of North American cities. When I was living in New Haven in the late 1980s there was a bearded young man I used to see frequently. He went around town barefoot, all year round. He also claimed he was Jesus, come again to judge the living and the dead. New Haven Jesus never explained why he chose to start his apocalyptic mission in a dilapidated university town on Long Island Sound with a high crime rate. Admittedly, there was plenty of sin there, but it hardly seemed auspicious. New Haven Jesus used to loiter, as I did, in the bookstore where my wife worked, so I had ample opportunity to observe him. When he turned thirty-three in 1988, he let us know he was convinced his death was imminent. I don't know if he imagined he was going to be crucified in the middle of New Haven (by whom?), but he didn't die that year, and so he suffered the indignity—for the risen God, I mean—of reaching his thirty-fourth birthday. He then noted, with admirable logical clarity, that the biblical accounts of Jesus' life were, as we all knew, notoriously unreliable. (Point to him.)

Less extreme, and probably saner, versions of the *imitatio Christi* are welcomed by Church authorities. There is a respected tradition in Roman Catholic theology of an act of identification with Christ, some form of self-abnegation or asceticism to follow the religious example of, and thus foster communication with, the human form of God. Jesus is God incarnate—that is, God embodied, encased in flesh—and mere mortals can thus hope to have some identification with the divine by following his example and decrying the flesh. The Augustinian monk Thomas à Kempis wrote his famous, and still widely read, ascetical treatise *The Imitation of Christ* around 1425, but the practice was popular well before then.

From the early eleventh century onward, self-flagellation was the most common form of *imitatio Christi*, a practice in which zealous true believers lashed themselves into a bloody state to encourage visions of God, to chastise their carnal desires, and to imitate the physical suffering of Jesus. This form of self-abuse also functioned as an atonement for the sins of the individual and the general perfidy of the human world; it was a sacrifice offered in hopes of appeasing an angry God or, if the end-times were coming, an act of self-purification marking the flagellant as one of the devoted preparing for the imminent Rapture. One might even speculate that many devoted flagellants masochistically enjoyed the pain, or anyway acquired a taste for it along the way, but that is perhaps to psychologize too much. Given this complex of motives and significations, it is not surprising that self-flagellation proved so popular in times of stress. In Italy during 1260—following famine in 1258, plague in 1259, and ongoing city-state wars—there was a mass outbreak of self-flagellation. A series of earthquakes then upped the millennial ante and sent thousands more running for their whips and goads. They also grabbed their weapons, which they used, between bouts of self-flagellation, to murder Jews.

Outbreaks of self-flagellation continued to mark the millennial fevers that ran through Europe in the Middle Ages. In 1348 the Black Death provided the strongest portent of apocalypse yet, wiping out as much as a third of the European population in a matter of months and throwing the surviving population into a paroxysm of panic, scapegoating, and political unrest. The nobleman Agnolo di Tura of Siena, who buried five of his own children, wrote of this new plague's enormous force in his chronicle of 1348. "And no bells tolled," he wrote, "and nobody wept no matter what his loss because almost everyone expected death.... And people said and believed, 'This is the end of the world.'" Flagellant cults sprang up everywhere, outlaw orders of body-abusing monks who performed public whipping rituals in an attempt to ward off God's wrath.

Given the widening gap between rich and poor and the accelerated proto-industrial culture of the fourteenth century, objective signs like the Black Death helped the dark dreams of millennium to coalesce into what Norman Cohn calls "a coherent social myth" that played across Europe with remarkable consistency of theme. The Millennium would see the rich and powerful punished, the poor and wretched exalted. Along the way, Church authority could be safely ignored, and the efforts of scholars and other enlightened forces to curb the fevers of whipping and pogrom could be confidently interpreted, and thus ignored, as last-ditch attempts to protect privilege. Obscure hermits and monks were elevated to positions of enormous influence in the blink of an eye, sometimes without their full co-operation.

It was, in consequence, a very good time for the canny and the opportunistic, or the merely devoted. Charismatic ideologues used millennial imagery to stir up political unrest which they then rode to prominence, wealth, and—typically—early and violent death. The English Peasants' Rebellion of 1381, for example, led by John Ball, was driven by envy of the rich reworked as God's disapproval of luxury. The German Peasants' War of 1525, later claimed by Marxists as a kind of prototype of proletarian revolution, was in fact an outbreak of millennial fervour driven by the vision of the Anabaptist Thomas Müntzer, an early associate of Martin Luther, who drove disapproval of established Church authority (and excess) into violent apocalyptic quarters. Luther himself saw the last days at hand, though he refused the path of armed revolt. "It is not to be expected that mankind will still see two or three thousand years after the birth of Christ," he wrote in 1540. "The end will come sooner than we think…. For my part I am sure that the Day of Judgment is just around the corner. It doesn't matter that we don't know the precise day…perhaps someone else can figure it out. But it is certain that time is now at an end." Luther's associate Phillip Melanchthon, addressing some students in a lecture hall in 1559, noted a prophecy that Gog and Magog would command Germany by 1600. "There will occur in times to come great and terrible changes and disorders," he said. "You young people are now yet living in the golden time, but there will soon hereafter follow much more horrible, more afflicted times. There sit here in this auditorium many among you who will experience it; may God then give you mercy."

For the Anabaptist followers of Müntzer, 1533 was the portentous millennial year, and in 1534 the prophecy looked to be fulfilled. A group of armed Anabaptists, led by the thirty-five-year-old prophet Jan Bockelson of Leyden, took over the town of Münster in Germany, declared it the New Jerusalem, and predicted it would become the centre of the New World Order that would arise when the papacy and aristocracy were destroyed in the imminent millennial conflagration. Bockelson was a charismatic and gifted actor who used his height and remarkable good looks to supreme advantage. He declared himself king, seized the possessions of the aristocrats, who had been driven from the town, and clothed himself and his fourteen young wives (the oldest was nineteen) in sumptuous clothes. He ruled his New Jerusalem according to a combination of personal whims and his unassailable claims of personal communication with God. The new regime demanded communal goods, polygamy, and the destruction of all books but the Bible. The streets of the town and the days of the week were renamed, prefiguring the tactics of French and Russian revolutionaries, and a strict reign of terror was instituted, complete with an elaborate propaganda effort and public displays of power. Challengers to his authority were regularly beheaded.

The displaced aristocracy eventually took its revenge on this strange theocratic state. Neighbouring landowners cut off all supplies of food and water to the people trapped within the walls. The people of the town suffered mightily under the scarcity imposed by the siege, while Bockelson and his court hoarded food and drink. When Bockelson declared himself "Messiah of the Last Days," he promised to perform miracles to rescue the starving people, but he failed to turn the cobblestones of the town into loaves of bread, and the starving townspeople wept bitterly.

When the townspeople trapped inside began eating human corpses, Bockelson sued for peace, but the displaced nobles were not in a conciliatory mood. The town was sacked, the millennial pretenders massacred, and Bockelson himself, along with his close associates, was tortured to death. He was drawn and quartered, and the four pieces of his body were sent to four distant German cities to advertise the adverse consequences of hastening the end-times—or, at least, of doing it by seizing the possessions of hereditary nobles.

Other celebrated millennial prophets have also come to a messy end. Prominent among them is the renegade Dominican monk Girolamo Savonarola, one of history's most famous self-flagellants, who was thrown into his frenzy of prophecy by events leading up to the strongly suggestive year 1500: a millennium and a half after Christ, and by some calculations, notably those of the Sibylline prophecies, the time of God's revelation.

There were many signs of impending change at the time. The explorer Christopher Columbus, writing to his friend

Juan de la Torres in that year, noted his own millennial role. "God made me the messenger of the new heaven and the new earth of which he spoke in the Apocalypse of St. John after having spoken of it through the mouth of Isaiah," Columbus said, "and he showed me the spot where to find it"—meaning, presumably, the New Mount Zion of the Americas. Then, in 1502, Columbus wrote to King Ferdinand and Queen Isabella in Spain of the parallels between his own voyage to the East (by way of the New World) and the Crusaders' treks to the East. "In this voyage to the Indies Our Lord wished to perform a very evident miracle in order to console me and the others in the matter of this other voyage to the Holy Sepulchre," Columbus said, suggesting how one crusade might substitute for another. In 1498, the master engraver Albrecht Dürer illustrated an edition of the *Book of Revelation*, then often distributed on its own as a pamphlet, with fifteen brilliantly macabre woodcuts. And the painter Botticelli nicely expressed the stakes when he signed his famous picture, *The Nativity*: "I Sandro painted this picture at the end of the year 1500 in the troubles of Italy in the half time after the time according to the eleventh chapter of St. John in the second woe of the Apocalypse in the loosing of the devil for three and a half years. Then he will be chained in the twelfth chapter and we shall see him trodden down as in this picture."

Like Botticelli, Savonarola believed that the troubles of northern Italy in the 1490s prefigured John's revelation of a final apocalyptic battle in the year 1500. The portentous date was backed up with significant human events. The powerful Medici ruler Lorenzo the Magnificent, whom the diplomat and philosopher Machiavelli had called "the greatest patron of literature and art that any prince has ever been," died in 1492, the year of Columbus's first voyage, throwing Florence into political turmoil. Lorenzo's death and some associated portents prompted Savonarola to write

that "as from his death the greatest devastation would short-
ly ensue, the heavens gave many evident tokens of its
approach; among other signs, the highest pinnacle of the
Church of Santa Reparata was struck with lightning, and a
great part of it thrown down, to the terror and amazement
of everyone."

Fearing the uncertainty to come, Savonarola welcomed
the invasion forces of Charles VIII of France when they
entered Florence on December 10, 1494. He saw Charles as
a messiah, the inheritor of God's mantle on earth—a role
European kings have been asked to play since medieval
prophets saw Frederick I, the Holy Roman Emperor, as
God's flaming sword in the 1100s. "This is good news to
the city," Savonarola wrote, "that Florence will be more
glorious, richer, more powerful than she has ever been.
First, glorious in the sight of God as well as of men: and
you, O Florence, will be the reformation of all Italy, and
from here the renewal will begin and spread everywhere."
The jubilation was short-lived. The French forces were
unwelcome and soon retreated. Florence established a
republic, in which the ever versatile Savonarola, switching
sides with admirable dexterity, managed to be a powerful
force. His self-flagellating followers, known as the Weepers,
continued to hold sway over large segments of the
Florentine population.

Savonarola now entered a new phase of millennial fervour, declaring God's law in Florence and preaching zeal-
ously against luxury and excess. Sumptuary laws, limiting
personal extravagance on religious grounds, were passed,
and Florentines gathered in large numbers to burn their
worldly goods in a huge "bonfire of vanities." Florence was
one of Europe's most luxurious cities, given to impressive
displays of personal and community wealth, and there was
plenty to burn. Draperies and embroidered clothing, gold
furnishings and finely worked leather goods, gorgeous works

of secular art—all of it was heaped on the massive fires in a paroxysm of collective remorse. It is a central millennial image, this outbreak of nearly insane public regret.

 ▬ ▬ ▬

Savonarola's spectacle gave Tom Wolfe a title for what is probably the quintessential novel of the rapacious 1980s, *The Bonfire of the Vanities*. Wolfe's 1987 novel chronicles the downfall of Sherman McCoy, a hapless but supremely arrogant Wall Street bond trader, as he is strung up by the righteousness, corruption, and hypocritical puritanism of New York City. Wolfe's morality play was millennial in prospect because he saw clearly that the excesses of the 1980s would necessarily bring in their turn the puritanical "family values" rhetoric of the 1990s. In 1987, Wolfe rounded off the implied argument by penning "A Eulogy for the Twentieth Century," in which he argued that ours has been a century obsessed, to the point of extreme violence, with the idea of "starting from zero"—including the prospective zeroes of that looming date, 2000.

It's certainly true that the glee with which harbingers of "family values" castigated the poor 1980s reached such a pitch, in the first half of the 1990s, that wiping the cultural slate clean seemed very much on the public agenda. This fever of self-laceration and new-found piety lives on. We knew "family values" were here to stay when they began emerging from the mouths of television commercial actors, whose rumpled, down-home appearance (blue chambray shirts, faded jeans for men; floral-print dresses, pastel cotton sweaters for women) is a semiotic clue to their sincerity. What products are they actually selling? It hardly matters. The real message is that greed and flash and insane careerism are out; virtues and values and family and conservation—all that is in. They tell us these things in earnest voices meant to exude mature good sense.

These revisionist robots are only the latest, and friend-liest, actors in the Evil Eighties morality play, a latent millennial theme still powerful in our culture. In the past half-decade we have seen The Yuppie repeatedly burned in effigy. Michael Millken and Ivan Boesky were sent to jail. Long shots of deserted Wall Street filled our televisions screens. Worse, the moralizing virus spread into the form of popular culture most likely to shape the thinking of the masses: Hollywood movies. An instant classic of the genre was *Regarding Henry* (1991), in which the mean, nasty—what else?—lawyer played by Harrison Ford has to be shot in the head, *twice*, before he becomes a nice guy again, the guy his lovely wife presumably married, the good father his daughter barely remembers. Ford's performance, which makes the head-shot Henry into a lovable younger sibling for his child, a kind of handsome and charmingly dopey Francis of Assisi, owes virtually nothing to the real experience of recovering from severe brain trauma. Do we see Henry losing control of his bowels? Do we see him dissolve into inexplicable rages? No. He follows lost puppies. He weeps affectingly. He is sweet and adorable.

In fact, *Regarding Henry* was just the first example of a trend toward what we must now call "Gumpism": that is, the identification of virtue with mental impairment. The 1994 hit *Forrest Gump*, in which Tom Hanks portrays the man of the century as a lovable mental deficient with a knack for making history, suited the continental mood. North American society has long been hostile to intellectuals, suspecting them of everything from moral weakness and dangerous scepticism to communist conspiracy and venereal disease, but never has it been quite so explicit in pursuing the opposite prejudice, the moral elevation of simple-mindedness. We North Americans find ourselves, on the brink of the third millennium, living in a high-tech society in which, paradoxically, stupidity is our brightest badge of goodness.

These cultural artifacts are part of a national coping exercise, a kind of twelve-step recovery from the greed-and-glory binge of the 1980s. People are trying, in this desperate way, to prepare themselves for what is coming. That the effort is mired in self-contradiction will not dampen the fervour of the Great Denunciation. Countless times, in countless ways, we have been told, since rounding the corner on the '80s and embarking on this ten-year pilgrimage toward the new millennium, that The Party Is Over. Has anyone missed the message? Listen to the Savonarolas of our own day, for they are everywhere, from Century City to Madison Avenue.

And good riddance! We all hated (didn't we?) those 500K-a-year Wall Street traders, with their Ivy League diplomas and red suspenders. We all hated the key figures of the '80s and '90s psychodrama, especially the two invariably described as "wolfish" Ivan Boesky and "wicked witch" Leona Helmsley—hated them, that is, with some of our most resonant images, culled from fairy tales. We all *really* hated the aggressively hair-gelled character played by Michael Douglas in Oliver Stone's *Wall Street*, Gordon Gekko, who famously intoned the message that Greed is Good. This was a man named, not coincidentally, for the little lizards New Yorkers keep in their apartments to eat cockroaches.

Of course, what really bothers most people about being told that The Party Is Over is that they weren't invited to The Party in the first place. What is more, I suspect that some of this new family-values morality might just be a diversion to draw our attention away from those people *still at* The Party. These people include every politician currently in office, the many people who are still happily making hundreds of thousands on the Street (Wall or Bay, as you like), and the plethora of endorsement-gorged professional athletes who continue to top all lists of popular heroes for

North American youth. Greed is still, for some people, awfully good.

History shows that responses to a new millennium, and to a lesser extent to a new century, are framed by an admixture of hope and dread. The first invites optimism, high spirits, loosened morality. The second involves dark prophecy, self-flagellation, the castigation of handy scapegoats, and the preaching of simplicity, plainness, and a puritanism that passes for good sense. In Florence, as in New York, they came close together—sometimes on the same street. But make no mistake. Our moralizing response to the 1980s had nothing to do with a real sea-change in values, or even a rational response to the downturn in the economy. We are merely doing what humans have always done: approaching a new era with deep misgivings and anxiety. Some try to lash themselves into shape with the goads of self-denial; others seek oblivion in celebration. Still others vacillate, purging only to binge again. We *all* wonder desperately what the future will bring. If the puritanical and scapegoating 1990s are so far any indication, we are poised to enter the new century and the new millennium like guests who drank too much too soon. At mid-party we begin to slump, and then we weep at the sound of midnight striking—already a little hungover, regretful, and punishing ourselves for our excess.

"O Florence, Florence, Florence," Savonarola preached in a similar vein in 1495, "for your sins, for your cruelty, for your greed, for your lasciviousness, for your ambition, you have yet to suffer many adversities and much grief." He enjoined the *flagellum Dei*—God's punishment for the city's sins. It was helped along by the personal flagellation of the Weepers. By this time, Savonarola was claiming to see visions and to receive prophecy directly from God. His Church masters finally called him on the various heresies. He was forbidden to preach in 1495 and, when he did not desist, excommunicated in 1497. A second bonfire of vanities in 1498 provoked riots throughout Florence, and the Medici family, united in resolve once more, forced Savonarola from power. He was captured by Roman authorities in the spring of 1498, tortured to confess his heresy (a confession he later repudiated), and eventually hanged and burnt on May 23 of that year.

━ ▄ ━

Not all the militant prophets have been Christian, of course. But while the Christian apocalyptics drew their inspiration from an already vibrant Jewish millennial tradition expressed in the prophecies of Baruch and Ezra, among others, millennialism has proved more popular with Christians than with people of other religious persuasions. (All forms of religious belief include an eschatology, a theory of last things, but it is not always associated with the mythic thousand-year calendar that has so dominated the western imagination.) The Hebrew pseudo-messiah Shabbetai Zev gained followers in Turkey in 1666—that good apocalyptic year—when he ignored the warning of the twelfth-century philosopher Maimonides, who had cautioned the Jews of Yemen that apocalyptic belief was dangerous. Shabbetai Zev's coming, which was supposed to lead to a climactic battle that would end the world, was halted when he was arrested by Turkish authorities. He was forcibly converted to Islam, given the Muslim name Mehemed Kapici Bashi, and released. But rumour had it that he was secretly practising his apocalyptic Jewish faith, and he, too, was eventually tracked down and killed in bloodthirsty fashion.

Other prophets have not been so evidently bent on seizing worldly power. History's most famous millenarian predictor, Michel de Nostredame, known as Nostradamus, was an otherwise unremarkable sixteenth-century chemist and physician who dabbled in cosmetics (his 1552 *Treatise on*

Make-Up is considered something of a classic) and was known for his confections, particularly a quince jelly of surpassing delicacy. But on Good Friday, 1554, Nostradamus took himself into his study and began twirling astrolabes and figuring complex Arabic sums, finally delivering himself of a multi-volume work called *Les vraies centuries et prophéties*, otherwise known as *The Books of Prophecies*, which predicted world events to the far point of the year 3797. Nostradamus's prophecies are still widely quoted in colourful supermarket newspapers like *The Weekly World News*. According to some modern-day followers, his books accurately predicted the rise of Hitler and Nazism and the assassination of John F. Kennedy. He also predicted the Lisbon earthquake of 1755 and the French Revolution of 1789, themselves events of grand millennial proportions.

The French Catholic prophet Suzette Labrousse, one of the few prominent female seers, saw the French Revolution as a harbinger of the New Age. "In 1792 there will be in heaven a meteor that all the inhabitants of the earth will see," she said, "that it will remain visible for a year, that then justice will reign on earth; the Pope"—that old bugbear—"will renounce his temporal power. If this does not happen, there will be great bloodshed in Europe." In 1792, when this did not happen, Labrousse went on a pilgrimage to Rome, where she was arrested for preaching and plotting against the Pope. Though she was freed in 1798, she remained in Rome for the "great things" she expected in the millennial year of 1800.

By that time the Americas had their own brand of end-time craziness, and the death of George Washington on December 14, 1799, threw many Americans into an apocalyptic tizzy. Thus began a brief but distinguished millennial tradition in the United States. Indeed, North America has had its share of apocalyptic religions—perhaps more than its share. Whereas those bent on creating a heavily armed City on the Hill are now drawn to Montana and Idaho, in the last century it was typical for people seeking a New Jerusalem to head for western New York. Not all of their visions were apocalyptic. The Mormons, who followed the prophetic vision of Joseph Smith, do not predict the end of the world. But in the 1830s, William Miller gathered a sect of disaffected Mormons around his prediction that the world would end on October 22, 1843. When it didn't, the date was revised to 1844, but that too failed, and this so-called "Great Disappointment" split the Millerites into two groups. One became the Seventh-Day Adventists, who no longer go in for concrete prediction. The other group, consisting of loyal Millerites, continued to set dates for doom. Each time the prophecy failed, the group split like a decaying radioactive molecule. One such group, headed by Charles Russell, predicted the end of the world in 1914—a prophecy that was supported, if only briefly, by events of the First World War. Today, the followers of Pastor Russell, who keep their prophecies to themselves, are known as Jehovah's Witnesses.

In Europe people approached the end of the nineteenth century with more aplomb, coining (sometime around 1886) the phrase "*fin de siècle*" to describe the decadence, ennui, and artistic outpouring of the century's final decades. Contradictory impulses have always marked periods of millennial anxiety—Florence's luxury goes hand-in-hand with Savonarola's asceticism; constraint and laxity twine together in the Ranters' vision—but the nineteenth-century *fin de siècle* took the contradictions to new heights. It was a notably topsy-turvy time, with a new licence in sexual matters lying closely alongside vicious sexual repression in elaborate codes of manners. An unprecedented technological outpouring, backed by new developments in the traditional sciences and the invention of new ones like statistics and sociology, was matched by waves of occultism and marginal belief in spirits, presences, and mediums. The Ouija Board, still the parlour game of choice among ten-year-olds when I was a boy living in Prince Edward Island, was patented way back in 1892 by a Maryland novelty company. More sophisticated otherworldly novelties—attempts to communicate with the spirit realm by the methods of the fashionable drawing-room psychic Helena Blavatsky, or exegesis of the voluminous revelations of the Swedish mystic Emanuel Swedenborg—entertained the inhabitants of North America and Europe.

It was a time of great expectations. Full-blown technological optimism and reformist fervour were visible in the Paris Exhibition of 1900 or the Columbia Exposition held in Chicago in 1892–93, and audible in Dvorak's *New World Symphony*, written to mark the opening of the Chicago fair. Ludwig Lazarus Zamenhof invented what he hoped would be a universal language. It was called Esperanto—etymologically, a suggestion of "hope"—and Zamenhof confidently predicted it would eventually end all human conflict. It was, indeed, only one of many international languages being invented at century's turn; the others—Balta, Bopal, Dil, Obra, Spolin, Volapük—are long since gone, while Esperanto struggles gamely on, holding the interest of a few earnest eccentrics. But these fevers of optimism were matched by deep gloom and the peculiar modern condition of millennial anxiety that Vicomte François René de Chateaubriand had labelled a century before "*mal de siècle*": the sickness at century's end. Philosophers and critics saw the world crumbling, the accelerated culture of the twentieth century carrying humanity into a dark, unknown future—a vision given brutal credence by the dull, prolonged viciousness of the First World War.

There were prophets, too. In 1899, an Englishman called John Hugh Smyth-Pigott announced that he was Christ returned to the world to dish out divine justice. He was subsequently jailed. Birsa Munda, a young East Indian educated

at German Protestant missions, announced the advent of
the millennium three times and, third time lucky, finally
sparked a rebellion in Delhi on Christmas Day, 1899. In
fact, millennial outbreaks were happening in many quarters
of the British Empire, from the Pathans of the Northwest
Frontier in 1897 to the followers of the Sudanese Mahdi
who defeated Charles George Gordon at Khartoum in 1881
and continued to afflict imperial forces in 1899. A quite different kind of prophet signalled the end of a less self-conscious period of human understanding when he published,
in 1899, a book called *Traumbedeutung*. Freud's *Interpretation
of Dreams*, at the insistence of his publisher, actually bore
the imprint 1900: it seemed a more fitting year of birth for
the revolutionary treatise.

There was scepticism about this millennial anxiety, of
course. A French magazine article of 1886 tried to define the
millennial mood, but managed to indicate only its own
ennui. "To be fin-de-siècle is to be no longer responsible," it
said; "it is to resign oneself in nearly fatal fashion to the
influence of the times and environs.... It is to languish with
one's century, to decay along with it." Impatient with all of
this, *The Atlantic Monthly* weighed in during 1891 with a fine
denunciation. "Everywhere," the editors complained, "we are
treated to dissertations on fin-de-siècle literature, fin-de-siècle statesmanship, fin-de-siècle morality.... People seem to
take for granted that a moribund century implies, not to say
excuses, disenchantment, languor, literary, artistic, and political weariness, and that in 1901 the world will make a fresh
start." The editors of *The Century*, writing in 1901, were
more considerate—and ironical—in hindsight. "The people
who tell us that a century is merely an arbitrary division of
time with no ethical significance are poor observers," they
wrote. "Else they would have noticed a cataclysm of Nature
which synchronized with the end of the year 1900.
Suddenly, absolutely, the Woman with a Past disappeared

from the stage. It is remarkable. We called her *fin-de-siècle*. The century finishes and she no longer exists."

This tough-mindedness about the calendar's vagaries is admirable. But our dreams, as Freud had so lately discovered, can exert enormous power, even—or especially— when they are "unreal." We store our hopes and fears in them, and the reality they then have is, for all its non-material origin, unexpectedly powerful. And so we discover that, contrary to the claims of journalists, the *fin de siècle* did not die in 1900; like the heralded messiah-kings of the millenarian tradition, who awaken from a magical slumber in times of crisis, she simply went to sleep for a time.

I am sitting on a railway platform in northern England, waiting for the train that will take me back to London. I have come up here, through the unsettling English countryside, to speak with some philosophers about the future. We did not discuss the millennium, however. We did not compare notes on portents and parallels. No, we talked of old questions, human questions: what is justice? what is morality? We did this with an air of assurance that the questions were going nowhere fast, that they and the people to ask them would still be around in the decades and centuries to come. We took the long view, we philosophers, and we took it in both directions.

Without warning I am buttonholed by a wandering oldster, an ancient mariner of the railway station. He sidles up to me on my bench and asks me, without preamble, what I think of privatization. I start thinking of something to reply when I realize that, as usual, this has not been a genuine request for information. He begins to regale me with an impressive, if not very coherent, diatribe against privatization. He is wrinkled and brown, bent in the shape of a human question mark, and sports a superfluity of wispy grey hair. This is all par for the course. Amazingly, considering where we are, he has excellent teeth. Hearing that I teach in a university, he shakes his head with infinite, pitying sadness.

"You see that lad over there?" he says, pointing to an obvious undergraduate nearby who is immersed in a thick hardcover book. "What's the matter with the bugger?" he demands rhetorically. "Head stuck in a book. No life in him. No interests. All this specialization, like. No life. What's the matter with him?" I sense more than mere general interest here, and suspect that perhaps my young scholarly colleague rebuffed an earlier approach. But I pass that by and offer another explanation. "Times are hard," I say, as if that needs saying in northern England in the 1990s. "He's probably anxious about the future."

This is to put it mildly. I fleetingly consider opening up an end-time theme for the ancient mariner, uncovering a few shards of apocalypse that are on my mind. For all I know, the young man, wrapped up so completely in his book, could be *wracked* by anxiety about the future. From the looks of him, he was probably born around 1975. It is entirely possible that he has no idea whether he's going to live even as long as I have, let alone reach the wizened state of the garrulous old duffer importuning both of us in the railway station. I think to myself: leave the kid alone. He just wants to get through his exams and then hope there might be something better on the other side of them than a useless degree, signing on to the dole every week, and spending the rest of his life in a pokey two-room flat in this bleak northern city.

I say none of this. In fact, I say absolutely nothing because my aged companion has already beaten me to it. "The future?" he says with yet another slow shake of his head, a gesture laced with *Weltschmerz* and the cheaply purchased wisdom of age. "There *is* no bleeding future. He hasn't *got* a future. *You*"—he pokes me in the chest, for emphasis, with a bony yellow finger—"haven't got a future."

The train arrives and I get in. My friend, his sermon delivered, walks away in search of new wedding guests to collar. I sit facing backwards and watch him through the window as we pull out of the station. I say to myself: as we go, I am looking into the slight but immediate past. I see the past of the road just travelled. There is no future. I have no future. I now have it on good authority.

As long as there have been people around to argue that the world is about to end, or that the future is empty, there have been others—smaller in number, perhaps, but hard-headed and articulate—who have found these predictions risible, even dangerous. This scepticism about bad millennial dreams, the "blind unreasonable whimwhams" of end-time fear-mongering, as one critic called them, is a valuable commodity. It keeps us from declining into millennial madness. It reminds us that every single apocalyptic prediction ever made has so far been proved false. Such scepticism should also remind us, however, that there is much to be learned from false prophecy. After all, as every first-year philosophy student knows, doubt is the engine of knowledge as well as of faith. Scepticism should also help us to remember that, as with so many of the shards of apocalypse, we are not the first generation to live through them. Our credulity and our doubt are to be found sharply delineated in other end-times. "The present moment teems with these anticipations of futurity, beyond the example of every former period," an anonymous author wrote in a book called *The Age of Credulity*, published in 1796.

There is some solace in this. It helps to keep our critical faculties operating; it helps us resist the attraction of the millennium's dark dreams. Of course, the situation is complicated by the fact that one sure sign of millennial fever is a widespread debunking of critical intelligence as an agent of Satan. The medieval hermits who exhorted disenfranchised peasants to attack the established Church also egged them on in book-burnings and the sacking of monasteries. Cleverness was associated then, as it is now, with unnatural destruction. This is yet more Gumpism: the celebration of a simplicity bordering on idiocy, which becomes a mark of moral purity. Here, a lack of intelligence is equated with virtue. By contrast, intelligence, that dangerous human failing, is associated with bad consequences: "smart" bombs that know how to find their targets, for instance, or the frozen cleverness of a technology that destroys old-growth forests or dumps oil on sensitive ecosystems.

In the nuclear age, smartness is sometimes seen as literally demonic: the insidious allure of technology, the "beauty" of the mathematics of atomic destruction, are the Devil's work. In Russell Hoban's post-apocalyptic fable *Riddley Walker* (1983), the Devil appears as a puppet figure known as "Mr. Clevver." Walter Miller's *A Canticle for Leibowitz* (1978) describes a post-nuclear future which is actually a return to the embattled Middle Ages: a metaphor that, as we shall see, gains more resonance by the day. A small band of monks tries to guard meagre human knowledge from the raging anti-intellectualism of the holocaust's deformed survivors. The marauding peasants, frightened and ravaged by technology they cannot understand, destroy all but a few scraps of human knowledge in what is called, proudly, the Great Simplification. Gumpism with a vengeance.

We have suffered no apocalypse yet, but we are well on the way to this degree of hostility to rational thinking. "Rationality, in general, has been out of fashion in the recent years," Wendy Kaminer writes in her 1995 book *It's All the Rage*. "New Agers condemn it as left brain thinking, some feminists consider it male-identified, while some self-styled radical academics are apt to dismiss it as a pretense of objectivity; on the right, religiosity is a much more potent political force than reason." Kaminer even had her own form of millennial prophecy: "I expect that we'll proudly become even less rational as the millennium approaches: more people will report being visited by aliens or abused by Satanic cults in childhood or graced by their guardian angels. In my worst moments, I imagine that this book would be taken more seriously by a broader audience if I claimed to be channeling the spirit of a two-thousand-year-old shaman or an extraterrestrial."

Our best antidote to a diminishing taste for rationality, when it comes to the dreams of millennium, is to explore the parallels between our own culture and the other end-times. What we find is that every single element of millennial madness evident in these apocalypic fragments has an expression in an updated form in our own times, from the new vogue for prophecy to the spectre of environmental collapse to the distrust of elites and focus on our bodies and genders. There are new guises, of course. We may find that the Antichrist now has an Internet address or cable-TV access, and that anxiety about the future prompts visions of abduction by space aliens rather than by God's minions. We may discern the lack of leaders not in well-publicized deaths—George Washington, Charlemagne, Lorenzo de Medici—but in disaffected voters and a vogue for touchy-feely seminars in "leadership studies." We may decorate our bodies in painful ways rather than flagellate them.

But these are just old worries in new clothes.

Two

The Prophet Zone

Who has once met irony
will burst into laughter
during the prophet's lecture.

Adam Zagajewski, "Ode to Plurality"

IN UNCERTAIN TIMES it is not unusual for people to seek guidance. The forms may differ. Some will prefer the accessibility and economy of late-night psychic hotlines, with their 1-900 numbers and images of LaToya Jackson, J. Z. Crystal, or the "famed international psychic" JoJo, who, in common with many of her cohorts, got her psychic powers after a car accident involving a severe blow to the head. She never says where she got the weird platinum-blond pigtails that wave from that head like ethereal antennae.

Others, who don't like to stay up that late, will opt for slick futurists' newsletters, polished publications cobbled together by demographers and mailed every month to anxious executives for a hefty subscription fee. Instead of horoscopes and Tarot, the newsletters sport graphs and pie charts, but the impulse beneath the two choices is really the same: we desperately want to know what the future will bring.

The desperation is increasing, even while—no surprise—the basic inability of anybody, psychic or futurist, to predict the future remains the same. Scrolling through the channels in an idle moment the other day, I noticed that psychic hotlines have recently moved from the graveyard shift of late-night television to the daytime slots formerly dominated by soap operas. The soaps are still with us, but they are now hard pressed by talk shows of growing incivility and witlessness and call-in infomercials in which knowledge of the future is sold alongside cubic zirconia bracelets and exercise machines. "Vision," said one religious leader portrayed in the 1995 film documentary *Prophecy*, "is the ability to see the things that are coming." What I see coming are more television channels that cheerfully abandon the pretence that they are about entertainment or information. Why retain the dramatic or comedic *vehicle* for advertising when you can just opt for the pure thing?

For myself, I prefer to get my prophecy in person. I also find, in these unsettled days, that pure wackiness is somehow a lot more compelling than considered futurism. Futurists are really just statistics geeks and trend-spotters, and while they may do their work well or badly, they are ultimately restricted to the message that the future is going to be very much like today, only more so. That may help you plot a sales campaign or plan an electoral strategy, but it won't equip you for the end-times. For that you need someone who has travelled further than the demographic projections. You need someone who visits the astral planes on a regular basis, someone who speaks with the other side, someone who is personally acquainted with your own guardian angel.

— — —

It is Easter Monday and the final day of the Psychic and Astrology Exposition at the Metro Toronto Convention Centre on Front Street in Toronto. I go with my wife, Gail, who among other things is a historian of psychology. We have done this before, visiting the psychics' fair, because you never know what you're going to learn from a palmist or aura photographer. Gail has been trying, without success, to find a Gall's head, one of those china or plaster models that were used by phrenologists to read character and ability from the bumps on one's head—the ones that carve up the surface of the skull into discrete territories like musical ability, or sexual attraction, or violence.

It's not without risk, going to psychics' fairs. At the last one we attended, at the old Automotive Building on Toronto's Canadian National Exhibition grounds, I spotted one of my students browsing through crystals, incense, and mandalas. Apart from being alarmed that she gave every indication of finding more wisdom there than in my lectures, it suddenly struck me that it is impossible to convey an attitude of ironic detachment from across a crowded exhibition hall. I had to skulk behind some Tarot posters until she'd moved on and the coast was clear.

The Easter Monday fair is smaller and quieter than the CNE event, and holding it in the airless, carpeted expanses of the Convention Centre seems a mistake. We get lost coming in and find ourselves standing uncertainly before a table of what turn out to be people from Abitibi-Price Inc., the forest-products giant. They are having a shareholders' meeting and are giving out annual reports that are titled "Up Into The Profit Zone." I am on the verge of asking for a copy, thinking I have arrived at the fair, when I notice a sign pointing the way to the real prophets. Then—a kind of delayed reaction—I smell the incense.

We stroll up and down the aisles, passing the reflexologists and acupressurists, the clairvoyants and seers and palmists, the Celtic and Chinese and Romany psychics, the "scientific ones," with their cheesy fake computer equipment that might just have impressed a set designer on "Lost in Space." We pass seers exhibiting a wide spectrum of backgrounds and pitches, from the standard eastern mysticism of Yogi A. S. Narayana to some kind of renegade western "contact with the spiritual planes in heaven" offered up by Sister Leona Hartman, of the Spiritual Science Fellowship. There are cute, would-be exotic psychics, like the woman calling herself "Gemstone," a name displayed in big silvery letters on her purple velvet banner. But there are also down-home banalities, presumably directed to a more white-bread kind of customer, like the guy whose banner simply read, in Gothic letters, "Keith," and—my personal favourite—the intent-looking young man who is sitting in front of a sign that reads "Numerology by Gordon."

All of them, even the (I imagine) normally serene Yogi Narayana, are showing some telltale signs of desperation for business. They all but leap over their little tables to offer us their insights and explain their unique methodologies. Prices are slashed everywhere: four separate kinds of prediction for five dollars, free demonstrations with no obligation, two for the price of one. It is cut-rate prophecy, and I am a bit disappointed. Sigmund Freud, no stranger to fortune-telling, once noted that it was important to charge people a lot of money for psychoanalytic sessions because otherwise they wouldn't believe they were getting anything of value. What kind of future can you predict for five bucks?

I am keen to find out what the professional prophets can tell me about the coming millennium, so I convince Gail to bustle past the aromatherapy displays and shelves full of Chinese tranquillity balls, Native Indian dream-catchers, pyramids, and aura photographers to the stand where Emile Verkerk, of Unicorn Systems Inc., is offering a combined palm analysis, electronic Tarot reading, biorhythm analysis, future forecast, and love scope. Emile asks me to spell my name, give him my birthdate, and then—the real deal—place my hand for a precisely specified length of time on a hand-shaped electronic sensor bank. As soon as I take my hand away from the sensor, Emile's computer starts chugging out the pages, which spill over the front of his stand with unseemly haste. But then, I figure this is the beauty of computer-generated prophecy. Sure, you *could* spend half an hour in a one-on-one clinch with a personal psychic, but it would cost you anywhere from forty to seventy-five dollars (cassette tape included) and you'd probably be no wiser than after three and a half minutes with Emile's patented Unicorn Systems Inc. program. The number of "scientific" astrologers at the expo is one change I notice from the last time. Even here, where you'd expect the appeal to scientific norms to be moot, the value of technology and accuracy, or rather the value of a *show* of those things, is highly prized. When even fortune-telling has gone high-tech, I figure you know for certain that the world is in the grip of a pervasive scientism.

Still, it works for me. I find out some interesting things about myself: for example, that I am exactly 11,735 days old that day and that my personal angel is called Barehiel. It also says the motto governing my life is "I believe," though I rather doubt this. (I can't really be sure, however, because apparently my intellectual biorhythm as I write this is about to hit an all-time low.) The Tarot reading isn't very interesting but the palmistry turns up a few worthy tidbits. "You express yourself to others with a view to being informative by way of facts, figures, and other assorted information," it says, a bit incoherently. "You're a veritable walking encyclopedia, full of all sorts of information that you have sorted out." It says, twice, that I am inflexible and resistant to change and mentions, with a blitheness I find troubling, that "many times you do not understand the complexities of the modern world."

But the fortune concludes on an up note: "You are a genius in your own right," it tells me, "waiting to bring your ideas to fruition." This jibes nicely with the future forecast, which notes that I "have good ideas and plenty of energy." It advises me to "set aside some time for 'production.'" (I don't know why that word is in quotes, by the way, so don't ask me; that is not part of the "all sorts of information" that I have sorted out.) The sex scope has some spicy things to say about my interest in fetishism (does it show?) but concludes with the unobjectionable claim that for me "The main sex organ is the mind."

Not bad for five dollars. I am in a spending mood now, so I plunk down another fin to get my handwriting analysed. I realize this has nothing to do with prophecy, but you never know where you might stumble on insight. Ellie George, my handwriting analyst, is an artist, and she takes longer than Emile's computer. Gail and I stroll around some more, lamenting the fact that the fair's transplantation from the Ex grounds to the Convention Centre means that you can no longer get a hot dog or a chocolate-dipped ice cream cone between predictions.

We stop by a free demonstration on past lives, which features the Reverend John C. White telling people in the audience what they have experienced in their earlier incarnations. The crowd is the weird assortment that I have come to think of as typical of psychics' fairs: the preponderance of overweight trailer-park types, who probably don't really need any more hot dogs or ice cream, brightened up here and there by one or two stunning young women dressed in Gothic-style basic black, and rounded out with a bunch of teenagers, male and female. These last look like regular teenagers, down to the Notre Dame sweatshirts and backwards baseball caps, but I wonder what bizarre demographic subgroup they actually represent. Do they have cool nicknames for themselves, and a kind of snowboarder-style insider slang? Is there such a thing as Astral Plane hip? Are there Adolescents for Angels? I'm afraid to ask.

A woman called Katherine asks Rev. White to tell her about her past lives, and he obliges, mentioning her time in China during the construction of the Great Wall and the child she bore by her husband, Joe, who was also, as luck would have it, in China at the time. Another audience member, Alison, has also been in Asia in the past, it seems; her husband Paul was along too, working in a rice paddy somewhere. "Which of you works with computers?" Rev. White asks Alison and Paul, who are sitting together on the little institutional chairs. They both look blank, and then exchange a gaze of bovine incomprehension. "Well, this will make more sense to you in, oh, a year from now," Rev. White says, without a perceptible pause. "I think January."

I am not so interested in past lives, or in hearing that Gail and I had both managed to be in Egypt during the time of the pharaohs. We go back to pick up Ellie's handwriting analyses, which are ready. They are brief and pointed. "You've got a sharp and quick mind just like a computer," mine begins. "You're clever and witty." This is getting to be pretty flattering, I think. It also mentions, though this time only once, my widely perceived aversion to change and outside authority. "You like to run your own show and call the shots," it says. "You're dedicated to your cause and beliefs— loyal." Well, it contains less information per dollar than Emile has given us, but Ellie throws in a free chocolate, which she claims is entirely calorie-free.

All this is diverting, in its way, but it still isn't what you'd call prophecy. I realize that when astrologers talk about the future they usually mean the next few weeks or months, not the next few decades. I have been looking for millennialism and I have found a lot of people who want to know whether they should sell their houses now or wait a year. It is all pretty banal, though it does suggest something I have long suspected about the cultural power of prediction, and the desire that goes with it. The natural reaction to global uncertainty, the fully human response to end-time prophecy, is perhaps most often the one in which you pull the covers over your head and think: What's going to become of *me*? The Psychics' Expo patrons, with their barely concealed longing for love and job information, the zest for prediction about their own annual incomes and marriages, are no different in this respect from anybody else. Even if the world is coming to an end, a lot of us really just want to know if interest rates are going up.

Then I find Hassan Jafer. Hassan is a professional astrologer, but he also has the kind of client base a database-driven futurist might envy. He publishes a monthly newsletter called "AstroTrends," which, he says, "is distributed throughout the world and is designed for timely and helpful advice for clients." Hassan's company, Astrograph Inc., also publishes a cool wall chart called "AstroTrends till the Year 2001!" which plots his astrological predictions about world events from 1990 to 2002. Hassan has some impressive successes on his c.v.: apparently (though I can't confirm it) he predicted the end of communism and apartheid, the dismantling of the Berlin Wall, and the New World Order.

Hassan is willing to admit he has made a few howlers, like predicting a final showdown in the Middle East in 1993 and the widespread use of environmental perfumes, released through office ventilation systems, to alter mood at work starting in 1991 (though this has been tried in Japanese offices, I'm told). He also thought we'd have a cure for AIDS by 1992. He saw computer secretaries as early as 1991 and still thinks there will be robot musicians sometime in 1996. According to Hassan, we're going to see breakthroughs in nuclear technology, new speed records set in aviation, better forms of education, space missions outside our own galaxy, an end to fundamentalism, a more just society, less social inequality, and quicker forms of mass transit. He sees no actual apocalypse in 2001, it seems, which shows admirable restraint for a psychic, but he does think that there will be a spiritual awakening, a focus on Jerusalem as the spiritual centre of the world, and a renewed emphasis on universal justice and divine truths.

Looking more closely at the "AstroTrends till the Year 2001!" chart, however, it strikes me that this careful mix of the obvious and the just slightly wacky is entirely consistent with the modus operandi of other astrological prophets. Hassan's focus is more global than personal, but he is nevertheless peddling the same mixture of plausible generalities and hopeful bright-side predictions. In fact, the message of all fortune-telling could be boiled down to something like this: "It may not look that way right now, but things are going to be slightly better." The message must not be so hopeful as to court disbelief, but it cannot be actually pessimistic either, for that would undermine the willingness of the clients to keep coming back. After all, the punters pay to hear a little good news. The thing to do is spice up the good news with some non-specific predictions of disaster or downturn—or, in the personal case, temper the flattery with some trait like resistance to change that can be put in a positive light—and make the whole thing appear considered and balanced.

I have come to the psychics' fair looking for some juicy predictions of the future, some professional doomsayers. I should have known better, of course. All I get is anodyne pap, the kind of intellectual and spiritual pabulum people like to suck on when they find, like me apparently, that they don't understand the complexities of the modern world. It is not a wholly despicable profession, feeding this way on people's insecurities. It is just, beneath the surface hocus-pocus, all the hokum of exoticism and mystery and danger, surprisingly bloodless. No wonder it draws the chubby suburbanites and the teenagers. It is, in the end, as comforting as a trip to the strip mall for a carton of milk.

▬ ▬ ▬

"Prophecy is not fortune-telling," Harry Rasky says in his film on prophecy, which happens to air on television the same weekend, on Easter Sunday, that we visit the psychics' fair. Summing up the history of prophecy, Rasky describes prophets as akin to cultural critics. They are gadflies, the film suggests, spiritual dissidents who refuse to remain silent as they see the world declining into actual or metaphorical disaster. For example, the great prophets of the biblical tradition—Isaiah, Jonah, Jeremiah—are rabble-rousers who call the people to account for their failings. They do not merely predict the end of the world; they draw a crucial causal connection between it and our behaviour. One of them, Jeremiah, even gave his name to the noun that means "lamentation, or doleful complaint." Thus their message is ultimately a proselytizing one: *The world is going to end, certainly, and soon. But then again, maybe not—especially if we change our behaviour right away. And let's say the world does end soon; wouldn't you rather be among the saved than among the damned?*

Prophets don't predict the future, Rasky's film tells us; they just say, in the most general terms, that bad things are coming. They report "signs" and "portents" of disaster, which their "vision" has allowed them to see. The environmentalist Hanne Strong, speaking to Rasky over the noise of an approaching storm (how many days did they have to wait to film that?), describes her meetings with all the great prophets on the planet. "They have told me of war, famine, drought, disease, earthquakes, fire, economic collapse," she says. It sounds to me as though she has been watching television—"vision" must really be a synonym for "cable." The film sought out modern-day prophets with a relentless zeal, looking for those with a positive message, but what Rasky found were prophesies of a brighter tomorrow only for those who are on the right path to God. In the end they communicated only tautology: optimism of this religious kind is fine if you're already a religious optimist, but it's not much use to the rest of us. When confronted by a sharp atheistic intelligence like that of James Watson, the scientist who collaborated on the discovery of the DNA double-helix structure, Rasky's idea of a cheery brand of prophecy breaks down. During his interview, Watson briskly rejects the whole issue of optimism and religion, claims not to understand the leading questions of the interviewer, and spends most of his time looking away from the camera, as if searching for a likely exit.

Still, when we veer away from the strictly religious prophetic themes, the search for modern-day prophets raises some important points about the state of our culture. The Yale humanities professor Harold Bloom talks with fine-honed disgust of the false prophets springing up with alarming frequency in these days, the Jim Jones or David Koresh types, charismatic leaders who take their people underground with stockpiles of automatic weapons or poison and thence to some self-fulfilling immolation. "Things are in many ways looking worse and worse," Bloom says. "There has never been any shortage of prophets, and I'm sure as the year 2001 approaches we will get an entire new ghastly crop of them."

Bloom also notes the consistent poll results that indicate almost 90 percent of Americans believe they have a personal relationship with God—or, as most of them would put it, "a Higher Power." This is fertile ground for sowing religious zeal, as commentators on American society have known since de Tocqueville, and for spawning strange marketing fads, like the angels boom of the early 1990s. Angels, like the nameless Higher Power, have a chummy, personal aspect to them that gives solace to all the children of dysfunctional families who populate self-help meetings and co-dependency seminars. This is religion without the tradition, the ritual, or the risk; it is commitment-free and, in the end, narcissistic. Your personal angel is really like the supportive big brother or sister you never had. For instance, my angel,

Barehiel, is so far being a little cagey with his (or her) appearances, but I figure that when we finally hook up he (or she) is going to want to know *all about me* and my feelings, my insecurities and aspirations, and probably my stat line in the pick-up basketball game I played last week.

False prophets like Jones and Koresh are at the horrible end of a spectrum that includes every person walking down the street with a sign telling us the end is nigh. Although such people are seen more often in *New Yorker* cartoons than on the streets of my city (where the signs people carry usually say things like "Crippled and addicted mother of two—please spare some change"), Bloom is right to note that these prophets have always been with us. They are more prevalent in times of cultural stress, but like cold sore microbes they never really go away. The particular talent of the modern-day variety is their ability to draw thousands of others into their apocalyptic visions, often with their life savings stuffed into suitcases.

In 1990, for example, Elizabeth Clare Prophet, of the Church Universal and Triumphant, convinced more than two thousand of her followers that the world was going to end in April of that year, probably around the 23rd. She heard this, she told them, in a communication with God mediated by a group of beings known as the Ascended Masters. Mrs. Prophet claimed to be a reincarnation whose previous past lives included St. Catherine of Siena, the fourteenth-century Catholic mystic, and Marie Antoinette. After the warning was issued, her followers hastened to a series of underground bunkers that were then under construction in Paradise Valley, a thirty-thousand-acre farm owned by the church along the Yellowstone River in Montana, an area near Yellowstone National Park known for its trout fishing and elk herds. Many of them were heavily armed and loaded down with supplies of rolled oats and dried beans to sustain them through the coming nuclear holocaust.

Mrs. Prophet, known to her followers as "Guru Ma" ("the mother who teaches"), had told them that the events of 1989, in which superpower tensions receded for the first time since the Second World War, was actually a Soviet ruse, designed to draw the United States into a false sense of security. (In terms of plausibility she might have been better advised to use the really scary scenario of, say, *Crimson Tide*, the 1995 film in which a renegade ex-Soviet republic gets its hands on a few nuclear weapons.) Mrs. Prophet's husband, Ed Francis, had been convicted the previous fall for the illegal purchase of $100,000 worth of automatic weapons, ammunition, and handguns. He claimed they were needed "for defensive purposes."

Members of the church paid up to $10,000 to reserve a space in the shelter, which Mrs. Prophet compared to "Noah's ark in the earth." At the time of the warning, the shelter complexes lacked sanitation facilities. They were, however, stocked with dried food, computers, bedding, medical equipment, blood supplies, diesel generators, cookware, and other survival gear. Local merchants reported a run on flashlights, batteries, aspirin and first-aid kits. "This is the time we have been told by Mother to be prepared," said one of her followers. "We must be prepared now because Mother says this is a dangerous time," said another. The followers were told to pray to lessen the chances of Armageddon. In fact, they said, if the holocaust did not happen on April 23, that could be interpreted as the positive result of their praying; Guru Ma would lose no credibility with them. It's a good thing they took this iron-clad escape-clause attitude, because most of them knew that Mrs. Prophet had declared the end of the world several times already, the most recent date being October 1989.

And in fact, when April 23 rolled around, the world was still standing and the bombs were still in their silos. Worse, Byron Robb, a Montana district court judge, had ordered that construction of the bomb shelter be halted and that 31,000 gallons of diesel fuel gasoline that had leaked from storage tanks near the shelter be cleaned up. The leaks, he ruled, constituted an environmental threat. This was a kind of local Armageddon Mrs. Prophet probably hadn't been thinking about when she predicted the world's end, despite the fact that she had condemned "the desecration of Mother Nature" as one sign of coming doom. (In a pamphlet issued in 1990 she criticized the slow clean-up of the *Exxon Valdez* oil spill in Alaska.)

Predictably, Mrs. Prophet grew cagey in her predictions of doom and expressed confidence that the shelter would be completed. Nuclear war could happen at any time, she said, but the day she had claimed the bombs would fall certainly inaugurated twelve years of "intense negative karma" that would bring "the four horsemen of the apocalypse" galloping near. Like all doomsayers, she claimed no personal desire to be proved right. "I pray regularly that this prophecy will fail," she said, giving a nice twist to her repeated false warnings. "I would be happy to be a fool for God." But if she is right, she at least has the solace of knowing that she and her followers were building "a state-of-the-art, masterpiece shelter."

And so it goes. Between August 1993 and October 1994, Neal Chase, the spokesman for a group called Baha'is Under the Provisions of the Covenant, issued a series of press releases predicting Doomsday from the sect's headquarters in (where else?) Montana. The releases were collected in the February 1995 issue of *Harper's* magazine under the headline "The End is Nearish!" Mr. Chase began by claiming that his group had correctly predicted "the day, the minute, the hour, the second that the World Trade Center was bombed" on February 26, 1993. "Now we are giving the date for the big one." Using biblical calculations from Ezekiel, Mr. Chase told the world that Saddam Hussein would take his revenge on the United States on September 4, 1993, by dropping a thermonuclear bomb on the United Nations building in New York. "We have warned you," he said. "The blood of the people is not on our hands."

On September 27, 1993, Mr. Chase reported that his calculations had neglected the added forty days mentioned in Ezekiel 4:6. New date: October 14, 1993. "The waiting is over," he said.

In a release dated November 1, 1993, Mr. Chase revised the date of the bomb to March 23, 1994, with the battle of Armageddon slated for forty days later. "WE DIDN'T MAKE A MISTAKE," he wrote. "We didn't make a mistake, not even a teeny eeny one!" The false date was owing to a discrepancy between the New Jerusalem Bible and the King James Version. "There shall be no more delay! God never makes a promise He doesn't keep," the release said.

The next release came on April 4, 1994. "All the dates we have given in our past releases are correct," it said. "Not one of these dates is wrong." But now Ezekiel's math had a new conclusion: 460 siege days since the World Trade Center bombing meant the big one was coming on May 2, 1994. "By now, all the people have been forewarned," Mr. Chase concluded. "We have done our job."

There was more. On October 9, 1994, another release was issued. "Exactly as we have been predicting, Saddam Hussein has now mobilized his forces to take his revenge for the Gulf War," it said, "full-scale thermonuclear destruction of the UN building and all New York City, scheduled to take place on November 26, 1994, give or take a week or two." The May 5 crash of a helicopter near the New Jersey entrance to the Lincoln Tunnel vindicated the May 2 prediction, the release said, and further suggested that the "silence in heaven for about half an hour" mentioned in Revelation, chapter eight, could be interpreted as half a year, or about 180 days. Hence November 26. "We are the only ones in the entire world guiding the people to their safety, security, and salvation!" the release concluded. "We have a 100 percent track record!"

It's easy to scoff at this kind of thing, and it is also easy to say that the approach of the millennium will make false prophets thicker on the ground. This obscures the genuine dangers posed by apocalyptic thinking. On April 19, 1995, news of a massive truck-bomb explosion in Oklahoma City began filling the airwaves. A fertilizer-based car bomb, exploding next to the Alfred P. Murrah Federal Building—which housed, among many other things, the regional offices of the Alcohol, Tobacco and Firearms Bureau—killed 168 people, making it the worst terrorist attack in American history. For weeks we were surrounded by images of the scoured-out office building, of bleeding babies and the waiting relatives, their faces drained of hope and colour.

Very early reports of the bombing took care to mention that it happened exactly two years after the fiery end of the Branch Davidian complex in Waco, Texas—a disaster that for weeks placed doomed ATF and FBI agents on our TV screens nightly, first storming the enclave and then watching as David Koresh and his followers torched themselves rather than surrender to Caesar's forces. Evidence of millenarian themes in Koresh's New Jerusalem was rife, from his mumbled television pronouncements that he was the Second Coming of Jesus Christ to his tangled written messages, complete with suggestive quotations from the Book of Revelation. This evidence was largely ignored by the besieging FBI and ATF agents, despite the warnings of biblical scholars imported to the scene to decipher the messages. In retrospect, David Koresh begins to take on his proper significance: he is our own late-day Jan Bockelson of Leyden, and Waco, Texas, is the twentieth-century version of Münster. Koresh, like Bockelson, issued whim-as-law pronouncements, slept with the female members of his community as if by *droit de seigneur*, and braced himself for the inevitable siege by gathering all the AK-47s and M-16s he could find. He never changed the days of the week or claimed to be able to turn cobblestones into bread, but let's be fair: his siege didn't last nearly as long as Bockelson's did. Government forces are not as slow to act as medieval noblemen, and they have better weapons.

The line of speculation connecting the Oklahoma City bombing with Waco was immediately quashed in early news reports, only to resurface when it turned out the bombers were Americans, not Muslim extremists, and had connections to a bizarre libertarian paramilitary group known as the Michigan Militia. Suddenly the airwaves were full of amateur video of these Uzi-toting anti-government weekend warriors on clumsy "manoeuvres" in the Michigan countryside. It was reported that more than 15,000 people nationwide belong to similar groups, which believe the U.S. government is populated by Jews and "Communists" bent on the destruction of individual rights. The ATF, we were reminded, as the agency responsible for the American "War Against Drugs," is now one of the most heavily armed government agencies in the country. And the Waco disaster—in which a God-fearing nutball had simply tried to map out an ideal society that acknowledged his status as the returned Christ, while incidentally stockpiling lots of firepower, only to be crushed by The Man—has fast become an anti-government rallying point.

Wider reaction to the Oklahoma City bombing ran a familiar, if bizarre, media gamut. There were shots of a tough-talking Bill Clinton, fading into long views of the wreckage of the building. The same news photograph, of a firefighter carrying the body of a dead child from the collapsed day-care centre on the building's first floor, appeared on the covers of *Time*, *Newsweek*, and *Maclean's*, and the grim, angular features of Timothy McVeigh, the crew-cut bomber arrested and charged by U.S. federal authorities after he was stopped for what is always called a "routine traffic violation," haunted the screen of my TV. His former army roommate was interviewed on the tabloid TV news program "A Current Affair," telling us (what else?) that McVeigh was "a loner" who always went about armed during his time in military service, even when he was off duty. Finally, in the strangest but somehow most appropriate twist, almost a week to the day after the bombing, television producers acknowledged that the storylines of three shows—the daytime soap "All My Children," its prime-time counterpart "Melrose Place," and the satirical cartoon "The Critic"—had to be altered after it was realized that plot devices featuring crazed bombers were "inappropriate" and "insensitive."

What is it about bombs, anyway? Certainly they have figured with unprecedented prominence in recent action films, especially several 1994 efforts about madmen given to elaborate, almost metaphysical, bomb attacks—*Speed*, *The Specialist*, and *Blown Away*. Indeed, seven of the biggest-grossing films of all time, all of them products of the last decade of Hollywood special-effects escalation, have featured at least one major explosion. It begins to seem, these days, that explosions are what Hollywood does best. Movie experts speculated, with cheerful—and probably correct—cynicism, that the Oklahoma City explosion would not lessen the public appetite for cinematic explosions; if anything, it would enhance it.

And of course there was a spate of reported bombings in the days following the Oklahoma City attack, giving rise to the usual confusion between cause and effect in the mass media. (Do more planes really start falling out of the sky following a big crash, for instance, or does it just seem so because the media's attention is focused there?) The summer of 1996 brought two bombings that could not be ignored, however—one the blast that destroyed TWA Flight 800 off Long Island, the other the pipe bomb attack that caused two deaths in Centennial Olympic Park during the Atlanta Olympics. Fear of further terrorism was obvious after these events, especially when mingled with rumours of a militia plot, foiled by the FBI, to disrupt the Olympics with a full campaign of bombings. But since Oklahoma City, we know that political violence can now come from within.

Indeed, that aspect of the Oklahoma City bombing raised to a fever pitch the hair-pulling and breast-beating of American media commentators. Not only was this attack—on innocent women and children—carried out in the middle of a sleepy southwestern city, it was the work of domestic terrorists: fringe wackos, perhaps, but ones connected to a thick vein of underground discontent. The racism of initial speculation that "Middle Eastern elements" were behind the bombing gave way to a strong undercurrent, almost palpable during panel discussions and phone-in shows, of anxiety. Was the country coming apart at the seams? Was it at war with itself?

The Oklahoma City bombing and its panicky aftermath was still fresh in my mind as, scrolling through the cable flow one night, I was suddenly riveted by a generically handsome newsreader saying "As Peter used to say, we'll see you next week—if the Lord doesn't come first."

Peter? Peter *Jennings* used to say that?

But no, this was nothing quite so prosaic. The Peter in question was Peter the Apostle. Peter the Fisher of Men. The show was something called "This Week in Bible Prophecy," apparently a regular seven-day roundup of the latest in what the old prophets had to tell us. It makes sense, of course, that the prophets would go to TV in our own millennial day to spread the message of imminent apocalypse. And what better format than that of a news magazine like "60 Minutes" or "Prime Time Live"—or, indeed, "This Week In Baseball," the show which apparently supplied the idea for a title. Here's the news, Bible fans: World About to End; Thousands Shocked.

In fact, it turned out that "TWIBP" was mainly interested, that week, in getting its viewers to buy a "revolutionary new video witnessing tool" that depicted what would happen after the Rapture John warned us of in Revelation: the end-time warm-up in which the righteous souls are hauled off this earth and taken to meet their Maker in Heaven just before the Judgment Day that closes out this earthly experiment. The video sported the effectively colloquial title "Left Behind: Where'd Everybody Go?" and retailed for $24.95 plus $3.50 for shipping and handling. It was ninety minutes long and proved, according to the anchor, that the Rapture was "not just a theological debating point but a reality." At exactly 4:59 p.m. Eastern Time, on a date to be revealed only later, the saved would be taken from this earth. This mass disappearance would then throw the rest of the world into a panic. There would be looting, riots, madness, self-immolation. Highlights of the video were shown, at first carrying a disclaimer that read "This is a simulation only, not an actual news report," but later unadorned. They featured yet another generically handsome newsreader gradually losing his studio cool as reports flooded in from deranged correspondents reporting the mass hysteria that had greeted the Rapture.

"There is terror and absolute panic," the reporters yelled as their feeds were interrupted by flashes of static and the sound of sirens. Stock footage of Parisian and South African riots was then overlaid with "interviews" with desolate "survivors." "My wife warned me about this," one lumpy middle-American said. "She said this would happen." And, turning to look deep into the camera, "I've been *left behind.*"

There followed shots of the world leaders panicking, sending out messages into deep space, massing military hardware. "Please tell us what you want," one politician's voice pleaded with the unseen power. But the faithless could never really understand the reality of their situation, the first anchor told us. They would posit all kinds of crazy and increasingly desperate explanations for the mass disappearances: teleporter beams, alien abductions, things we couldn't yet imagine. These explanations would all be false. The truth was that God had, as promised, taken the righteous from the earth in preparation for the Last Things. The faithless could resist that conclusion as much as they liked, but it would not change the fact that they would be *left behind* if they did not find faith now. The signs that the Rapture was coming could hardly be resisted, he said. Look at the scriptures, and then look at the world around us. "When we look at the news headlines, we can reach no other conclusions than that this generation will see the return of the Lord," the anchor said. "This powerful and terrifying video will help you reach your unsaved loved ones for Christ so they won't be *left behind.* Give someone the greatest gift of all—the gift of eternity."

One point not addressed in this edition of "TWIBP" was the possibility that the sudden disappearance of all the born-again Christians in the world might be a very good thing, and hardly something likely to throw those of us "left behind" into a mortal panic. I for one wouldn't expend much energy casting about for explanations. The show also didn't offer a view on the fact that John limits the number of the righteous to twelve times twelve thousand—a symbolic rather than real number, perhaps, but often quoted with some emphasis by literalists. And, for that matter, who decides which biblical numbers are real and which symbolic?

In any case, the shameless fear-mongering of this program and its "video witnessing tool" is troubling. It is also likely to escalate. Whereas in the 1100s, even in the 1490s, communication of millennial prophecy was limited to those a prophet could reach by his own speech, and the fear he could generate limited by his own eloquence, nowadays the prophet zone is populated by people with lots of media savvy, files of horrifying footage of political unrest—unrelated to chiliastic eschatology, but no matter—and, most important, the money and brains to gain access to cable television.

The violence depicted in "Left Behind" is all borrowed from other, real-world events. It is also all incidental, in that it follows from the Rapture but is not carried out by the Christian believers. In this scenario, the disastrous consequences of the Millennium are the result of overreaction and panic by the unbelievers who have been "left behind," not by those carried off. The producers apparently ignored one incidental danger of the Heavenly Gathering, inscribed on an actual bumper sticker seen in the United States of late: "Warning: In case of Rapture, this car will be unmanned." That's presuming a little on God's judgment, but still, don't tailgate those guys. You never know.

There has recently been a disturbing proliferation of millennial violence that is both real and carried out by the believers. It happened halfway around the world and in a culture that is not predominantly Christian. On March 20, 1995, the deadly nerve gas sarin was released into the Tokyo subway system, killing 12 people and hurting thousands more. A group known as Aum Shinri Kyo, or the Supreme Truth sect, was connected with the attack, which was followed by two more: one on April 19 in the main train station at Yokohama, which sent 509 people to hospital, and another two days later, injuring 25. The sect, invariably described in news reports as "a doomsday cult," denied any connection with the attacks but grew vocal when police shut down some of the buildings occupied by cult members and carted their screaming children off to police custody.

As the drama unfolded, it grew weirder. Ten days after the March 20 attack, the police officer heading the investigation was shot and seriously wounded as he left his Tokyo apartment building. A few days before Easter, police in Los Angeles arrested two Japanese men who they suspected were involved in a plot to release nerve gas at Disneyland during the Easter weekend. The men, who the police believed were cult members, were stopped at Los Angeles International Airport. Incredibly, they were carrying an instructional videotape on how to make sarin. When a cult member was arrested on suspicion of having masterminded the Yokohama attack, he was fatally stabbed as a wild scrum of media people jostled him and his police escort. In true contemporary style, the murder was captured entirely on videotape. The man wielding the knife, a member of a Japanese right-wing gang, pushed his way toward the front of the crowd. There was a new energy in the scuffling: something was happening. The arrested cult member moved to one side with a jerk, then collapsed to the ground, where cameras fought to capture a close-up of his agonized face. The attacker threw his bloody weapon defiantly on the ground and stood calmly as a space suddenly opened around him and then closed as police moved in to arrest him.

— ■ —

We have an enduring fascination with the prospect of apocalypse. The sane among us do not really take it seriously, but beneath the (in some ways) infantile desire for apocalyptic stories lies a more rational worry, one based on real events and trends in the world. Many of us feel, with good reason, that things on earth are getting worse—if not worse instantaneously, as in the standard doomsday scenarios, then worse very quickly indeed. Cities around the world are crumbling; dangerous gaps are opening up between rich and poor; population is growing without heed to the gradual, and inevitable, decline of non-renewable resources like fossil fuels. Immersed in these real-world forms of apocalypse, it is hard to see our way clearly to a more hopeful place.

In this frame of mind we look to the experts with something of the same mixture of hope and dread that the old-time prophets aroused in their audiences. Indeed, some thinkers who have an eye on the crumbling earth environment are now hailed as visionaries of the apocalypse as we edge nearer to the brink of 2000. Are they the true prophets for these end-times? And is their vision one of reassurance, or one of despair?

I decide to pay a personal visit to someone recently touted as a real Prophet of Doom, a genuine Harbinger of the Apocalypse. His office is nearby, in one of those Romanesque nooks that abound in the thoroughly nineteenth-century University College, part of the University of Toronto, a place that was built in a time when people still thought learning had to be done within heavy stone walls, preferably in a basement. To get to it, I must descend into a positively medieval corner of the college quadrangle.

As I climb carefully down the uneven steps, the blackened stone suddenly opens out into a routinely institutional set of offices—computers there, photocopier here, everything painted the requisite beige. The warren of little offices is full of people clacking away on their electronic keyboards, poring over articles. The Prophet of Doom, the Harbinger of the Apocalypse, has his office at the end of the corridor. He is expecting me, but I am not quite expecting him. He is tall and good-looking, smiling amiably and sending off no vibes of dark portent. He is wearing dark chinos and a red cotton sweater. In fact, he looks a bit like a Gap model. He smiles warmly and asks me to call him "Tad."

The Prophet of Doom is actually Thomas Homer-Dixon,

professor of political science and director of the Peace and Conflict Studies program at the University of Toronto. He is the author of influential research on the relationship between imminent environmental disaster and social violence. What Homer-Dixon's findings indicate is that increased stress on the environment will more and more be a factor in the sorts of social violence evident in the world's so-called "hot spots." The prose of his journal articles conforms to the scholarly norms of considered academic discussion, but it describes a world of upheaval and discord. It is replete with images of what Homer-Dixon likes to call "acute conflict": "conflict involving a substantial probability of violence," to use his own laconic definition. To some, the low-key tone is actually the most frightening thing about these works: in fevered imaginations, Homer-Dixon's quiet academic voice seems to take on the considered menace of one of those film villains lately so popular, the educated terrorism of Alan Rickman or Jeremy Irons in the *Die Hard* movies.

Homer-Dixon's early research hypothesized that various kinds of environmental collapse—cropland depletion, rain-forest destruction, soil erosion, decline of fish population—were imminent in many places around the planet, and that the threat of its happening elsewhere would grow as the world's population passed nine billion in the next fifty years. In the view of some observers, these environmental scarcities would lead to violent conflict: fights for food and greater instability within underdeveloped countries, roving gangs of marauders, the devastation of marginal groups, national instability, possibly even open conflict between countries.

"There are fundamentally disturbing trends, especially with renewable resources," Homer-Dixon says. In person, the laconic quality of the academic writing is absent, replaced by an enthusiasm, a richness of knowledge, that is at once breathless and articulate. Ideas and facts pour out of him with impressive speed; he requires no warming to his subject—he's in full flight from word one. "There are real reasons to be concerned, whether you're talking about the ozone layer or fisheries. There is good research to indicate that frogs are dying off around the planet because of UV radiation; we're seeing major changes." I point out the irony of this fact: the precise reversal of traditional apocalyptic portents, in which frogs rain upon the earth, but he is already hurrying on to the next point.

"Then you get outside those global problems, the ones that manifest themselves at the biospheric level, and look at what's happening to cropland, water supplies," he says. "And there are multiple effects here. You have a shrinking of the resource pie, because the resources are degraded or depleted; you have increasing demand, because people's consumption rates are going up and the populations are larger; and you have structural inequalities in the distribution of the resources, which makes the shrinking of the pie and increased demand that much more serious for marginal groups. So the marginal groups are getting forced out." The immediate result? "This is creating huge cohorts of young unemployed, highly alienated, urbanized men, who are extremely dangerous in any society. They don't have a stake, any opportunities, and they are ripe for exploitation and doing all kinds of nasty things."

In some parts of the world, he suggests, this factor is already a major contributor to social violence. "Ecological and population factors don't act independently of social and political, cultural and historical factors," Homer-Dixon points out. "Nonetheless, we're making a grave mistake if we ignore them. The most pernicious outcomes that we see in the world are usually the result of an interaction of population and ecological stresses with, say, unequal land distribution or unequal power distribution within a society, which may have its roots in colonial history or traditions of a predatory state or something like that. You simply can't say that one factor is more important than another."

Because the worst effects of such environmental degradation are rarely confined to their original sites, this is dire stuff for the 20 percent of us in the so-called First World, comfortably enjoying a standard of security far above the global norm. Homer-Dixon has used the image of a stretch limousine on the potholed streets of New York City to illustrate his sense of the situation. Inside the limo, he says, "are the air-conditioned post-industrial regions of North America, Europe, the emerging Pacific Rim and a few other isolated places, with their trade summitry and computer-information highways. Outside is the rest of mankind, going in a completely different direction." For anybody who has seen those limos, which debouch their fur-clad occupants into the fashionable restaurants that are the only bright spots in blocks of bombed-out apocalyptic regions of lower Manhattan, the image is unforgettable. We are the world's limo passengers? We will be the targets of resentment and, increasingly, violent attack?

Homer-Dixon is convinced that people must feel some threat to their personal security before they will take environmental issues really seriously, and his research has been instrumental in doing just that. You don't need to invoke anything like James Lovelock's controversial "Gaia hypothesis"—the idea that the planet is a single complex organism, whose health can be threatened by one part of it, namely voracious old *Homo sapiens*. No, this is about famine, disease, and violence, and no New-Agey "If you love this planet..." hand-waving seems nearly as compelling.

"There's been a tendency over the last few years to try and broaden the conception of security so that it almost means socio-economic well-being, everything under the sun: health, quality of life, income per capita," Homer-Dixon says. "I define security narrowly, in terms of violence.

If you can get across to people that there's a plausible case that environmental problems will increase the incidence of violence, then that makes environmental issues more than just lifestyle, or quality of life, or aesthetic issues."

It is not a coincidence that Homer-Dixon's field, peace and conflict studies, found new sources of scholarly interest in the late 1980s, just as the Cold War declined and the Great Clash of Ideologies played itself out in the crack-up of the Soviet Union and the resulting pro-capitalist triumphalism of the West. Nor is it coincidental that his research into the possible environmental causes of conflict gained such attention. Here, after all, was a kind of threat to security that came not from a rival political philosophy (and the massive cache of weapons the standard-bearers of that philosophy could deploy) but from something deep within the logic of capitalism, from our own rapacious denuding of the Earth's resources in pursuit of comfort and profit. Homer-Dixon's influential articles, published in the early 1990s, have ridden a growing wave of environmental dread.

"I propose," he wrote in an article published in the respected but largely professional journal *International Security* in 1991, "that poor countries will in general be more vulnerable to environmental change than rich ones; therefore, environmentally induced conflicts are likely to arise first in the developing world. In these countries, a range of atmospheric, terrestrial, and aquatic environmental pressures will in time probably produce, either singly or in combination, four main...social effects: reduced agricultural production, economic decline, population displacement, and disruption of regular and legitimized social relations." Bad enough, you might think, but the knock-on effects of these developments would be even more devastating. We might expect to see "several specific types of acute conflict," Homer-Dixon wrote, "including scarcity disputes between countries, clashes between ethnic groups, and civil strife and insurgency, each with potentially serious repercussions for the security interests of the developed world."

To get this message to a wider audience, Homer-Dixon co-authored in 1993 a more accessible article on the same topic in *Scientific American*, "Environmental Change and Violent Conflict." That in turn led to a *New York Times* op-ed article, later reprinted in the *International Herald-Tribune*. Soon stories trickled down of people reading his original *International Security* article on Air Force One. Copies of the article were said to be circulating to American embassies and consulates. U.S. vice-president Al Gore had expressed some interest. (Homer-Dixon would later be invited to the White House for briefings.)

Homer-Dixon managed to have the right—if unpleasant—idea at the right time. In 1993, the writer Robert Kaplan happened to meet him at a conference in Europe, and when he decided to write his next article for *The Atlantic Monthly* Kaplan drew heavily on the research Homer-Dixon was quietly publishing. Kaplan's alarmist cover story "The Coming Anarchy," published in May 1994 and later part of a 1996 book, was based on his visits to West Africa and discussions with Homer-Dixon. Kaplan boldly predicted a world ruled by "disease...unprovoked crime, scarcity of resources, refugee migrations, the increased erosion of nation-states and international borders, and the empowerment of private armies, security firms and international drug cartels." What was observable in West Africa, Kaplan argued—the youth gangs, the political disintegration, the imminent famine—was just a foretaste of what the whole world would experience in a matter of decades.

"Nations break up under the tidal flow of refugees from environmental and social disaster," the magazine's cover blared. "As borders crumble, another type of boundary is erected—a wall of disease. Wars are fought over scarce resources, especially water, and war itself becomes continuous with crime, as armed bands of stateless marauders clash with private security forces of the elites. A preview of the twenty-first century."

Kaplan was immediately attacked for writing a deliberate polemic in place of considered discussion; he was also called racist for his suggestion that the West African nations could not manage their own problems. Homer-Dixon himself disputes some of Kaplan's claims, but he thinks the article did a good job of shaking people up. "If you look around the world, you can trace out fairly clear links between ecological pressures and resources scarcity and all kinds of social pathologies. It's always a unique story, because it's combined with particular cultural and historical factors, but those things are underneath the surface," he says. "[Kaplan] has very vividly described a possible world that is now part of our range of thinking about where we might be thirty or forty years from now. It may be that only a portion of the world experiences that outcome—maybe nobody will experience it—but as one of the leading demographers in the United States told me, even if he's only 20 percent right, that's bad enough. So it's good to get people thinking about this."

Judging by the reception given such arguments, the prospect of environmental conflict is strangely compelling to people on both the left and the right of the political spectrum. But among certain sections of that spectrum, it also prompts an odd ideological version of having your cake and eating it too. It happens this way. While warnings of environmental apocalypse have in the past mostly been the property of reformers—the well-intentioned zealots of Greenpeace, say—they are now welcomed by anti-reformist elements, too. For example, Newt Gingrich's right-wing rhetoric borrows a lot of dire portent about the moral collapse of North American culture in an attempt to play up fears of the end-times. The spectre of political collapse in dangerously overpopulated, underdeveloped countries—and the related Kaplanesque worry that hordes of displaced Third World refugees may soon be showing up at our immigration offices, or already are—strikes the same note as Gingrich's adapt-or-die political rhetoric. This in turn allows citizens to see themselves as threatened, and, as a result, to send their weaker cohorts into social oblivion without a second thought. The Contract With America is simply the Rapture described in John's Revelation played on the level of cuts to social-program spending: the righteous will be saved, and the sinful shall perish.

At the same time, the less biblically inclined parts of the Right are able to pass off genuine environmental challenges to market-driven economies if they happen to come from leftists with a doom-saying bent. They simply claim that warnings about environmental threats to security are really nothing more than the product of overheated millennial imaginations. In an article published in 1995, Marcus Gee, an editorial writer with *The Globe and Mail*, took Homer-Dixon to task by challenging the warnings of "coming anarchy." Gee's long article, "Apocalypse Deferred" (with the witty subhead "The End Isn't Nigh"), began by summarizing Kaplan's warnings in the *Atlantic* article of a second, environmental Cold War. "It is absorbing, fascinating, frightening stuff," he said, sounding a bit like Dana Carvey's send-up of Johnny Carson. "It is also dead wrong." Gee then went on, at considerable length, to argue that "[b]y almost every measure, life on Earth is getting better."

Gee's real target in the article was the active doomsayer school of thought in political economy, the group of gloom-merchants given to predictions of population explosion, resource depletion, and growing global instability. In the academic trade, these people—who include Paul Ehrlich, author of the 1968 best-seller *The Population Bomb*, and the Club of Rome, which published a report in 1972 called *The*

Limits to Growth—are known as "neo-Malthusians." That is, they follow the lead of Thomas Robert Malthus, the English economist whose 1798 *Essay on the Principle of Population* predicted that population growth would soon outstrip crop resources, resulting in famine and war. "[T]he power of population is indefinitely greater than the power in the earth to produce subsistence for man," Malthus wrote in the *Essay*. "Population, when unchecked, increases in a geometrical ratio. Subsistence increases only in an arithmetical ratio. A slight acquaintance with numbers will shew the immensity of the first power in comparison of the second." Without curbs on population growth, the results would be devastating. (Aficionados of utopian and dystopian literature may recall the birth-control devices in Aldous Huxley's *Brave New World* that were known as "Malthusian belts.")

In other words, though increases in resources, resulting from, say, more efficient farming techniques, actually encourage population growth, the resulting increases are too extensive to be accommodated. The new population boom disturbs a natural equilibrium, which must be, in extreme cases, reestablished through sharp decreases in population. "Famine," Malthus wrote in his dispassionate eighteenth-century way, "seems to be the last, the most dreadful resource of nature. The power of population is so superior to the power in the earth to produce subsistence for man, that premature death must in some shape or other visit the human race." He could have been talking about Somalia, you think, only Malthus didn't know the word "ecosystem."

Malthus himself was not without hope—he was an Anglican clergyman as well as an economist—and in the conclusion to the *Essay* he wrote that "Evil exists in the world not to create despair but activity." But nevertheless he did think there was a rigid upper limit to population growth, which no amount of Christian activity could change.

The rival anti-Malthusian school, of which Gee and the *Globe and Mail*'s editorial board can be considered amateur members, are sometimes known as "cornucopians." The world is an ever-increasing basket of resources, they say; take it easy. The market can expand the resource pie in ways unimagined by rigid old Malthus, and the proof of the claim is everywhere obvious. Though the world population is five and a half billion and growing fast, life is better now than ever before. Or, as the American humorist P.J. O'Rourke put it in a lecture in Toronto last year: "I have just two words to say to people who think we're worse off than before: dental care." This split isn't necessarily or always left-wing versus right-wing, of course, but there are some obvious affinities. Neo-Malthusians are concerned about the environment, the vast numbers of poor in developing countries. Cornucopians preach a brisk business-as-usual line that suggests, underneath it all, a dislike of regulation and a faith in the global market's beneficent powers.

Homer-Dixon wrote a reply to Gee's article that offered various counter-sallies in the form of statistics and graphs, and he suggested that Gee was wrong to extrapolate aggregate numbers (statistics taken as averages from a number of countries) and to assume that economic growth is the only thing that matters in keeping people secure. One point, graphically presented, was that the coming apocalypse might be one of water scarcity. The supply of fresh water in many African and Asian countries might decline well below current minimum standards over the next thirty years. The decline will be global: according to a 1995 World Bank report, eighty countries now have water shortages that threaten health and the economy, and 40 percent of the world's population—more than two billion people—has no access to clean water or sanitation. But whereas Canadians, for example, will see their annual supply of fresh water slip from 109,389 cubic metres to 90,880 per capita, Libyans will have to make do with 60 cubic metres (down from 160), and Jordanians will try to get by on 80 cubic metres (down from 260). Many experts estimate that 1,000 cubic metres per capita is required for a modern, industrialized country. "The wars of the next century will be over water," not oil or politics, said Ismail Serageldin, the World Bank's environment vice-president, in a 1995 report.

Homer-Dixon's *Globe and Mail* rebuttal made an even more important point. Focusing on big countries like China and India shows that a problem doesn't have to be a trend to be serious. "India, China and Indonesia make up 45 percent of the world's population," he says. "If even one of those countries goes, it's going to have a staggering effect on the rest of the world. In some sense, we shouldn't do the standard political science thing, which is to try and figure out what the probability is, the frequency. Maybe the probability is really low, but if it happens in one important country, we're in trouble." In fact, though Homer-Dixon has often been identified with the neo-Malthusian side of the debate, he actually claims to find the whole thing "sterile" and has tried in recent years to move beyond the limitations of an optimist/pessimist dichotomy.

This desire to transcend pessimism suggests that Homer-Dixon is unwilling to inhabit the Prophet of Doom role with any real conviction. Indeed, his latest work has centred on the ability of human societies to adapt to a crisis of scarcity, and he no longer uses the same strong terms he did in articles published a few years ago. Malthus, he now implies, was not nearly subtle enough: he forgot to factor human intelligence into the survival equation. We are smart enough to adapt to scarcity; we are not mere prisoners of our resource situations. But there may nevertheless be real limits, because scarcity itself may make ingenuity less plentiful—by encouraging, for example, brain drains or squabbling among elites. This is what in recent work he has called "the ingenuity gap," and he points out clear instances: Haiti, Somalia, Rwanda. "We have to hope that countries like China and India don't end up in that kind of trap."

The elements that make Homer-Dixon's work so provocative in the current climate of thought are not hard to identify. The hypotheses mooted in his early articles play into very real fears, fears heightened by both political and cultural factors. Thus he has been vaulted into a position of cultural prominence precisely because his findings arrived just in time to fill what we might call an "anxiety vacuum," created by the late-1980s decline of the Cold War, with another, less obvious threat: environmental collapse. "I think people now have space in their brains to think about other things, things that have longer time-horizons," he says. There is, too, the growing sense that, as an ex-Marine of my acquaintance once put it, drawing a contrast to life inside the military, "Nobody's in charge out here." Homer-Dixon's work feeds directly into the kind of non-specific fear we can now call "millennimania." "People are bewildered by life," Homer-Dixon says. "They're bewildered by the idea that three kids could go and beat two old people to death with a baseball bat."

Certainly "bewildered" seems to describe the seekers at the psychics' fair well enough, but they'd probably have been equally bewildered by life as peasants in the Middle Ages. The question is, how widely shared is their unease? In these times of random violence, when some people seem to act out of motives that are literally incredible, I have an idea that Homer-Dixon is all too right.

I recall the day I left New Haven, after four years of graduate school. I pulled the van onto the highway, feeling suddenly nostalgic for this clapped-out post-industrial town, and I heard a radio newsreader announce the murder the previous night of a Chinese food delivery boy, a teenager. Two other teenagers, younger than himself, had ordered the food so that when he came to the door they could open it, shoot him repeatedly, and watch him die. I won't say that I almost crashed the van in my shock; on the contrary, I felt a bizarre twinge of recognition, as if a metal engine piece were snapping into place. It was what Wayne Koestenbaum, a Yale English professor, once called "the unmistakable sound of *proof*." There it was, arriving as if fully expected: a concrete demonstration that the moral universe was crumbling.

Homer-Dixon himself cites, in addition to these factors, the overwhelming objective evidence that environmental crisis is happening faster, and with more devastating effects, than ever before. "You look around the world and there are stress signs in lots and lots of places," he says, "and I think the attention to these issues is a subliminal recognition by the public that things are happening on a scale, with a complexity and unpredictability, that is really new."

But perhaps the biggest factor in Homer-Dixon's current vogue—and the one that encompasses these others—is the obvious millennial overtones people find in his research. We all suspect, in our weaker moments, that this benighted late-century world is coming to an end. When we hear that the decline of arable land is going to lead to gang wars, or that countries are in danger of long-term destabilization for lack of water, we figure the end-times really are upon us. From this point of view, the fact that Kaplan's article and some of Homer-Dixon's work centre on Africa is just par for the course. That's where AIDS and Ebola came from, too. Africa: cradle of the apocalypse.

Of course all prophets, even nuanced academic ones, fight off any personal stake in their analysis. "I would like to be proven wrong about a lot of this stuff," Homer-Dixon insists. "I hope that China and India make the transitions into prosperous, stable societies with sustainable populations, living within the resources they have in their own territories. I have no interest in being right; I would like to be put out of business." A pause. "But I have this feeling that in the end I'll probably win the debate. I may not win it in my own lifetime, but looking back from the year 2100 or 2150 over the trajectory of economic development during the twentieth and twenty-first centuries, we will see a period of unbelievable rapaciousness, in which we squandered most of the resources on the planet. And we will think: if only—if only we'd had the political will to prevent some of that."

Shades of the apocalypse again, I think, though clothed in lots of academic caution and a more nuanced scenario: Savonarola with a doctorate and a database. Homer-Dixon strongly dislikes the millennial thematic, and discounts it as a factor in the popularity of his work. "The least significant thing is that we really are coming to the end of the millennium," he says. "People don't come up to me at my talks and ask, 'Do you think this has got something to do with the fact that we're coming to the end of the second millennium?'" But that's hardly the point; Homer-Dixon is mistaking cause for effect. Environmental collapse isn't happening *as a result* of this being the end-time. It would be happening anyway. Our deep fascination with its happening, however, our overwhelming feelings of dread and helplessness—not to mention the notoriety that people like Homer-Dixon and Kaplan now enjoy—*these* are indeed cultural effects of the end of the millennium.

He may not like it, but Homer-Dixon has become the Prophet of Doom for many people, not so much because his research is good, but rather because, as he would say, people now have space in their brains to think about the prospects of environmental apocalypse. The ideas his research encourages, even if they are not what he sees himself saying, rush in to fill the newly created anxiety vacuum. If he has done nothing else, Homer-Dixon has shown that environmental apocalypse won't simply be about some old-growth forest being destroyed, or even global warming. It will happen in places, like Somalia, where violence is proximate and common. People will be starving, and then other people will shoot each other in order not to starve too. In the end, then, the real danger for many of us is not that we will have too few resources to survive, but rather that somewhere, sometime, someone with a gun may just want our resources badly enough to kill us for them.

Since it's not often you get to meet a Harbinger of the Apocalypse, and my time is (of course) running out, I ask the blunt question that hangs in the air, the one he has tried to fight off. I realize it's all very complicated, but when it comes to the future most people are really pretty primitive. Is the end nigh? If not apocalypse now, then apocalypse soon? *Is anarchy coming?*

"I don't know," the Prophet of Doom says, laughing at the very idea of predicting such a thing. "I just don't know." He laughs again, and pauses. "And I think anybody who says they know is an idiot."

THREE

To Have and Have Not

> The rich have become richer, and the poor have become poorer;
> and the vessel of the state is driven between the Scylla
> and Charybdis of anarchy and despotism.
>
> Percy B. Shelley, *A Defence of Poetry* (1821)

*O*NE IN THREE
U.S. teenagers believes he or she will be shot to death
before reaching old age. In 1993, the murder rate in
Washington, D.C. was fifteen times the rate in "troubled"
Northern Ireland. Almost three-quarters of U.S. prison
space has been built since 1984. Guns are manufactured in
America at a rate of 360 *an hour.*

When I moved to New Haven in 1987, I knew a little
about the place. I knew it was poor, that the formerly busy
factories were now mainly idle, the former employees out of
work. Even the Winchester Repeating Arms factory, just
down the street from the first apartment I rented, where
they used to produce the U.S. Army's standard-issue M-16
rifle, was not working up to par. As one acquaintance
described it, the city of 125,000 was "the armpit of the Ivy
League," an urban wasteland wildly different from the
bucolic idylls of Princeton or Dartmouth.

What I wasn't prepared for was the fact that the university is a fortress, an island of privilege and learning in a sea of
poverty and crime. The buildings of Yale, with their elabo-
rately ugly neo-Gothic stone carvings, rise up from the New
Haven Green like a medieval monastery, walled and gated
and filled with the contemporary equivalents of habited

monks: preppy kids, most of them white, and tweedy academics—nearly all of them white. To many of those inside,
the walls serve to keep at bay a barbarian horde given to
trading in drugs, listening to primitive, bass-dominated
music, and killing each other. The cloistered show all the
controlled terror and outward bravado of clerics hoarding
manuscripts against the Dark Age.

New York, the great violence magnet, is about a ninety-
minute drive away. It beats New Haven in sheer disparity of
rich and poor, of course. But Connecticut, with its bedroom
communities and pockets of wealth in Darien and Litchfield
and Greenwich, reported the highest average income of any
state in the United States during the late 1980s. I certainly
saw no evidence of wealth in most of New Haven; it was
run-down saltbox houses and untended lawns. Here and
there—in the Prospect Hill neighbourhood, where I lived
during my final year, and in a few other places—the ugliness
gave way to stately Federal and Victorian houses, some of
them massive enough to be called mansions and to recall
the carriage-trade heyday of the town. Like many northeast-
ern cities, New Haven had boomed and busted, and its
manufacturing era was over. The black families who moved
there from Georgia and South Carolina during good times
earlier in the century were now stranded in very bad times.
There was unemployment and boredom. There was posturing and violence. There was a thriving drug business,
marked by the usual turf disputes. As evidence, residents
were constantly reminded that New Haven had the highest
per capita murder rate of any city in the United States—a
statistic that I have been unable, in nine years, to confirm.

Despite all this, during my years at Yale I persisted in the
belief that I was not implicated in the town's obvious haves-
versus-have-nots class division—that its urban violence was,
somehow, not about me. As a graduate student who lived
off-campus, outside the protective walls of the university, I

did not identify much with the rich undergraduates, with their skiing weekends and J. Crew wardrobes and parents who rolled up to the residence hall in September in their Range Rovers. They were in some ways as different from me as the gold-draped black kids who patrolled the mall in surly posses or tooled around town in their souped-up Mercedes, Volvo, and Saab crackmobiles. And yet I have been unable to shake the feeling that I was on the wrong side of one very important line. Studying political theory in the midst of life-threatening poverty, devoting myself to abstract arguments about social justice as gunfire sounded outside my Prospect Street windows, gave new meaning to the phrase "living in an Ivory Tower." It also reminded me, as little else could, that privilege is not always about money. To have the leisure to live what Hannah Arendt called "the life of the mind"—to be able even to imagine, as a real choice, a life of thought and writing—is privilege as surely as driving a Lexus sedan.

Living in New Haven taught me one other thing, something I knew from countless books but not yet from real experience. The poor hate the rich. They hate them.

And they will hurt them if they can.

<hr>

What makes the reports of the environmental doomsayers so unsettling is not simply their familiar tale of depleted resources—terrible though that is. It is rather the suggestion that environmental security threats seem to lead to the loss of what economists like to call "stake": the sense of communal commitment, or responsibility to your society. In other words, when the gap between those who are comfortable and those who are exposed to hardship becomes too wide, large segments of the population will begin to defect into violence. After all, what have they got to lose? The scarcity of arable land or drinkable water is hardly the only, or even the major, factor in social violence, but when people lack for the basic materials of life, they are more likely to deal harshly with those who have them.

This situation was exposed with brutal clarity in the Los Angeles riots of 1992. With the added powder keg of racial hostility, those riots—prompted by the treatment of Rodney King, the black man who was seen being viciously beaten by white Los Angeles police officers on a now infamous piece of amateur videotape—managed to touch off "sympathy" riots in many North American cities, including the usually peaceful Toronto. These riots uncovered once more the racial faultlines in North American society, but they also, crucially, demonstrated the fact that socio-economic differences are often inseparable from racial ones. The riots seemed to be as much an expression of economic resentment as they were a statement of black anger—witness the looting of Asian-owned stores in South-Central Los Angeles, the taking of possessions from people who, from a racial perspective, had nothing to do with Rodney King's oppression.

There are exceptions, of course; not every black issue is an issue about socio-economics. Reaction to the O.J. Simpson murder-trial verdict in October, 1995, for example, appeared to show race trumping money as a factor. Poor black men and women, who should perhaps have thought twice about cheering a proven wife-beater, rejoiced at the "liberation" of one of the most privileged men in the United States. The hatred that bubbled up in the wake of the verdict, as angry whites jammed the phone lines of call-in radio programs even as blacks cheered from rooftops and church naves, also prompted some of the most obviously millennial commentary yet to appear in North American public discourse. "Welcome to the United States of America at the tail end of the Century of Progress," New York Times columnist Bob Herbert wrote of the racial divisions. "We are living in a land that has lost its reason."

Environmental doomsayers suggest that sub-social out-breaks of hostility like the 1992 riots could soon be replicated at the international level. The engine of conflict in a borderless world is, they argue, just the renewed tribalism that was evident in the otherwise pointless attacks on whites who strayed into the danger areas of Los Angeles. We know all too well that powerful forces of ethnic nationalism have already torn apart the Middle East and the Balkans. National borders mean far less today than our schoolroom maps would suggest—the real lines are those of blood, colour, and tribe. As Robert Kaplan says, where and how the next vicious tribal conflict will occur is finally less significant than the global change "in which the classificatory grid of nation-states is going to be replaced by a jagged-glass pattern of city-states, shanty-states, and anarchic regionalisms." The nature of this new world is opaque to many of us in the First World, because we cannot understand the hatred that leads to setting a raped ten-year-old girl aflame in Grozny or executing a young man in Monrovia by placing a burning, gasoline-filled tire around his neck. We also cannot understand that a life of ethnic war might be preferable to the available alternatives, the camaraderies and conviction of the barracks more desirable than simply starving to death.

"The intense savagery of the fighting in such diverse cultural settings as Liberia, Bosnia, the Caucasus, and Sri Lanka—to say nothing of what obtains in American inner cities—indicates something very troubling that those of us inside the stretch limo, concerned with issues like middle-class entitlements and the future of interactive cable television, lack the stomach to contemplate," Kaplan argues. "It is this: a large number of people on this planet, to whom the comfort and stability of a middle-class life is utterly unknown, find war and a barracks existence a step up rather than a step down." The stark economic facts bear him out.

World Bank statistics show that fully a billion people on the globe live on less than one U.S. dollar a day—that's about one person in six. Worldwide, one person in one hundred and twenty-five is a refugee, a person without the security of home or country. These things do not make for stability.

These warnings are culturally significant. They tell us a lot about the shape our political fears now take. The link forged between environmental scarcity and political conflict, while not always borne out in practice, communicates a powerful message of our ever-dwindling control of the future. Even the most jackbooted political regime, we now clearly see, cannot eliminate unrest forever, not if that unrest cuts to the heart of human existence: the basic availability of the things we need to survive. Though some of us may seek refuge in the idea that we can control political events through force of will, "natural" factors, like population growth and resource depletion, do not seem so tractable.

This is especially so if political change, which has been fast and vast even since 1989, continues to accelerate in the years remaining to 2000 and beyond. The blithe faith of an Adam Smith, that the market will regulate this changing world to a more or less just equilibrium, will look ever more absurd as the world mutates beyond the imagination of any single mind, let alone one raised in eighteenth-century Scotland. It does not take a psychic gift to see that, given the ethnic basis of much of the world's present conflicts, and given, too, the resource scarcities that can be expected to prompt or worsen those conflicts, the exportation of the gospel according to market freedom is unlikely to be the answer to a violently divided world. "Do not assume," the U.S. Navy scholar Michael Vlahos told Kaplan, "that democratic capitalism is the last word in human social evolution."

The fall of the Berlin Wall in 1989 and the break-up of the Soviet Union were greeted by supporters of democratic capitalism as the dawn of a triumphant new day for the ideas of property, individualism, and the global market. The dark underside of market liberalism, once obscured by capitalist triumphalism, is now coming into view again. The security threats pointed out by environmental gloom-merchants like Kaplan actually reinforce a trend to social violence that has an even more disturbing, and basic, source: the growing disparity between those who enjoy material comfort and those who don't, especially as that disparity is viewed as a result of differences in ability or intelligence. Here the prophets of environmental doom join forces with a more familiar breed of socio-economic doomsayer.

So, for example, the London-based *Economist* magazine reported in 1994 that the divide between rich and poor is now larger than at any time since the Middle Ages. At the same time, national debts have grown to monstrous proportions: the United States, which was carrying $1.557 trillion in 1984, was in hock to the tune of $4.77 trillion in 1994. This figure will reach something like $6.831 trillion by 2000, according to projections made by James Dale Davidson and William Rees-Mogg in their book *The Great Reckoning*. Population growth is also accelerating. Tokyo, which supported 6.9 million people in the 1950s, had reached 25 million by 1990 and is expected to grow to almost 30 million by 2010. In 1995 the population of the United States was almost 265 million; at current rates of growth it will pass 400 million by the year 2050. By 1994, not one of the world's twenty most populous cities could claim to meet the World Health Organization's clean-air standards.

— ▬ —

In February 1991, as I was writing the last pages of a doctoral dissertation on justice and dialogue, a murder took place just a few blocks from my house. It was like a lot of New Haven murders. Late at night, one young man was killed by another even younger man in an apparent dispute over cash or drugs or both.

But there were a few significant differences. For one thing, the young man who was killed was white. In fact, he was more than merely white; he was, as it were, super-white, the apotheosis of white. He was a Yale sophomore, the nineteen-year-old son of a prominent Washington lawyer who hailed from Chevy Chase, Maryland. He was an athlete, tall and blond, a devotee of the ultimate preppy game, lacrosse. His name, remarkably enough, was Christian Prince. The boy later charged with the assault, James Fleming, Jr., was a black sixteen-year-old from the beleaguered Newhallville neighbourhood of New Haven.

According to news reports, Prince was returning to his apartment after an off-campus party when he was stopped by a small group of black men on Hillhouse Avenue, a beautiful elm-lined street that is the site of New Haven's Roman Catholic church as well as the mansion belonging to the president of the university. What happened next is a little unclear. When the body was discovered, a wallet, containing forty-six dollars, was in the victim's back pocket. Friends of Fleming, in police statements taken later, said he had borrowed a gun earlier that night "to do some stick-ups" or to "shoot a cracker." But Fleming was acquitted of the murder charge in 1993 when no evidence was presented to link him definitively with the crime. Rumours circulated that Prince had been carrying hundreds of dollars, suggesting a dispute that, as the New Haven television reporters liked to put it, marked "a drug deal gone wrong." But there is no evidence of this drug connection. What is clear is that someone—maybe James Fleming, maybe one of his friends, maybe somebody else—fired a gun. The bullet hit Prince square in the middle of his chest. He died there, bleeding, on the sidewalk of Hillhouse Avenue.

It was the first murder of a Yale undergraduate in New

Haven since 1974. I was nearing the end of my time in the
city, and I started to feel like one of those "short" conscripts
in Vietnam: the ones with only a few weeks left in their
hitch, waiting with heart-stopping anxiety for release day to
arrive. My wife and I had lived in New Haven for almost
four years and we had not yet been the victim of any kind of
crime. We hadn't had a car stolen, a window broken, a wallet demanded. We hadn't once had to talk to the combat-
ready New Haven police, with their commando outfits and
wicked nine-millimetre sidearms. We were clean. But this
became itself a source of a weird statistical anxiety. Our
streak of luck couldn't possibly last. The longer we went
without some kind of crime marking our lives, the more likely it seemed that something bad was just about to happen.

Wherever rich and poor live in close proximity, there
will be violence and there will be fear. You don't have to
visit South-Central Los Angeles to see this. You don't even
have to visit Manhattan, where the gap between top and
bottom income levels is the widest of any county in the
United States—excepting a leper colony in Hawaii. You
can learn it first-hand as part of an expensive Ivy League
education.

▬ ▬ ▬

The internal logic of capitalism means that market-based
economies are unable to provide justice for all their citizens—unless, that is, the freedom of the market is supple-
mented or controlled by regulation. In an entirely
unregulated market, we inevitably decline into a kind of
winners-win/losers-die equality of economic opportunity
that resembles the Hobbesian state of nature much more
than the civil society most of us hope to inhabit. The vaunted *self*-regulation of the market, the dangerous old idea that
justice will be realized by fair competition and spending
freedom, is not proof against the essential inhumanity of

capital, especially as the population grows beyond our comprehension or control. The reasons for this are tangled in the early history of what the Canadian political theorist C.B. Macpherson famously called "possessive individualism."

At the root of the liberal democratic experiment—the political ideology that is dominant in the industrialized world—is a conflicted vision of the human individual. On the one hand, this individual is conceived primarily as an owner with a naturally equal claim to whatever goods are available: someone who possesses property that requires protection from the threat of envious others. In contrast to earlier notions of ownership, which were based on merit or virtue or bloodline, this new kind of owner, who was more or less invented by English political philosophers in the 1600s, requires no further traits or characteristics to justify possession. The possessive individual acquires, simply by virtue of being an individual, the right to have and hold material possessions. Indeed, this right is itself the most basic form of property, something that belongs to the individual without reservation—in the language of the U.S. Constitution, the right to property is *inalienable*.

If equality lies on one side of possessive individualism, liberty is on the other. According to this liberal view, the individual is conceived as fundamentally free, at liberty from threat or domination. True, one might have to strike some kind of bargain in order to protect what one possesses as a matter of equal rights: I sacrifice some power to the state in order to protect what I own by natural right. However, freedom is still basic to this conception of the individual, because it is precisely on the basis of being self-determining that the individual has property (and the right to property) in the first place.

And yet these attempts to bolster liberal individualism do not resolve the basic conflict between equality and freedom. The freedom of each person is—when expressed acquisitively in the right to property—constantly in friction with the freedom of others; when unregulated, exercising that right leads inevitably to inequalities. Liberal democracy works by granting status to everyone who manages the common, if lucky, feat of being born; nothing further is required for us to have political (and indeed moral) status. But the freedom enshrined at the same time means that, under some definition of success, the cream must eventually rise to the top. I have to be free to distinguish myself from others, in achievements or riches or something. Thus there is a basic tension in a democratic society between the egalitarianism of "All people are created equal" and the inescapable fact that some people are stronger, smarter, taller, richer, more beautiful, or more talented, than others—and hence are free to gain advantages others can probably not enjoy.

This tension, which is deeply buried in the liberal view of the world, is becoming more obvious as the resource scarcities and social violence of the last decades sharpen the prospect of material conflict. Put simply, the issue is this: will people be content to remain liberal democrats as we turn the corner on the millennium? If the prophets of economic extremity are to be believed, the signs in the culture are hardly favourable. Our darkest dreams seem on the verge of coming true.

One important root of our current democratic crisis is the uncomfortable notion of *elites*, the idea that the better, smarter, richer, or more beautiful among us should lump themselves into a social subgroup. This lumping is what a Marxist would call class consciousness. But contrary to any crude Marxist view of things, class is not always a simple function of capital. There can be classes in looks and athletic ability as much as in money and social position. That fact can get lost in the shuffle, because it is one of the peculiarities of capitalistic societies that we tend to reward people for their looks or athletic ability by giving them more money.

As a character says in David Mamet's play *Glengarry Glen Ross*, "This is how we keep score, bubby."

So, even as we are all created equal in political terms—one person, one vote, etc.—freedom allows some of us to outdistance the others in comfort and power. The potential for conflict in this situation has always been great. Lately it has grown to dangerous proportions. One response now favoured is to level differences by force—that is, the valiant "anti-elitist" attempt to eliminate not only social inequalities but inherited ones, too. This has been tried before, with little success. In the 1790s—another millennial hotbed—the fledgling U.S. government experimented with social levelling in the business of diplomacy. Thomas Jefferson's "Pell Mell Etiquette" called for the obliteration of all distinctions of rank and birth. Pecking orders all abolished, visiting dignitaries would be treated just like other down-home folks. The effort was a policy disaster. It achieved only one egalitarian goal: it succeeded in giving everyone equal offence. The reason is simple. Democratic equality does not, and cannot, mean that everyone is the same. It's not just that systems of rank are necessary to realize certain kinds of efficiency (in the military, say, or the diplomatic corps). The genetic lottery is not committed to equality, and some people just seem to be more genuinely gifted than others. So the question is not: Are there intractable differences between people? Of course there are; there always have been. The question is: What are we going to do about them in these straitened times?

There is no shortage of answers on offer. We have recently been told, for example, to refuse all judgments of "quality," for they are really just expressions of class interests. We have been told to foster self-esteem instead of achievement in schools, for education is really about feeling good about yourself. We have been told to play down the achievements of exceptional and extraordinary people because these paragons threaten the self-image of the less able, for the point of a human life is not to feel intimidated by people who are better at things than you are.

From these bizarre judgments, of course, it is not much of a step to what Paul Fussell calls, in his book *Class: A Guide Through the American Status System* (1983), "revenge egalitarianism": the envious cutting down to size of the exceptional. This is the resentful tendency satirized, all too plausibly, in L. P. Hartley's novel *Facial Justice* (1960), in which "the prejudice against good looks" is taken to a logical policy conclusion: government plastic surgeons are charged with making everyone equally plain. Or consider the dystopian vision of Kurt Vonnegut's science-fiction story of phenom Harrison Bergeron, a gifted athlete and genius who is killed by the "U.S. Handicapper-General" after he throws off the scrap-metal harness and enormous earphones designed to impede and distract him, and thereby render him equal to everyone else. Revenge egalitarianism is a product of envy; it is not democracy. "Democracy demands that all of its citizens begin the race even," Roger Price sums up in his book *The Great Roob Revolution* (1970). "Egalitarianism insists that they all *finish* even."

Recent political events strengthen the case that democracy is in conflict with itself over the ideas of elites and equality. If North American pundits agreed on anything during the national elections of the early 1990s, it was that *elites were on the run*. The voters had spoken, and they had expressed their disgust with experts and professionals of all kinds. The elites were distant from real people, from the true concerns of the nation. More than half of Americans, 52 percent, told *The Washington Post* that they would rather spend a week in jail than be president. Ironically, it was the experts and professionals who populate the mass media who seemed to find this anti-elitist sentiment particularly satisfying. In fact, the elites of punditry were so gleeful about the public's denunciations of what was usually called the "political and business" elite (as if those groups were always united in aim) that they let the debate slide easily into cliché: elites were self-evidently bad groups of arrogant and condescending privilege-hoarders. In a witty send-up of the increasingly twisted denunciations, the cartoonist Lind, in the July 1995 issue of the Toronto-based *This Magazine*, depicted a "rich people's protest march," complete with slogans ("Don't say 'rich'—say 'poverty-deprived'!") and interest-group signs ("Elites Against Elites Against Spending Cuts").

In this sort of charged rhetorical atmosphere it is hard for someone to speak up and seriously defend elitism, but a few brave souls have done just that. One of them is William Henry III, a *Time* magazine culture critic whose 1994 book *In Defense of Elitism* attacks the politically correct denunciation of quality with all the anger and wit of a dying man. Henry died, of cancer, before his book saw the light of publication, adding some poignancy to his bitter polemic. Friends of mine who read pre-publication excerpts of the book thought this was probably just as well; the enemies of plain speaking wouldn't have Henry to kick around. *In Defense of Elitism* is indeed a provocative book, and one out of step with these careful times. It ruthlessly mocks the banality of victim politics in the halls of power and "special pleading studies" in the groves of academe. It rants against stupidity and the lowering of standards in American life. Above all, it defends one simple idea that is increasingly without able (or willing) defenders: that society benefits from "the willingness to assert unyieldingly that one idea, contribution or attainment is *better than* another."

The willingness to make and defend intellectual distinctions is for Henry the healthy core of elitism, what gets lost in routine denunciations of the elite. But that willingness leads inevitably to the politically unpopular (and now largely unutterable) view that some people are better than others.

This view, which used to be widely accepted, is what has given elitism its bad name. Henry opens his book with a telling observation: "Somewhere along Bill Clinton's path to the White House it dawned on me that the term 'elitist,' which I had matter-of-factly applied to myself and most of my fellow liberal Democratic friends for decades, has come to rival if not outstrip 'racist' as the foremost catchall pejorative of our times."

This is doubtless true. The epithet "elitist" has become an all-purpose argument-stopper, one of the new class of self-evidently unconscionable things. My undergraduate students, whose good grades gained them entry into one of the country's best universities—de facto elitists all, in other words, whether they like it or not—routinely invoke it when they ask why they have to study reactionary old duffers like Plato. Yet they seem to have no problem with some elites, like the sports heroes they admire, perhaps because their achievements are so visible (you can't argue with a home run). Nor do they balk at another elite that has a strong hold on the popular imagination: the one based on the pure genetic good fortune of physical beauty. No, it's mainly intellectual elites that receive the scorn these days. According to Henry, a society that denies the need for a stimulating intellectual elite, in favour of a relentless celebration of the ordinary and the average, is a society in deep trouble.

He pursues the thesis with verve, even glee, and one of the book's incidental benefits is its rich catalogue of horror stories, culled from recent headlines. There are distressing tales of Stanford University undergraduates who have never heard of the New Deal, can't date the American Civil War, and think that failing students is "un-American." There is mockery of declawed fairy tales, cleaned up to send more positive messages to children—a trend lately sent up with some verve in several volumes of *Politically Correct Bedtime*

Stories "collected" by humorist James Finn Gardner. (Little Red Riding Hood is saved not by the male hunter but by her newly empowered grandmother.) There is also a controversial letter from George Plimpton, editor of *Paris Review*, asking for "the very best work" from writers, and also "worthy pieces by women and minority writers."

Henry's book is not, however, simply another the-walls-are-crumbling lament about relativism from some disgruntled conservative hack. Henry is a liberal, though admittedly a well-heeled one. For him, "To speak in defense of elitism is not to tilt the balance of national life but to seek to restore it." Since the Second World War, he argues, American society has been gripped more and more by the sort of incoherent egalitarianism that marks Garrison Keillor's Lake Wobegon, "where all the children are above average." In democratic thinking, "equal" does not mean *the same* but rather equal before the law or in the polling booth. More subtly, it has meant equality of opportunity, what liberal theorists call "the career open to talents": the idea that anyone should be allowed to compete for, and perhaps even get, any job they are qualified to do. Legislating equality of outcome may palliate the less able, but it also apparently works to punish the gifted and hard-working. And it obliterates distinctions: when we all get A grades, an A ceases to have any meaning. As Paul Fussell puts it, "In the land where everybody is somebody, nobody is anybody."

In a way, it is really too bad that Henry isn't around to continue the debate. We need more people willing to argue that the widespread attack on the notion of social elites is actually a virulent strain of Gumpism. What he ultimately suggests is that the idea of elites be divorced from social position and attached to ability and intelligence, creating thereby a worthy elite, the so-called "cognitive elite" of brains and ability.

Of course, it turns out that such a meritocratic elite is, in these tortured days, no more immune from attack than any other.

— — —

Elites of physical beauty, athletic ability, and facility in memorizing and repeating other people's words in front of a camera are numerically tiny, the talents they muster evanescent. They pose no deep threat to equality. The problems posed by the elite of intelligence, however, are different and harder to deal with. To aggressive levellers of social distinction, in other words, what is troubling about the elite of cognitive ability is precisely that it claims to be based on merit. Not surpisingly, there has been little clear thinking about the issues. And sometimes what presents itself as clear thinking creates far more heat than light. In their now notorious book, *The Bell Curve: Intelligence and Class Structure in American Life*, the Harvard psychologist Richard J. Herrnstein and the conservative polemicist Charles Murray offered some gloomy—and brutal—reflections on this New Elitism of intelligence. Herrnstein and Murray start where Henry's more graceful and humane discussion left off. Let's take seriously the idea of an elite based on merit, they seem to say. What consequences does the idea really have for a democratic society?

What they found was not reassuring to most people who read the book or observed their claims being discussed. In fact, the "truth" Herrnstein and Murray discerned was so ugly that they were attacked without mercy by a host of writers who saw the book as incendiary, racist, and, not least, bad science. The attacks, written by illustrious critics including Stephen Jay Gould and Henry Louis Gates, Jr. mostly appeared in upscale "intellectual" magazines like *The New Yorker*, *The New York Review of Books*, and *The New Republic*. What was all the fuss about? The United States, Herrnstein and Murray argue in *The Bell Curve*, is indeed now dominated by a "cognitive elite" of high-IQ managers and professionals. What's more, these people are increasingly more powerful than, and isolated from, an intelligence-deficient underclass in which crime, poverty, and political apathy are rampant. And, oh yeah, this underclass happens to be predominantly black.

Herrnstein and Murray say they recognize the dangers of a cognitive elite separated from the rest of society. Yet their policy suggestions say nothing about eliminating or integrating such an elite; instead, they are all about how to expand the cognitive elite rather than control it. Immigration should be limited, they say, to counter the lowering effects of population expansion. And, to avoid "dysgenesis," or intelligence dissipation through breeding, birth control should be made more widely available to those at the low end of the bell curve. They defend these attempts to fatten the high-IQ end of the bell curve by gesturing toward economic competitiveness, but the effects are clearly discriminatory and, on their own evidence, racially targeted.

In fact, the program is eugenic in inspiration, and it raises the ugly spectre of IQ testing in the early part of this century, when it was used explicitly to defend sterilization programs for people of "sub-standard" intelligence. The racial bias, which virtually discounts social and environmental causes for differences in IQ scores, also sounds an unwelcome echo of past debates about the inferiority of blacks. Thus conditioned by the past, *The Bell Curve* is also oddly futuristic; it has its own kind of millennial anxiety in the picture of a United States overrun by less intelligent people, many of whom are brown and black, while smart white people waited to have children until it was too late, concentrating on their careers, their leisure time, or their relationships. Thus, the authors imply, a once powerful nation falls behind smarter, stronger nations like (who else?) Japan in the tough world of the twenty-first century.

The book exudes a strong dystopian aura that is eerily reminiscent of other fertility dystopias, like P. D. James's *The Children of Men* (in which, by 2022, fertile men have gradually disappeared from the earth) or Margaret Atwood's *The Handmaid's Tale* (in which a brutal right-wing theocracy takes over the United States by freezing automatic teller machines, then implements a biblical "utopia" where young fertile women, the handmaids, are birth-slaves to powerful but infertile wives). These fertility dystopias represent what might be, in its way, the ultimate Malthusian control. If increases in education and birth control don't stop the world population from reaching 15 billion in 2050, maybe male or female infertility will. Some evidence of dramatic declines in sperm counts has already been recorded by Danish researchers, who also found increases in deformities and cancer in reproductive organs during the last few decades of the twentieth century. And in seventeen countries worldwide, according to UNICEF figures, fertility rates have declined at least 50 percent in the last generation.

The Bell Curve steers clear of this kind of general zero-population-growth nightmare, concentrating instead on evidence of a growing gap in reproductive activity between the smart and the "less" smart. There is therefore, to my mind, a hidden but powerful eugenic message from the book's authors to members of the cognitive elite: Do your duty, smart (incidentally, white) people! Get out there and breed a little faster!

Such an analysis comes gift-wrapped for anti-welfare conservatives, especially if they also happen to be closet racists. Dinesh D'Souza, the former Reagan policy adviser who made his reputation attacking the politically correct dogmatism of American university students and professors in his book *Illiberal Education* (1990), weighed in with a neo-racist tome called, with somehow typical late-century overstatement, *The End of Racism*. D'Souza argues that

American whites have mostly given up their formerly racist views (or at least given up uttering them), even while black-on-black racism seems to be on the rise. This leads him to the dangerous conclusion that the end of American racism is in sight—if only blacks will pull themselves together, turn their backs on the welfare state's debilitating handouts, and stop having babies out of wedlock. Racism is not America's problem, D'Souza says in a twist worthy of his spiritual mentor, Charles Murray (there is a long and sympathetic chapter on *The Bell Curve* in D'Souza's book); America's problem is really welfarist liberalism. Well-meaning government intervention, the Democratic "Great Society" experiment, merely ends up trapping blacks in poverty, even while providing careers for various well-meaning "race merchants" who support affirmative action programs, minority scholarships, and other condescending forms of patronage.

Such thinking plays to a receptive, and apparently growing, gallery of middle- and working-class American whites who profess themselves tired of hearing about black suffering. (No white liberal guilt for *them*.) It also appears to ground the widespread fear of blacks, who remain a 12 percent minority in the United States, in "evidence" of their inferior intelligence and predilection for violent crime. If whites fear blacks, D'Souza seems to suggest, it is not because of racism but because crime statistics bear them out. If some whites despise black English, rap music, the wearing of African dashikis, or the invented Afro-Christian holiday Kwanzaa, then once more this is evidence not of racism but of the belief that black culture just isn't very impressive. The implication of such arguments is clear enough: whites are just being rational; now blacks have to stop blaming everyone else for their problems and get with the program.

The fear that has poisoned black-white race relations for decades shows no signs of diminishing. In a July 1995 article in *The Nation*, which argues that most cost-cutting measures adopted under Newt Gingrinch's Contract With America seem to target blacks, political scientist Andrew Hacker notes that these decisions arise from new kinds of social fear. Hacker regularly presents his white university students with a hypothetical choice to illustrate the problem: They could either lose $300 to a white mugger, or $100 to a black robber. "Almost all select the first option," Hacker wrote, "and give essentially the same reason. They would gladly pay the extra $200 to avoid a black assailant. It is not simply that they feel blacks are more drawn to violence. Far more at issue is the fear that the man in front of them will take another moment and do something horrible, to repay the white race for what it has done to his people." This, Hacker concludes, "is the same fear slaveowners had of being slaughtered in their beds."

It is also the fear that I found myself, all too unwillingly, feeling during the years I spent in New Haven. The thought is ugly; it is repellent. But it is natural—and this despite the heavy bombardment of recent Hollywood films depicting easy, joshing friendships between blacks and whites (*Pulp Fiction, Die Hard With a Vengeance, Speed, The Shawshank Redemption, Forrest Gump, Driving Miss Daisy, Philadelphia, Unforgiven,* the *Lethal Weapon* movies, *48 Hours,* etc.). Not only do these films tend to obscure the reality of black oppression in North America by suggesting an easy social mobility—as the writer Benjamin DeMott forcefully argues in his 1995 book *The Trouble with Friendship: Why Americans Can't Think Straight About Race*—they also create bizarre expectations on the part of whites. You want to say, as you walk down that street or through that mall, passing those tough-guy black kids: "I am not like the others; I am not your oppressor. Let's be friends, like Mel Gibson and Danny Glover." But your white skin talks before you do. It says almost all there is to say.

When it comes to race in America, books like *The Bell Curve* and *The End of Racism* only compound the confusion. Invoking apparently irrefutable genetic support for Murray's contention, in the 1984 book *Losing Ground*, that welfarism is a social dead-end, these new works suggest that we now know the real reason the underclass is mainly black. It is not that blacks have been historically disadvantaged, or even that government regulation has proved a less powerful force than a free market where privilege begets privilege. No, they say, the real reason is that quota-based affirmative action programs, welfare, and most forms of social assistance are doomed to fail by Mother Nature. No amount of standard-lowering or monetary gifts can alter a person's genes. Biology is not exactly destiny, but it's pretty darn close.

Good polemicists all, D'Souza, Herrnstein, and Murray shamelessly manipulate statistics and history in pursuit of these conclusions. (D'Souza is especially unconvincing in his tales of the handful of Southern free blacks who owned slaves before the Civil War: such owners were a tiny minority and often of mixed race. They hardly qualify as strong historical evidence of black-on-black racism.) Their arguments often confuse correlation with causation, apparently with deliberate intent to provoke. Nowhere do they acknowledge that among the lingering social effects of slavery could be persistent economic and social disadvantage, and the so-called "black pathologies" D'Souza dwells on. In the case of *The Bell Curve*, the authors artificially and controversially limit the notion of intelligence to that which IQ tests can measure, substituting "intelligence for moral worth," in the words of one critic. And their weak palliatives emphasizing the *positive* aspects of racial "clans" (saying, for example, that blacks are better athletes and should be proud of that), or suggesting America's "real" racism problem is all a matter of black special pleading and self-hatred, are just cheerful conservative hooey. *The Bell Curve's* numbers, finally, like all statistics, leave no room for individuality and invite the reduction of everyone to his or her group.

All true. The unpalatable fact, though, is that North American society *does* seem organized to reward intelligence and not moral worth. If this were not so, IQ would not be one of the most reliable predictors of worldly success. And likewise, of course, there would not be such a good market for books that make these kinds of arguments. *The Bell Curve* and *The End of Racism* are sure signs of the times; they are in the business of undermining the social programs that a more hopeful nation, the socially conscious America of the 1960s, thought worthy of construction in pursuit of justice. Revisionist tomes like these make it easy to forget that this optimism, so easily parodied now with tales of affirmative-action abuse and third-generation welfare recipients, was a powerful social force. The only thing that matches it in influence today is the utterly cynical manipulation of racial hostility for political purposes: the enshrined Republican strategy of playing on white, especially Southern, fear and resentment to buy what must henceforth be known as "Willie Horton votes."

To be sure, *The End of Racism* and *The Bell Curve* have bigger fish to fry than any mere presidential election campaign. They claim to be telling us the way the world really is. *The Bell Curve* in particular wants to provide scientific (therefore acceptable, indeed virtually irrefutable) phrasing for the unpleasant reality that, in a society based on free-market liberalism, brighter people should be more likely to succeed than others. (It also says a great deal, along the way, about what free-market liberals understand "bright" to mean.) *The End of Racism* accepts those claims and takes them further, into the realm of cultural policy and normative judgment, suggesting that blacks are only getting what they deserve. These modern American "conservatives," then, who attack the welfare state with such vigour, are not really conservatives at all, in the sense that, say, Edmund Burke was. They are not interested in the inherent worth of institutions or traditions. They are actually old-fashioned liberals, the political descendants of Locke and the other possessive individualists who placed so much faith in a barely regulated society ruled by property. But the strange thing is that these modern scions seem so unwilling to defend their politics on the merits: they don't defend the genuine moral disapproval they feel for black culture. They resort instead to superficially powerful, but in fact quite flimsy, claims about the nature of genetic predisposition. They hide their ideology under a blanket of biological determinism and cant about individual freedom.

Indeed, *The Bell Curve*'s argument is in a way oddly reminiscent of the "noble lie" of Plato's *Republic*. To preserve the caste system necessary for social harmony, Plato suggests that rulers should tell citizens a mythic story about different metals being mixed in the souls of different classes of people. Citizens will not accept a ruling class based on a claim to superior wisdom, he notes, but they *will* accept a divine ordinance that gave the rulers "golden souls." Our own scientistic culture prefers a statistical ordinance, but the impulse to sugar-coat inequality is ultimately the same. These days we soothe ourselves with the thought that, if the graphs show it, it cannot be otherwise.

— — —

Despite all the hand-wringing about *The Bell Curve* (and, to a lesser extent, *The End of Racism*)—despite, that is, all the finely honed prose of the critics, despite the accuracy of many charges of slipshod analysis—it remains difficult to denounce the idea of a genuine cognitive elite. If we are willing to gloss over the cultural prejudices embedded in *any* judgment of intelligence—a controversial assumption, admittedly, but one many people seem willing to make for IQ tests—"braininess" seems not only a good trait but an honest one: a difference we can all respect. Isn't this precisely the "aristocracy of merit" that philosophers and politicians have long demanded from a just society? Isn't the cognitive elite simply another way of saying the best and the brightest, the ones who will do good things for everyone?

Unfortunately it is not. The problem posed by the New Elite is not, as it was with bloodline elites, mere existence. The problems are, instead, the elite's growing social irresponsibility, and, even more dangerously, its growing control of the social machinery. As the cognitive elite has grown in power through the decades following the Second World War—the decades creating a world ruled by information—it has increasingly set itself apart from society at large in a well-protected enclave of power. A number of keen observers of American society have recently, without indulging in knee-jerk anti-elitism, shown us the dark future of North American society. It is a future that *Harper's* magazine editor Lewis Lapham calls "the new feudalism."

In his 1995 book *The Revolt of the Elites and the Betrayal of Democracy*, the American historian and critic Christopher Lasch advanced the elitism debate by going beyond the simple-mindedness of *The Bell Curve*'s statistical analysis and exposing the uncertain future of a political culture dominated by a cognitive elite. Lasch noted that the cognitive elite, precisely because it is (and knows itself to be) merit-based, has begun to defect in large numbers from the responsible social role privileged classes formerly occupied. Like Henry and Herrnstein, Lasch is no longer around to expand on his views: all three analysts of elitism died in 1994 while awaiting publication of their respective books. (The statistical significance of that doesn't bear thinking about.) But his book probes what *The Bell Curve*, *The End of Racism*, and even *In Defense of Elitism* seem happy to ignore: the possible dark underside of *any* intelligence-based meritocracy.

Twenty percent of the American population now controls between half and 80 percent of the country's wealth, Lasch notes. The disparity between rich and poor in industrialized countries is wider than at any time in the last fifty years. In other words, what the First World is to the developing world—Homer-Dixon's air-conditioned limousine—the so-called upper-middle class is to the rest of European and North American society. The important difference is that this dominant class is now composed not of blue-bloods but of what U.S. labour secretary Robert Reich has called "symbolic analysts." In other words, it is, Lasch writes, "a 'new class' only in the sense that their livelihood rests not so much on ownership of property as on manipulation of information and professional expertise." The new elite includes bank managers and businesspeople, but also information managers like journalists and academics. It is apparently diverse and often, as the media's denunciations of elites makes clear, in conflict with itself. But these surface conflicts are merely distractions. They obscure the essential sameness of the majority of office-tower inhabitants, even as they deflect attention from the plight of the less-gifted majority.

Bolstered by a world ruled by information, the symbolic analysts—the new "credentialed overclass"—enjoy a style of life that is lavish, even decadent, in these late-century times. They are also increasingly insulated. They work in towering glass buildings, dine in expensive, opulent restaurants, shop in gourmet food stores, and live in exclusive neighbourhoods. Because their colleagues and friends may hail from family backgrounds of different social strata, they do not see just how similar their education and success have actually made them. They even, according to Michael Lind, senior editor at *Harper's* and author of a sharply critical book on the overclass, manage the impressive legerdemain of denying that they constitute a class. Lind's book *The Next American Nation* was also published in 1995, making it the unofficial Year of Hand-Wringing About the Elites.

Lind, once known for his intelligent conservative views, begins to sound like a Marxist when he launches an attack on the social irresponsibility of an American overclass that denies it exists. "The most remarkable thing about our new American oligarchy," he writes,

> is the pretense that it doesn't constitute any-thing as definite as a social class. We prefer to assign our good fortune to our individual merit, saying that we owe our perches in the upper percentiles of income and education not to our connections but solely to our own IQ, virtue, brio, genius, *sprezzatura*, chutzpah, gumption. Had we been switched at birth by accident, had we grown up in a ghetto or bar-rio or trailer park, we would have arrived at our offices at ABC News or the Republican National Committee or the ACLU in more or less the same amount of time.

Thus united only by wealth and ability, the credentialed few lack a common political outlook, other than a desire to pro-tect their positions, but share a vivid disdain for those less able. "Simultaneously arrogant and insecure," Lasch writes in the same vein, "the new elites regard the masses with mingled scorn and apprehension."

That scorn and apprehension is returned in spades, as we know. And this mutual enmity in turn leads to defection—not of the downtrodden, perhaps, palliated and distracted by the sports and movie equivalents of Aldous Huxley's "soma shows," but of the elevated. On this view, the Los

Angeles riots were an aberration, and one, as I noted earlier, in which blacks attacked and looted not the secure homes of Beverly Hills but the corner stores and discount shops of their recently arrived Korean neighbours. It is really the *revolt of the elites* from social responsibility that we should observe, not just the *revolt of the masses*.

Lasch is, in his work, consciously alluding to Ortega y Gasset's famous book of that title. But even *The Revolt of the Masses*, written in 1930, finds less to fear in open armed revolt than in the insidious triumph of "the commonplace mind." "The mass crushes beneath it everything that is different, everything that is excellent, individual, qualified, and select," Ortega writes, sounding a lot like William Henry. Or like Paul Fussell, in fact, who labelled the phenomenon in question "Prole Drift," which he defined as "the tendency in industrialized societies for everything inexorably to become proletarianized." The result? "Bestseller lists, films that must appeal to virtually everyone (except the intelligent, sensitive, and subtle), shopping malls, and the lemming flight to the intellectual and cultural emptiness of the Sun Belt."

We could easily multiply the examples: The proliferation of country-and-western music channels on television and radio. The virtually complete baseball-capping of North America. The juggernaut market invasion by restaurants selling high-fat, high-sodium, high-calorie food. The $400-million (U.S.) spent by fans on stock-car racing merchandise (shirts, caps, belt buckles) in 1994—not to mention the $3.15-*billion* (U.S.) spent on goods bearing the imprint of the thoroughly prole National Football League. Paul Blumberg calls this kind of thing the Howard Johnsonization of America. We can now also call it by another name: Gumpism.

This picture of the generally revolting quality of our times has, then, two related sides: on the one hand, a mass of bemused wage-slaves whose power is entirely in their shopping habits, eliminating quality and discrimination by sheer force of numbers; and on the other, a shrinking enclave of the rich, pampered, and besieged. The hostility running through this two-class society is obvious. The new managers of information and money—unlike the old elites of blood-line and land—feel no sense of attachment to community or devotion to such traditional virtues as prudence, obligation, charity, or loyalty. We cannot imagine them caring for indentured servants, taking part in village fêtes, or collecting for rummage sales. Worse, their vaunted meritocracy is, according to Lasch, "a parody of democracy," in which the privileged take refuge in abstract equality of opportunity when confronted with the less well-off. Because success is predicated on the merit of intelligence, they think justice has been served if there are, say, open scholarships to Ivy League universities. Everybody has the chance to be smart, after all. Such a defence of equal opportunity conveniently ignores what is known as "legacy preference": the well-known and well-documented tendency of elite universities to prefer children of graduates, even if their test scores are on average lower. According to a recent analysis of admissions figures, a "legacy" is three times more likely to be admitted to Harvard than someone with the same, or better, scores whose father went to some other university—or no university at all. As the ads say: Membership Has Its Privileges.

Insulated by its good intentions and bad delusions, the overclass effectively siphons off talent from the lower classes with a handful of minority scholarships to elite schools. They grant success to this tiny, hand-picked subgroup of the minority, who have now attended the same schools they have. This sort of "affirmative-action patronage," as Lind calls it, leaves the lower classes in America leaderless and stagnant. In fact, as Lind observes, the overclass has gotten so good at perpetuating its position that it has become like the ruling guild of an Italian or Dutch city-state. "Our latter-day oligarchs (lawyers, bankers, publishers, anchorpersons)," he says, "are the contemporary equivalents of the plump and goateed syndics, haloed by starched collars, who gaze smugly back at us through honeyed veils of impasto from the paintings of Rembrandt and Hals." In these and countless other ways the rich and talented, in Lasch's words, "retain many of the vices of aristocracy without its virtues."

The new aristocracy of brains and education is also increasingly and aggressively isolated. Its members begin to seek shelter behind the gates of private suburbs, patrolled by private police forces, their garbage collected by private contractors. There are now more privately employed security guards in the United States than publicly funded police. Federal spending on law enforcement and government dropped by 42 percent during the 1980s; on transportation infrastructure it dropped by 32 percent. Increasingly anxious about their privilege, the overclass has begun an effective—and massive—retreat behind castellated walls. Private toll roads, to replace a national highway system, are now being discussed by ten states. Tony suburban neighbourhoods have applied for permission to erect gates—a move that one California judge condemned as an illegal "return to medieval times." Not only does the overclass feel no sense of attachment to the less well-off, they regard them as a positive threat.

Many members of the overclass, especially those of the youngish upper-middle class, protest their innocence in this new Class Cold War. As evidence of their freedom from taint they point to their own version of the white-knuckle life. Yes, they say, we are young, smart, and well-educated—as privileged as it gets in late-century North America. But we also know that Social Security will go broke in 2029 and that Medicare will have no spring in its financial step when we become seriously ill in a decade or two. The most affluent members of a generation born in the 1950s and '60s now live, if they can be believed, in fear of a poverty-stricken old age. "The market runs on fear," writes the financial journalist Ted C. Fishman in an article on why more and more Americans are pursuing high-risk / high-return investments (*Harper's*, October 1995). "Although I am a thirty-seven-year-old white, Ivy League-educated, married man, and thus, by any reckoning, enjoying nearly every advantage one may have in American society," Fishman says, "I do not expect, necessarily, to be able to retire with sufficient wealth to maintain my present standard of living. I belong to a generation that not only is hooked on stock investing but also grudgingly embraces speculation as the last best hope against dying penniless." Fifty-one million Americans play the stock market, Fishman tells us, many of them because they believe that only aggressive, even capricious, investing is all that stands between them and bleak retirement in a dingy, single-resident-only apartment. Where thrift is bankrupt as a survival strategy, fear rules. And damn the even less fortunate others, the ones who cannot even scrimp enough to make a call to a mutual fund manager worthwhile.

In this retreat of the affluent into cocooned and fearful isolation—an isolation which, moreover, feels to them entirely justified—we are veering dangerously close to the nightmare third-millennium visions of recent ultraviolent, ultra-trashy cinematic science fiction: the contracted-out Detroit police force of the *Robocop* movies, the brutal "rule of law" megacities of *Judge Dredd*, or the haves-versus-have-nots scenario of *Demolition Man*. The last two films star the absurdly over-muscled "himbo" Sylvester Stallone, who seems to be making a late-century career of portraying good—which is to say *pro-order*—men who wield suitcase-sized guns in a chaotic future of massive cities and rampant criminal evil. The message is clear. In the future, tougher and tougher measures will be called for to deal with property crimes and violence. The supporters of these "measures" will pride themselves on remaining on the right side of the law, but the rule of law will be, inevitably, ever more repressive and all-controlling. In *Demolition Man* the result is particularly egregious: the starving underclass of Los Angeles actually lives underground, in the sewer system, while the surface world is an anodyne "utopia" that manages to combine Orwellian and Huxleyan elements. (Arguably worse is the Prole Drift evident in the fact that the overworld supports a single chain of restaurants: Taco Bell.)

"The underclass is stalled in place," the Harvard economist John Kenneth Galbraith told Harry Rasky in *Prophecy*, summarizing the analysis in his book *The Culture of Contentment*. "And this is a dangerous situation. We live in a world of private affluence and public squalor. We live in a world of quite expensive television programs and quite poor schools. We live in a world of clean houses and filthy streets. We live in a world where law and order in the suburbs is quite good and in the inner cities quite bad. A world of enormous inequalities."

We have chosen consumerism over well-being in framing our society. We have placed all our faith in a market that is indifferent to individuals and their hopes. We have appeased ourselves with material goods and worried about access to a greater share of them. And in doing so, we have ignored the stress fractures and faultlines in the social edifice. Even the chorus of claim and counter-claim that has become the dominant theme of North American discourse—the so-called culture wars—does nothing more than deflect attention from the small minority that lives in outrageous comfort. To Lind's eyes, for example, the media attention on issues of race and culture is really a red herring that allows the overclass to shift the focus away from massive debt loads. Servicing those debts, he notes, functions as a de facto transfer of wealth from the poor (that is, non-investing citizens) to the rich (the roughly 20 percent of the population with money to place in mutual funds).

Despite the much-ballyhooed collapse of Soviet communism, then, the harsh reality is that Marx really was right about the social world: understood properly, class is everything.

The analyses of Lasch, Lind, Galbraith, and others are in many ways accurate. But like so many warnings of impending economic collapse, they simply leave us grasping once more for elusive solutions—and incidentally subject to debilitating feelings of helplessness and dread. Like a lot of prognostication of the present day, they combine social, economic, and moral threats in such a way as to suggest no hopeful alternative. Sensitive readers might be tempted to react like medieval peasants or threatened Renaissance Florentines: by diving to the floor, curling into the foetal position, and hoping the walls don't crumble on top of them.

■ ■ ■

Even when the economic doomsayers offer positive suggestions, the payoff is invariably slim. Lasch's suggestions for improvement, for example, are no more helpful (though they are certainly more palatable) than Herrnstein and Murray's. Lasch thinks that elites would feel more attachment to society if they cultivated the values of the lower-middle class—a holdover from his argument in *The Culture of Narcissism* (1979), which criticized the penchant for therapy and victimhood among the well-educated and privileged. But this is really just romantic nonsense. No bank manager or lawyer is going to feel more commitment to the poor by going bowling or watching "Roseanne," getting a sense of their "bourgeois virtues." The condescending emphasis on the vaunted "loyalty" and "tradition" of stolid working people is the kind of delusional perspective that used to afflict only Marxist intellectuals educated at Oxford. At the same time, the most vibrant culture of narcissism right now, as any watcher of daytime television can attest, seems to be the one of abrasive talk shows, whose audiences are disproportionately lower class and black. The people who clamour to make their confessions and air out their pain to Phil, Sally Jesse, Leeza, Jerry, Ricki, Vicki, and the rest are not the well-bred wasters of Lasch's imagination—they are the people in whom he invests all this misplaced hope. Lasch's rosy, family-values view of middle America is too Disneyfied, too sanguine. There is no social-democratic promised land in the middle of the bell curve. The hard questions are still unanswered. How can a large and powerful cognitive elite be reconciled with the egalitarianism at the heart of democracy?

The social elites are not going anywhere. And anyway, despite the cries of the modern-day levellers, elimination of elites is not the answer. John Stuart Mill, no friend to conservatives, knew that true elites (as opposed to self-styled ones—admittedly a fine, often impossible, distinction) provide an important example to society. They help it flourish through innovation and effort. Therefore neither spasmodic disapproval of elitism nor the retreat of elites into self-interested enclaves of privilege is of any use to society. They are two sides of the same coin. What we need instead is an elite that supports a culture of modified noblesse oblige. (Or, accepting that intelligence determines the new aristocracy, intelligence oblige.) In other words, we need a body politic in which privilege—even when meritocratic—implies obligation; where success—even when the result of hard work—demands devotion to community. We need a return to what Michael Lind, overstating the case a little, calls in his book "the old American republican ideal of civic obligation."

The republican ideal has always been alive in American

society, still more in "communitarian" polities like Canada and Great Britain. But nevertheless it sits uneasily with the individualism and freedom of the dominant liberal idea. The problem for us is simple: Can the social obligations of the gifted and well-off be made compelling to them? Can they be convinced that they must have a stake in the well-being of the whole society? Certainly one way to do this, though a risky one, is to revert to the kind of security analysis offered by Homer-Dixon. In a society of severe economic inequality, it becomes harder and harder to enjoy the privileges one has. Therefore the privileged should work to diminish inequality just to the extent that they crave security. As Benjamin Disraeli famously said in 1848, "The palace is not safe when the cottage is not happy." Yet this sort of benign Tory largesse can backfire, for when "acute conflict" is imminent, the barricades of the gated suburbs may begin to look better than well-meaning claims about social justice. How do you guarantee that the security threat is severe enough to call the privileged to account, without being so severe that isolationism and privatization look like more rational options?

Consider another kind of argument, one that has the benefit of being both plausible and ameliorative. In 1971, the Harvard philosopher John Rawls published a thick book called *A Theory of Justice*, which made an elaborate argument for a very simple conclusion. The genetic lottery, Rawls argues, is just that—a roll of the dice. Nobody knew before the fact who or what they would turn out to be. This includes relative wealth at birth and the allotment of talents that we associate with genetic traits, including intelligence.

But now ask yourself: what if, not knowing how the dice would roll for you, your social position and allotment of talents, you could nevertheless be party to the construction of your society's basic structure? What kind of principles of justice would you support *then*, placed behind a notional "veil of ignorance"? How would you choose to organize the society in which, on the other side of the veil, you might not be one of the able or privileged? The answer, Rawls suggests, owes much to our basic intuitions about fairness in distribution. In a way, his thought-experiment is analogous to an old device for solving dinner-table disputes. We both want part of the remaining cake. So we agree that I will cut the cake, but you will choose the first piece.

According to Rawls, then, behind the veil of ignorance we would support equal liberty and access to social positions—meritocratic equality of opportunity. From this point of view, we will not insist on strict equality of outcome— that would not be rational, given the inevitable differences in ability between people and given the value we place on freedom and effort. But we *will* demand that any inequalities of outcome be constrained by a crucial rule: they must make the worst-off class as well off as possible. After all, there but for the grace of the gene-gods go you.

A powerful conclusion. And yet, given the presumption of the New Elitism, that privilege accrues only to merit, it is hard to defend basically egalitarian ideas of justice in terms of what elites *owe* their fellow citizens. The privileged just won't buy that argument. After all, they say, they worked hard to get where they are and everybody else can just *get off their butts and get a job*. This myth of merit is not accepted only by the well-off, either. Nor is it always accepted in the apparently rational form of equating intelligence with success. According to the New York pollsters Louis Harris & Associates, fully 70 percent of Americans believe that their financial situation is "at least somewhat" reflective of "God's regard" for them.

At the same time, current means of holding the privileged responsible—graduated income tax, for example, which in effect regulates differences between people with the implicit threat of state force—are actively resented.

Such uses of the sovereign power, even when only implicit, can actually serve to encourage the very defection of elite social elements that Lasch feared. The more we perceive progressive taxation not as part of our collective bargain as citizens but rather as, say, an imposition of a regime that bolsters weakness, the less the able among us will be content to continue playing the social game. The retreat into gated communities is only the beginning of what could become a more and more vicious form of wealth-based separatism.

But then, nobody said creating a just society was going to be easy. As the liberal ideology of market freedom percolates down through all levels of society, even while the means of realizing market success slip away, it is, if anything, getting harder all the time.

I am tempted to end this stage of the discussion right here, on a more or less positive note, so we can move on in the terrain of millennial dread with at least one beachhead of hope secured. But I am aware, as much as anyone is, that this kind of philosophical argument about justice often fails to convince us of real-world obligations. This kind of theoretical defence of equality, the sort of thing academic political philosophers routinely trade in, appears to have little or no practical clout, even among those who find their theoretical underpinnings appealing. The reasons are simple to state but difficult to address. If the worriers are correct—and I include myself in that group, at least now and then—it is possible that it is already too late for this, or any, vision of justice.

Consider the potential problems. Democracy as it is usually practised is subject to all kinds of pathologies that tend to reinforce dominant interests. The franchise may be universal in most countries, but that does not stop powerful groups from exerting an undue influence in the day-to-day business of government. Anyone who doubts this need only consider the fact that there is no capital-gains tax in the United States, even though only the top 2 percent of the population, in terms of income, declares a capital gain in a normal tax year. After the Reagan years, in which tax reform was a constant theme, three-quarters of Americans owed more tax than they would have under 1977 tax laws; only the richest 5 percent of the population received any significant cuts. And new tax-reduction laws in Newt Gingrich's vaunted Contract With America will mean that families earning $350,000 a year will get annual cuts of $13,000 while families earning $30,000 a year will enjoy a reduction of only $180—about 50 cents a day.

More money, of course, means more airtime and more political clout. Overwhelmingly, contributions to political action committees come from business, not issue-based interest groups. In the first two months of 1995, the Republican National Committee was receiving $123,121 *every day* from corporate donors. In some cases, individual candidates racked up totals of more than a million dollars each during the 93-94 campaign cycle. As Michael Lind puts it, "Labor does not balance big business; consumer groups do not balance big business; *nobody* balances big business.... Citizens vote occasionally; dollars vote continually." According to a report from Citizen Action, an independent consumer group quoted in Lind's book, "Thirty-four percent of the money spent by federal candidates was directly contributed by no more than one-tenth of one percent of the voting age population." Civics classes, Lind notes, teach children that American democracy is a balance of powers, with no single interest or group overwhelming the others. Yet, taking seriously Deep Throat's famous advice to "follow the money," he finds a different story, of deep corporate influence in Washington and tax cuts designed to benefit the fortunate few. "We were lied to," he concludes gloomily of the myths promulgated in the classrooms of America's primary schools.

On one of my infrequent trips to the ugly federal building in New Haven, I was stopped by a young black man trying, like me, to fill out a form for a social security card. The trouble was, he could not read the form. Nor could he write his own name. He asked me to fill in the form for him. But I had never heard of his birthplace, a town apparently in Georgia, and I had trouble understanding him. We struggled along, deeply mired in frustration and, for both of us in our different ways, humiliation: he because he lacked this basic life-skill and needed to resort to asking me for help; I because I felt strangely ashamed of my own learning, the subtle rebuke implied by the apparent ease of my literacy. And the tragedy was that we could not, even together, complete the form. For a man like that, I often thought later, what possible stake is there in the business-as-usual ethos of America? Why would he go to the polling booth when he cannot read the candidates' names, let alone distinguish one set of meretricious promises from another? As Disraeli wrote, from troubled 1870 Britain, the rich and the poor are now very much like "[t]wo nations; between whom there is no intercourse and no sympathy; who are as ignorant of each other's habits, thoughts, and feelings, as if they were dwellers in different zones, or inhabitants of different planets."

Increasingly, then, we can expect the unrest of less powerful groups to be expressed not in electoral action, which they (correctly) regard as bankrupt—in 1994, only 23 percent of Americans with a household income between $5,000 and $10,000 bothered to vote—but in violence. The distractions offered by consumer capitalism and a sensation-hungry media will not keep a large and suffering underclass tame forever. Immigration, though it is being severely curtailed in the United States, will mean that new members of the underclass will pose an increasing demographic and social threat to the elite overclass. According to some prophets, these developments effectively signal the end of the western democratic experiment begun in the 1780s. Apparently, you cannot grant moral and political status to every single human being and expect a society—still less a globe—to function peacefully forever. "Those societies that continue to allow themselves to be administered by individuals whose only qualification is that they were able to win a popularity contest," argues Patrick Kennon, an ex-CIA operative whose 1995 book *The Twilight of Democracy* summed up this line of thought, "will go from failure to failure and eventually pass from the scene." Democracy is over, Kennon and his ilk suggest, and what is coming is bound to be worse for a lot of people who are now living in comfort. To combat anarchy, various forms of fascism are beginning to look more and more attractive to those with possessions and privileges they want protected.

Are we really headed for either anarchy or jackboot repression? The clues in the culture are not reassuring. The violence we have seen in North American cities has failed to shake the stronghold of elite privilege. That is, the threat of violence has not led to more elite responsibility, partly because the elites still (as Lind notes so eloquently) refuse to see themselves as such, and partly because the focus of violence has not been clearly enough on class. Instead, civil unrest appears to be motivated by racial and cultural differences that pundits allege are separable from class. As a result, the social violence has led only to more isolationism and hiding on the part of the comfortable. The well-off do not want to be recognized for what they are, which is, in the all-too-apt metaphor of the writer Michael Lewis, *piñatas*. Like the colourful papier-mâché animals stuffed with presents, Lewis wrote in *The New York Times Magazine* in 1995, the rich appear on our streets as objects in need of a clubbing, so that their nice insides will spill out. *Feliz Navidad.*

Sensing that conspicuous consumption is an invitation

to violence, the rich are reacting with more of what Martin Amis suggested in *London Fields* would be a ruling preoccupation of the coming millennium: *envy-preemption*, or, in other words, the conscious attempt to forestall attack by not looking too elevated or privileged. So the fabulously wealthy deliberately dress down when they venture into public spaces. Drive battered cars. Or create—a disturbing real-world example—what the critic Mike Davis has called "carceral architecture": so-called "stealth buildings" designed to look plain on the outside and thus disguise the outrageous opulence within, making prisoners of their owners in the process. All of this is alarming—and, in the carefully expressed views of socio-economic jeremiahs like Kaplan, Lind, and Lasch, meant to be so.

Yet, at the same time, even as the gloomiest cultural critics are lamenting the death of democracy, the dream of "direct democracy" offered by Internet converts is building. This is the great promised land of a future democratic explosion, where every voter gets to express a lightning-fast preference on every issue: governance as constant plebiscite, with every voter armed with a full-colour monitor and a modem. Yet even if we welcome this development in theory—and, I should hasten to add, there is good reason not to; you don't have to be an authoritarian like Plato to believe that sometimes the people don't know what is in their own best interests—the rosy visions of direct democracy really offer small comfort.

Individual voting, via personal computer, will not only fail to generate greater social stability; it will also focus the tensions of existing society and foster anarchy. For one thing, in an even more pronounced way than at present, access to power will become the main issue of contention. At the moment, Internet access is effectively restricted to a tiny minority of very young and extremely well-educated people. They are in the main academics, students, businesspeople, computer technicians, and children of wealthy homes. They are also disproportionately male: recent studies indicate that the population of regular Net visitors is almost 80 percent male. Despite the rhetoric of anarchist liberation that is associated with the Net, the dreams of cyber-democracy are empty. Our technology, as a response to a political situation beyond easy control, will hasten, not slow, the breakdown of society.

The fixation with the "democratic" possibilities of the Internet and television relate to a second issue, another piece of capitalism's inner logic, that threatens the survival of the society we know. Certain features of political life— the merger of politics and entertainment, the electoral advertising culture—are themselves part of this political breakdown. Actors now speak for candidates as glibly as they offer up tired exit lines. This is not news, but it is worth saying once more. What does this hollowing out of the electoral process mean for us? It means that politics has *become* advertising: the imagistic manipulation of vote-spending citizens in favour of campaigning products that, like Procter & Gamble brand competitors, are different only in name. When democracy—the idea that power lies with the people governed—has become self-defeating, the image-consciousness of today's politicians is an entirely rational response to the fickleness of citizens who vote with their preferences. And those preferences are becoming less and less the genuine property of those who express them.

Worse, they are becoming less and less real. They are becoming, like so much of the late-century world, virtual.

Four

The Virtual Future

> The technophiles are taking us all on an utterly reckless ride
> into the unknown. Many people...think it is inevitable. We
> don't think it is inevitable. We think it can be stopped...
>
> The Unabomber Manifesto, August 2, 1995

FOR SOME TIME
I have been tempted to compose my own personal manifesto, which I will then distribute to newspapers, threatening dire consequences if they don't publish it within three
months.

I am a carbon-based organism, I will say, and I like it
that way. Linear thinking, not montage, built the world.
Books are harder than television for a reason. In *Wired* magazine, you can't tell the ads from the articles. My e-mail
address is like a phone number, not an alternative name—
I'm not giving it to you. Faster isn't always better. Chatter is
still chatter even when it's electronically mediated. There is
more to life than information...

These are, I know, slightly Luddite thoughts in the world
of mid-1990s North America, the world of the Great Dream
of Interconnectedness. This, after all, is the world in which
techno-anarchism and the decentralization of communication are supposed to lead us into a new promised land of
democratic thought, the world in which we will transform
ourselves into a new form of being, evolving beyond the
limitations of our corporeal bodies into a sort of half-
human/half-machine creature that will plot an ascension
into the brave new virtual future.

"A recurring vision swirls in the shared mind of the Net," says Kevin Kelly, executive editor of *Wired* magazine and one of the loudest voices in this dream, "a vision that nearly every member glimpses, if only momentarily: of wiring human and artificial minds into one planetary soul." In their pursuit of this vision, Net-users are the ground-floor revolutionaries, the pioneers, the mystics. They sense that they are *out there*, on the edge of something really, really big. Everyone says so. "When I first got a sense of the Net, I went around saying that it would have a greater consequence on what it is to be human than movable type," chipped in Kelly's friend John Perry Barlow (Net guru and lyricist for The Grateful Dead), writing to the editor of *Harper's* in August 1994. "I'm now inclined to think this is the most transforming technological event since the capture of fire." Barlow even thinks—with impressive arrogance—that the *Wired* crowd are, in fact, the "spiritual descendants" of the French theologian and anthropologist Pierre Teilhard de Chardin, who plotted the course of human evolution into a collective mind "sufficiently interesting to provide company for God."

"Netheads" have been talking this way for a while, of course, but the dream of a transcendent technological moment seems focused and intensified by the advent of the millennium, with its long cultural history of spiritual transformation now mixed indiscriminately with the newer baggage of science-fiction imagery in which bodies fuse with machines. Evolving past the base physical need for bodies by stringing oneself through a cat's cradle of telephone lines and computer connections is really no different in scope from imagining oneself to be a High Attainer in the Ranter mode, an acolyte of a vague, but thoroughly invigorating, pantheism: the Net is God, and the Net is everywhere. That the contemporary form of pantheism runs on a nervous system of fibre-optics and printed circuit boards does not alter the desire for transcendence that lies at the centre of the dream. Nor indeed does it temper the arrogance and fanaticism of the initiates. The messiah of the Second Coming is not a man; the messiah is the Net itself.

The transformative dream of the Netheads also includes a crucial democratic element, a dream of hooking up everyone into a vast network of instant political decision-making. A powerful connection is therefore made here between religious and political aspiration, a connection typical of the earliest millenarian thinking. The attraction of an extra-human saviour grows in direct proportion to our sense that the political world has forsaken our interests. Spiritual hope is nurtured by material dissatisfaction. As a result, some people now dream of a fully wired, virtual world that will think with one vast collective meta-brain. According to them, the earth will reconstitute itself as a single thinking entity, a mass of interconnected atoms in constant communication. Salvation will be thus both temporal and heavenly. And then, who knows about being interesting enough to keep God company? As the old gospel song says: Operator—get me long distance.

Even as we should be struggling with the very idea of the Net, though, the wiring of the world has almost been completed. A recent IBM advertising campaign, which offers (with typical humility) "Solutions for a Small Planet," plays vividly on the pervasiveness of computer technology. Cloistered nuns, rustic shepherds, rug merchants in an Islamic bazaar—all are shown discussing the latest technological developments with the savvy of M.I.T. graduate students. The series reached a sickening climax in the summer of 1995 when the latest installment showed a group of saffron-robed Tibetan monks, communicating via telepathy, who marvelled at the ability of IBM technology to bring the entire world into communion.

Who needs the Buddha when you have IBM?

The first thing you notice about debate concerning the Internet is how much of it actually happens in books, the medium Netheads keep predicting is going the way of the dodo. Kevin Kelly once said of Marshall McLuhan's ideas, for instance, that "[n]obody reads McLuhan, because he was right. If you're getting your information about McLuhan from books, you're not getting it." That sounds clever, but Kelly reads books, and he writes them. His technophile friends read and write books. In fact, more than a hundred Net books were published in eighteen months during 1994 and the first half of 1995. And people continue to read McLuhan's books. Those who do not—those who know McLuhan only as *Wired*'s "patron saint," author of the Zen-koan-like "probes" or aphorisms on the magazine's masthead each month—can be said to "get" him only minimally.

True, McLuhan's work does force you, as George Steiner noted in a 1962 review of *The Gutenberg Galaxy*, to confront the act of reading. "The question of how to read McLuhan, of whether reading him is in itself an obsolescent mode of contact, is implicit in McLuhan's own work," Steiner wrote. But that question can only be raised if you *are* reading him; you cannot have this productive intellectual encounter elsewhere than in a book. There does seem to be something the extended written work offers us that we simply cannot get in any other form. "Perhaps it is a sign of our millennium's end that we frequently wonder what will happen to literature and books in the so-called post industrial era of technology," Italo Calvino said in his *Six Memos for the Next Millennium*, published in 1988. "I don't much feel like indulging in this sort of speculation. My confidence in the future of literature consists in the knowledge that there are things that only literature can give us, by means specific to it."

Nobody would call the spate of recent Net books literature, of course, but it does seem significant that their
authors feel compelled to use the old technological miracle
of the printing press to make their positions known. That
suggests a kernel of instability in the aspirations of the Net
culture, even a kind of ambivalence among some of its
members. And indeed, by early 1995, the first wave of giddy
Net enthusiasm had crested and an intellectual backlash of
sorts was becoming visible. The most powerful voices of
objection were precisely those of people who had ridden the
bandwagon only a few years earlier. Technological gee-
whizzers like Nicholas Negroponte, for example, who
penned the bestselling *Being Digital*, were confronted by
apostates like Clifford Stoll, whose book *Silicon Snake Oil:
Second Thoughts on the Information Highway* appeared to
illustrate a rigid law of cultural dynamics: for every popular
movement there must be an equal and opposite counter-
movement. Call this latest move the Netlash.

The Netlash also illustrates the power of nascent
technophobia even in otherwise devoted Netheads. J.C.
Herz, a recent college graduate who wrote a 1995 book
called *Surfing on the Internet: A Nethead's Adventures On-
Line*, tells us how she moved from budding enthusiasm for
the Net's communication possibilities to an awareness that
free and easy access to the thoughts of thousands of other
leisure-laden undergraduates like herself was, increasingly,
her vision of the Inner Circle of Hell. The writer William
Gibson, widely considered the father of "cyberpunk" science
fiction, sensed this growing ennui among veteran users and
accurately noted the essential reason for it. The bulk of
Internet communication is, Gibson said, "crackerbarrel
stuff"—aimless chatter among people you'd be grateful to
escape at a cocktail party. Fans of his fiction are frequently
surprised to learn that Gibson, the man who created Johnny
Mnemonic, Count Zero, and the Neuromancer, has no

Internet address and no modem on his computer.

Stoll, a professional astronomer, includes this "cracker-barrel" point in his exhaustive list of objections to Net culture. His other complaints will be familiar to users and non-users alike. Computers, he says, often replace perfectly good existing technology with fancier, more expensive, and less useful alternatives. They do not, as advertised, improve worker productivity or business competitiveness. Computer networks are hard to set up and they are "brittle": sensitive to problems, unreliable. You can't take computer books to the beach. Computer-manipulated photographs make deception virtually undetectable. E-mail is so fast and easy it destroys the old-fashioned rhythm of correspondence—not to mention the physical beauty of writing and stationery and stamps. It can also prove overwhelming: a few companies, worried about the myriad distractions and triviality, now forbid workers to use e-mail during most of the work day. The terminals themselves are cold and impersonal, designed to be identical—hence the rather desperate attempts of users to "personalize" their terminals with homey doodads like cutesy mouse pads, witty screen-savers and quilted dust-covers. What is worst, finally, is that Net interaction is strangely addictive.

This last point, obvious to anyone who owns a computer game, was illustrated with heavy irony in the August 1995 issue of *Harper's*, which was devoted to a discussion of the Net's cultural possibilities. The roundtable discussion by pundits and cheerleaders was punctuated with real excerpts from an on-line discussion group devoted to those who felt they were addicted to on-line discussion groups. "I have lost hundreds, maybe even thousands of dollars in unearned income due to unfinished proposals and projects, late payments on bills because I just didn't take the time to make out the checks," moaned one man into the electronic ether. "[I have] lost rapport with friends and associates, missed deadlines on discount travel and air fares, [been late for] appointments (I was a punctual person until I got this Net habituation). I've spent countless hours typing out messages like this to people I don't know and will probably never hear from." More pathetic still was another man, diagnosed with lung cancer, who went on-line to "slowly say goodbye to my friends here, curse my enemies one more time...and otherwise wave a bit at the rest of you until it's just not time to do so any more." What's next? E-mail suicide notes?

In general, Stoll worries, as many of us do, that devotion to the Net takes you away from real life. "You don't need a keyboard to bake bread, play touch football, piece a quilt, build a stone wall, recite a poem, or say a prayer," he writes. This is an important reminder that the scope of computer culture is actually quite limited; most of the world gets along just fine without it. As recently as February 1995, for instance, 58 percent of U.S. adults were reporting that they had "never heard" of the Internet. Given this, the power of "cyberbullies" to make us feel we are missing out on a technological revolution should be seen for what it is: largely chimerical. And yet the sense of unease they instil in us remains a powerful cultural force. A 1994 Associated Press poll showed that 46 percent of Americans felt they were being "left behind" by advances in technology, especially computer technology—illustrating, I suppose, a late-century twist on anxiety about the Rapture. (A world-weary 16 percent, by the way, apparently past the point of no return already, said they "didn't care" that they were being left in the dust.)

The reader might be forgiven for thinking that Stoll's list of pastoral ecstasies is a little disingenuous, however, coming as it does from a professional astronomer and writer who probably hasn't played touch football since he was twelve. *Chaos* author James Gleick, reviewing Stoll's book in *The New Yorker*, was even more dismissive. "There must be people left in the world who genuinely prefer quilt-making or wall-building to playing with computers," he writes, "but Cliff Stoll is surely not one of them. He owns five computers, checks into six networks on an average day, and his e-mail archive, at fifty megabytes, is ten times as large as the complete works of Shakespeare."

Stoll's second thoughts, in other words, actually betray a dangerous elitism. He appears to want the Net for himself and for his "good" uses of it, but he cannot bear the abuses and, especially, the "dumbing down" of the culture that has occurred, with relentless swiftness, as more and more people have gone on-line. While it is true that most of us still lack a working relationship with the Net, there are apparently already enough "cyber-rubes" making their way onto the wires to make old-style Netheads nostalgic for the good old initiates-only days of 1991 or '92. Stoll and others talk about the loss of quality and personality while on-line, but what really seems to bug them is that the toy they played with in comforting solitude for so long is now the plaything of every kid with a dial-up modem and a cloned PC.

In the early days of the Internet, more than a decade ago—when it was still the preserve of high-level professors, technology experts, and hackers who loved to crack military-industrial security programs—the extravagant political claims made for the Net had the ring of at least partial truth. A small quasi-anarchist subculture had indeed developed among dedicated users, for whom defiance of authority, free flow of information, and dislike of social norms were important ideological commitments. (This subculture, especially its hacker wing, is at the centre of the darkest visions of the future we have, William Gibson's futuristic fictions of technological ennui.) If these early techno-anarchists were in the end more elite than revolutionary, and more dedicated to cracking codes than to social change—well, so be it. They never claimed to have a particular agenda. Freedom is what you make of it, after all.

The problem is that the core promise of individual freedom has not been maintained as the Net's connections have become more elaborate in the last half-decade or so. The dream of "the largest functioning anarchy in the world," as devotees proudly called it, has drastically mutated in the ether of electronic communication. We have been given, in place of meaningful individual liberty and the freedom of escaping social bonds, merely the freedom of unimpeded information flow. What kind of freedom is this? The freedom to be overwhelmed? The freedom to be afflicted by the clamouring voices of a million other users? If genuine freedom means greater control over one's life, a greater ability to direct oneself and make choices, then the freedom offered on the Internet is hollow indeed.

The skeleton of the Internet was actually created at the height of the Cold War when the U.S. defence industry lobbied successfully for a "nuke-proof" communications system. The mainframe computers of universities, think tanks, and government agencies were linked via telephone lines and packet-switching computer architecture. The idea was to create a computer communications system that would deliver messages even in the event of extensive damage to the physical system, because all messages would travel to their destinations by numerous simultaneous and diverse routes. This network existed for a long time before anyone outside the specialized departments knew about it. Even when it was discovered by a slightly wider bandwidth of university and computer workers, they still had the Net pretty much to themselves for a long time. Indeed, the bulk of the people you would encounter on the Net were until very recently just exactly what you would expect: white males, attending or teaching at big universities, who would probably have been better off doing something more social. And while the vaunted democratization of the Net has changed this profile a bit, it has mostly just added more voices of a similar kind to the existing elite population. Not that the veterans see it that way.

By mid 1995, stories were appearing in the tonier magazines and journals about the Great Net Defection: what more than a few commentators called the "Net Loss." The veterans of the Internet, the leading-edge scholars and thinkers who had pioneered the use of the network for information-exchange, were logging off—sometimes for good. "As the masses plug into the Internet, some of its original inhabitants are fleeing—including scientists and scholars who made it such a valuable resource in the first place," *The Wall Street Journal* reported in June. These same scholars and scientists then said, with appropriate apologies for the undemocratic tenor of their remarks, that the Net, especially the formerly useful newsgroups located on the wide-open section known as Usenet, were becoming impossible places to find information or ideas. "The sludge got pretty intolerable," a California technology officer told the *Journal*, explaining his decision not to visit Usenet space any longer.

Usenet is home to more than ten thousand newsgroups or bulletin-board services where subscribers can read or post any message remotely aimed at the stated topic. It is a cacophonous bazaar of voices, special interests, and bizarre interactions. There are no restrictions on what you say here and there is absolute anonymity while you say it. For apologists, this is the beauty of the Net. "Because of [the] impermanence," Kevin Kelly wrote from the still-rosy perspective of 1994, when his book *Out of Control: The Rise of Neo-Biological Civilization* was published,

> the type of thought encouraged by the Net
> tends toward the non-dogmatic—the experi-

mental idea, the quip, the global perspective, the interdisciplinary synthesis, and the uninhibited, often emotional response. Many participants prefer the quality of writing on the Net to book writing because Net writing is conversational, peer-to-peer style, frank and communicative, rather than precise and self-consciously literary. Instead of the rigid canonical thinking cultivated by the book, the Net stimulates another way of thinking: telegraphic, modular, non-linear, malleable, cooperative.

But the "freedom" of the Net leads to some disgusting exchanges, from escalating sexual interest to escalating insults, all of it expressed in "frank" (and ungrammatical) "peer-to-peer" style. Mostly the newsgroups merely remain in the realm of the banal. You can find ones devoted to everything from Lisa Simpson's college of choice to foot fetishes, alien abduction tales, and Jean-Luc Picard's sexual tastes. Most of these "cultural" discussions run under the "alt" banner (as in, say, "alt.sex.fetish.foot"), the section of Usenet devoted to "alternative" topics. And while the dangers of cyber-porn and cyber-violence have been much overrated, it is true that neo-Nazis, anti-Semitic conspiracy theorists, anti-government militiamen, and gangs of other wackos are using the Net the same way everyone else is: as a cheap means of spreading The Word far and wide. It just happens that their Word is about hate and racism, not the peace, love and understanding that the IBM ad-makers apparently (I don't say really) believe will come from full networking.

The sheer number of users and the ease of communication mean that the level of Net talk is depressingly low. "Even without the cranks, many participants in unstructured Internet conversations have little of interest to say but a lot of room in which to say it," Gary Chapman wrote in a

1995 *New Republic* essay. "The new electronic Acropolis seems to foster rhetoric stylistically closer to Beavis and Butt-head than to Pericles." Chapman, director of something called The 21st-Century Project at the University of Texas in Austin, was wringing his hands about the increasingly unmannerly character of the Net. He saw that the tendency of such incivility—the conversational bravado born of no accountability—was to undermine the democratic promise of the new communication medium. Strong expressions of opinion bring swift, sometimes nasty replies (known as "flames"), and threats of violence are common. Mark Dery, who edited the 1995 collection *Flame Wars*, on the increasing incivility and vapidity of the Net discourse, offers these choice examples of the flame: "You syphilitic bovine harpy." "You heaving purulent mammoth." "You twitching gelatinous yolk of rancid smegma." This sort of talk confirms many people's worst fears about the Internet, namely that it is still the preserve of just the sort of people you really wouldn't want to know, let alone spend time with.

Some apologists view all the rudeness as a simple growing pain: the unruliness of an adolescent medium on its way to maturity. Others see it as merely par for the course in an uncharted new world of communication. "Cyberspace is as much a frontier as the New World was to seventeenth-century Europe," writes James Gleick.

> Frontier worlds are known to be rude, ugly, and lawless. Too often, there is a degenerative *Lord of the Flies* mood. People lie shamelessly and other people believe them. Angry teenagers screech at one another from behind pseudonymous masks. I've had some shockingly unpleasant electronic encounters.... Just the other day, a disgruntled young man whom I've never met

posted a public message expressing the desire
to see my hands blown off in an explosion.

Still, even the sanguine agree that a decisive turning-point
was reached in 1993 when commercial services like
America OnLine hooked up their paying customers to
Usenet. Now you couldn't even be certain that another user
was a university student, let alone another professor or high-
tech worker. Talk about Prole Drift: it was happening on the
Net!

The result was otherwise apolitical scholars suddenly
getting an attack of elite's revolt. "I hate to sound undemocratic, but if you're going to have valuable discussion, you
have to limit it to people with valuable knowledge," said
Michael Slater, a computer expert, to *The Wall Street
Journal*. "The beginners can have their beginners' group."
But as long as there are no restrictions on access, no begin-
ner is going to stay on the bunny hill when he can cruise
over to the black diamond runs without much risk of permanent injury. A newsgroup devoted to microbiology recently
showed, among other things, a grade eight student looking
for help on a science project, several college students seeking summer jobs, and a heated debate over the plot details
of the film *Outbreak*.

The scholars, fed up with the noise, have begun to move
to subscriber-controlled groups, edited groups, or off Usenet
altogether. Some have gone back to old-fashioned print
media like academic journals and newsletters. Many now
employ subordinates, if they have them, to act as Internet
"sludge" or "bozo" filters—people who wade through all the
garbage to find the worthwhile nuggets. Still others pin
their hopes on the World Wide Web, a newer section of the
Internet that supports graphics as well as text. But alas, the
Web, because it is sexier than text-only parts of the Net, is
where commercial forces are concentrating their energy in

the drive to make the Net a kind of grand home shopping network. In the end, the exit of these elite users can only "raise the proportion of nuts, creeps and boors," Gary Chapman writes, adding that, unfortunately, "[t]his all sounds like an anti-democratic trend, in contrast to the democratization that computer networks are supposed to both exemplify and support. Is cyberspace already sorting itself into two camps, a jaded, invisible elite and a teeming mass of wrassling rubes?"

This two-class character of the Net is real enough, as is the degeneration of discourse into name-calling and pointless sexual posturing. But let's be honest about the democratic possibilities of the Net. The things Chapman describes—growing incivility and the revolt of Net elites—are unsettling developments only when set against the rosy background painted by him and other supporters of the Net democracy vision. However much long-term users may balk at the widening user bandwidth, the Net is still dominated by a clique of highly educated people, most much younger than the continental average, still vastly over-representing men, and many of them without the usual appurtenances of a wider life. These facts are painfully, depressingly obvious to anyone who spends even an hour cruising newsgroups or receives e-mail from a list-server.

The Net is not a democratic medium because access is controlled economically. At the moment, if you are not a university professor or student, a journalist, or in some part of the computer industry, you must at least possess a home computer, modem, and requisite subscription fee to hook up with commercial services like CompuServe, GEnie, or America OnLine. If you do that, you will, it is true, face the painful knowledge that more-privileged users regard you with immediate scorn. But this is a two-class system only in the sense that, say, four-year colleges form a higher class than junior colleges, or that owning an Acura puts you one up on someone with a Chevrolet. There are hundreds of thousands of people on the Net, yes, but there are hundreds of *millions* of people on this continent. Even with the appalling voter turnouts now characteristic of U.S. politics, the Net is far less democratic than any election ever run.

There is an even deeper problem with the dream of a democratic Net. Suppose you could open up the channels of communication to literally everyone who wanted to say something. Would this make for a more successful polity? That is the dream of a certain form of democratic theory, to be sure, a sort of brave new world of direct rule by the people, for the people. "No one has been more wrong about computerization than George Orwell in *Nineteen Eighty-Four*," Kevin Kelly writes. "So far, nearly everything about the actual possibility-space that computers have created indicates that they are not the beginning of authority but its end." Yet democracy seems to reach a kind of *reductio ad absurdum* when it is practised too completely. Let us imagine a scenario in which every citizen of a large diverse nation is instantly given a computer and modem at no expense, the central government is disbanded immediately, and all decisions of governance are switched over to individual users acting on a vast network in which there are no political action committees, no advertising, and each citizen's terminal counts for exactly as much as anyone else's. What would the result be?

Chaos. Claims and counter-claims would pile on top of one another. If there was inter-terminal communication, it would soon be dominated by bitterness and hostility. If decisions were ever reached, they would be strongly motivated by conglomerations of self-interest, and probably short-term self-interest at that. John Stuart Mill's nightmare vision of the tyranny of the majority, expressed so eloquently in *On Liberty*, would come crashing into being. Small and weak pockets of interest would be quickly dominated, and then eliminated, by powerful blocs of voters. With no one to make hard choices, to balance short- and long-term interests, the very idea of citizenship would rapidly become meaningless. And lest the techno-anarchists think this would be a good thing, consider what happens to racial, class, and cultural hostilities when there is even a localized breakdown of social authority, as in the 1992 Los Angeles riots.

The technophile's dream of direct democracy is actually undemocratic: it threatens the freedom of the few by appearing to accede to the interests of the many. Centralization of power, while often dangerous, is necessary if we want to protect threatened minorities. (Do cyber-intellectuals really think their tenured university posts would be safe once direct democracy was instituted?) It is also necessary for accountability. While nobody believes that professional politicians are necessarily motivated by noble goals, or even that they are more competent at governing than other people, we at least know who they are. Direct democracy will be functionally invisible. Decisions that affect us will be made by sheer force of numbers. True, we can use our own terminals to protest a decision, but when the protest ends, so does our freedom. There will be no capitals to march to then, no legislatures to picket.

When you engage in a numbers game, which is exactly what any form of genuine democracy is, it is sometimes best to limit the influence of those numbers. Numbers have a way of crushing dissent beneath their rolling wheels. The British and Canadian parliaments, the American Congress and (still more) Electoral College, are devices by which democracy is precisely made *indirect*. The business of governance is left in a few hands, with the proviso that some form of wider approval be required.

We may condemn our democratic forebears for their elitism, their aristocratic distrust of the great unwashed masses, but we ought to realize that they also knew a thing or two about the hard realities of governing citizens who fail to agree on many things. The hopes of the Net-democracy visionaries are curiously one-sided: they condemn the existing system for its pathologies, yet they refuse to see the pathologies of equal or greater magnitude lurking in their dreams.

■ ■ ■

The implications of the Internet revolution are therefore paradoxical. A decentralization of power, the cherished dream of the hacker, has created only political confusion and cacophony. The new medium of electronic communication has become, in the event, candy floss for the mind—quick, sweet, lacking in nutrients. Like television, it actively discourages coherent thought. And it has the added danger of providing the illusion of interaction. (At least with a television you are—more or less—aware that you are being passive, slumping without protest into an alpha-state coma.)

More deeply, we are not moving closer to a single planetary soul. Instead, as the Net grows, it begins more and more to take on a mind of its own. Naturally this pleases some people, like John Perry Barlow, who think fighting the evolution of the Net resembles some form of presumptively doomed neanderthal resentment. "When the yearning for human flesh has come to an end," Barlow sententiously writes, "what will remain? Mind may continue, uploaded into the Net, suspended in an ecology of voltage as ambitiously capable of self-sustenance as was that of its carbon-based forebears. It's not a matter of embracing this process. It has already embraced us and may, in fact, have designed *us* for *it* in the first place."

But if some of us have lost sight of the dangers of technology that no longer serves our interests, it is precisely because the information revolution has been so stealthy. It has managed to co-opt almost every possible source of cultural resistance. The hacker culture is no longer the preserve of nerds and weenies in high-level computer science programs, as it was just a few years ago. Ultrahip magazines like *Mondo 2000*, the quarterly bible of techno-shamanism edited by a man called R.U. Sirius, have forged a cultural link between computer-users and the alternative youth culture of body-piercing and gender irreverence. *Wired* magazine, though more corporate in style and more rah-rah in its support of computer technology, brims with sharp critical writing and irreverent comment on the world—all of it nestled in amongst slick ads from IBM and Microsoft. Youthful rebels are no longer inclined to refuse the empty promises of new technology. They are instead finding new, hipper ways of buying into them.

The promises are, to be sure, intoxicating. Otherwise sane people are thrown into paroxysms of enthusiasm for the Net. "Networks aren't made of printed circuits, but of people," Clifford Stoll gushed in 1986, before his recent second thoughts. "My terminal is a door to countless, intricate pathways, leading to untold numbers of neighbours." Some people even claim that, as virtual bodies, they have actually begun to exist in many places at once—global creatures strung out across the vast network, becoming somehow otherworldly and, yes, *more powerful* than mere humans. For them the Net has become a new kind of silicon-supported out-of-body experience.

Probably they have just read too much second-rate cyberpunk. In a way, though, Internet enthusiasm actively invites cyberpunk's dangerous confusion of technology and spirituality. Why dangerous? Because beneath the dream of a Great Human Network there lurks a darker vision of flesh-silicon amalgamation, one in which our bodies, and the world in which they exist, begin to appear less and less real. The resulting threat is not spectacular, or even obvious much of the time, but computer technology slips out of human control just as surely as the atom bomb did. The dark inner logic of technology, the desire for mastery that nestles within the hopes of emancipation, comes back to haunt us, aided by the cheerleading of those the Unabomber so vividly calls "the technophiles."

Arthur Kroker is one Net-savvy intellectual who has seen this danger clearly. He is also one of several Canadian thinkers now vying for the much-coveted title of "the new Marshall McLuhan." (A 1995 newspaper article suggested that, with *Understanding Media* back in print, a CD-ROM and various commentaries available, and his name on the masthead of *Wired*, McLuhan had been resurrected. The truth is more technological. He has been *cloned*.) Kroker teaches political science at Montreal's Concordia University, and he is an above-average McLuhan clone. His books, which include *The Postmodern Scene: Excremental Culture and Hyper-Aesthetics* (standard po-mo cultural theory) and *Spasm: Virtual Reality, Android Music and Electric Flesh* (an innovative fugue-like combination of jargon and industrial music, CD included), are strange crypto-academic performance pieces that largely eschew discursive clarity in favour of locutions like the following: "Always schizoid yet fully integrated, the hyper-texted body swallows its modem, cuts its wired connections to the information highway, and becomes its own system-operating software, combining and remodulating the surrounding data storm into new virtualities." Or: "Virtual positivism for the era of windowed culture: a recursive space of ambivalent signs that slips away into an infinity of mirrored, fractalized elements." Or: "Virtual reality skin-grafts the logic of the ambivalent sign onto the 'standing reserve' of the social."

Those examples are from Kroker's 1994 book *Data Trash: The Theory of the Virtual Class*, a work co-authored (entirely on the Net, mind you) with Purdue University political scientist Michael Weinstein. The rather annoying performance-art ambience of this book—the recurring sense that it was written by Laurie Anderson after a crash course in Hegelian dialectic—does not completely obscure its central thesis, a timely reminder of the dangers in the heart of technology. Here, the authors argue, the world is subjugated to a dream of "technotopia"—the *Wired*-IBM-Microsoft vision of a digital world of wonders. But the utopian part of the dream, in which technology builds a better future, actually collapses down into what they call "the will to virtuality": a self-destructive desire to exchange our corporeal human flesh for the perfection of wiring. Kroker and Weinstein suggest that our enduring fascination with computer culture indicates a desire to *become virtual*, to leave the unsatisfactory (and dangerous) real world of bodies behind and upload ourselves forever into the cyber-stratosphere.

This technotopian ideal is further strengthened by what Kroker, among others, has called the "doctrine of technological inevitability." The doctrine, which is a central tenet of our culture's dominant ideology, says that we must submit to the in-built technological demand to upgrade constantly. Technological inevitability is, in its way, a version of an evolutionary imperative: you must adapt (to the new versions of your technology) or die. And though we, not Mother Nature, have created this new quasi-evolutionary doctrine, it nevertheless now functions with the same insistence as any environmental imperative. It insists that we cannot rationally resist technological development. We cannot even slow it down. It's like the old nerd joke about gravity: *It's not just a good idea; it's the law.*

The trouble is that most of us, once transformed into data by our own technology, are entirely dispensable. We are "data trash" at the mercy of the new power-brokers, the virtual class, who rule with a kind of soft fascism of technological energy. "In virtual reality," Kroker and Weinstein say, "flesh vaporizes into virtuality as (twentieth) century bodies are repackaged with (twenty-first) century cybernetic

nervous systems for speeding across the electronic frontier."
Here the flesh-silicon integration of cyberpunk or the car-
bon/iron integration of Isaac Asimov's *Robot* novels is
revealed as a nightmare third-millennium scenario. "The
twentieth century ends with the growth of cyber-authoritar-
ianism," they write,

> a stridently pro-technotopia movement, par-
> ticularly in the mass media, typified by an
> obsession to the point of hysteria with emer-
> gent technologies, and with a consistent and
> very deliberate attempt to shut down, silence,
> and exclude any perspectives critical of tech-
> notopia. Not a wired culture, but a virtual cul-
> ture that is wired shut...determined to exclude
> from public debate any perspective that is not
> a cheerleader for the coming-to-be of the fully
> realized technological society.

The twist in the tale is that, at some level, we ourselves pursue this nightmare. We begin to consume the logic of technotopia just as we consume the products advertised on our
television screens. Desire is instilled in us like an invading
parasite. "By wanting to be 'virtualized,'" the journalist John
Oughton writes in the same vein, "we end up just re-com-
modifying ourselves—more bar-coded bodies washing up on
the cyber-shore, awaiting disposition by big.brother@power-
net.global."

If you doubt that this time is coming, just listen to the
words of John Battelle, managing editor of *Wired* magazine,
as quoted in *Data Trash*: "People are going to have to realize
that the Net is another medium, and it has to be sponsored
commercially and it has to play by the rules of the marketplace," he says. "When the Time-Warners get on the Net in
a hard fashion it's going to be the people who first create the

commerce and the environment, like *Wired*, that will be the market leaders." The result can only be a new and even more powerful form of television, ruled by the lowest common denominator, a place where, in Oughton's words, "we just lie back and run our direct-payment cards through slots wired to the bank balances of high-tech business interests, who think the best use of chips is munching them along the couch-potato tollway." Perhaps it has already happened to a larger extent than we know.

Paradoxically, though, because our media-saturated culture is "recombinant" in nature—that is, all images or events are simply fodder for further media allusion and manipulation—we find that even our nightmares of a virtual future are oddly lacking in substance. They have no genuine prophetic power, no ability to urge us on to resistance. Nothing real or actual underlies the dark allusiveness of our *fin-de-millénium* culture; everything is "like" something else, or experienced in images already mediated and layered with numerous interconnections. Movies are based on video games. Television offers reports on its own role in politics. Characters in situation comedies refer to rival situation comedies to raise a laugh. Conversations among certain people consist entirely of references to films and TV shows they have, by common assumption, seen and digested. There is therefore no pure experience, no vision free of cynicism and self-consciousness. The world itself, understood as something both unmediated and genuinely real, has, in short, disappeared. The world is now virtual too—and we simply long to join it in that state.

"Unlike the 1890s with its romantic invocation of catastrophe scenarios," Kroker and Weinstein note in *Data Trash*, "the 1990s emerge as an era of general cultural recline: a time of cynical romanticism and cold love, where the body disappears into a virtual imaging-system, and where even catastrophes are reversed by the media-net into specular publicity for a crash that will never happen.... This is the fate of the body electronic in the interminable countdown to the Year 2000." Cultural *recline* is not cultural *decline*. We are too sophisticated, Kroker suggests, to accept the image of decline, with its suggestion of a diametric opposite, progress. We are instead in what he calls a "crash culture": "contemporary society as it undergoes a simultaneous acceleration and terminal shutdown." We are always speeding up to a standstill.

And so, they suggest, the prospect of apocalypse may even become unexpectedly *boring*. We all suffer in varying degrees the restless enervation brought on by too much television, the seen-it-all-before faux-cynicism of the perpetual teenager. This ennui now threatens to infect our sense of the future. "The next millennium stretches out before us as a fatal scene where things disappear only to the extent that they are more (virtually) present than ever before," Kroker and Weinstein write in *Data Trash*. "And not just things, but the third millennium itself has already disappeared under the weight of future-boredom, and will only make one final appearance as a resurrection-effect of the next 1,000 years as raw material for VR generators."

At first glance, that last claim strikes me as exaggerated. Our millennial anxiety has not yet peaked, and most people show no signs, so far, of finding the prospect of the future boring. On the contrary. There is a good deal of surface cynicism, yes, and lots of what passes for ironic comment on the sorry plight of a culture that focuses on the trivial (the O.J. Simpson trial, endless struggles of overfed people to lose weight) at the expense of genuine human suffering (the insistent demands of a dying underclass, the war in Bosnia). But beneath that surface, is there not a good deal of genuine anxiety, deep cultural uncertainty?

Wading through the dense prose of *Data Trash*, I begin to feel compelled to meet Kroker, to talk about his ideas. No Luddite, Kroker is easily available via the Net, where he spends a good part of his life. But I decide I must pay him an off-line—that is, actual or *in the flesh*—visit. I'm not data yet; neither is he.

He meets me at the door of his Montreal house, an elegantly renovated brownstone near a pedestrian district of cafés and boutiques in the fashionable Carré St. Louis neighbourhood. No computers are evident in the house. There is lots of hardwood flooring, stained glass, and agreeably worn Oriental rugs. A small stack of books, mostly well-thumbed paperback volumes of Nietzsche, lie on the coffee table. In fact, but for these and the garlanded Elvis bust in one corner, this could be the home of an assistant bank manager or junior law partner. Kroker himself is more what you'd expect of the 1990s media icon, the intellectual as hipster nerd. Born a half-century ago in Winnipeg, he is slight, bespectacled, a bit dweeby, and clad all in *de rigueur* theory-guy black. He talks in a quiet but penetrating voice, quickly carving off big chunks of prose that are virtually indistinguishable from his writing.

"Millennial consciousness," he says in response to the objection I have come here to voice, "is a form of obsession which has a two-fold effect. It simultaneously creates an immense speed-up, which is palpable in the air—this sense of let's-get-it-over-with. At the same time, there is also a counter-movement of inertia, an immense slow-down. If you look at the popular media, it's all about dumbing down, bunkering in." He mentions "The Simpsons," *Forrest Gump*. He might also, I think, have mentioned the rich vein of recent television ads that play on themes of safety and control: getting your immediate environment (your car, your office, your house) into a less-threatened state. Because, after all, social disorder seems everywhere to be getting closer.

Cultural recline is intensified by the millennium, Kroker suggests. The imagined event of 2000 acts as a kind of "spasm" of intensity in the general movement of speeding up to a standstill. "The millennium creates a change in the psychology of time itself," he says. "The change it creates is almost a centrifugal pressure to put human consciousness under. The time of the millennium is a time for apocalyptic possibilities. There's a feeling of a settling of accounts." That settling is typical of late-century moods throughout history, but in our recombinant culture it's not as simple as killing unbelievers or even whipping ourselves into frenzies of self-denunciation. "The sense of millennial obsession is itself a pretty carefully staged obsession," he adds. "I like what Jean Baudrillard said once, that the *banality* of the millennium is upon us. He said in the late 1980s that we should take a vote to jump immediately to the year 2000, get it over with, and move immediately into post-millennial consciousness."

Kroker mentions an art exhibit running at the Montreal Museum of Fine Arts. The show, called "Lost Paradise," is a massive exhibition of Symbolist works from *fin-de-siècle* Europe. In its display of Klimts, Rossettis, Hodlers, Beardsleys, Munchs, Gauguins, and other artifacts of a great moment of cultural self-consciousness, when obsessions with death and decay lay side-by-side with transformative visions and hopes, Kroker says he glimpsed what was missing from the current *fin-de-millénium* malaise: genuineness.

"In some ways, I view the 1990s as the opposite of the 1890s, because the 1890s was the age of Mahler's music and the emergence of Symbolism, and the age, really, of melancholy and anxiety," he says. "In Symbolism you have the aesthetic prefigurement of fascism, in terms of the immense hatred towards the human body, for example—some of its offshoots were grisly trends in twentieth-century politics. But the 1990s are about *cold* melancholia, *cynical* melancholia. Melancholy itself becomes a kind of commodity. The notion of melancholia as an authentic form of longing and remembrance seems to have been eviscerated by the movement of entertainment technologies. Today melancholia has been taken over as another form of seduction. The forms of remembrance themselves have come to us in prepackaged ways." He mentions, as an example, TV coverage of the war in Bosnia. "You sit through a weekend and see these vivid images, which should be melancholy images, of human suffering and authentically feel that. But within a twenty-four-hour cycle you can see that form of melancholia fed and retranscribed into any number of things. The remembrance of the event disappears."

Television displacement is instant, and the "world" it delivers to us twenty-four hours a day is no world at all. This pervasive destabilizing of the world has the effect of hollowing out the substance of even our deepest emotional responses. The 1990s situation, then, is one in which authentic forms of anxiety are unavailable. Driven instead by the will to virtuality, we are leaving not only the world but also our bodies behind. In this sense, Kroker says, we "are in fact creating a successor species to human beings. And not coincidentally, this happens in time for the millennium. It's almost like humanity has given itself a gift: it has willed its own disappearance."

I don't know about that, but it seems true enough that our bodies have been thoroughly colonized by the electronic media they use. Our sensory expectations have changed, for example, creating corresponding mental changes, like the seven-second attention span evident in MTV-watchers or the "hyper-texted" ability of younger people to hold multiple stories in mind at once. To people educated in the age of accelerating media, watching old newsreel footage, or even tape of old television shows, can have the oddly displacing effect of suggesting that people in the past were all morons: they seem to talk so slowly (albeit in complete sentences) and it takes them so long to get to the point! "These are not technologies that remain outside," Kroker says, matter-of-factly, of the entertainment media. "They put their hooks into flesh and come inside the body. We don't have pure bodies any more; we have electronic bodies."

Like the Unabomber, however, Kroker thinks the technotopian domination is far from inevitable. "The doctrine of inevitability is a false bill of goods that's sold by the technological class because it serves its own interests," he says. "It wants people to feel impotent because when you feel impotent, you forget the central fact about any technology: that it involves social choice. We need to reactivate a discussion of what should be the social choices that will guide our use of technology. Nothing is inevitable when it comes to technology." When we no longer believe in the technotopian dream, then—when we are overcome by a crisis of faith evident even now among the Silicon Valley disk-jockeys in what Kroker calls "the burn-out of data trash bodies"—we can finally begin to ask the hard questions about our tools. Which is to say, how are technology and democracy related? How can technological advances be made to serve the cause of justice? How can we channel our vast resources and cleverness, not into more and more self-perpetuating technology, but into deeper forms of cultural life?

These political questions, which are indeed the hard ones, find no solution in the world of the Net, as it is now colonized by commercial and even non-commercial interests that are hostile to the basic ideas of social justice. And in the end, despite the nuance of his diagnosis, Kroker has little to offer in the way of response beyond a new version of the old dream of a more thoroughly democratized Internet, with terminals and modems for everybody. Such widening of the user bandwidth might possibly stave off the quick reduction of the Net into just more TV, but could it ever cut deeper than that? Will it liberate us from our domination by the technophiles and their debilitating dreams of ultimate control? Will this post-technotopian dream really come about? Are we strong enough to resist the lures of the will to virtuality? Not to resist them in a rearguard and paranoid technophobia, that is, but to pursue technology in better directions?

"After what has happened so far in the twentieth century and is still going on in the way of technological carnage," Kroker and Weinstein say in *Data Trash*, "it is amusing to realize that there are still techno-fetishists filled with enthusiasm about how technology is going to fulfill their prepubescent dreams, which they assume unthinkingly that everyone inevitably shares with them." I don't know if "amusing" is the right word. That enthusiasm, though, is the ultimate Revenge of the Nerds, with Microsoft chairman Bill Gates presumptively crowned as King. Or, if you prefer your doomsday imagery to be biblical, as Antichrist of the Techno-Millennium. In 1993, an anonymous letter posted to the Internet made the case explicit. The letter quoted the famous passage in Revelation 13:18: "Let anyone who has intelligence work out the numbers of the beast, for the number represents a man's name, and the numerical value of its letters is six hundred and sixty-six." Gates's full name is William Henry Gates III, and so, the writer argued, converting the name into ASCII values, you get the following:

$$B \quad I \quad L \quad L \quad G \quad A \quad T \quad E \quad S \quad 3$$
$$66 + 73 + 76 + 76 + 71 + 65 + 84 + 69 + 83 + 3 = 666$$

Now you know. Fear him.

Do the Nerds really harbour secret aspirations of total global control? Scott Adams, a worker at Sun Microsystems and author of the popular cartoon strip *Dilbert*, which is about a lonely computer engineer, thinks they don't even need to. His witty discussion of the issue made the point clear: technological inevitability does all the work. "I think it's a Darwinian thing," Adams said in an article that was posted on a Net bulletin board service. "We're attracted to the people who have the best ability to survive and thrive. In the old days it was important to be able to run down an antelope and kill it with a single blow to the forehead. Now all that matters is if you can install your own Ethernet card without having to call tech support and confess your inadequacies to a stranger whose best career option is to work in tech support."

It's obvious, Adams went on, that the world now has *three* distinct classes of people, each with its own evolutionary destiny. That is, there are: "(1) Knowledgeable computer users who will evolve into godlike non-corporeal beings who rule the universe (except for those who work in tech support)." They are supported by: "(2) Computer owners who try to pass as knowledgeable but secretly use hand calculators to add totals to their Excel spreadsheets. This group will gravitate toward jobs as high school principals and operators of pet crematoriums. Eventually they will become extinct." And finally there are: "(3) Non-computer users who will grow tails, sit in zoos and fling dung at tourists."

━ ▪ ━

Before leaving Montreal I spend an afternoon at the "Lost Paradise" exhibit myself, to see if Kroker is right about the emptiness, the virtuality, of our millennial anxiety. Entering the vast cool halls from the steamy street outside, I immediately see that his argument has some substance. Certainly there is a depth of feeling about the works, especially in the anguish of Edvard Munch's paintings, say, or the golden hopefulness to be seen in those gorgeous Pre-Raphaelite women, that seems missing from the cultural ephemera that express current millennial feeling. The images of young girls, their breasts barely formed, run together with dark works of satanic and thanatic theme, chilling images of death from tuberculosis, cholera, syphilis. Most significant for me is a big bronze sculpture of Friedrich Nietzsche's head (1904) by the German artist Max Klinger. This piece, set on its own in a small, square gallery bounded by billowing gauze curtains, is imposing, dense, impossible to ignore. For me it somehow captures all the intertwining of nostalgia and pessimism that marks the 1890s *fin de siècle*. Nietzsche's triumphant vision of the "Overman" being perverted into the Nazi storm trooper seems an appropriate judgment on the hopes and dreams of a confused end-time.

I do not see any vivid contrast to our own day, however, at least in the feelings and ideas expressed. If anything, the parallels strike me more forcefully. We would not choose these means of expression, perhaps, and the mass-media products of our anxiety will probably find no place in a fine-art museum (maybe an anthropological museum), but the commingled impulses of control and surrender, the enthusiasm and dread, are everywhere similar. The problem is not really, as Kroker argues, that 1990s millennial anxiety is cynical. That cynicism is a form of coping as transparent as any erotic or thanatic image of the nineteenth-century *fin de siècle*. We are very much aware of our own cynicism, our lack of connection to the world—and we are alarmed by it. No, our enduring problem, the one that will carry us into the third millennium, is the same one that afflicted the 1890s, and, further, has afflicted every end-time culture in our history. It is that we appear to have no way of coping with uncertainty about the future that transcends the dichotomy between hope and dread. Our millennium is, like all the others, necessarily Janus-faced. And so when it comes to the future of technology, no effective middle course has yet been mapped between the technotopia of fetishists, with its apocalyptic consequences for data trash, and the foredoomed refuse-to-use backlash of neo-Luddites. We still do not know how to use our tools in a way that keeps them from using us.

Our anxiety about the coming millennium may be staged, recombinant, mediated, or virtual. It may be all of these. This kind of anxiety may be more sophisticated, or further deflected, than the simpler kinds experienced in other eras. But it is real, and there is no escaping it.

▬ ▃ ▬

Technology is a word of Greek origin. The systematic study (*logos*) and exercise of skill (*teknai*) has been with us as long as primates have used tools—including, significantly, weapons, like the crude club snatched up in the opening scene of *2001: A Space Odyssey*. The fetishizing and worship of technology, on the other hand, is something apparently peculiar to recent times, in particular the centuries since the "new science" of empirical observation and control swept the West, beginning around 1580. We have not always believed that we could bring the world to the mat using the tools we had invented, or that we would usher in new forms of consciousness by virtue of the communications media we developed. Now our tools seem tools no longer. We do not use technology; it uses us. Rather, it *is* us—and we it.

In various nascent forms, from the Ford assembly lines to the Nazi death camps, this vision has dominated the age in which we live. Its dark underside has never been far from view, and some of the ablest minds of the century have devoted themselves to what the German philosopher Martin Heidegger simply called, in a landmark essay, "The Question Concerning Technology." Despite the nuance of his understanding of technology—he saw clearly that the technological project was, for both good and ill, a matter of mastery of a world that otherwise seemed brute in its given-ness—Heidegger's own checkered life, with its infamous Nazi flirtation and the refusal to acknowledge this complicity after the fact, might seem to exemplify the ambivalence of the modern age. We are simultaneously drawn to and repelled by the peculiar logic of techno-modernity, and the deep interior instability of Nazism, with its dreams of emancipation and nationhood played out in mass manipulation, armoured Panzer divisions, and systematic racial murder, marks a kind of apotheosis of that logic.

It is easy to distance ourselves from the horrors of Nazi technophilia, but our own symptoms are less easily dodged. Since the fall of the Berlin Wall in 1989 we have almost managed to forget that this was and is the Nuclear Age, an age of constant apocalyptic anxiety. Our stock images of doomsday are still nuclear in tenor: the bombed-out cities, the seas of melted glass and concrete, the charred bodies, the invisible radiation poison gradually ravaging survivors. For most of the last five decades we have needed no millennial resonance to make the dream of a fiery end seem real. Now that the end-time thematic begins to take hold of us, the nuclear threat is, ironically, precisely the one we find least prominent.

Except, that is, on certain occasions. On a hot August weekend in 1995 we were confronted again by the stock images of mushroom cloud and flash-burn human outlines. The fiftieth anniversary of the bombings of Hiroshima and Nagasaki brought the usual forces of cultural manipulation into play: the television specials and earnest discussion groups, the endless op-ed essays and magazine symposia. The same arguments about the necessity of dropping the bomb were rolled out. The only significant change was the absence of any high-profile protest activity. The bombings had become, finally, the preserve of history, subject of heated protestations and justifications by old duffers, editorialists, and other makers of memory. The very intemperance of some of the arguments—What should Truman have done? Did Hirohito try to surrender? Was one bomb enough?— demonstrated that the issues were somehow dead ones. None of it really seemed to matter.

Things were quite different when I was an undergraduate during the first half of the 1980s, when we took the prospect of nuclear armageddon seriously enough not to make it the focus of glib debating techniques. It is probably impossible for anyone under thirty to know how it felt, then, to live under this threat. And it is possible that those now over, say, fifty might be a little inclined to minimize the sense of doom that back then gripped those of us in our teens and early twenties.

We weren't simply being paranoid. In 1981, in the midst of a growing arms race and tension in various parts of the world (Afghanistan, Poland, South Africa), the "Doomsday Clock," which first appeared in 1947 on the cover of *The Bulletin of the Atomic Scientists* to represent the proximity of a nuclear war, stood at a mere four minutes to midnight. Then, in 1984, as the arms race accelerated, the clock moved nearer still, to three minutes away. (The clock has been closer than this to the midnight of nuclear destruction only once, in 1953, when the United States tested the first hydrogen bomb and the nervous scientists placed the minute hand a scant two ticks from disaster.) "Arms-control negotiations have been reduced to a species of propaganda," the editors of the *Bulletin* said in 1984. "The blunt simplicities of force threaten to displace any other form of discourse between the superpowers."

I was editing an undergraduate newspaper at the time, a job that heightens one's political awareness well past the comfort level, and I remember the muted dread I faced each day when I opened the morning papers to see how the world was doing. It would be inaccurate to say that my friends and I actually went around expecting nuclear war at any moment. We were young, after all, and spent far more time drinking, listening to Clash records, and thinking about (or, less often, engaging in) sex. But I can recall some friends of mine agreeing on a rendezvous point should the sirens begin to wail. I was afflicted, now and then, by genuine seizures of

dread that I would not live to see thirty. They usually subsided by themselves—or, of course, when thoughts of liquor,
pop music, or sex once more intruded.

The 1995 Hiroshima weekend carried me back to this
period, but it wasn't the pundits' polished phrases that took
me there. It was Peter Sellers. Watching a TV double-bill of
the films *Dr. Strangelove* and *Fail-Safe* on August 5, I was
struck by the well-known similarity of the plots: in both
films, an "error" sends American nuclear bombers into
Soviet airspace; when they cannot be recalled, a "doomsday"
scenario is created in which both sides must suffer destruction. But even more striking was how short the distance
seemed between the serious drama of *Fail-Safe* and the overt
satire of Kubrick's film. Sellers, in one of three brilliant por-
trayals in the same film (he also plays the U.S. president and
an ineffectual RAF group captain), depicts the character Dr.
Strangelove, an ex-Nazi bomb expert who advises the U.S.
Joint Chiefs of Staff, as a half-smiling lunatic with an absurd
accent, cigarette-holder, and blond coiffure. Twitching
maniacally in his wheelchair, Strangelove struggles to control the leather-clad right hand that, with a mind of its own,
threatens by turns to strangle him or stiffen into a Nazi
salute. Once it is clear that the errant nuclear bombers cannot be deflected from their course, Strangelove argues, the
only rational option is for the United States to launch an
all-out attack. After all, if they do not, they will surely be
destroyed by retaliating Soviet missiles.

The *Fail-Safe* counterpart is Professor Groeteschele, a
hawkish political scientist played with straight-faced but
nevertheless hilarious menace by Walter Matthau. In this
version of events, the bombers winging their way into
Soviet airspace have been misdirected by a computer, not,
as in *Dr. Strangelove*, by the deliberate act of a deranged military man (General Jack Ripper, the man who fears for his
"precious bodily fluids" and believes that fluoridation of

water is a Commie plot to weaken the West). Nevertheless the drama is the same. When it becomes clear that the planes are on course to bomb Moscow and cannot be turned back, Groeteschele turns in a creditable Strangelove imitation and cuts through the humane dithering and ineffectual hand-wringing of his military colleagues among the Joint Chiefs of Staff. "Don't you see, sir?" he tells the President (Henry Fonda, looking avuncular, stricken, and Ivy League all at once). "This is our chance! You must not recall those bombers! History demands it!"

Which says something about what might happen if political scientists made all our political decisions. It also says something about the impossibility of genuine satire about nuclear destruction. Sellers's Dr. Strangelove is a kind of parody of Professor Groeteschele, to be sure, but the effect is limited because to our eyes Professor Groeteschele is so clearly a madman already. Both films were released in 1964, when I was just learning how to crawl, and seeing them three decades later reminded me of something that events since 1989 have allowed us to forget: our lives really have been lived under a nuclear shadow. It may be hard for us to recall the paranoia of the early 1960s, when a Communist lurked under every hedgerow. And perhaps the threat of "mutually assured destruction"—the doomsday scenario—has decisively receded in our minds, even all but disappeared. The "Doomsday Machine" mentioned in both films, in which massive retaliation for a first-strike attack is automatic and unstoppable, is no longer our nuclear reality. We no longer hear how the weapons stockpiles could kill us all three times over, four times, whatever. But nuclear weapons have not been eliminated. There are caches of them all over the world, and not all in the hands of powers with enough stake in the idea of peace and order to make their use unthinkable. There may even be a sort of doomsday machine still. The doctrine of technological inevitability is in one crucial way just like the renegade nuclear bombers: it has been launched, and it cannot be recalled.

Of course, as much as the relentless nature of technological "progress" disturbs many of us, the truth is that nobody today could be a thoroughgoing follower of Ned Ludd. An enigmatic figure whose historical reality has been much disputed, Ludd was at the heart of the anti-technological rebellion that spread through northern England in 1811 and 1812, and his followers, cottage hand weavers and combers, donned masks to smash the power looms and torch the textile mills they felt were destroying their way of life. The Luddites were right about that, but they found out, to their detriment, that you cannot really halt progress. English lawmakers responded to the property crimes by making the destruction of machines a capital offence. By 1813, twenty-four Luddites had been hanged for their attempt to slow the march of technology.

No response so simple as smashing a machine is available to us now. When *The Net*, a 1995 film in which Sandra Bullock is drawn into a government conspiracy through her idle computer hacking, is described as "the first neo-Luddite thriller," or when a bookish intellectual indulges in an intemperate outburst against machines on television, we are forced to realize that contemporary Luddism remains a cultural phenomenon both elite and selective. Much as we think we might like to, at least selectively, none of us can really escape the reach of technology.

For example: I now conduct the bulk of my personal correspondence on e-mail. I have spent time on Usenet newsgroups and list-serve discussion groups. I don't enjoy it much, but I read *Wired* magazine. I do enjoy writing on my computer, of which I am inordinately fond. The computer is installed in a room whose temperature is controlled by electric heating and cooling devices, lit by electric light bulbs, with an electronic stereo playing in one corner. I am, like all of us, through and through a devotee of technology. We cannot avoid it; technology is the air we breathe, the medium we swim in. I may occasionally want to toss a machine across the room, but that's usually a function of frustration, not an attempt to turn back the clock.

Naturally we decry the big disasters of technology: Bhopal and *Exxon Valdez*, Chernobyl and Three Mile Island. We may even, sometimes, rage against the machine in a more generalized way. Kirkpatrick Sale, for example, in a recent book celebrating the Luddites (*Rebels Against the Future*), fingers computer nerds as our ultimate enemy. "It is the computer and those who feed and handle it who reign supreme," Sale says, articulating a common sentiment. He goes on to say, rather obviously, that "control of information is control of power." But even if these things are true, we all know that rebellion against the future is just a fast track to oblivion. None of us would willingly surrender *everything* the hyper-technological world has to offer: air travel, air conditioning, refrigeration, radio. We are therefore caught in inner conflict. We can even identify a kind of "Inner Luddite" here: the little voice inside our heads that expresses, now and then, ambivalence about the swift transformation of our culture into a rah-rah machine where technology uses us rather than the other way around. As the writer Daniel J. Kevles noted in a perceptive *New Yorker* essay, neo-Luddism's sympathizers are "a group that includes some of us all of the time and all of us some of the time." Accurately identifying the scion of the Inner Luddites, Kevles's essay was called "E Pluribus Unabomber."

When the Oklahoma City bombing happened on April 19, 1995, there was for a time speculation that the person responsible was the man known as the Unabomber, a clearly demented but also very clever urban terrorist who has sent sixteen mail-bombs to various people during the past seventeen years. His bombs have killed three people and injured twenty-three. His favourite target seems to be university professors of various kinds, with a special preference for scientists. His bombs are homemade but meticulously crafted, with highly polished metal parts and hand-carved wooden pieces. There was no evidence to link the Unabomber to Oklahoma City, however, and the truck-bombing was far from his usual modus operandi. The line of speculation was discarded when other suspects turned up. He produced a small blip on the cultural radar screen and then dropped from view.

Then, later that summer, right around the time of the Hiroshima and Nagasaki anniversaries, the rough police sketch of a hooded man wearing sunglasses appeared once more on our television screens. For the Unabomber had in June sent two major newspapers, *The New York Times* and *The Washington Post*, a single-spaced, sixty-two-page document outlining his reasons for the bombings and indicating that by publishing this manifesto within three months, and publishing three annual updates, the papers could forestall further bombings. On August 2, the *Times* and the *Post* printed extensive excerpts from the manifesto. They said they did so for the sake of "newsworthiness"—that is, what the manifesto could tell law-enforcement types about the Unabomber's identity—and not in response to the Unabomber's demands. At the same time, FBI sources suggested that the Unabomber might actually be the man known as Kilgore, bomb expert for the short-lived but intensely hyped 1970s terrorist group called the Symbionese Liberation Army, who had kidnapped Patricia Hearst and given her the *nom de guerre* Tanya.

The excerpts from the Unabomber Manifesto make fascinating, if bizarre, reading. They are full of academic jargon and the ponderous judgments of scholarly writing ("The two psychological tendencies that underlie modern leftism we call *feelings of inferiority* and *oversocialization*..."), as well as routine they're-all-in-it-together conspiracy rhetoric ("The

nass media are mostly under the control of large organiza-
ions that are integrated into the system…"). There are
numerous denunciations of special interest groups, with
trendy academic leftists singled out for special hostility.
There is even a kind of wistfulness. Because the mass media
are controlled by those large corporations, the Unabomber
writes, "[t]o make an impression on society with words
s…almost impossible." Hence his resort to other, more spectacular methods. "If we had never done anything violent and
had submitted the present writings to a publisher, they probably would not have been accepted," the manifesto goes on.

> If they had been accepted and published, they
> probably would not have attracted many read-
> ers, because it's more fun to watch the enter-
> tainment put out by the media than to read a
> sober essay. Even if these writings had had
> many readers, most of those readers would
> soon have forgotten what they had read as
> their minds were flooded by the mass of mater-
> ial to which the media expose them. In order
> to get our message before the public with some
> chance of making a lasting impression, we've
> had to kill people.

It was statements like these that gave FBI agents the idea
that the Unabomber was a resentful former graduate student. (How could they tell?) If nothing else, sending the
manifesto to the papers gave new meaning to the phrase
"publish or perish."

Most strongly of all, though, the manifesto shows deep
and violent anti-technological feeling. The Unabomber is
the King of the Neo-Luddites. "The technophiles are taking
us all on an utterly reckless ride into the unknown," the
manifesto says. "Many people understand something of

what technological progress is doing to us yet take a passive attitude toward it because they think it is inevitable. But we don't think it is inevitable. We think it can be stopped..." The Unabomber thinks technology has twisted people's lives, robbing them of dignity and autonomy, even as it damages nature and creates numerous social pathologies like crime and poverty. He thinks we can return to a civilization of "small, autonomous communities."

The Unabomber—who may be the former math professor, Theodore Kaczynski, arrested in April 1996—tells us something important about ourselves, about our ambivalence towards the technology that dominates our lives. For, deranged though he clearly is, he is right about so many things that afflict us. There is indeed a little of him in all of us. Insanely one-sided, his tale of techno-woe nevertheless strikes a chord with the Inner Luddite. Technology does steal our dignity and twist our lives about. Most people would indeed rather watch television than read a serious essay about the ills of society. We will soon forget the message of the manifesto in the onslaught of sludge the culture throws at us more effectively than ever before. In fact, the situation is even worse than the Unabomber appears to believe. He thinks that killing people will force others to stop and listen, to take his ideas seriously. Of course it won't. But not because they will dismiss any and all ideas of his as crazy. Nothing so straightforward. They will, instead, dismiss his ideas routinely, for no reason at all, simply because he is no longer, at some point, considered sufficiently "newsworthy."

These days, not even killing people is enough to get others to pay attention to you, or your ideas, for more than a brief moment.

—_—

"When you sit in the force field of a television set, you may not be aware of it, but your cellular structure is being rearranged," Arthur Kroker once told an interviewer for the Vancouver-based magazine *Adbusters*. Kroker denies that this image of altering biology is a metaphor. Our bodies are actually being rearranged by media exposure, he says. The same issue of *Adbusters*, an invaluable publication that subverts advertising by close satirical imitation, depicts a fifteen-second TV spot called "The Product is You." Images taken from the spot show a man basking dumbly in the grey-blue glow of his television set. "Your living room is the factory," the ad's voice-over says. "The product being manufactured…"—cut to shot of the man's neck, which sports a consumer bar code—"is you."

What does it really mean to say that television is altering our cellular structure, or that prolonged computer interaction is transforming our bodies into data for "the harvesting of flesh," as Kroker likes to say? In one sense, any idea or piece of information could be said to alter the flesh: my brain cells, or at least my brain chemicals, are in a constant state of flux as my senses receive and analyse data. But there is also the powerful idea, first explored by the British biologist Richard Dawkins, of "memes." Memes are coded, nonphysical information that Dawkins argues can "nest" in physical organisms. Like genes, they reproduce as a function of relative adaptiveness to an environment: some live and some die. The philosopher Daniel Dennett, a follower of Dawkins, once defined the human brain as "a meme nest." Our physical bodies, in other words, play host to any number of self-reproducing ideas, not all of them beneficial to us, which we help to survive. Examples of pro-human memes might be, say, monogamy and "adaptive" virtues like loyalty, sociability, and honesty. These are ideas whose reproduction and flourishing symbiotically aids the reproduction and flourishing of the human species. Examples of anti-human memes might be the excitement aroused by explosions, the dangerous conviction that problems can be solved with weapons, or the belief that the planetary environment is entirely at human disposal. To the extent that these ideas flourish, our biological existence is actively threatened.

Here, then, the will to virtuality actually meets the biological talk of evolutionists. In some cases, we actively help to reproduce ideas that are harmful to our own survival. Unlike most other species, humans possess the capacity to be self-destructive. We are also complex enough in our mental architecture to entertain—and be entertained by—many new and interesting ideas. Such ideas, and the means of delivering them, can be dangerously seductive. And as new ideas present themselves to our (non-physical) minds, there is a sense in which new memes may actually take up parasitic residence in our (physical) brains.

I have never been sure how literally to take this meme-talk. Dennett and others insist they are not using this physical language metaphorically, while Kroker, he of the flesh harvest, says that the meme-speak is "a biological metaphor." But in the end the issue of strict literality hardly matters, because the point is clear enough. We are being altered by our technology and our media of communication. This is true in obvious ways when, using some forms of technology, we actually "wear our machines" in the form of technological improvements on the body: prostheses, hearing aids, glasses, even cosmetic implants. It is also true in less obvious ways when we seem to spread ourselves out through the electronic ether by means of computer networks or, conversely, sit still while the networks bring what we fancifully call "the world" to us by means of television. In our little rooms, we are indeed becoming virtual. We are becoming a new form of being that is, as Kroker insisted, half-flesh and half-data.

It is not, however, a very welcome prospect. Some of the more suggestive recent science-fiction dreams are on the verge of coming true. In David Cronenberg's grisly film *Videodrome* (1983), for instance, the main character, played (with typical intensity) by James Woods, taps into a pirate television station that broadcasts scenes of brutal torture. He finds himself becoming addicted to the vicious images, drawn into the sick dramas of humiliation. Even as he does so, he finds his body altering in various bizarre ways. It seems that beneath the pirated television signal there flows another kind of signal, a mind- and body-altering beam that transforms Woods into a new form of being. (This development is explained with positively scholastic obscurity by someone called Professor O'Blivion, who exists entirely on videotape in a vast library.) Part conspiracy thriller, part murder mystery, and part technophobic manifesto, *Videodrome* also offers some trademark disgusting Cronenberg special effects as Woods's body is altered by the signal. An ugly slit begins to appear in his stomach, from which he can draw out new forms of himself: a gun fused to his arm in place of a hand, a grenade in place of the arm. Woods's character, initially horrified, eventually becomes a kind of devotee of his new, television-altered body. "Long live the new flesh!" he yells at one point.

The second image may be more familiar. In the course of "Star Trek: The Next Generation" it appeared that the only genuine threat to the humanistic goody-goody utopia of the United Federation of Planets was something called "the Borg." Old familiar enemies from the original series— the Klingons, the Romulans—were either on-side with the Federation or uneasily at peace. Only the Borg, a half-flesh, half-metal collective entity bent on the "assimilation" of all substandard forms of life, posed a serious danger. Driven by a relentless desire for technological perfection, the Borg was dedicated to stamping out all forms of carbon-based (that is, mortal) life and soaking up their usable technical knowledge. The threat of the Borg was one, significantly, that came from within. The Borg's assimilationist imperative is really a violent manifestation of techno-capitalist ambition, in which new models must always supersede old ones—even if the old ones are perfectly fine. The Borg also represents a kind of nightmare of internal human destruction. It illustrates with vivid clarity the possibility that, in a desire to bond more and more closely to our machines, we will find that they take us over in some insidious—and then violent—fashion. When Captain Picard is captured by the Borg, made into one of them (complete with various mechanical prostheses and weird body armour), they very nearly succeed in wiping out the human race as we know it.

Of course, the storylines of the episodes featuring the Borg did not pursue this theme of technological self-destruction very far. Instead they preferred to emphasize, in practically McCarthyite manner, the dangers of mindless collectivism as against the joys of individualism. The theme was hammered home with typical "Star Trek" ham-fistedness in a late episode in which a single Borg member is "tamed" by the crew—and even given an individual name. The "reformed" individual Borg, known as Hugh, then returns to the Borg collective and spreads individualism through the functioning collective like a virus, creating a "good" Borg strain of proto-individuals who split off from the collective: a kind of heavy-handed fable for the American Revolution or, better, the break-up of the Soviet Union?

Yet the real danger of the Borg is not the old Cold War worry that collectivism is deadening. It is rather the very new worry that our bodies are being colonized by our own machines; that the Borg is already with us, in the forms of transformative mass media that denigrate the real world and in computer networks that take us out of our bodies. And the threat to our physical bodies is as real, and as deep, as any bomb we could create or imagine.

Long live the new flesh.

FIVE

Our Bodies,
Our Selves

> The transgression does not deny the taboo but
> transcends it and completes it.
>
> Georges Bataille, *Erotism*

THE VIDEO FOR
David Bowie's single "The Heart's Filthy Lesson" shows the
singer performing with apparent equanimity in a dingy
slaughterhouse. Displaying his habitual elegance, Bowie
sings and dances to the Brian Eno score with a host of
human corpses. Another troupe of zombie-like human forms
joins the dance, sticking sharp objects into one another, as
the camera cuts away to images of hangings and the dismemberment of a dead body.

Bowie is not alone in asking us to enter the slaughterhouse. Nirvana's video for the song "Heart Shaped Box" features images of human fetuses hanging from trees or
suspended inside a hospital drip bag. Tom Petty, in the video
for his song "Mary Jane's Last Dance," goes to a morgue to
steal the body-bagged cadaver of a woman, played (if one
can say so) by Kim Basinger. The London, Ontario, band
The Gandharvas won an award for their video of a song
called "The First Day of Spring," which shows a man
strapped into a torture chair, his head covered with a cage,
plastic tubes leading into his torso in a manner reminiscent
of the Borg prostheses in Captain Picard's "assimilated"
body. None of these videos was banned by MuchMusic, the
Canadian all-video channel, when they were released during

1995. But "Delia's Gone," a bizarre necrophilic ditty by Johnny Cash, of all people, was too much even for the new generation of video programmers; its release was blocked.

The existence of such "video nasties" is anything but new, especially in the overheated jump-cut world of MuchMusic or MTV, where scenes of torture and exploding buildings have long been cinematographic staples. But the intense body-consciousness of these recent offerings, the clear emphasis on corporeal mutilation and decay, seems to strike a deeper note of unease. Indeed, to some, the new flesh-consciousness of music videos, a popular art form rarely taken seriously by critics but which reaches an immense young audience, suggests an increasingly desperate sense that the body is under attack, threatened by the hard, depersonalizing machines that surround it. The videos seem in turn to reflect the recent fashion among young people for what can only be called extreme body decoration—the tattooing, piercing, scarring, and branding that border on self-mutilation.

In a strange way, these trends can all be seen as attempts to *get the body back*, to reclaim the messy physical organism from the virtuality of current technology.

"Man loses his sense of private identity when computer banks and networks dissolve the human image," the McLuhanite thinker Nelson Thall said in *The Toronto Star* in a 1995 interview with rock critic Peter Howell. "We become genderless and sexless through technology, and the mind loses the image of itself as a human being." Trends of extreme body awareness can be understood as a reaction to what McLuhan once called "the discarnate effect" of technology—the way ever-changing machines divorce us from our bodies. When flesh is rendered virtual and personal integration is shaken, the body becomes a natural site of cultural resistance, perhaps the last meaningful place to resist electronic encroachment. Here, body mutilation, a self-conscious toying with primitiveness, is a political act; it marks a rejection of civilization's norms, but also a rejection of the increasing mechanization of the world. To decorate the physical body, especially in painful ways, is to reclaim its material reality, its existence as flesh that can be burned, pierced, marked, lashed to bloodiness—and, of course, ultimately enjoyed. The pierced or tattooed body takes us away from the cyber and back to the simply material: the flesh as site of pleasure and pain, pleasure and pain as means to truth. And that truth is simple: *I am material.*

The anxiety evident in this resistance is strongly enhanced by general late-century uncertainty, the free-floating anxiety of a culture that provides few secure footholds. According to the artists themselves, the attempts at fleshly reclamation even have a sacrificial quality, the ritual purification of the *imitatio Christi*, in which bloodshed is a form of appeasement.

"I think people have this fear of the future, far more than they ever have before, and I think the fear also is brought into focus because of a lack of belief that there has been a history," David Bowie told Peter Howell. "As things move so fast, it becomes harder and harder to put yesterday into place. My intent [in the video] was possibly that there's a kind of ritualization going on, a kind of deviant or mutated understanding of the pagan ritual in appeasing gods. If we're to let blood before the end of the century, then everything will go right in the twenty-first century." In this view, body extremists are, as Norman Cohn said of the medieval prophets who practised rites of personal mutilation, "an elite of self-immolating redeemers." (Other rock musicians are less forthcoming, or simply less articulate: "I haven't really thought about it," Trent Reznor of Nine Inch Nails said when asked about the millennial resonance of his band's videos. "I'm not smart; I just make music.")

There is an even more straightforward apocalyptic allusiveness in the self-inflicted mutilation of the modern primitives who now patrol our urban streets. For the most part, recent devotees of painful body decoration circle around its S&M or tribal origins and point instead to a particular kind of millennial dream: the standard-issue post-apocalyptic future in which blasted urban landscapes are patrolled by badass punks dressed in designer leatherwear—*The Road Warrior*, say, or *Blade Runner*. Wearing a nose ring or prominent tattoo in the mid 1990s is in this way an example of just how recombinant North American culture has become. The wearer is not so much alluding to some non-western tribe or even marginal sexual group; he—or, increasingly, she—is really quoting the art director of a bleak science-fiction movie. Call it "dystopian chic."

Still, the desire to reclaim the body's materiality is an important sign of cultural unease. Body mutilation has often functioned, in cultures both pagan and Christian, as a form of penance: no pain, no spiritual gain. It has also had an important prophetic role. In 1490s Florence, Savonarola and his Weepers lashed themselves in public even as they denounced the luxuries of the Florentines, drawing their own blood in frenzies of enthusiastic self-flagellation. The blood was for them a sign of prophetic seriousness, a mark of good faith: *The end really is nigh, you sinners! Just look at my self-mutilation!* Today, bodily transgression retains this element of critical seriousness—and arguably the hint of masochistic release—even as its targets shift. Whereas the flagellants of other end-times tied their public suffering to religious purification, and met the uncertainty of the Second Coming with self-abasement and violent denial, the young extremists of our own day link body decoration to a purification of social expectations, and meet the uncertainty of their own futures with a refusal to invest that future with expectation or meaning.

Body decoration is in effect the creation of an alien body within the culture, something carefully created to shock and unsettle. It expresses a wish to overturn the strictures of both biological and cultural determinism. The freedom promised by these forms of social transgression can be very exciting. Yet we also notice that the desire for freedom, when so blatantly expressed, is itself an expression of uncertainty, and one that says much about the individual's defeat in the face of powerful mass culture. Highly visible contraventions of the social rules reveal a new and more subtle lesson about cultural unease. In an obvious sense, transgression is simply a way of coping with anxiety, an attempt at getting cultural insecurity under control. Yet at the same time, when it is stage-managed with great care, transgression functions paradoxically to reaffirm the value of the norms it would transcend. Shocking gestures of body decoration and gender playfulness thus reveal an odd two-sidedness. They are *straightforward* expressions of anxiety, a rejection of society's standard promises. But they are also *perverse* expressions of anxiety, because they contain the hidden wish that those standard promises of social security be solid and real—that is, things that can be genuinely rejected by an act of will.

The decline of straightforward anxiety into perverse anxiety is the movement of a culture that has lost faith in its promises of security. The decline is also a sign of the multi-layered forms that anxiety about the future now often take. It is no coincidence that we are, in the anxious 1990s, playing out social dramas of the body found in other end-times, the complicated dance of threatened body and uncertain self. What we find is that recovering our on-the-brink bodies is anything but easy.

Heterosexual men are notoriously lacking in self-awareness, and in common with a lot of my cohort, I have a pretty positive body image. This is to say that I am, unlike most women and many gay men, inclined to think that my bod, while certainly no work of art, is *more or less okay*. "Inhabiting a male body is much like having a bank account," John Updike wrote in a 1993 essay called "The Disposable Rocket": "as long as it's healthy, you don't think much about it." (The disposable rocket is Updike's image for the questing, reckless sperm-delivery aspect of male physicality: the male body will climb into the air, burn itself into a cinder, and happily fall away dead if there is even a slim chance of getting some semen where it is supposed to go.) Like most straight men, then, when I think about my body at all, I usually think it's not too bad, really *nothing to be ashamed of*. This is what we think—sometimes rather unrealistically. Statistics show that straight men are inclined to overestimate drastically their degree of physical beauty, with about half ranking themselves in the top 10 percent.

These are some of the things that pass through my mind as I stand naked in front of the mirror in my bedroom. The mirror is actually two big sliding doors that hide the closet. It is full-length and covers most of one wall of the room. (I should say right away that I am not responsible for this. The mirror was installed by the previous tenant, who apparently liked to watch himself as he worked out on an exercise machine, a Soloflex or Rider-Man or Torture-U-Like.) Despite the unforgiving nature of this big mirror, I am here now of my own free will. I am taking stock of my body, taking its measure so to speak, looking it straight in the eye to see which of us blinks first. I am doing this because I feel it is in the air, body-consciousness, and I think I had better not resist it. I feel my flesh these days to be somehow under permanent threat. If it is not altered at a molecular level by computer and television signals, rendered disposable by the onslaught of the digital world, laid low by a debilitating disease, or transformed into a carbon/iron compound, it will find itself in a disagreement with someone from the wrong side of the winners/losers economy, someone carrying a gun.

At the very least, I think, my body is getting bulkier and less pleasing by the day. Also weaker. Like everyone else over the age of eighteen or so, I am in the process of decaying—enacting, through the temporal fact of my body, the great circle of life. For these and other reasons, I feel I must *reclaim* that body in some way. I remain unsure how to do this. For one thing, the very idea of "reclaiming" makes it sound as if my body is at the Left Luggage counter of a railway station. If only it were that straightforward. And though we seem to be in the midst of a raging body-consciousness, a New Corporeality, the art of getting the body back, rescuing it from the terrors of the age, is something few have really mastered.

For example, though I have no sleek black exercise machine in the bedroom, I see them, in their considerable glory, during the interminable television infomercials that haunt my insomnia. Awake at four or five in the morning, I turn on the television and sit in its cold blue glow as fitness instructors, enthusiastic to the point of manic violence, extol the machines' virtues, screaming at the camera "Technique! Technique! Technique!" and indicating the abs that have been isolated, the quads that have been crunched, the delts that have been flexed. (No wonder, when the average American every week consumes an amount of fat equal to six sticks of butter—that's almost eighty pounds a year.) I see strangely primitive "fitness" contests in which muscled young women walk across the stage in bikini and high heels, flexing washboard stomachs and smiling about the grim wonders of 3 percent body fat. They are not freaks of nature, they insist to the gelled interviewers, and they are definitely not body-builders. Body-building is sick. They are merely *into fitness*.

I think they should maybe be *into therapy* instead. But who am I? I'm just a guy with a persistent lack of upper-body

development and probably 15 percent body fat. I look at my
body, I look at myself, the body that is me. It is—I am—
about five feet and eleven inches tall. (Or, as my driver's
licence metrically insists, 180 centimetres.) My body weighs
something in the neighbourhood of 165 pounds. I don't
know for sure because I haven't actually weighed myself
since I was in college. I'm fairly healthy and not obviously
overweight.

I look again, more closely. I see a head of ordinary proportions set atop slight shoulders, which are rounded a bit
in a nascent scholarly stoop. I see a reasonable chest (no
pectoral implants needed there, yet) which sports an
acceptable amount of hair, stopping well short of the ursine.
The longish trunk ends in a stomach still more or less flat
but slightly thickened at the sides, in a definite suggestion
of love handles to come. I see heavy thighs and calves with
the decent muscle definition I acquired as a jogger. The legs
themselves are covered in quite a bit of hair, really, but what
are you going to do? And finally, the weird duck-like feet,
those orthopedic nightmares. The feet have been giving me
problems since I was a kid. Spade-like and almost triangular
from heel to toe, they build to weirdly high insteps which
force me into oversized shoes. They're practically pyramidal,
the feet.

Guys actually do flex their muscles when they are alone
in front of mirrors, so I do that now. I raise my arms in the
classic Arnold-as-Hercules pose, curling my hands into fists
over my shoulders. The wimpy upper arms spring into some
kind of life. Then I suck in my stomach a bit and flex my
abs, doing what body-builders call a "crab" pose—arms
down at the sides, hands still in fists, turning the body
quickly back and forth, grinning maniacally. The crab
requires a sort of hold-your-breath, try-to-implode effort
that makes the skin turn red and the face contort. I give this
up pretty quickly, but not before I convince myself that I see

ome abdominal muscle definition beneath the thin layer of
at around my middle. Really, quite objectively, thin, I say
o myself. That's not really fat at all, just a kind of *padding* or
hickness.

I recount the small catalogue of injuries and aches that
ire troubling me at the moment. Twisted right ankle, suf-
ered stumbling down what can only be described as a grassy
knoll. Sore left knee—need new running shoes. Stiff right
elbow—cause unknown. And the sharp inexplicable pain
under my left shoulder blade that causes me to grimace as if
I have been shot when I turn my body the wrong way.
There are also the usual marks and blemishes, tales of a boy-
hood of routine and modest violence. A long angry scar
snakes down one of my legs, the result of being levelled by a
car while riding my bike down Wellington Crescent in
Winnipeg the day I graduated from high school. There are a
couple of smaller scars from the same incident mixed in
with the miscellaneous graffiti of cuts and tears that decorate both knees. There are some faded scars on my abdomen
from childhood operations. I have a couple of noticeable
moles on my chest, lots of little ones scattered elsewhere.

I have a hole in my left earlobe, made when I was nineteen, in which I used to wear a small hoop and, on occasion,
a cross; but, thanks to a nasty infection some time ago, it no
longer sports anything, reduced now to a mere decorative
dimple. Beneath the skin, there is the knitted-up hairline
fracture on my left forearm, broken playing basketball when
I was thirteen. My hands are covered in numerous minute
scars, the record of cuts and nicks dating back three
decades. The brightest ones are along the side of my left
index finger, which I almost managed to slice off with an x-
acto knife during a seminar in newspaper layout, and in the
corner between my pinkie and third finger, which I slashed
open while trying to cut a hot dog bun.

Not very honourable wounds.

Looking at your body this way, like a patient etherized upon a table, produces an odd feeling of personal dizziness, a brief spin into the heart of what philosophers call the mind-body problem—a form of McLuhan's "discarnate effect," in other words, but brought on by simple reflection, not by proliferating video images or expanding computer networks.

The effect can be acute. I *am* a body, I might say. There I am in the mirror. But then, it also seems as though I simply *have* a body. I can assess it, look it up and down. Is that *me* in the mirror? Or is it simply the material apparatus by which I perambulate through the world? Looking so closely at my body, I begin to feel like the space alien played by Jeff Bridges in the movie *Starman*, who steered a human body around like it was an elaborate assault vehicle. I ought to feel that I inhabit my body all the way down to my fingertips, all the way down to the toes of those oddly shaped feet, but my relationship begins to feel like one of pilot to craft.

It is a mysterious situation, really, that my consciousness should find itself shackled so completely into this material form, the soft six feet of flesh. The philosopher René Descartes said that mind and matter were two entirely different kinds of stuff—the only two kinds of stuff in the world. The human being was for him a miraculous conjunction of these two substances—a sort of superb psycho-physical confection. Descartes also said, rather less plausibly, that the connecting surface, the interface if you like, between body and mind was located at the pineal gland, deep inside the brain. This was the place where the non-corporeal mind translated its many directives into the material movements of the physical world.

Philosophers have long since rejected this dualistic picture of the world—Gilbert Ryle derisively called it "the ghost in the machine"—but they have shown some difficulty in replacing it with a convincing alternative. None of their answers really seems to grab the matter by the throat. Is our consciousness something that "supervenes" on the causal chain of the physical world, for example? Or is mind "epiphenomenal," something that happens as a by-product of physical events? Is it perhaps an "emergent property" in physical organisms of a given complexity, something that just begins to emanate from a brain that has a certain vast quantity of processing power? Or, even more simply, is mind just reducible to neurological function, to the impossibly complex concatenations of synapses and brain-wave fluctuation? In other words is there, perhaps, no separate mind-substance there at all, just a very intricate physical one?

The problem is that we don't really know, and that lack of knowledge disperses any comfort we have had about our embodied selves. Indeed, some philosophers have become so vexed and troubled by the persistent disagreements that they have given up the search for a solution. The mysteries of the mind, they suggest, are beyond the powers of the mind to understand. We are just not built with enough central processing power to understand our own programming. According to these people (sometimes pejoratively called "the New Mysterians"), the mind is—and must remain—beyond our ken.

Nevertheless, most of us remain crude and unreflective dualists of a sort. That is, we think of ourselves as being selves that have bodies, and here mental states typically seem closer to the heart of our personal identity than physical ones. So, for example, we speak, without much reflection, of our bodies *failing us* in some way, succumbing to illness or fatigue when we need to work. We view our bodies as the site of unwelcome decay or disease, or as something susceptible to alien invasion. As we look at the body reflected back at us in the mirror we see something that probably looks and feels a little substandard, a smidge sluggish. It is

lumpy here, it sags there. Perhaps there are dark circles of
fatigue permanently etched under the eyes. It moves less
quickly, less gracefully, than it did. Our bodies, it seems to
us, are forever *letting us down*.

At the same time, we are prone to abusing them. We
bash into things, pursue dangerous pastimes, stay up too
late, eat poorly. We have one too many alcoholic drinks and
fry some of our fragile brain tissue through dehydration. We
slaughter brain cells all the time, cavalierly, by the thousands. And yet we do not typically think of this brain-cell
murder as abuse *of the mind*. Brain cells are bodily; they are
corporeal. While someone may well (if his slang is very outdated) speak of something "blowing his mind," he certainly
does not mean it literally, and would probably stop immediately if he did. We alter the chemical balance in our brains
in various recreational ways, yes, but only because we like
the way this makes us feel. Which is to say, we like the way
those chemical imbalances affect our states of mind.

Even in medieval times, according to the sociologist
Richard Sennett, people were drawn to a form of crude dualism. They understood their bodies as "garments of flesh" that
clothed a divine soul. Of course, this separation of soul and
body can have unforeseen effects. In his 1995 book *Flesh and
Stone: The Body and the City in Western Civilization*, Sennett
notes that the mechanistic world-view that arose in the early
modern period—the period in which Cartesian dualism was
first mooted—gradually drove the soul from its fleshly clothing. In 1628, William Harvey, a rival to Descartes in the
study of anatomy, proved that the heart was actually a sort of
mechanical pump and not, as had been previously thought, a
centre of mysterious divine heat. And so began the modern
anatomical study that would reduce the mysteries of the
body to explicable, if miraculously complex, pumps, tubes,
and fluids. This new picture of the body as a complex
machine was a deep challenge to human self-image. Because

of it, the soul has finally been reduced to the spongy grey matter of the brain, our selves cut down to complexes of neurological function.

Nevertheless, we resist this reduction. The critic Robert Everett-Green recently cited, as evidence of this, the popularity of Oliver Sacks's vivid and moving tales of neurological dysfunction, in books such as *The Man Who Mistook His Wife for a Hat*. Though Sacks is a scientist, his portraits of people dealing with brain problems are deeply revealing of the human soul, of the person. Sacks's "popularity may be an index of how little satisfying we find the mechanistic view of the body," Everett-Green writes. "After all, if we are *only* machines of flesh, then we have no value once those machines fail." Thus "Sacks's clinical tales recount how the soul-like qualities of the self can actually surmount grave damage to the body's last great mystery zone, the brain." There remains an irreducible quality to our first-personal experience, our sense of ourselves as self-conscious individuals—hence our persistent sense of the "mind's I."

Even as we resist reductionism, though, complete integration of body and mind continues to slip through our fingers. Still in the grip of crude dualism, we begin to feel our rational selves distracted and beset by physical desire, and so desire must be expunged. Denigration of the body's urges can lead in turn to neglect, the sort of otherworldly academic pose in which attention to personal adornment, sometimes even personal hygiene, is prima facie evidence of frivolity, a fatal lack of mental seriousness. A friend of mine, deciding to bail out of graduate school, said she could no longer stand to be around people "dead from the neck down." The disembodied mind is not, finally, stable. It loses its bearings, its physical groundedness.

Yet the denial enjoys a long tradition. It is, for example, a central element of the Platonic system—Socrates called the body the soul's prison—that was carried into the

Christian world by intellectual synthesizers like St. Augustine. There it found a congenial place in the midst of that other tradition of bodily denigration, the one alive in the New Testament. Pleasure is condemned as a temptation that pulls a lowly sinner off the true path. Desires must be stifled, sometimes violently. (How these early thinkers *worried* about pleasure.) The will must be strengthened to fight off the pernicious joys promised by the body's urges. Christian denigration of the body goes even further, for here physical suffering is actually seen as the royal road to the soul's salvation, and pain is wisdom's highway. In this way the Greek philosophical quest for wisdom, accomplished through denial of the body, is transformed into the Christian quest for salvation.

A later intellectual achievement of the denial tradition is the powerful idea of impartial reason, articulated clearly during the Enlightenment. Here the goal of denial is transformed from salvation or wisdom to sheer knowledge. Now the true seeker, in addition to denying the body's routine temptations of desire, must eliminate from his mind all extraneous distractions, including nuisances like emotion or sentiment. The western icon of the impartial observer, the scientist or thinker as emotionless hero, is often thought to be an entirely modern creation, but it is in fact rooted in the much deeper historical ground of the mind's ancient quarrel with the body, dating back at least as far as Socrates.

It is no coincidence, then, that the popular brain-box heroes of our own age are in the main physically and emotionally ascetic. Conan Doyle's Sherlock Holmes, with his feats of intense deductive logic, fuelled by pipe tobacco but not, significantly, by food. Or "Star Trek"'s Mr. Spock, who denies himself both emotion and luxury as though they were viruses that afflict the logical brain. The apotheosis of this modern self-image, of the truth-seeker as disembodied, is perhaps the robot or the computer. Thus Data, in "Star

Trek: The Next Generation," is a perfect conjoining, for he is the computer in human form: an android. He even bears a name that simply means factual information. (Data's evil twin brother has by contrast a darker, more mythological name: Lore.) Data is a vast storehouse of information and computational power walking around in what appears to be a body but is, in fact, a highly complex machine. He is a sort of super-human, innocent of desire or passion, unaffected by base motives like deceit or revenge and not susceptible to easy physical defeat. Numerous "Star Trek" storylines hinge on the rather cheesy plot device of having some misfortune affect everyone in the crew except the impervious Data. He can reason at immense speed; he is physically powerful; and he is not, as some aliens once called the "Star Trek" humans, an "ugly bag of mostly water."

The image of the non-corporeal seeker is never perfect, for the creators of these hyper-rational images are themselves human and usually enjoy playing on the essential humanity beneath the icy-cold demeanour of thoroughgoing rationality. Holmes, for example, is "humanized" by his cocaine addiction, his execrable violin playing, his susceptibility to both love and envy. In one of the many *Star Trek* movies, the noble Mr. Spock sacrifices himself, dying a slow and horrible death by radiation, only to explain (as his skin peels yuckily away) that logic, not honour, demanded his sacrifice. "The demands of the many outweigh the demands of the few," he hacks to a misty-eyed Captain Kirk. The creators of the super-human marvels likewise hasten to show the often humorous limits of the logical cast of mind. One of Data's running gags is that, when some other character muses rhetorically "What are the odds of *that* happening?" he actually calculates them, to six or seven decimal places.

To the denizens of a workaday world, the world where bodies obtrude, such single-minded pursuit of knowledge must indeed appear risible. In these moments Data becomes a close relative of the ancient philosopher Thales, who, Socrates tells us in Plato's *Theaetetus*, was so intent on studying the stars above that he stumbled and fell down a well.

In this worldly-wise inversion of the mind-body problem, the hyper-rational being is made a figure of fun. Yet the inversion does not really solve the problem, for whether we emphasize the mind to the body's detriment, or vice versa, we have surely not succeeded in integrating the two. Even as we try to reclaim the body from the mind's denigration of it, we find that the body is not ready to be accepted without further ado.

— — —

The late-century human body is a complex, intellectually constituted thing. Beset by threats and influences, altered by surgery and technology, it is no simple material fact lying ready to hand. It is instead a rich cultural achievement, laden with disputes and struggles over gender and power and selfhood. It has been built into its current shape over several centuries, and that shape is now thoroughly conditioned not only by obvious social power relations but also by cultural and subcultural forces whose true influence we sometimes only dimly perceive: the mass media, the fashion system, the state of reproductive technology. You cannot escape the body by retreat into the mind; but neither can you avoid the mind in pursuit of the body.

"The body is being rethought and reconsidered by artists and writers because it is being restructured and reconstituted by scientists and engineers," William A. Ewing writes in his 1994 book *Body: Photographs of the Human Form*. Ewing's point seems to echo the New Corporeality obsessions of David Cronenberg and Arthur Kroker. The fascination with the body is both a function and a pursuit of uncertainty. We alter the flesh because the flesh seems so threatened, so vulnerable—and so deeply integrated, as time goes on, with our machines. We wear prostheses, alter bones and skin surgically, even engineer births and splice genes. Modern conveyances carry our bodies at hundreds of miles an hour, and, more unsettling still, intricate computer networks extend our vision and carry our minds to far parts of the globe at speeds approaching warp. Our minds are thus in one sense finally unshackled from our bodies; we have left them behind in our offices or studies and entered the noncorporeal space of the cyber-world. The great mortal fact of life, the body's contingency, is no longer a simple given.

We shrink from this knowledge, even as we realize its inevitability—hence the desire to find the body once more, to get it back in the foreground, violently or painfully if necessary. The return to the body is thus an expression, perhaps the deepest one, of anxiety about what the third-millennium human will be. What new shape will the human body have? Are we evolving past the need for bodies altogether? We are looking for some kind of security, the warmth and familiarity of what used to seem, without much effort, closest to me: the body in which I am housed. But the fear evident here, the rearguard nature of the action, is (to use a fleshly metaphor) palpable.

Once again, though, what we find in a return to the body is not always reassuring. Bodies are prey to disease and they are vulnerable to their own functioning. Cancer is nothing more than cellular growth gone out of control; viruses simply take advantage of the developmental capacity of cells. Bodies can also be deformed, ugly, freakish. Even as the ideal forms of the supermodel or Soloflex-user become more inescapably visible—on urban billboards of startling explicitness, on television at all hours—our own bodies begin to look, inevitably, substandard. The images of bodies that bombard us in the New Corporeality suggest standards of beauty that only an infinitesimal portion of the population can aspire to, and even they can sustain them for only a few years.

This escalation of standards has the unsettling effect of stimulating our desire even while rendering our own sites of desire less acceptable, even repulsive. This is particularly true when it comes to the ideal of female beauty, which in our time has combined the visible-ribbed thinness of near-anorexia with the bustiness of a wet nurse. But it is more generally true of the ideal of youth, which we celebrate as insistently as any culture that fears for its future. The pore-less unwrinkled models now gracing fashion magazine covers are rarely older than twenty-five, often as young as fifteen or sixteen. Despite feminists' objections, the manu-facturers of cosmetics, the editors of magazines, and the pro-ducers of fashion television go on insisting that they are doing nothing more than reflecting reality, not constructing it. In a way they are right, for if the rest of us were not so complicit in the maintenance of these bizarre standards of beauty—if we did not find these starving youngsters so beautiful—they would not persist. Don't just blame Revlon; we all have a stake in this.

In response to these increasingly unreal standards of beauty, some elements within the culture have begun to play on the very idea of the "normal body." Freak shows like the Jim Rose Circus Sideshow, in which tattooed "geeks" perform disgusting feats of body awareness—eating nails, burning their flesh, hanging weights from their genitals—are once more touring the continent, drawing a new genera-tion of the curious into smelly taverns and beer halls with an oddly trendy combination of old-fashioned circus weird-ness and alternative music. Not all the freakishness is so sensationalistic. The Toronto writer Barbara Gowdy, for example, whose story collection *We So Seldom Look on Love* was published in 1992, is the literary high priestess of the refusal of the normal. Gowdy's vivid stories, of four-legged and two-headed people in search of themselves and places they can feel at home, are late-century parables for all of us who have found the body cumbersome, alien, somehow obtrusive.

Also vulnerable. The critic Elaine Scarry notes in her book *The Body in Pain: The Making and Unmaking of the World* (1985) how brutal practices of torture and war, which have become impossible to ignore in our bloody century, confess their corporeal essence. Torture is the stimulation of pain in human tissue to elicit information; war is the destruction of human tissue to effect political change. In Scarry's unflinching gaze, Cartesian dualism is brought into horrible political focus. We influence, change, and perhaps even destroy minds by heating, electrifying, cutting, or tearing the *bodies* in which those minds are encased. The mind may be strong in its own terms, and may run from affliction to the Platonic forms or the Christian Heaven, but its basic, inescapable weakness is clear to soldier and torturer alike: it must have a body to live. Socrates was renowned for his ability to withstand hardship, walking barefoot during winter campaigns and working for days without sleep. Would he have proved so sanguine in the hands of a Nazi torturer?

Or consider art where bodies are prominent, for example, the gorgeous work of the much denigrated bisexual photographer Robert Mapplethorpe. Off the cultural agenda for a time after the early '90s controversies concerning posthumous exhibition of his art (he died in 1989 at age forty-two), Mapplethorpe returned to prominence when a shabby 1995 biography by the journalist Patricia Morrisroe called forth a passionate defence by his friend and former lover, rock star Patti Smith. The defence also helped renew interest in Mapplethorpe's brilliant, evocative photographs of muscular bodies. The homoerotic elements of his art are ultimately less important than their sheer physical beauty and the morbid awareness they provide that bodies, by their very nature, do not persist. Here, overt concern with sex is matched by an awareness that a plague of gigantic proportions has made real bodily pleasure for many people a distant memory. Mapplethorpe—so corporeal in his art, so dead of AIDS—is emblematic of the age.

The increasing eroticism of advertising and publishing seems to parallel a loss of hope in the act of love itself. That act now seems either dangerous, a time-bomb of disease, or merely disappointing, a full flight to desire rendered less than ideal by its failure to achieve the beauty of a (heavily retouched) magazine ad. We soothe ourselves with our candy substitutes. In erotica everything is promised and nothing delivered; consuming it, we subsist on a sugar diet of pure stimulated desire. And our bodies are as distant as ever—perhaps even more so, since now we labour under the illusion that the eroticized culture has brought them closer.

In the midst of our devastating plague—that common millennial trope, now rendered sexual—others have simply disregarded the dangers and returned to the fraught pleasures of unprotected sex. *The Village Voice* reported in 1994 that many gay men, in New York and elsewhere, were making a conscious choice to shed their condoms. One way to reclaim the body's corporeality, certainly, but one without much future.

■ ■ ■

Like many people who live in North American cities, I have lately grown used to seeing more of other people's bodies. Among other parts, I see a lot of navels and the rings that are installed in them. Body-piercing fashion has been marked by a kind of escalation, a sort of ring race. It started, it seems to me, with women adding more holes to their earlobes, climbing steadily up from the lobe and into the tough cartilage above; men added right-side holes to the left-side ones that were fashionable when I was an undergraduate.

Then the rings moved from the lobe to other parts of the ear, to the nose, the lips, the eyebrows.

The jewellery has also gotten bulkier and more obviously primitive. Barbells are now punched through the brow over the nose. Big shanks of silver are installed in holes punched right out of the ear itself. Thick rings are put through the middle of the nose, like livestock. Bulky lumps of steel are stuck through the thick part of the lower lip, or—Jesus!—in the middle of the tongue. I once heard a much-pierced woman, who was maybe twenty-two, confess that she had experienced no problems with any of the piercings—until she had her tongue done. "Kind of freaked me out," she said. "But if you can get over the first five days, when your tongue is really swollen and eating is a bit of a problem, you're laughing." Laughing?

More extreme and clearly sexual piercing has emerged from subcultural obscurity. Nipple rings are apparently useful when you want to string a fine silver chain from your ear, through your nose, and down to your chest. Penis and labia rings are also very much the rage in certain circles, though I suspect more people talk about them than actually get them installed. With penis rings we have arguably left behind the swirling shoals of fashion, where anybody might want to conform for the sake of sending the message of hipness, and entered the world of those who like to dance along the line between pleasure and pain.

The difference is a subtle one these days, and that says something significant about us. Twenty, even ten, years ago, people who openly sported rings in their faces would have been considered candidates for commitment. People who sported them in their genitals have always had more choice about secrecy, but had it been known they would probably have been ostracized. Of course, many people hold this view of body-piercing even now, but their disapproval is apparently doing nothing to slow the desire of urbanites under thirty-five to adorn themselves with jewellery in the most unlikely places. Most of us have seen Dennis Rodman's navel ring. I recently saw an ad for Fodor's travel guides, a picture of the Mona Lisa, but with a ring through her nose—"because it's not the Old World anymore." Today a fortysomething father can describe, with hilarious self-deprecation, the new rite of adolescent passage: his thirteen-year-old daughter's "first piercing." "This is a scene my parents could never have envisioned," law professor Tom Singman wrote with true dad-guy bafflement in *The New York Times Magazine* in 1995, "dad and daughter watching a half-naked man demonstrate the proper care of a nipple pierce. Yet, there I was, gobbling down pierce-care hints, as if this were the most normal thing in the world. Then it hit me: This *was* normal."

Perhaps contrary to expectation, a lot of the piercing you see on downtown streets and in clubs is very becoming. The vertiginous combination of a pretty face and a piece of barbarous jewellery can be deliciously unsettling, and a small, well-placed tattoo sometimes has a sexual edge that pleases the eye as much as any other bodily feature. But despite that, I experience mounting feelings of unease as I walk through the First Annual Toronto Tattoo and Bodypiercing Convention, held on a hot weekend in May. Unease not because I find what I'm looking at repulsive—though, to be honest, there is some of that: the big guy with about six things installed in his nose looks to me like a slave at auction, and the stark black-and-white photos of penis and scrotum rings being installed make my empty stomach flutter and dive in an unpleasant way. No, the unease is mostly the result of feeling as though I have entered a world in which I am a tourist, a spectator at a cultural zoo in which those on show have the edge.

The convention is really no more than a gathering of a dozen or so tattoo and piercing "artists" in a music club called the Opera House, a cramped and dingy establishment on Queen Street East in Toronto. Like alternative music clubs the world over, the place has an unmistakable stench of sour beer and stale cigarettes permanently emanating from its ancient floors. It seems a good place for this group. It goes without saying that they are an odd bunch, but the oddities multiply as I move through the crowd gazing at tattoo designs and picking up pamphlets on piercing "aftercare."

I notice, for example, that there is a small representation of a traditional tattooing constituency, bikers. There are a couple of spiffy, polished-chrome hogs parked arrogantly in front of the club, and their undoubted owners, tricked out in leather chaps and vests, are inside comparing tattoos with the bonhomie of fishing buddies. Good, good, I think; the *bikers* are here. This tattooing thing isn't just a weird youth fad, an urban hiccup. There's a link with the tradition, the real outlaws. I wonder if there might be any *sailors* here, too, with anchors on their arms. But looking closer I realize there is something a little stylized about the bikers, and I notice that their moustaches are just a bit too carefully trimmed. These are not bikers. These are leathermen, homosexual S&M aficionados for whom the biker look is iconic and charged with sexual energy. I see that there are a couple of what might be real bikers nearby, but they are frumpy by comparison, older for one thing and wearing bad leather jackets, hilariously out of date designer jeans, and sporting faded blue tattoos on their pale, scrawny arms.

Most of the convention-goers are what you would expect, young people of varying degrees of beauty who have decorated their bodies in quasi-extreme ways. A tall thin woman, a spiky blonde, is walking around wearing a bra and miniskirt, showing off some delicate tattoo work on her upper body. Her finely toned abs are rippling under the dead-pale skin of her torso, and I find that somehow more impressive than the body decoration. Nearby a couple of guys, both in their early twenties, are advertising their piercing clinic. They both have extensive facial piercing, including multiple pieces running through their noses, big barbells on the lip, and so on—the sort of rig that would set off an airport security portal. They are selling T-shirts that show a face, its nose bisected by several tusk-like steel spikes; underneath it says "DIDN'T HURT."

The ground zero of the body-decoration quarter of the New Corporeality is a now infamous 1989 publication, much in evidence at the convention. It is a special issue of the pop culture journal *Re/Search* with the title "Modern Primitives: An Investigation of Contemporary Adornment and Ritual." *Re/Search* is the regular publication of a San Francisco-based editorial collective whose reports on strange and lesser known elements of North American culture have become legendary. The journal began publishing in the 1970s, reporting on punk music, conspiracy theories, surveillance technology, sadomasochism, and perennial late-century counter-culture heroes like William S. Burroughs and J. G. Ballard. The appearance of each issue, on such topics as "Incredibly Strange Films" and "Incredibly Strange Music," soon became a subcultural event. The much-reprinted "Modern Primitives" number has become the gospel of the tattooing, body-piercing, and ritual scarring crowd.

I snag a copy for closer review. The editors have some pretensions to scholarly investigation, tracing historical tattooing cultures and making some tentative links to Polynesian and African practices of body decoration, but the bulk of their "investigation" is in the form of interviews with tattoo and piercing enthusiasts, accompanied by stark up-close-and-personal photographs. The insights offered by the devotees range from the philosophical to the pragmatic—like the woman who says she can only reach orgasm when having sex with a man whose penis has been pierced with a metal barbell. There is also much talk of altered states of consciousness, of pain taking you outside your body, and the ritual release of primal or atavistic energy.

The most explicit of the profiles in "Modern Primitives" is of an aging San Francisco advertising executive known as Fakir Musafar. In the interview with the *Re/Search* editors he says he borrowed the name from an old "Ripley's Believe It or Not" item about a nineteenth-century Indian fakir who spent his life with horseshoes tied to his arms and daggers plunged through his skin. Musafar began his extreme practices early in life, drawing inspiration from old *National Geographic* features on African tribes who narrowed their waists, elongated their necks, or suspended weights from body parts, including the penis. His photos of himself with a nineteen-inch waist, or suspended horizontally from a dozen fishhooks inserted into various parts of his body, are enough to turn your stomach. They are compelling, though, you have to grant that—you can hardly take your eyes away. And the interview, in which Musafar recounts in loving detail the extremities to which he has taken his body, is a model of unintentional hilarity. He talks about suspending a three-pound weight from his penis or elongating his scrotum with thick metal rings as though these are just fun things to do.

Musafar is also a consultant for the California-based magazine *Piercing Fans International Quarterly* (PFIQ), which was first published in 1977 and thus became one of the earliest centres of the body-piercing subculture. *PFIQ* features photos and stories of piercing both routine and extreme, from male nipple rings (popular with Caesar's soldiers, apparently), to the ampallang (a barbell through the penis head), to the "Prince Albert"—a ring through the penis tip. "Called a 'dressing ring' by Victorian haberdashers," we are told, the Prince Albert "was originally used to firmly secure male genitalia in either the left or right pant leg during that era's craze for extremely tight, crotch-binding trousers, thus minimizing a man's natural endowment." Nobody is certain that Prince Albert himself wore one, and I frankly doubt the stated purpose of the ring. "Piercing is through the base of the penis head," the magazine explains. "The procedure is quick; the pain, minimal; the healing, rapid; and the pleasure, lifelong." If that is not enough, PFIQ also features photos of clitoris rings, labia rings, and a penis that appears to house more than thirty barbells and rings ranged along its length. There was even on one occasion a penis split lengthwise, each part of which was pierced by a metal loop attached to a chain leading to rings in other parts of the body. Musafar himself seems bemused about that one. "Somehow he did it, and it worked," he told the Re/Search interviewers. "He sent us some photos, we printed them, and that's all we know."

It is probably more than most of us want to know. PFIQ was banned in New Zealand and in Australia, where the split-penis man lived—proving that there are still some things you can do to your body so extreme they'll give most people the willies. A victory for those on the edge.

The single common denominator among those who favour extreme body decoration seems to be social transgression. One sociologist has called the tattoo and pierce "voluntary stigmata." They are also attempts at individuation in the midst of pressure to conform. There is a strong rite-of-passage feeling to tattooing and piercing: pain endured in public as an entry into community. Subjects of the "Modern Primitives" interviews speak repeatedly of sexual initiations involving nipple or labial piercing in front of assembled groups. There may even be redemptive elements to the act, where the pain is used as a cleansing ritual, a physical displacement and venting of emotional suffering.

Tattooists and body-piercers like to emphasize that tattoos and body jewellery have been a feature of every culture since the dawn of time. Even in "civilized" society such adornments have been popular—but, I notice, especially at moments of cultural upheaval, like the nineteenth-century *fin de siècle*. Lady Randolph Churchill had a tattoo of a small coiled snake on her wrist, starting a small craze for them among fashionable Victorian ladies. Winston Churchill bore his family's coat of arms on his body. Leo Tolstoy enjoyed showing off his body art at fashionable dinner parties. Nipple rings were also popular at the time. Certainly the duelling scars of upper-class Germans are a form of visible body decoration, artfully acquired and maintained—they opened the scabs and poured wine into them to make them heal more visibly. Czar Nicholas II of Russia wore a tattoo. So did Archduke Franz Ferdinand, whose assassination in Sarajevo touched off the First World War; legend has it that his attacker's bullet went right through it.

— — —

I walk a little farther through the convention and see some impressive bodywork being done by the assembled tattooists. A guy in his twenties, lying sideways on a table, is having his lower leg decorated. Another guy, close-cropped and stripped to the waist, is having a massive dragon tattoo installed on his upper body. The head and upper part of the dragon are already complete, vividly coloured in greens and reds on his broad back. The lower body and tail of the dragon swirl in outline around his right shoulder and down his right arm, where the tattooist is at the moment putting some bright orange colouring on the scales of the tail. I am fascinated by the care with which he does this, painting tiny patches with his buzzing gun and wiping the excess ink away constantly. The comparisons to painting are not overstated, I decide, though it may be most akin to painting of the black-velvet school. Still, it is painstaking work, laborious and time-consuming. I look closer to appreciate the artistry. Then I look up at the face of the subject, the canvas for all this elaborate body art. I am shocked to discover that I am looking into the eyes of one of my philosophy graduate students!

The feeling of surprise is mutual, and though I congratulate myself that I betray no outward sign of shock, inside I am reeling. His name is John Doran and I remember him as a smart guy, not overly talkative, who attended a seminar I gave on contemporary political theory the previous year. He looks older than me, but then lots of graduate students do, and he has a certain tough-guy thing going for him with his shaved head and the heavy arms and shoulders. But I never had him pegged as a tattoo enthusiast. Now I say to myself: Of course. He always wore long-sleeved shirts to class.

"Is this just a passing interest for you?" he asks me, as I look at him rather stupidly, working my mind around the situation. It's a good question. I used to think about getting a small tattoo, but I understand the disdain somebody with a whole dragon snaking around his body would feel for a dilettante who once contemplated adding a little heart or rose to his biceps. John is all too evidently a serious tattoo person, and serious tattoo people, while not generally excitable, are a bit fanatical—you'd have to be, wouldn't you, to spend thousands of dollars and dozens of hours getting a whole patch of your body covered in ink designs? Dabblers like me and fashionable kids probably just piss them off. On the other hand, people with tattoos have something important in common, a bond that sets them off from the pristine majority. It might be a tough call for him. Speak to me, in solidarity for our shared interest? Or refuse to take me seriously, the purist's disdain for the merely curious?

Solidarity wins out, and we chat a bit more. It's odd talking to somebody having tattoo work done on them, because they are suspended somewhere between posing for a portrait and undergoing a painful surgical procedure. John isn't even wincing, but I know that even as we speak the tattoo gun is punching a dozen small ink-filled needles into his flesh five times a second. I ask him the dumb questions that cascade into my mind. How long has it taken? Months of weekly sessions, each several hours long. Is it expensive? Yes— $3,700 altogether—but "you get what you pay for," John says. I see his point. What price art, after all? Because I'm not a complete dork, I don't ask him if it hurts. I know it hurts, for God's sake; I've heard the stories about tough-guy bikers keeling over in faints or vomiting.

I wonder what moves a guy like John to cover his body, the only one he'll ever have, in a design that might seem excessive on a dressing gown. A few weeks after the convention I call him and we agree to meet for lunch. He appears wearing a T-shirt with the single word "ANARCHY" printed on it. Despite his threatening appearance, he is as thoughtful and articulate as always. He tells me some surprising things about himself. Before coming to study philosophy at the university he spent some time in a Franciscan monastery, training to be a priest. He is still a devout Catholic who doesn't drink or smoke. He works as a bouncer at a downtown bar, likes comic books and ultra-violent action movies, hasn't yet told his parents about the tattoos (so far he has three), and is considering getting more. "It is an itch," he says, about the designs proliferating on his upper body. "But I think in the end my aesthetic considerations will outweigh any desire to get more pieces." Pieces. Serious tattoo people call them *pieces*, as in "of art."

Aesthetic considerations? Yes. The tattoo is a "visible personality trait," he says, a kind of statement of who you are, so it has to be carefully considered, and your body must be treated with the respect accorded a canvas. "I wouldn't want all my actions to be visible to people," he adds, "but this is something that is with you like nothing else is." Like many serious tattoo people, he prefers the term "body art" to "tattoo." And he waves off objections that this very permanence will come back to haunt him when the brightness of the tattoo's colour fades. He is twenty-three years old; how will he feel about the dragon, people ask him, when he is forty? Irrelevant. "At a certain point the question 'Why?' becomes unintelligible," he tells me. "It's like any desire: if you have it, no explanation is necessary; if you don't, no explanation is possible."

This makes the whole thing sound intensely personal—and intensely opaque. I'm still grasping for reasons, for an explanation. "I didn't do this as a statement of allegiance to any tribe or subculture," he says. "It's a matter of satisfying a personal desire." In fact, he has no deeper theory to offer. Is there no meaningfulness in the tattoo fad except this piece of anxious nihilism? Lots of young people are trying to satisfy desires that they, no less than we, find difficult to understand. If an educated, precise mind like John's cannot clearly explain his own tattoos, is there any hope that the rest of us can understand them?

I put it to John that millennial anxiety may be caught up in the mainly inarticulate craze for painful body decoration. "I don't know," he says, thinking it over. "I do know that it scares me to death, the millennium. It's going to be rife with craziness. I think I'll lock myself indoors on December 31, 1999." We talk about some of the craziness that's already evident: senseless urban violence, religious fundamentalism, the loss of hope among his peers. "People want to believe in something," he says, "but I don't think our culture offers people anything to believe in. You know, I'm an optimist. But I live day-to-day. I've stopped thinking about the future. I just don't know how much of the future is there."

▬ ▬ ▬

John is reluctant to offer explanations for his desire to decorate the body, but I found other cognoscenti more forthcoming. Many of the exhibitors at the convention spoke to me of their customers' desire to become what the *Re/Search* editors suggest: modern or urban primitives, cultural rebels trying to reclaim the basic fact of the body within the highly industrialized contemporary city. The exhibitors showed me tattoo designs from Polynesian tribes and African power symbols that are most popular with their younger clients.

"What is implied by the revival of 'modern primitive' activities," the editors of *Re/Search* argue, "is the desire for, and the dream of, a *more ideal society*. Amidst an almost universal feeling of powerlessness to 'change the world,' individuals are changing what they *do* have power over: *their own bodies*. That shadowy zone between the physical and the psychic is being probed for whatever insights and freedoms may be reclaimed."

This utopian impulse is ___n yoked to more familiar motives, like the transg___ion of social norms that date back to Old Testame⸗ ⸗rohibitions of body decoration in Leviticus 19:27–2ˤ . You are not to round off your hair at the edges nor ˊ ⸗ the edges of your beard.... You are not to gash your ¹ ⸗es when someone dies, and you are not to tattoo yˢ ⸗ives. I am Yahweh.") Transgression of norms is plˢ ⸗able; it marks off the transgressor as special, daring. ⸗t he or she is also, in this political theory of bodily extremity, a kind of cultural guerrilla, a harbinger of an imagined better future. The tattooed or pierced person has always been motivated by the pleasure of being different, of having permanently altered the virgin body in a manner both socially unacceptable and painful. Now the motive expands from the merely narcissistic to embrace a form of cultural revolt. To stress individuation in this way is, in a world of mass-produced and mass-consumed images, in effect to break a lance for the anti-modern and irreducibly personal.

My pain, after all, is purely and immediately *mine*. You can't take it away from me. It is not, as with so many other of my experiences, already mediated and filtered by the stock of images lodged in my brain. "Our minds are colonized by images," the *Re/Search* editors say, in a sentence that could have been written by Arthur Kroker. "Images are a virus." This viral colonization, which makes of the brain a nest of memes ingested without thought or choice from TV and movies, renders unique personal experiences almost impossible. Everything I do, from visiting a famous museum to having sex, is always coloured in advance by images of the act nestled in my cultural memory. And this fact of modern life threatens my authenticity; it challenges the essential project of finding and exhibiting my true self. To decorate the body becomes, in this view, a way of snatching authenticity from the clutches of a "rational" and "scientific" culture that would increasingly destroy the self.

The refusal of that culture also takes us back to the roots of the dominant anti-body view of rationality. The recovered body begins to appear to us, in the words of British sociologist Chris Schilling, "an island of security in a global system characterized by multiple and inescapable risks." Control of one's body is a symbolic refusal of the all-seeing powers of orthodoxy. Yet this remains by definition a highly visible refusal. "Youth subculture forms in the space between surveillance and the evasion of surveillance," the sociologist Dick Hebdige suggests. "It translates the fact of being under scrutiny into the pleasure of being watched." Control of the body, then—the only control available to the marginalized young—is central to this transcendence of taboo. "If teenagers possess little else, they at least own their bodies," Hebdige says. "If power can be exercised nowhere else, it can be exercised here.... To wear a Mohican or have your face tattooed is to burn most of your social bridges. In the current economic climate, when employers can afford to

pick and choose, such gestures are a public disavowal of the
will to queue for work."

The permanence of the act of body decoration, the pain
it brings, and—not least—the eroticism of the final product
thus set off body decoration as perhaps the one remaining
utopian gesture. It brings us back to ourselves in numerous
important ways: as individuals, as bodily creatures, as mortals whose "body art" is of necessity both permanent (I can't
take it off) and fleeting (it dies with me). "In this
Postmodern epoch in which all the art of the past has been
assimilated, computerized, advertised and replicated," the
Re/Search editors conclude, "the last artistic territory resist-
ing co-optation and commodification by Museum and
Gallery remains the Human Body."

Critics have noticed some difficulties with the body as
site of resistance, though. As the practices of extreme body
decoration become more widespread, the kind of mix-and-
match appropriation of primitiveness and iconography
makes the urban version of body decoration a little suspect.
People wear ankh and yin-yang tattoos because they "look
cool," or they flip through *The Dictionary of Symbols* to find
hip designs as though the world's cultures were a kind of
fashion sourcebook. (Which, tragically, they then become.)
Merely fashionable body decoration can become a form of
consumerism, a branch of the "Third World chic" in which
South American peasant dresses or Middle Eastern kaffiyehs
are trendy fashion accessories. Young urban consumers of
body decoration take on Melanesian tattoo designs or
Hebrew characters entirely for their surface aesthetic value.
They are just diversifying the global market to include a
new product: pictures painted on the flesh.

The body-art gesture also risks being too extensively and
perhaps illegitimately replicated, especially by people who
otherwise exhibit no trace of spiritual guerrilla warfare.
Even as far back as 1989, the editors of *Re/Search* professed

themselves worried that fake non-piercing nipple rings were being sold by some New York department stores, in models that ranged from a $500 gold hoop to a $10,000 diamond-encrusted effort. A friend of mine, a human resources manager for a large multinational soap merchant, recently had her navel pierced. She finds this small gesture of individualism still unsettles some of her more strait-laced co-workers, but she was recently pleased to discover that a group manager in her company, a fortysomething male engineer based in that great white-bread enclave, Cincinnati, had gone even further and gotten one of his nipples pierced. Pretty soon we'll have boardrooms full of suits, all of them secretly thinking, "If only those guys knew I have a nipple ring under all this pin-striping..."

In this way, the mass-media assimilation of all things fringe threatens to submerge even the transgressive elements of body decoration. The pain remains, but it is now the routine pain of ear-piercing or wearing high heels—the pain of fashion. Mass culture can be too powerful a force to be challenged effectively by small gestures of individuation. Either they are taken up by the great, pervasive machines of cultural consciousness and reduced to flavour of the month; or they collapse down into mere narcissism. Or, unfortunately, both. The genuinely utopian thought is then threatened with pure extinction—and with it, the ideal of the authentic individual. We are confronted by a central paradox of popular culture: a movement or trend is always over the very moment it becomes visible as one. We are constantly chasing a vanishing point on the spectrum of what is cool, the eternally promised land of true hipness.

Ultimately, however, the moral of the story proves to be familiarly McLuhanesque. Even when the tattoo images are substantively empty or when the pierced body is common, it does not really matter. The medium is the only real message here. The significant thing about extreme body decoration is not the decoration itself, in other words, but the irreducible fact that it appears on the body, the soul's fragile housing. No message, however radical, would have the same force if transmitted merely via T-shirt, ballcap, graffito, or hoarding.

All the same, we might reasonably expect to see more and more extreme acts of cultural rebellion acted out on the last great canvas, the body. Just as rock videos have gotten faster and nastier in recent years in order to snag the wavering attention of an enervated, image-soaked audience, so gestures of cultural defiance may have to get more extreme to make their point of refusing conformity. Even as it gets harder and harder to shock those who toe the line, the desire to shock will get stronger. Some people will want to alter the body beyond all recognition.

■ ▬ ■

Bodily extremists try to overcome social expectations of proper appearance. Other kinds of extremists, drag queens and drag kings, and many kinds of cross-dressers in between, have, in a similar vein, begun to play with the expectations of gender and sex. There is some significant overlap between the two groups, especially in the gay and lesbian communities, and a shared mission of social emancipation draws them together in the midst of proliferating threats. They both seek the authentic self, the self that is not limited by accidents of birth, norms of social control, or dominance by machines.

Ironically, though, perhaps the ultimate challenge to the determinism of biology is precisely one that welcomes technological advances rather than refuses them. Instead of reclaiming the body's materiality in a flight from technological encroachment, some people are using technology to overturn the materiality of the body—by transforming one sex into another. Like the Japanese-Australian performance artist Stelarc, for instance, who straps himself into elaborate virtual-reality machines that create a new electronic body, or the advocates of "ThinkWare" Internet uplinks that are worn on the body like Sony Walkmans, these people seek freedom by embracing technology, not fleeing it. But here the dreams of the few can begin to clash with the desires of the many, turning the joyful vision of a trans-gendered future into a nightmare of confusion and licentiousness. Where some people see only greater freedom in a world no longer ruled by sexual divisions and strong gender roles, others see anarchy and doom, the unfettered bacchanalia of Sodom and Gomorrah just before God's wrath is finally unleashed.

We must not allow ourselves the myopia of imagining that the bending of gender and sexual expectations is new. There are, in both the West and East, long-standing traditions of cross-dressing and deliberate gender confusion, especially important for cultural occasions when anxiety needs assuaging. The ritual confusion of the Jewish holiday Purim, for example, or Mardi Gras are social means of reaffirming normality by playing with it. Or consider the early light comedies of Shakespeare—*A Midsummer Night's Dream, Much Ado About Nothing, As You Like It*—with their themes of identity won and lost, gender roles switched, and lovers gained or misplaced. These plays, all written and performed in the waning days of the sixteenth century, as Shakespeare and his company struggled to succeed despite an outbreak of plague that closed all London theatres between 1592 and 1594, are playfully topsy-turvy. Unlike Shakespeare's darker comedies and bleak tragedies of the early 1600s, when James I had replaced Elizabeth I as his primary patron and the Bard evidently fell into a more depressive mood, these are late-century holidays from social censure. The light comedies, all premiered before 1598, allow us to overturn the normal in a carefully controlled way, and with revealing effect.

However interesting the effects, in essence these inversions of the conventional world function as a way of reassuring ourselves that "normal" is still the norm. Social and cosmic order are eventually restored, the traditional marriage dance performed at play's end to illustrate a new equilibrium. Though these departures from social convention are naturally comic rather than tragic, there is nevertheless catharsis here, the ritual purgation of fear—purgation in these cases through laughter and celebration. It is catharsis of a special sort: the fear in question is not of violent endings and tragic mistakes, as in Sophoclean tragedy, but rather fear of the mysterious Other.

The decadence of the 1890s, when waves of social and cultural transgression coursed through *fin-de-siècle* Europe, went further in its challenges. Faced with a great turning of the calendar wheel, people began to discard accepted gender divisions and standards of sexual propriety. Writing amidst the confusion, in 1892, the German psychiatrist Richard von Krafft-Ebing coined a term to replace what he felt was the unduly judgmental label of "sexual inversion." The term was "homo-sexuality," which Krafft-Ebing spelled with a hyphen—a hyphen you can still sometimes hear in the pronunciation of those hostile to sexual licence. Three years later, Oscar Wilde, arguably the most famous homosexual of the modern era, went to jail for the "abominable crime" of intimacy with his young friend, the callow Lord Alfred Douglas, son of the Marquess of Queensberry. Wilde is in many ways emblematic of the ironies in gender inversion, for he was highly visible, a kind of social superstar, yet widely reviled. After he was released in 1897, Wilde spent the remaining years of the century wandering through Europe. His celebrated life, and his even more celebrated death in Paris in 1900, had the peculiar double effect, characteristic of end-time gender confusion, of promoting an ethos of aestheticism (Wilde's ideas on interior decoration were widely admired and copied), even while his notoriety provoked reactions that drove homosexual culture further underground—where it remained for a long time. (Sex between men remained a criminal act in Britain until the Wolfenden Report was released in 1957.)

When you start to play with gender or sex, the effects cannot be easily controlled. The norm does not necessarily return to its position of prominence. In our own time, transgressions of the normal are virtually constant—we are a culture on permanent holiday. Anticipating the future, some people are even now preaching the value of deep confusion over gender and sex. "Our sexual identity hasn't stabilized, and the good news is it may not," writes the American author known as "Eurydice" in the November 1995 issue of *Spin* magazine.

> The future belongs to radical inter-sexuals, those who defy definition. There will be a shift from a homo-hetero split to a kaleidoscopic perversity, where one will proudly say "I'm a pervert" like one might now say "I'm a father." Dirty words will lose their power to intimidate. Children will study sex. Overpopulation, sperm banks, and in vitro walk-ins will finish the job the Pill began, divorcing sex from procreation.

Eurydice foresees a new millennium in which we transcend the limitations of masculine and feminine—and even of male and female. "Post-millennial eroticism will be inclusive, incoherent, and transgressive," she says. "We'll each make up our life like a work of art, out of imagination and desire."

Is this already happening? Some people think so. Bisexuality, for example, once thought a fringe orientation even among the gay and lesbian community, where it is often shunned as "residual denial" or "lack of commitment," is garnering more social visibility and more political clout. A *Newsweek* cover story on bisexuality in July 1995 challenged that magazine's presumably middle-of-the road readership to confront this new kind of sexual expression—at a time when the majority were probably congratulating themselves for a grudging toleration of gay men. Marjorie Garber's chatty book about bisexuality, *Vice Versa: Bisexuality and the Eroticism of Everyday Life*, appeared around the same time, suggesting to the impressionable that they were surrounded by people ravaged by indeterminate sexual longing.

With the continuum of gender differences and sexual preferences under this kind of popular challenge, maybe it's no surprise that there is a small chorus of voices who want to do away with sexual differences altogether. These "trans-gendered" prophets don't want to play with gender; they want to destroy it in an androgynous millennial vision.

One of the more colourful residents of my diverse Toronto neighbourhood is a beefy transsexual jogger I see three mornings a week huffing and puffing by in matching pink satin shorts and tank top. He/she favours red nail polish and has upper-body musculature to shame a prizefighter. For a while, whenever I saw him/her, I would think, Who does he/she think he/she's fooling? Then finally I realized: fooling people doesn't enter into it. Like it or not, we're all becoming ever more familiar with challenges to hitherto stable categories of race, sexuality, gender, physical ability, even age. If some of us resent the enforced tolerance of political correctness, most nevertheless recognize the basic desire that lies at the heart of these challenges. People badly want to break the connection between biology and destiny. They want to be free.

There are those willing to take an axe even to the most resistant of biological categories. Martine Rothblatt's thesis in her 1995 book *The Apartheid of Sex* is that "sexual dimor-phism"—the deeply embedded notion that the sexes are two—should be jettisoned just as surely as the racial segre-gation of apartheid. "Genitals are as irrelevant to one's role in society as skin tone," Rothblatt writes. "The division of humanity into two sexes is the most long-standing and rigidly enforced of all stereotypes." Stereotypes? The last time I checked, it wasn't stereotypes that appeared to divide humans into two sexes. Genitals may be irrelevant to social role, but surely they're not simply irrelevant. Has Rothblatt confused *gender*, the traits and expectations we label "mas-culine" and "feminine," with *sex*, the biological division into male and female?

No, she hasn't. The challenge of *The Apartheid of Sex*, it turns out, is even more drastic than more familiar attempts to loosen the bonds of gender expectation. If we take chal-lenges to gender roles to their logical conclusion, Rothblatt suggests, the distinction between *male* and *female* disinte-grates just as surely as the distinction between *masculine* and *feminine*. The reason? Try as we might, we can find no differ-ence between the "male" and "female" members of the species that is not susceptible to change. The biology of one's birth is less definitive than it seems at first glance. In this view, the male/female division in genitals is really no more than a crude evolutionary strategy for species sur-vival—and one that our late-millennium technology has rendered moot.

Not that many people are willing to believe this, even now. In his 1995 book *To Renew America*, Newt Gingrich offers the following backward-looking take on recent chal-lenges to gender roles and the resulting hostility between the sexes. "One of the most absurd of modern practices," he writes, "is that 'war between men and women'—as if God didn't make us both male and female, as if both were not necessary for the propagation of the species." Newt hasn't been paying attention. One of the most evident challenges to biological determinism is precisely the fact that with the development of in vitro fertilization, men and women are no longer, as individuals anyway, necessary for that propagation. We still need males to produce sperm to fertilize eggs, but—as a lesbian couple I know proved with the birth of their first child some years ago—that's not much of a scientific trick compared to, say, designing a stable jet airplane or creating an affordable personal computer.

Meanwhile, attempts to localize deeper male-female differences in brain size or functioning have been at best inconclusive. Males do seem to show greater ability to conceptualize space, for example, while females are better at making thematic connections, but it is impossible to be confident that these differences are genuine artifacts of biology and not caused by other factors like selective socialization or even just the in-built biases of the tests. There is a minute difference in average hippocampus size between men and women, but no evidence to suggest this means anything, particularly since there is much more difference within the sexes than between them. Anyway, there is no accepted correlation between brain size and intelligence. In short, when it comes to mental function, we clearly share much more than we don't.

For the critics of sexual division, it follows that sex is just as much an artifact of society as gender. We have organized the species into male and female groups, Rothblatt says, not because there is anything fundamental to the division, but because it has suited our social and political purposes to do so. If those purposes are now changing, among other things to accommodate the claims of women and previously marginalized sexual groups, why not go further? Why not begin to replace sexual dimorphism with a *sexual continuism* that recognizes a potentially infinite variety of sexual identities and orientations, not to mention partners?

Rothblatt even proposes a continuum of colours to describe them: "In the rainbow lexicon of sexual continuity," she writes, "the aggressive element of sexual identity may be represented as yellow, the nourishing element of sexual identity as blue, and the erotic element as red." From these three primary colours, we can construct a multi-hued table of paint-chip sexual orientations, ranging from the comfort of pine green ("a slightly aggressive but mostly nourishing person who does not try to appear sexy") to the edginess of orange ("a non-nourishing person, equally aggressive and erotic"), and pausing almost everywhere in between. Even white and black are included on Rothblatt's table, the former as "a person who feels genderless" and the latter as "a person who feels all elements of gender are constantly in flux."

"A person's nature has nothing to do with gonads," Rothblatt boldly continues. "Natures are transgendered." Thus "manhood and womanhood can be life-style choices open to anyone, regardless of genitalia" and "from the apartheid of sex shall evolve the freedom of gender."

Rothblatt is nothing if not a forward-looker. She knows that even in the anything-goes atmosphere of the mid-1990s the resistance to the proposed paradigm shift will be great—"it will take decades," she acknowledges, perhaps a little optimistically. She offers rejoinders to standard objections, like the "bathroom bugaboo" (that is, who pees where?) and the need for stable government categorization of citizens (just like South Africa's need?). Mostly, she argues, the issues come down to a desire for convenience and sheer resistance to change, neither of which makes a good case for retaining the dimorphic world.

Less compelling are her suggestions for linguistic innovations, like calling marriage partners "spice" (as in, "Are spice invited too?"), replacing "Mr. and "Ms." with the honorific "Pn." (for "Person"), and using the trans-gendered pronouns "heesh" (instead of he or she) and "hirm" (instead of her or him).

Dismantling sexual identity is a steep challenge to the status quo. It's also a challenge to certain kinds of separatist homosexual activism or the forms of feminism based on "womyn's ways of being." The trans-gendered option suggests that these agendas of separateness are regressive; they keep us mired in existing divisions. That may suggest a reactionary tendency in the trans-gendered position, since it appears to undercut some forms of emancipatory political action. But the genius of the view is that it is so far out there that it has simply moved altogether past the dominant rhetoric of male and female, heterosexual and homosexual, mapping out a new world where many of the old grievances have been rendered moot. While the comparison to racial apartheid is a little overdrawn, the confidence of trans-gendered visionaries like Rothblatt is oddly infectious.

It is at the end of *The Apartheid of Sex*, when Rothblatt gets personal in an afterword about her own trans-gendered status, that the issue really comes alive. In fact, this revelation—which will come as little surprise to anyone who has glanced at Rothblatt's author photo, which shows off her prominent Adam's apple and stevedore hands—might have been better placed at the beginning of the book. Like Kate Bornstein, whose own trans-gendered status is the heart of her affecting performance-art pieces and a deeply personal 1994 book called *Gender Outlaw: On Men, Women, and the Rest of Us*, Rothblatt should have had faith that, when it comes to challenging accepted norms, the personal is the political. The fact that Martine used to be (perhaps sometimes still is) Martin strengthens her argument. It shows what many of us perhaps find difficult to grasp: some people have already gone beyond the destiny of their original biology. The trans-gendered option is distant from most people's lives and concerns, but, like many fringe movements, it has effects at the periphery that may, eventually, make their way to the centre.

Nobody said gender revision would be easy, however. Changing power relations and the social definitions that accompany them is always a tricky business. Even going beyond the impasses of recent gender wars between men and women, with their acrimonious cacophony of claim and counter-claim, is proving painful. (This despite Newt Gingrich's well-meaning contribution.) Before those wars are over they will doubtless loose further chaos on our received nostrums and play havoc with existing social relations. Attempts like Rothblatt's to map out new options of gender and sex are even more troubling, especially to those inheritors of the medieval Crusaders' judgmental orthodoxy we know nowadays as the Religious Right or the Christian Coalition.

Increasingly, in a world of constant revision and technologically driven freedom from physical limits, we don't know what to do, what to be. There is great freedom, but also great uncertainty. We can probably expect further rearguard actions, violent attempts to turn back the clock, new and more vicious backlashes. When the challenges push as aggressively as the trans-gendered revolutionaries want them to, the likelihood of nasty reactions is high. Despite all the joyful rhetoric of emancipation among the converted, expectations are hard to change. "For all I know," Eurydice confesses in her look to the future, "in 30 years the death penalty will be due punishment for abortion, civilians who fornicate more than thrice weekly will be caned, erotica will be burned in public, and sodomites will live in catacombs." A recent informal survey of bathroom graffiti at my university showed that the vast majority of pejorative remarks written on the walls were not about those of different races or religious persuasion, but about gay men.

Fear of the Other runs deep. Whatever new forms of

gender or sex the visionaries construct for the third millennium, the hardest task will remain the old one, of accepting those who are different—sometimes in hitherto unimagined ways.

- _ -

There is lots of transgression—of body, gender, and sex—to be seen at the Gay Pride Day parade that Gail and I attend in Toronto in the summer of 1995. "Heterosexuality isn't normal," one man's T-shirt proclaims. "It's just common."

Watching the Pride Day parade, with its array of ever more particular sexual subgroups and special-interest covens—gay and lesbian teachers, gay and lesbian parents, drag queens, Asian drag queens, Asian drag queens who are parents riding motorcycles—it strikes me that if one were moralistic about our culture, one might well view this display as strong presumptive evidence that the world is, in fact, coming to an end. The *decadence* of it all is inescapable. The great bodies, the obvious sexual power, the gleeful refusal of presumed normality—it all seems so apocalyptic, so *fuck you* in its perverse joy.

I find myself enjoying this display of sexual exuberance, but I don't kid myself that mine is a majority view. I imagine my parents, for example, suddenly airlifted into the crowd massed along the street, and I find it surprisingly easy to picture their faces as the waves of shock and disapproval wash over them. They would probably drop dead on the spot. Still, I think most people should go to a Gay Pride Day parade now and then, just to see the array of otherwise cloistered subcultures brought out in strength. The parade has a Mardi Gras air to it, the atmosphere of delighted and defiant overturning of social conventions. It is all tempered, deepened, by a melancholy awareness of those who are not there, the many thousand young men—and women and children—dead of our modern-day Black Death.

The pathos of the missing dead is not confined to the mourners and the AIDS Memorial near the parade route, either. The paraders hold up signs that say "Find a Cure." But these protests seem more obligatory than fervent. The slogan has the weariness of a routine, ongoing search for a cancer cure. These days, the lack of a cure is an accepted fact of medicine's late-century inadequacy, no longer so obviously political an issue.

In the midst of death, we celebrate life—of course. But there is something a little forced, a little fearful about the parade's exuberance. Before my eyes, the celebration becomes a stylized warding-off gesture, an avoidance ritual reminiscent of the crowds of self-mutilating, sexually licentious enthusiasts who followed medieval prophets from town to town in hope of the Messiah's imminent arrival. Gradually, the excesses of the assembled throng—the hyper-feminine drag queen make-up, the whips and leather of S&M slave and master—begin to take on a darker aspect. Because these factors of joy and grief combine so oddly and yet so naturally, a Gay Pride Day parade has, to the fanciful mind, the bizarre and unsettling resonance of a medieval masque or Death March.

These people aren't actually leading us into apocalypse, of course. In fact, maybe, as with other cultural dreams of apocalypse, the causal connection runs the other way: these previously marginalized people are the harbingers, not the causes, of a widespread uncertainty. Perhaps they are the front lines, the avant-garde, of a new millennium in which old sexual certainties—which are really neither that old nor that certain—actually will collapse and be replaced by something far more fluid, more flexible, more unsettling.

As these thoughts are swirling through my head, a dancing parader with the usual washboard stomach of toned abs pushes a leaflet into Gail's hand. I peer over her shoulder to read it. It says, "The Raelian Movement invites you to live the love of differences." Now, I happen to know about the Raelians from following regular reports about them in the undergraduate newspaper published at my university. They are a group of marginal religionists who follow a prophet called (no surprise) Rael, who claims to speak regularly with space aliens called the Elohim. Rael's followers regularly visit college campuses around North America to pass on the good news he has collected from them.

Elohim is actually a Hebrew word that means "those who come from the sky"—C. S. Lewis called the space creatures of his *Silent Planet* science-fiction novels "elohim," and it is, for some people, a synonym for angels. There is even a weird paramilitary group of white-supremacist conspiracy theorists in eastern Oklahoma, led by a Canadian-born preacher named Robert G. Millar, who live in a compound called Elohim City. (Timothy McVeigh, the Oklahoma City bomber, made a telephone call to Mr. Millar two weeks before the April 1995 bombing. Mr. Millar later denied any connection to the attack.) Rael, for his part, says the Elohim are real. He should know; he has talked to them. He even wrote a book about their conversations. It is called, pretty straightforwardly, *The Message Given to Me by Extraterrestrials.*

Why are the Raelians in the Gay Pride Day parade? Since when has the gay and lesbian community been invaded by that other queer subculture, the one in which people claim to converse with space aliens?

Nobody around us seems to know. I look more closely at the leaflet for clues. It is advertising something called "The Awakening Seminar," which seems to be a kind of Raelian rap session designed to increase bodily awareness and, incidentally, self-esteem. The seminar teaches a "technique" called The Awakening of the Mind Through the Awakening of the Body. "After using the techniques that will be taught during this seminar," the leaflet says, "you will notice a marked improvement in your quality of life and your creativity, in your professional as well as the sexual and philosophical life."

Looking around, I think there is plenty of sexual awareness here already, thank you, and nobody seems to be having any trouble at all awakening his or her body. In fact, most of the bodies are, even as I read, half-naked and dancing to a pounding disco bass line.

Six

The Truth Is Out There

It is undesirable to believe a proposition when there is
no ground whatever for supposing it true.

Bertrand Russell, *Sceptical Essays* (1928)

ANTICIPATION HANGS THICKLY
in the room, like mist. Already all the available plastic seats
are filled, several hundred of them, in neat rows of ten.
People are still spilling in from the concourse outside, step-
ping over television cables, staking out sections of floor or
leaning against the walls. I check my watch. It is ten minutes past eight on a rainy Friday night in October. We are
waiting for the chosen ones. They are late.

A few more minutes pass; then the chosen ones at last
appear. In they come, five ordinary-looking people and the
moderator, the journalist John Robert Colombo, walking
through the crowd and onto the little stage. From the people around me I hear an audible sigh or gasp of before-the-
fact appreciation. *Here they finally are.* A man sitting in
front of me, driven to express his emotion further, actually
rubs his hands together. I look around at the rest of the
audience. The usual human mix, I think, young and old,
slim and fat, fashionable and frumpy. It seems entirely normal, as if this were a Friday-night movie screening or a baseball game. They do not, in other words, look like the lost
and confused, the credulous and deluded.

But appearances can deceive. These people are not normal, at least in one crucial respect. With the exception of a

few merely curious spectators—among whom I count myself—the members of the audience are all true believers, dedicated followers of arguably the weirdest prophets of a very weird time. For the people we have all come to see are not the usual brand of celebrity, renowned for ability or insight or looks. They are not even run-of-the-mill prophets, merely claiming to know something the rest of us don't. No, they are the chosen ones, an elite hand-picked by a force beyond human agency. That's right: the five people trooping into the hall have all been "touched" by space aliens. They have been contacted or abducted or simply permitted to observe the silvery space vessels of the visiting extra-terrestrials. They are, as the program says, members of a special subcultural club whose members are known as "alien experiencers."

Waiting for them to arrive has given me ample time to reflect on the role experiencers now seem to play at the fringes of North American culture. Like charismatic medieval prophets, I think, touched by the hand of God and singled out as messengers of doom, these chosen ones are here to tell us what they have seen, to convey messages, to offer reassurances and hope. Like those prophets, too, they have attracted a wide audience of the uncertain and the anxious. The old tales of visions and divine visitations have been altered in their hands, though. They have seen the fire in the sky, yes, but they have changed the foundation of that experience from evidence of God's intervention to proof of the arrival of extra-dimensional visitors. Otherworldly they remain, but in a new spirit.

The people gathered in this hall tonight—and people across the continent—seem all too ready for this post-Christian transformation of the old millennial dream. They understand the new meaning of the sign written across the heavens. In fact, they like the sign's new air of technological promise, evident in those faster-than-light spaceships. They like its oddly comforting confirmation of other intelligence, however hostile, in a universe now known to be unimaginably vast. They are, as Norman Cohn said of medieval Christians who also lived in expectation of visitation from beyond, "at once terrified and enthralled at the imminence" of the visitors' arrival.

Certainly, new communications technology has proved ready to aid the new prophets in their mission. No longer do the chosen ones need to career through cobbled streets shouting their exhortations and declaiming their experiences to the gaping serfs and villeins. No longer is their sphere of influence limited to, say, the Rhine Valley or the English Midlands. Now they tour the continent on a conference circuit run with near-military precision. They publish laser-printed personal newsletters, dominate Internet newsgroups, even broadcast on public-access cable television. And they sport visible signs of their status as chosen ones. In place of the birthmarks or deformities that in simpler times confirmed God's selection, these people display surgical scars on the knee, or in the buttocks, where the aliens have implanted communications chips or otherwise left their calling cards.

But the chosen ones we have come to see tonight seem most like those earlier prophets in one other respect. They claim to have had a distinguishing experience, to have been personally chosen, but they remain, to the naked sceptical eye anyway, entirely self-appointed.

They don't see it that way, of course. No, the aliens have selected the experiencers for a reason, based on some kind of criteria: their insight, their willingness to believe, who knows? Amidst all the confusion—the violence and bewildering complexity of the culture we inhabit, the loss of authority and faith—the chosen ones are messengers of the coming changes. They want to help, to warn. It is not too late—if we are only open to the truth. And the truth *is* out there.

This symposium of experiencers is part of the regular ESP and psychics' fair that I have attended before. This time the fair is held not in the shiny corporate Convention Centre downtown but rather in the distantly suburban International Centre, one of those cheerless exhibition palaces littered like discarded concrete boxes along the strip near Toronto's international airport. The International Centre is actually a glorified bingo hall, with shabby display areas and overpriced food, but it has the overriding virtue of ample size. Its wide expanse is packed with people on the autumn night the other-worlders are in town. The main attractions, the usual psychics and seers of the fair, are already drawing customers in good numbers. More than a hundred such mystics and soothsayers have set up their booths and tables, hung their banners from the cinder-block walls, and begun the characteristic big shill of the psychics' fair: palms read for five dollars, auras photographed for ten, cards deciphered for twenty.

Jostling among the seekers and acolytes, I am pleased to notice that many of the faces behind the tables are familiar. Sister Leona Hartman is here, as is Yogi A. S. Narayana. The psychic known only as "Keith" has a stall set up, and so does Gordon, of "Numerology by Gordon" fame. Hassan Jafer, he of "AstroTrends till the Year 2001!," is hanging around too. The whole gang. Even the Raelians have made the trip, apparently eager to get in on the UFO and alien program. Their presentation, "UFOs—The Truth Revealed," promises little more than further details about Rael's conversations with the Elohim, but I am glad to see them anyway.

I don't see any of my students this time, or anyone else I know personally, but the assortment of gut-heavy middle-agers and quasi-gothic adolescents, complete with their eyebrow rings and purple hair, is the same as before, and I start picking out a few faces familiar from other visits. The regulars, I think; I know them now. But then I realize that they probably recognize me, too. Coming suddenly to mind, this is a deeply disturbing thought: I have become a regular at psychics' fairs in and around Toronto.

The UFO and alien exhibits and displays are new features of the standard psychics' expo, something the organizers have not attempted before. They certainly know which way the *Zeitgeist* has begun to blow by late 1995, though. There is vast crossover potential for them in the UFO and alien theme, lying as it does so close to the cash-down prophecy of the psychics. The desire for other-worldly truth that drives the regular customers here, their fierce need to hear what the future will bring, is shared by this other constituency, whose members believe that the small greys (or the large whites) are coming, from Zeta Reticuli (or the Pleiades), in their saucer-shaped (or cigar-shaped) vessels, to save (or destroy) the Earth. The people in the International Centre cafeteria even mark the momentous occasion of the first-ever UFO and alien symposium by offering some new, though no less exorbitantly priced, dinner specials. In addition to Psychic Chicken Extraordinaire, the menu this evening features Solar Vegetarian Soup and something called UFO Pie, which bears a passing resemblance to the agreeably mundane comfort food my mother taught me to call shepherd's pie.

By the time I arrive, it is clear that the UFO and alien exhibit has instantly become the most popular part of the whole convention, siphoning people away from routine astrological attractions and even, for now, drawing more attention than the real money-maker at any psychics' fair, the chocolate-dipped ice cream cone concession. People are huddled in their dozens around televisions showing a video documenting a celebrated "alien autopsy," performed (as legend has it) on a dead alien found in a spaceship crash near the Roswell Air Force Base in New Mexico on July 4,

1947. Film footage shot after the crash—for years explained by government officials as a weather balloon gone astray—is now the subject of several serious investigations, including one by the respected British documentary filmmaker John Purdie. The video showing at the fair includes interviews with people who witnessed the scene of the crash, and one even shows two short black-and-white film sequences, recently discovered, of what appear to be alien post-mortem examinations, complete with full detail of an egg-headed little grey alien, conducted in the gory aftermath of the crash.

"If it's fake, it's a brilliant one," Dr. Chris Stringer, of the Natural History Museum of London, said of the recovered autopsy film in an interview with *The Guardian* of London. According to the UFO conspiracy theorists, the film was shot by a U.S. Air Force technician and then suppressed for decades by government forces. "But the trouble is that it's an old black-and-white film, and you can't really conclude anything from it," Stringer added. The implications of the question of the film's veracity are huge. This, after all, is the best-documented UFO incident of all time. "If there is even one credible piece of evidence that Earth has been visited by aliens, it changes everything," Richard DeMotto, national security aide to U.S. Senator Robert C. Byrd of West Virginia, says of the Roswell incident. "It only had to happen once."

People around me nod their heads in silent agreement as expert after expert reiterates Stringer's point about the brilliance of the fake. *Who could fake something like that? Who would want to?* It's true that the setting of the filmed autopsy looks genuine enough, with accurate war-era medical technology and a squad of bustling doctors draped in full protective gowns. But the alien himself, his right leg apparently shot or torn away, is to my eye all too obviously constructed of plastic or clay. The film begins to take on an air of unintentional hilarity as the begowned figures stride purposefully around the operating theatre looking grim and scared. They tentatively prod the exposed abdominal cavity of the alien. They lift a clear, retina-like film from the large eye cavity in the bulbous head. The alien's face is frozen in a rictus of simulated pain. It's an *elaborate* fake, certainly, but hardly a brilliant one.

Nearby are even cheesier examples of what initiates usually insist on calling "ufological evidence." Tacked to the wall are a number of colour photographs, taken over the years by a Swiss man called Eduard "Billy" Meier, apparently showing alien spacecraft hovering over the European countryside. Meier has taken more than a thousand of these photos. He also claims to have ongoing contact with the aliens, who come to visit us from the Pleiades star system, thousands of light years away. "As can be expected," the official guide to the exhibit says, "his story has been met with a great deal of resistance. Debunkers and critics alike have been busily at work for nearly two decades trying to expose him. Ridicule and enmity are not strangers to Billy, who as of 1994 had suffered no fewer than thirteen assassination attempts." I can't imagine why anyone would want to kill someone who makes photographs that are about as convincing as the special effects in Ed Wood's *Plan 9 From Outer Space*. Who is he hurting, after all? But in ufological circles, emotion runs deep.

As does conviction. Standing near these people, who examine the Meier photographs with all the attention of art experts in the presence of a Goya and watch the alien autopsy footage with wide-eyed attention, can be a disorienting experience for anyone naturally given to even modest scepticism. It is hard to know how to respond. Clearly, bursts of derisive laughter are not an acceptable option in this company, and anyway the evident seriousness of their attention commands a certain face-value respect. The experience is strongly reminiscent of the mixture of feelings I used to have while attending church as a teenager.

After a time in the presence of the ufological believers, though, I begin to feel a bit like an alien myself, a lone rational being suddenly airlifted into this den of the primitive and the convinced. I look just the same as these people, sure, but inside my head the wiring must be—mustn't it?—all quite different. Suddenly I have a strong sense of identity with the character played by Kevin McCarthy in *Invasion of the Body Snatchers*, running onto the highway in a panic, running from the invading pod-grown aliens *who look just like us*, trying to tell the passing motorists that the world is no longer what they think it is. His panic is the panic of inversion: the alien infiltration has been so successful that now he, not they, is the odd thing out.

Don't panic, I say to myself; *if you don't make a sound, they won't know you're not one of them.*

As I wander through the exhibits and listen to the earnest conversations of the people there, the scene shifts its reference from old science fiction to new. Maybe it's the rainy streets outside, the almost cinematic sheen of the asphalt as I arrived, or maybe it's just the straight faces around me, but I begin to feel as though I have been unwittingly drawn into an episode of the hit television drama "The X-Files." I am in the realm of the paranormal, the unexplained.

"The X-Files" climbed out of cult obscurity during the early 1990s to become a genuine prime-time hit. Its storyline of a government conspiracy to cover up widespread alien abduction was at first glance lifted straight out of bad pulp sci-fi, but it struck an immediate chord with an audience of mostly young, well-educated viewers who came to be known as "X-Philes." The devotion of its early viewers is legendary, and they observe the investigations of the two renegade FBI agents, Dana Scully and Fox Mulder, with an attention to detail as intense as any biblical exegesis.

By 1995, "The X-Files" was one of the most popular shows on television—so popular, in fact, that long-term viewers began to abandon ship because the show was in grave danger of losing its cool edge. On various Usenet newsgroups and Websites, the integrity of new storylines, and the show's new fans, were openly questioned. Bitter arguments broke out among disaffected "X-Files" nerds, just as they had between rival Kirk and Picard factions when "Star Trek: The Next Generation" hit the airwaves in 1987. We all know what happens when a cult goes mainstream: the original cultists, with their unerring instinct and need for novelty, abandon ship and move on to something else.

The fascination of "The X-Files" is still lost on many people, who find it difficult to relate to a show in which two FBI agents, played with admirable woodenness by David Duchovny and Gillian Anderson, gamely struggle with the machinations of their own superiors (and, in the case of Anderson's character Scully, with her own rational scepticism). Moreover, the questions at the heart of the drama seem to many straightforwardly absurd. *Are* there extra-terrestrials living quiet lives as American citizens? *Have* hundreds, maybe thousands, of Americans been transported to outer space for bizarre experiments? *Do* some people indeed have microchips of alien design implanted in their sinuses or buttocks or necks? Occasionally the show gets even crazier than that, with plotlines that veer off into the nutty preoccupations of a supermarket tabloid—fluke-like creatures living in city sewers, people who spontaneously combust, satanic rituals in small-town America. Through all this, though, the dominant theme remains the struggle to wrest information from a brutally secretive, and complicit, government.

The oddness of this quest, in which two licensed government agents battle their own agency, is not lost on devoted viewers. On the contrary, it gives the show its basic counter-cultural appeal. Supported by excellent special effects and the brittle interplay between Scully and Mulder, the show is among the most diverting and intelligent series to emerge from 1990s television. The show's plot development has progressed at impressive speed, restlessly introducing new layers of conspiracy and new oddball characters: an informant called (what else?) Deep Throat, an ubiquitous chain-smoking enemy nicknamed Cancer-man, even a trio of wacko conspiracy theorists who publish a magazine called *The Lone Gunman*. When Mulder, during one show, asks these guys to consider the possibility that the Gulf War was a staged cover-up for UFO landings, one of them laughs and says, "That's why we like you, Mulder. Your ideas are weirder than ours." The show's knowing wit, which trades effectively on the post-Kennedy-assassination memories of its audience, has added even more subversive appeal. In one confrontation with Mulder, Cancer-man utters a classic line: "Don't try and threaten me, Mulder," he says through a cloud of cigarette smoke. "I've watched presidents die."

Mulder himself is a fascinating late-century character. Well-heeled (his family lives on Martha's Vineyard) and well-educated (a doctorate in psychology from Oxford), he is also very cool: he gets to confront the unknown while carrying a gun and wearing a Giorgio Armani trenchcoat. Mulder is a credulous paranoiac, of course, but that's precisely what makes him so good at his job. He feels in some intimate way the pull of wacky explanations, the wild theories offered up for levitations, gory deaths, self-immolations and the like, all the while apparently remaining just this side of outright madness. Innumerable scenes in which he expounds plausible-sounding theories of "the paranormal" to a sceptical Scully are the show's stock-in-trade—and often a source of apparently intentional camp humour. Scully's feisty rationality provides a perfect foil for Mulder's credulity; they are a perfect double-act. And she's not always right, either. In one episode, she was actually abducted herself, presumably by aliens, and examined in the usual fashion described in actual abductee "reports": excruciating brain scans, rectal probes, the works. Scully claims still to be a scientist at heart, but that kind of experience could test a girl's conviction.

Mulder's fanaticism is, by contrast, deeply ingrained and unassailable. It actually reaches back to a formative childhood experience in which his sister Samantha was, according to his hazy memories, bathed in light and carried out the window by a mysterious force. His Washington office is dominated by a standard-issue poster of the aliens-are-among-us subculture, the motto recently sighted too on bumper stickers and T-shirts. Its message? *I Want To Believe.*

Doubt and belief thus twine through "The X-Files"; they are the show's dominant tropes. Its twin mottoes, both utterances of the doomed Deep Throat (he was taken out by government enforcers at the end of the second season), are "The Truth Is Out There" and "Trust No One." In fact, these might be considered the signature tags of a 1990s version of the spiritual quest. Here we seek wisdom by hunting the hidden danger, tracking the threatening sociopath or alien. (One of the most frightening of recent episodes pitted Mulder against an alien hit-man, a sort of off-world terminator, sent to Earth to knock off various renegade aliens living quietly as American citizens.) In this way, the FBI has oddly enough become, under the influence of "The X-Files" and also Jodi Foster's powerful performance as an FBI hunter of serial-killers in *The Silence of the Lambs* (1991), the home of modern paladins, those seer-knights of the old romantic tradition. These film and television paeans to the ideals of FBI integrity are in effect the closest thing we have to the old ballads like the epic *Chanson de Roland*, which praise the dedicated spirit of the First Crusade. The apparently debilitating irony that the FBI is precisely the agency responsible for shutting down anti-government communes like the one immolated in David Koresh's Waco compound is, in "The X-Files" anyway, overcome by Mulder's go-to-hell attitude to his superiors. He affirms that they, not the aliens, are the real enemy.

Not surprisingly, Mulder is wildly popular with the straight-arrow, toe-the-line G-men of the real FBI, who wouldn't be caught dead arguing with a superior, never mind sporting a good haircut or a Hugo Boss tie. Mulder thus becomes an unlikely anti-hero. He is a lonely, paranoid knight for this dark age of unseen dangers, conspiracies, and campaigns of lies. To those of us weaned on Saturday morning cartoons that were broken up by hourly reports on the Watergate scandal, Fox Mulder is somehow completely believable and, what is more, intensely charismatic. His appeal is the paradoxical one of being a hero for a generation without heroes, an isolated government agent in a time when government has increasingly come to represent danger and betrayal rather than protection or honour. Mulder is us.

Then there is the deep, visceral pull of the alien-abduction theme itself. Sightings of UFOs have been common for decades in North America—just as they were also a notable feature of life in the last end-time, the Martian-dominated 1890s, when the artful science fiction of H. G. Wells and others was a powerful literary equivalent of "The X-Files." By the early 1990s, though, mere UFO sightings were apparently no longer enough. Thousands of people were now claiming, sometimes vehemently and in considerable detail, that the UFOs had landed and taken them away for bizarre experiments. These were, as the ufological aficionados like to say, close encounters of the *fourth* kind: not just contact, but hostile contact.

"The victims underwent mind scans," the writer James Wolcott reports of the burgeoning abduction phenomenon.

"[B]lood, semen, and fetal tissue were extracted from them by medical instruments almost medieval in their primitive force. Some had monitoring devices implanted in their sinus cavities. Many abductees—or 'experiencers,' as some preferred to be called—underwent regressive-hypnosis therapy to recall the trauma in full Technicolor, and joined support groups." Wolcott, setting out this list of brutal medical procedures in his review of a thick 1995 book called *Close Encounters of the Fourth Kind: Alien Abduction, UFOs, and the Conference at M.I.T.*, by C.D.B. Bryan, manages to identify not merely the cultural phenomenon of the abductees, but also the strangely serious attention they now seem to garner from otherwise impeccable journalistic and scholarly sources. In fact, the incidence of serious journalistic and academic interest in abduction tales constitutes, as Wolcott suggests, a phenomenon worthy of its own X-File.

Bryan, for example, is the author of *Friendly Fire*, a well-regarded book on the Vietnam War, and also of a straightforward, detailed history of the National Geographic Society. The book jacket of *Close Encounters* describes him accurately as "a much admired journalist" and makes much of the fact that one such as he should find the M.I.T. conference, a formal gathering of abductees, worth considering, at length and with a straight face, in his brick-like work of first-person reportage. *The Atlantic Monthly*, which anyone would regard as a serious magazine, published in 1991 a long, deferential article about an annual gathering of abductees in Wyoming. The philosopher Charles Fort, appearing in mid 1995 on a television show with the aptly nutty title "Mysterious Forces Beyond," urged "systematic observation of paranormal phenomena"—a phrase straight out of the Fox Mulder lexicon. John E. Mack, a renegade professor of psychiatry at Harvard Medical School, has written several books on abductee experiences, including the hot-selling 1994 effort *Abduction: Human Encounters With*

Aliens. Mack is, in Wolcott's words, "to alien abduction what R.D. Laing was to schizophrenia: the magnet, the rebel visionary, the throbbing brains."

These well-known examples are really just the tip of the iceberg, however. According to J. Allen Hynek, a former adviser on UFOs to the U.S. Air Force and founder of something called the Center for UFO Studies in Chicago, anywhere from thirty to two hundred "respected" academics now form what Hynek calls an "Invisible College" devoted to abduction studies—the wide range of numbers indicating, I suppose, just how invisible some of them must be. Though these shadowy alien academics fear academic reprisal with a degree of anxiety approaching paranoia, their wariness is probably entirely rational under the circumstances. The important thing is that these people are not obviously loony or otherwise unbalanced, which is precisely what makes the seriousness of their investigations so unsettling. Like a few other observers of the recent abduction phenomenon as a cultural trend, Wolcott is well aware of the irony in this serious interest in the paranormal. His review of Bryan's book is adorned with the nicely turned subhead "Strange but true: Ph.D.s get serious about U.F.O.s."

That the medical procedures described in the abduction tales are so ridiculously primitive, not to mention rooted in very down-to-earth fears—"Why," Wolcott asks, "would entities capable of transcending space-time and wafting people through walls be conducting rudimentary Roto-Rooter rectal exams and siphoning semen?"—seems not to have occurred to Mack and the other serious investigators of the abductions. Or, if it did, it apparently made no difference to their willingness to believe abduction narratives. Mack for one is a believer already, at least in the sense of finding the reports of abductees psychiatrically plausible. For him, they pass the so-called "sincerity test." In other words, by all standard indicators these people actually believe that they were laid out on shiny alien tables and poked and prodded. Whatever else is going on, they are not lying—that is, uttering deliberate falsehoods. But how far does that judgment of sincerity really carry us? James Gleick, reviewing Mack's last book about abductees in *The New Republic*, summarized the argument with the following mock syllogism: "People think they were abducted. They don't seem crazy. We're experts on mental illness. Therefore, people were abducted."

Bryan's tome mixes in a little bemused humour at the beginning, but the book's overall tone is one of genuine sympathy and respect. Through the course of the conference, Bryan tells us, he found himself coming to treat the abductees with more and more seriousness. He eats meals with them, listens to them talk, hangs out with them—and decides that they are not deluded. In the end, he dismisses his own initial dismissiveness and reaches the conclusion that, at the very least, "something mysterious is going on" in the heavens. A decisive turning point in his change of heart comes when he hears a woman describe how an alien tried on her high heels; this detail convinced him, he said, that she was telling the truth. "*What possible reason could the woman have to make up an incident like that?*" he wonders, in slightly hysterical italics.

■ ▄ ■

Compared to that kind of exquisite detail, the Toronto abductee symposium starts off a little weakly. John Robert Colombo opens the proceedings by expressing his own mod-estly sceptical view of abduction and contact reports. "Though there is a great deal of evidence of alien contact with humans," he says, "there is no proof." This telling observation, which is meant to express the important dis-tinction between what is merely reported and what can be demonstrated, is seemingly lost on the audience, at least where I'm sitting. My neighbours begin to grumble and enter into whispered disquisitions about the vast number of sightings. Over a million people have been abducted in North America, one man says. One in ten people has had some contact with aliens, another adds. If that's not proof, what is? (According to statistics collected by the U.S. Air Force, the numbers *are* quite shocking: about 3.7 million Americans, or about one in a hundred, actually claim to have been abducted.)

The first panelist, Drew, a tall man in his thirties, brings us back to the first-personal essence of the matter. He saw a UFO only once, he tells us, while caddying for his father on an Alberta golf course in the late 1960s. It was July, and he was twelve years old. The ship was, he says, "a spherical metal object that was not moving and had heat waves emanating from it." Appreciative murmurs from my neighbours. Drew, who is now an investigator with the Toronto branch of the Mutual UFO Network (MUFON), goes on to say that the incidence of alien reports is going up: MUFON-Toronto gets between 150 and 200 a year, mostly from southern Ontario. But most of the reports, more than 90 percent, are proven to be hoaxes or otherwise explicable.

The audience, evidently keyed up for tales of semen-siphoning and the rectal probe, is not pleased to hear the news. Drew and a fellow MUFON investigator called Tom are politely applauded, but the general disapproval is obvious.

Joyce, a chunky woman with shoulder-length hair and a rather grating voice, offers more of what the crowd is here for. A former newspaper reporter—and therefore, she seems to suggest, a sort of reformed or converted sceptic—Joyce begins her recitation with what she regards as a crucial distinction. She says the abduction language is too hostile to describe what happened to her when she was a six-year-old girl nestled comfortably in her bed one night. "I am not an abductee," she tell us, "I am a contactee."

Joyce's story is a classic of the genre. "They came through the wall, picked me up and the next thing I know I'm hovering above my house," she says. "It's bright, bright, bright as day. I saw the ship above me, with red, yellow, and blue lights." She was then effortlessly conveyed into an aperture that opened up in the bottom of the hovering ship. The aliens, who were about five feet tall, then moved Joyce into a dark area of the ship, where they waited while their large sensitive eyes adjusted to the dim light. They then began the fabled medical experiments, though in this case the procedures were oddly benign and mostly painless. Instruments were held near Joyce's eyes as the aliens attempted, she thinks, to feed important information directly into her mind. But this force-feeding of data failed to take hold in the six-year-old Joyce's brain. "It gave me a headache, quite frankly," she tells us. The next thing she knew she was back in her bed, waking up to the morning sun.

I like the simplicity of Joyce's tale—even if its details are oddly familiar. Joyce tells us how she came by these memories of this early experience with the aliens, which has not been repeated since. ("They couldn't lift me up now," she jokes to the audience, "that's why they haven't been in touch since then.") It seems that she "recovered" the memories of the incident, repressed for so long as a result of (yes) post-traumatic stress disorder, by regressing to her earlier stage of development through the agency of hypnotic therapy. She recovered these important memories, she tells us, by entering the hypnotic trance on three occasions only, and she offers a stern warning to the many people who are now seeking early abduction memories by excessive use of hypnotic method. "I do not condone repeated use of hypnotic regression," she says with emphasis. "Forty times is *too many*."

Still, now that Joyce has recovered the memories, they are as bright, bright, bright as day. She speaks movingly of her "sense of mission" and the "deep, ingrained" certainty she now has that she was specially chosen by the visitors. "I'm an edge," she says, comparing developing human consciousness to a jigsaw puzzle that is gradually being assembled by forces beyond us. "I'm an awakener."

Okay. But what was the aliens' message to the planet, anyway? Did she manage to haul in any concrete information before the headache blocked off further saturation? "Mostly it was just peace, love and understanding. And what's wrong with that?" she demands in response to an unvoiced challenge from the audience. "We could all use a bit more of that, you know." She swivels her head around, her eyes a searchlight for potential objections. Joyce then concludes her recitation of the experience with a neat psycho-spiritual twist that makes alien abduction out to be rather like an extreme form of self-realization therapy. "This experience taught me that we're all important," she says. "Don't let anyone tell you what to do. *You're important.*"

Another woman, Kathy, has also been in close contact with the aliens, and she now begins to recount her tale with the flat precision of an oral examination. Kathy is young, perhaps in her mid-twenties, and sports a neat outfit of plaid blazer, turtleneck, and slacks. She has sharp features and puffy, quasi-big hair. She is, she says, "an experiencer and a futurist" and comes from a long line of people who talk to extra-terrestrials on a regular basis. "Our family has been in contact with the higher intelligence since 1970," she says. "I just keep a record of everything that comes in—the transmissions—usually in the form of automatic writing."

The aliens Kathy knows are seven feet tall, not five, and they are "beautiful, bright creatures" who "are strictly interested in the evolution of this planet and the solar system." They worry that "we're accelerating natural disasters on the planet" and they want to help. "They're going to come in great multitudes," she goes on. "They would love to be in contact with more people, but you have to be open and receptive to them. If you haven't been contacted yet, you will be. You will know them by their light. We should," she concludes, "be prepared for the acceleration of our spiritual gifts" in the years that remain before the millennium.

This is all a bit touchy-feely, and like Joyce, Kathy is insistent that the aliens are up to only good things. Her recital prompts a shouted question from a young man in the front of the audience who is dressed all in black. What about all the stories of painful medical experimentation, he wants to know. Even Joyce has mentioned the eye-probes and her resulting headache. What do the aliens really want?

Errol, the final member of the panel, is a member of MUFON who had his own UFO experience while serving in Libya with the British Army's Royal Signal Corps in the 1950s—asleep one night in his tent, he saw the standard bright light and hovering silvery shape. Errol grabs the microphone and answers the young man. "They need our bodies because we're genetic experiments for them," he says. "They need our females for their eggs, for cross-breeding purposes. They are here to treat us like lab animals."

A general stir in the gathered audience. But why has this not come to the world's attention, the man in black wants to know. "A great deal of scientific work has been done on this, very quietly," Errol replies, "and it has been suppressed by the government." The questioner looks unconvinced, but Fox Mulder would know exactly what Errol is talking about. There must be some kind of high-level government conspiracy going on, because only that can explain why there are so many first-person reports but no accessible documentation of alien visitation. "*Obviously*," Errol says, "obviously, there's something going on that somebody, somewhere, knows about. And if I die before I find out what's going on, I'm going to be extremely pissed."

His comment brings a hugely positive response from the crowd. In fact, Errol's matter-of-fact claims about egg-stealing and cross-fertilization seem to initiate a free-for-all among the panelists. There is some sharply stated disagreement. "The ones *I'm* in contact with have nothing to do with experiments and sticking things in people and all that garbage," Kathy says to Errol a bit testily. "They're so far beyond that. It makes them sound *ridiculous*."

"There are so many different kinds of beings, entities, extra-dimensional presences," adds Joyce. "I don't hang out with bad people on Earth and I don't hang out with bad entities either." Tom, silent for some time, pipes up. "But it's all coming from one source," he says. He mentions his research showing that certain gene configurations and disadvantaged socio-economic groups are apparently targeted for contact. The others look at him and nod warily.

The floor has now been opened up to questions and a long line quickly forms behind the microphone. A teenager in baggy jeans and a T-shirt wants to know if the aliens have indicated to Kathy or anyone else the truth of something that he's heard, namely, that the Oklahoma City bombing was actually masterminded by the Japanese. "I don't know about Japan bombing the United States," Kathy says matter-of-factly, as if he had just dialled up directory enquiries. "I haven't been given that information." A fat guy with late-Elvis sideburns wants to know if a recent increase in meteor activity is actually alien ships being shot down by U.S. Air Force missiles. Tom thinks not, otherwise there'd have been a much more violent response from the aliens; big battles, major casualties, the whole deal. "You can't shoot down the space brothers," Joyce tells the questioner in a slightly condescending tone. "They're extra-dimensional, and they're really fast."

Some people in the audience are no longer interested in

asking questions. Instead they are elbowing their way to the microphone and, all unbidden, sharing contact or abduction experiences. The atmosphere in the lecture changes from a routine panel discussion to something like an old-time revival meeting or one of those charismatic televangelical healing sessions. A large man with thick glasses recounts his experience of sighting a UFO that was, remarkably, neither saucer-shaped nor silvery. "It was large and square," he says, "sort of like a low-rise apartment building." A beautiful young woman with a crystal-and-silver necklace and an aura photograph pinned to her dress approaches the microphone and tells of her battle with a group of evil aliens she calls "the core mutants." "They attacked me with evil energy, but I'm a psychic and I enveloped myself in white light to protect myself and I struggled with them for two hours," she tells us in a quavering voice. "I managed that night, but other people may need to know."

The panel is silent for a moment. The core mutants? Then Kathy, apparently never at a loss for long, comes to the rescue. "Those particular ones are being driven out," she tells the woman, who appears genuinely terrified—she won't even say the phrase "core mutants" more than once because she says it gives her the creeps. "The planet is beginning to attract more advanced space beings." Adds Joyce, in what appears to be a gloss on the whole egg-theft issue Errol raised earlier: "This is actually genetic upgrading they're going through. They're trying to enrich their own species, to bring it back."

"But are they like prospectors?" a woman in her twenties now wants to know. "Sometimes I feel like we are just a piece of real estate to them." "No, no," says Kathy, "the earth is a free-will zone" and we will not be overrun because we have the spiritual wherewithal to resist any colonization. Alternatively, our spiritual evolution will render invasion undesirable. "The awareness on this planet *is* growing,"

Joyce chimes in.

The talk of spiritual growth and free-will zones seems to reassure some of the younger people in the audience. But one teenage boy now grabs the microphone and asks whether the aliens have said that Toronto in particular is in any kind of danger. The man next to me snorts in some form of disgust at this naiveté—as if the aliens care about Toronto!—but I can't help thinking it's a pretty good question. "Toronto is definitely in a precarious position," Kathy tells us, catching my neighbour and much of the audience off-guard. She mentions a coming wave of devastating "underground fires" and earthquakes. "But my purpose is not to instil fear," she quickly adds as people begin to shift uncomfortably in their chairs and gaze toward the door. "You have to trust your own inner guidance. There will be warnings. If you're in touch with your higher self, there will be lots of time when things are imminent."

This hint of apocalypse alters the discussion's tone in interesting ways. The anxiety that has been in the room from the beginning is now suddenly obvious, explicit, no longer muted or politely tucked away. By this time, too, the young man all in black has worked his way through the line again. I decide I like him; he's a worrier. He is now visibly upset and gives voice to a concern that has seemed to hover, unspoken, throughout the discussion. "We hear all these predictions, in Nostradamus and elsewhere, about the bad things that are coming," he says, his voice rising in an open display of millennial anxiety. "*Something's* going to happen in the next few years. *What do the aliens have to do with it?*"

"It's true," Joyce concedes, "that we're living in a tremendously polarized time—in the weather, in society, in the culture. This is like a revolution. There's turmoil, there's all kinds of crap. But in the end there's going to be something tremendously good."

"They have come to help," Kathy says soothingly. "But

we have to clean up this mess that we have created. They just want us to evolve."

"Remember *The Day the Earth Stood Still*," Joyce adds, referring, a little obliquely, to the classic science-fiction film in which the alien called Klaatu, bringing only a message of peace and goodwill, is destroyed by paranoid earthlings who think he must be dangerous. "The assistance will come," Kathy says. "But you have to be open."

— — —

Like Bryan, I admire the high heels detail provided by the woman at the M.I.T. conference, just as I admire the barefaced confidence of Joyce and Kathy, snapping out their answers to tentatively sceptical questions. But I suppose to my ear these pat stories smack more of well-oiled imaginations than a telling sincerity of belief. If you told a tale often enough, it would almost certainly begin to take on the filigree detail of truth. You might just come to believe it had actually happened even if it hadn't. ("What I say three times," said Lewis Carroll, "is the truth.") Indeed, James Wolcott reports that many of the abductees he interviewed, for a book project later abandoned, were slick master-narrators of their tales. "Their confessions didn't need to be wrested from them," Wolcott writes, "they were eager to expound their ardent monologues—so full of fetal imagery, from the womb-like interiors of the spaceships to the baby-headed aliens, and so similar to accounts of being 'born again.' They felt similarly 'chosen.' For them, the aliens were agents of spiritual growth, guardian angels zooming around like the Jetsons."

Are the hovering aliens targeting certain social groups for contact? Maybe. But maybe it's simply that the members of these groups are predisposed, for social or psychological reasons, to believe that they have been contacted. Of course, experiencers claim that the aliens only contact those who are "open" to their visits, handily explaining why, like ghosts and vampires, the aliens never show themselves to those, like John Robert Colombo, who really care about proof of their existence. In any event, this exclusivity of the contact experience is regarded as a clear advantage among the contacted. They represent a select group who speak frequently and passionately of their feelings of having been singled out for an all-important mission.

It is also significant in this regard that the details of the abduction experience are so remarkably similar from case to case. This convergence of detail suggests to some, of course, a telling case for prima facie plausibility—the tales *must* be true if they all report the same things—but it hints to others of a deeply recombinant culture in which individuals, knowingly or not, "borrow" details, even whole experiences, from the free-floating grab-bag of the popular imagination. The standard imagery of alien abduction is both obviously and intensely religious—it comes straight out of an old copy of *Illustrated Bible Tales*. The abduction experience carries strong messages of uplifting singularity and old-fashioned salvation. The abducted individuals are forcible converts, like Saul on the road to Damascus. Knocked from their beds or lifted from their automobiles, they are bathed in white light, transfixed by a powerful beam, then lifted and drawn through the air to the waiting Mother Ship. Abductees speak of being called away, in the grip of a vocation, of being sucked up to a literally higher power. This aspect of spiritual awakening in the alien-abduction fringe, something strongly in evidence during the Toronto symposium, begins to suggest that abduction tales really function as the newest, and the most unanswerable, form of personal religious experience. The tales show, indeed, yet another new shape that the Rapture described in John's Revelation can take in our times.

Typically, too, as Wolcott cannily remarks, the experience has a fetal aspect—abducted experiencers enter the hovering alien craft through a slit or aperture or other quasi-vaginal openings. Once inside the ship, whose interior is almost invariably dark, murky and warm, they are tested and probed, sometimes almost tortured, but often simply examined with well-meaning curiosity. Though it can be painful, the abduction is experienced as a kind of return to the womb. The experience is one of helpless release, of surrender to something bigger than oneself. It is also, of course, a stiff challenge, for the return to this world has all the sharp discomfort of birth.

So far, the alien abduction scene has remained cosily small. The experiencers gather at conferences like the one at M.I.T., the annual abductees' hoe-down in Wyoming, or the Toronto symposium. Collected together, they offer each other support even as they continue to argue about the details. If the Toronto meeting is anything to go by, though, we can, as the decade advances, predict that more and more people will be elbowing their way into this newly appreciated abduction fraternity, giddy with spiritual wonder and the prospect of a slot on daytime TV. It is a growth industry, especially so long as otherwise sane people like journalists and Harvard professors give it the time of day.

C.D.B. Bryan speculates about some of the possible causes of the recent growth in stories of alien abduction, surveying the suggestions from the psycho-spiritual (the bare need to believe) to the political (those well-meaning messages of human goodwill), but he entirely ignores the millennial influence on the abduction phenomenon—an explanatory dimension that in a way encompasses all the others. He cannot see that people are desperately seeking the visitations of the aliens, at least in part because they can no longer easily understand their own fellow humans or the situations in which they find themselves. The sense of helplessness that pervades ufological gatherings, while initially caused by disturbing events in the wider world, is powerfully reinforced by the great cultural turning-point the millennium represents—even (perhaps especially) if that reinforcement is largely the result of cultural pressures and internal, conventional expectations rather than anything real about the coming event. These people *want* something to be happening out there. The calendar's turning-point strongly heightens that sense of expectation.

So caught up is he in the will to believe the scarred veterans of alien medicine that Bryan opts in the end for a generalized fuzziness of well-meaning credulity. So many people appear to believe, he says, that there must be something to it: the sincerity test writ large. But in effect, like Fox Mulder, he really just *wants to believe*, and that leads him astray. Missing the connection to 2000 is, as Wolcott points out, "a major omission" in Bryan's discussion, and one that appears to prevent him and others from understanding the cultural meaning of the abduction phenomenon. Wolcott, citing historical studies like Hillel Schwartz's *Century's End* that detail popular delusions and widespread credulity in fraught times, concludes that "[s]ince we're coming to the end of not only a century but a millennium, no doubt even more daemons and phantoms are about to flood the portals." Imagining that the aliens are coming—that, in fact, they are already here among us, and have been for some time—is just the kind of thing we humans have always done when faced with the uncertainty of the future. That this future is marked by an admittedly arbitrary deadline does nothing to change this particular quirk of human nature.

The fleets of alien ships that abductees suggest are lying in wait just out of Earth's orbit become, like so many features of millennial dreams, simultaneously reassuring and terrifying. The prospect of a close encounter hovers uncertainly—and perhaps inevitably—between a third-kind close encounter of cosiness and spiritual communion, in which the awestruck individual gets to be like Richard Dreyfus walking into the brightly lit music-machine spaceship, and a fourth-kind close encounter of horror, alien experimentation, vicious dissection, dismemberment, and torture: a prolonged visit to the demon proctologist in hell. Do you want to believe?

▬ ▄ ▬

The duality of reassurance and terror, the third-kind / fourth-kind dialectic, surely explains much of the mid-1990s appeal of "The X-Files." Yet this travelling roadshow of the abduction community, which has to be seen not to be believed, makes it hard to imagine where a show like "The X-Files" can now go. For some time, the show maintained a high level of viewer interest by branching out from alien abductions to other reported areas of the "unexplained" to find new sources of weirdness. Already Mulder and Scully have investigated voodoo, cannibalism, cattle mutilations, killer viruses from outer space, genetically altered people whose shadows destroy anyone they touch, and Damien-like possessed children.

But, like all forms of speculative fiction, the alien-abduction genre that the producers of "The X-Files" tap into is one increasingly obviated by actual events that outstrip its ability to shock and entertain. When the real world is even weirder than the world of "The X-Files," in other words, the show might come to seem outdated, like science-fiction stories from the past: why bother? It is even possible that the weird feedback loop the show has established with its fringey audience has encouraged further reports of alien abduction and other paranormal events—even as the show continues to draw its plotlines from earlier reports. A two-part episode in November 1995, for example, hinged on the discovery of an alien-autopsy videotape—a real-world analogue that had already been used by the "Star Trek" producers, who the month before had had a ship of aliens crash-land in

1947 New Mexico. Not surprisingly, abduction tales recounted at North American conventions are now taking on the nuance and texture of the special effects created by the state-of-the-art technicians of "The X-Files." You can't help thinking that it is only a matter of time before the show folds back on itself completely by doing an episode on, I don't know, millenarian cults that flourish among TV-saturated pop-culture scavengers.

To this point, the genius of the show's writing has lain in its ability to dance nimbly along a line separating plausibility and paranoia when dealing with these phenomena. Almost everything that's happened to Mulder and Scully since the show began could admit of both paranormal and scientific explanation, and that finely maintained tone explains the show's enduring appeal even among savvy and sceptical viewers. Mulder and Scully are in this respect like the publishers of well-meaning critical investigations of the paranormal such as the Toronto-based monthly newspaper *The X Chronicles*, whose editors I met at their booth at the psychics' fair.

The paper is, according to its director of research, Martin McLean, "the official publication of the Canadian Registry of Paranormal Activity." Martin, a lanky man in his late twenties who bears an odd and to me unsettling resemblance to David Koresh, is a member of this registry; he even lists the initials CRPA after his name on the paper's masthead as proof of his accreditation. *The X Chronicles*, he tells me, has been publishing since March 1995, and its researchers investigate all manner of paranormal activity, from animal ESP and levitation to crop circles and theosophical claims. "The strange and bizarre, the revolutionary and outrageous, the factual and the fraudulent, the ancient and the modern—all catch and hold interest, however briefly, in the great sprawling storehouse of the unknown," the paper's publicity material says. "Yet, there exists in this remarkable repository, so rich in odd occurrences, unusual claims and provocative theories, a constant presence. That presence is the human mind."

Despite this suggestion that "the unexplained" might be explained as various forms of mental illness, the editors of *The X Chronicles* remain resolutely open-minded about reports of weirdness. "Progress owes much to the willingness of such brave people as Newton, Darwin, Mme. Curie and Einstein to pursue unthinkable thoughts down seemingly non-existent avenues," they say. "The unknown did not send men scurrying for cover but drew them onward." "Please," they conclude, "tell us your encounter with the strange, unknown, bizarre, or paranormal."

This spirit of open scientific inquiry is in some ways an admirable posture from which to assess reports of the unexplained. Yet there are unforeseen dangers in taking them too seriously. The line between the plausible and the bizarre can actually slip from view as one delves more deeply into the fertile ground of paranoia in which the alien-abduction and conspiracy communities flourish. This is already evident in the very latest plot developments of "The X-Files," which have taken us into alien clones of human subjects, Nazi and Japanese experiments with alien-human hybrids and mountain vaults housing detailed records for everyone born in the United States since the Second World War.

This risks becoming silly, and that would certainly kill the show's delicately balanced entertainment value. In one crucial sense, though, "The X-Files" is already a cultural artifact. A network TV special on the show was aired in the spring of 1995, a sure sign that its stock on the cool index is rapidly falling. Various spin-off shows of similar self-conscious weirdness—"The Outer Limits," "Dark Skies," even one called "Millennium"—have begun appearing on the Fox network and elsewhere, and several alien-invasion films have made their way into cinemas. By early 1995, entire

"X-Files" conventions were beginning to happen in the dire "Star Trek" mode, complete with appearances by bit-part actors and assorted computer geeks in costume wandering through the lobbies of airport hotels.

Nevertheless, "The X-Files" has crystallized a particular form of end-time anxiety. It provides a focus for aimless expectation of visitation and distrust of government—standard features of millennial unease—even as it draws an audience from a young and well-educated minority who feel themselves generally out of step with mainstream culture. These people are not so much the much-discussed twentysomethings as the slightly older and arguably more cynical half-generation now in their early thirties. The members of the group, who are really the ones Douglas Coupland was talking about in his novel *Generation X*, are the Watergate kids, the leaderless lump caught between the massively self-obsessed Baby Boom and the new generation of Nintendo-educated youngsters who Coupland tells us hail from a place called "Shampoo Planet." The uncertainty, even paranoia, many of them feel is exactly mirrored in the subtle contours of "The X-Files." In short: X meets X.

—–—

The experience of listening to the experiencers at the Toronto convention convinced me that, in our culture, anxiety is what sociologists like to call "overdetermined." That is, there are so many things to be anxious about, so many ways to be it, that anxiety sometimes detaches from real causes and becomes (as Sigmund Freud put it) free-floating, without particular referents: angst. Existentialist philosophers argued that such aimless anxiety was simply "a condition of being." Whether angst is really a condition of being, I don't know; I do know that it is frequently accentuated by events in the world. Non-specific anxiety attaches itself to isolated or partial truths and causes us to erect, on that basis, full-blown theories of external control and personal helplessness.

One staple theme of "The X-Files" has always been Mulder's frequent encounters with other conspiracy theorists, most of whom regard him as a de facto hero and leader. Social cast-offs, the sort of people who in another era would have been hippies, they wander around the country in motor homes equipped with satellite hook-ups and computer scanners for tracking the movements of hostile and secretive government forces. In their wanderings they may encounter another marginal community, the one building compounds and stockpiling automatic weapons. Here a curious overlap emerges, in which the extreme anarchist left-wing, often pierced, tattooed and decked out in sandals and army surplus clothes, crosses into the political territory occupied by the extreme libertarian right-wing, with its shaved heads, marching boots, and genuine mail-order fatigues. According to the show's producers, "The X-Files" appeals to these two marginal groups with about equal force, even while now pulling its largest audience share from among the merely curious and modestly sceptical mainstream.

And little wonder, for the show now vividly depicts the very world of interconnected government power-grabs and repression that these people have constructed in their own minds. Given the show's excellent record of picking up strange cultural ephemera, the regular appearances of these lunatics on the show suggests that there is a small but formidably well-equipped and computer-savvy subculture of cover-up-busting vigilantes. And it's true. The numerically tiny conspiracy-theory fringe in North America and Europe is very active. Fox Mulder is not the only one who is actively trying to bring the news of government perfidy with respect to alien visitations.

When I was in London in May 1995, the death of one of the pillars of this community received prominent attention in the serious daily newspapers. He was, after all, a peer of the realm: Brinsley LePoer Tench, otherwise known as the eighth earl of Clancarty. Lord Clancarty's family motto, *The Guardian* noted at the time, was "By Counsel and Prudence," but, the writer suggested dryly, the peer "refused to allow himself to be beset by these narrow horizons." "He could trace his peerage back to Galway in 1793," the article goes on, "yet he dated his true inheritance much earlier, to 65,000 B.C., when aliens landed on Earth and seeded the human race."

"The Earth was colonized by space travellers and we are all descended from them," Clancarty once said. "We all came from different planets originally, that's why there are different people with different coloured skins." He believed that a conspiracy of presidents (American, French, and Russian), aided by the film director Steven Spielberg, was preventing this knowledge from becoming common. In his seven books and many articles in the *Flying Saucer Review*, Clancarty outlined his belief in Shamballah, a mystical island in the Gobi desert where advanced beings make their home. He also believed in a civilization beneath the Earth's crust, reached by tunnels from the North and South Poles and Tibet—a weird echo of the believers in Atlantis, who think the fabled civilization lies beneath Antarctica. "From what I can gather," he once said, "these beings are very advanced." Clancarty was not a talented debater. Once, challenged to prove that aliens were on Earth, he said, "Well, you do see a lot of strange people about, don't you?"

His death, at the age of eighty-three, was greeted with sympathy and even respect in the House of Lords, where he had more than once debated the need for government to prepare for an imminent space-alien visit. In 1979, with false UFO sightings widespread following the success two years earlier of Spielberg's film *Close Encounters of the Third Kind*, Clancarty tried to keep the debate on track. "Suppose the UFOnauts decided to make a mass landing in this country tomorrow," he said. "There could be panic because our people have not been prepared." The reaction of Clancarty's peers provides support for a long-standing suspicion about British class divisions: upper-class madmen are "noted eccentrics" who enliven slow afternoons in the Lords; lower-class madmen rave on street corners and risk being hauled away to brutal incarceration. They die forgotten, not eulogized in *The Guardian*.

Like "The X-Files," Clancarty's example underlines the strong, even crucial connection that exists between believers in alien visitation and devotees of worldwide conspiracy theories. The connection stretches at least as far back as the Project Bluebook conspiracy of the 1960s, which I remember as a hot debating topic among the dough-heads in my junior-high schoolyard. The CIA, we learned, had covered up extensive evidence of alien visitation, including the material compiled after the Roswell crash—evidence gathered by the U.S. Air Force and contained in a group of files known collectively as "the Blue Book." The Bluebook Project is therefore one important real-world inspiration for what Mulder and his fictional FBI cohorts know as the X-Files. Another such source is the clutch of military documents known only by their official designation "MJ 12." I heard about the MJ 12 documents at the UFO and alien symposium, where a small fat man wearing a baseball cap told a group of people that these documents contained the real key to government repression of abduction evidence.

The writer Scott Van Wynsberghe recounted some of his experiences as an unwilling member of this conspiracy subculture in a couple of 1995 newspaper articles. A long-standing JFK junkie, Van Wynsberghe had begun devoting his time to pursuing the truth of the Tragedy in Dallas while still a young man. He was moved by quasi-scholarly interest and at first found many serious companions on this particular road to knowledge. But then he quickly found himself surrounded by less stable researchers. "Ice bullets and agents provocateurs were not what I expected when I entered the JFK field back in 1983, all eagerness and credulity," he wrote in *The Globe and Mail*. "Sure, I figured, there would be some awkwardness around the margins, but the rest seemed solid enough. Then came international banking plots, giant penises, flying saucers and the abominable snowman."

Soon Van Wynsberghe was receiving copies of publications called *Conspiracies Unlimited* or *The Conspiracy Tracker*, which laid bare Nazi-satanic plots to stockpile gold, international conspiracies of Jewish bankers, or cabalistic attempts to exploit UFO hysteria as a means of social control. There was even—echoes of *The Lone Gunman* in "The X-Files"—something called *Grassy Knoll Gazette*, which moots such theories as flying metal darts fired from an umbrella gun and the idea that Kennedy was killed by Freemasons. (There was an obelisk, standard symbol of international Masonry, in Dallas's Dealy Plaza—just as there is on U.S. money: the Washington Monument. And we all *know* George Washington was a Mason.) Van Wynsberghe says he began to feel like the character Causubon in Umberto Eco's conspiracy satire *Foucault's Pendulum*. "There exists a secret society with branches throughout the world," Causubon says at one point in that novel, "and its plot is to spread the rumour that a universal plot exists."

The same kind of head-spinning *reductio ad absurdum* is evident in, say, Thomas Pynchon's tales of cosmic conspiracy: *The Crying of Lot 49*, *V*, *Gravity's Rainbow*, *Vineland*. The interconnections depicted here are so involved, so detailed and self-referential, that they begin to resemble mental gridlock. ("If they can get you asking the wrong questions," reads one of the "Proverbs for Paranoids" scattered like candies through *Gravity's Rainbow*, "they don't have to worry about the answers.") Like Eco, Pynchon has a diverting inclination to introduce new layers of ironic possibility into what is outwardly a straight conspiracy tale. One is never entirely sure whether the narrators of these oddly comic novels really believe in the proliferating degrees of control, or are merely satirizing those who do.

Or consider Donald Sutherland's weirdly compelling performance in the film *JFK* (1991), the one redeeming feature of that overlong piece of cinematic fiction. As he unfolds with almost insane glee the depths of the Kennedy-assassination plot to Kevin Costner, Sutherland betrays a level of self-consciousness otherwise absent from the typical conspiracy theory—and completely absent from the rest of Oliver Stone's paranoid pseudo-historical film. Here we enjoy not just the interconnections of the tale but also the perception of irony that opens up a distance between the tale and our own feelings of paranoia. This double-edged enjoyment of wacko ideas is a delicious kind of pleasure, and perhaps one peculiar to our own credulous times.

The danger in seeking this pleasure, though, is that it can sometimes stimulate intellectual vertigo even in the normal. Like most people who are both sane and interested, Van Wynsberghe soon found, as he penetrated more deeply the mysteries of worldwide plots, that all the conspiracy theorizing was beginning to fall in on itself in his mind. "I bailed out of assassination theories when I realized that all the wild theorists had drawn together into a single, pulsating mass of cosmic silliness," he says.

> As I attuned myself to the ways of the JFK set, it became obvious why the door is open to every popeyed wahoo shivering with The Truth. First, the people who should be guarding the door are not up to the job, and some of them are similar to the twitchy characters who are getting in. Second, the realm of

occult-tinged conspiracy paranoia is so extensive that even serious theorists never stand a
chance. By staking all on the existence of hidden meanings and shadowy, murderous forces,
they position themselves in an intellectual
wilderness whose residents gobble up that sort
of thing for breakfast and howl for more.

Van Wynsberghe notes with horror the long list of previously serious JFK theorists and publications who had, throughout the 1980s, declined into a madness of occultism, fear of
aliens, and—a standard delusion of schizophrenics—suspi-
cions of microwaves or death beams directed at them from
the World Trade Center. It's as if routine conspiracies of
government, money, and power are no longer enough; we
have to enlist extra-human agencies, too.

The final substructure of such tales is the kind of ultimate, hyper-real conspiracy theory lampooned by
Causubon's international plot to spread plot rumours, a
place where theories of connectedness become so far-reach-
ing that they mutate into all-encompassing self-referential
madness. This logical terminus of conspiracy thinking is
what the writer Michael Kelly, in an article in *The New
Yorker* on the fringe theorists in the American militia movement, called "fusion paranoia." Fusion paranoia, Kelly
argues, is a phenomenon that afflicts both the far Right (the
anti-government militia crowd so much in evidence after
the Oklahoma City bombing) and the far Left (Noam
Chomsky *et alia*, long-time critics of the meshed interests of
capital and power). The minds of fusion paranoiacs are
dominated by an irreducible, ever blossoming idea that
Everything Is Connected. Or, as Christopher Buckley
recently wrote, also in *The New Yorker* (which seems to
make this phenomenon a kind of informal department), the
message of the times is "in the sort of language we now get

courtesy of Mark from Michigan—*it's all part of the plan.*" From this perspective, every bad thing, or even just every thing, full stop, is somehow connected to everything else, and, further, controlled by someone evil somewhere else: the great omnipotent "They" of the New World Order, Big Government, or whatever.

This is, it seems to me, the very same They referred to in recent cinematic sentences like this one from the 1995 compu-conspiracy thriller *The Net*: "If They can get to me," Sandra Bullock hopelessly says, "They can get to anyone!" Since the fact that They exist is far more important than who They really are, I think we should agree to call this worldwide conspiracy simply The Evil They Corporation, Ltd. We all know who They are. We also all know that They are everywhere—for being everywhere is just what They do. Next stop, a compound in Montana.

We should not miss the fact that this nightmare vision of ultimate interconnectedness, the staff of life to fusion paranoiacs, is actually deeply satisfying to the rest of us as well. When displaced by a world of apparent meaninglessness, it is natural to crave explanations, however unlikely, for events that defy normal categories of understanding. In the hothouse atmosphere of the late twentieth century, a crazy explanation begins to seem to many people better than no explanation at all. It is easier to believe that, say, the German corporate giant I.G. Farben engineered the Second World War in conjunction with U.S. business interests, or that the CIA ordered and directed the entire Vietnam War, than to accept the idea that nobody is ever really in any kind of control of nasty real-world events. Such belief is the centrepiece of some forms of popular madness. It is also, as philosophers of science like to say, entirely unfalsifiable: you can never gainsay a given feature of the Ultimate Conspiracy, because it carries with it no parameters for its own disproof. Therefore every objection can be recast as merely further evidence of how successful the conspiracy has become. *They've gotten to you, too, haven't They?*

The Latin root of "conspiracy" alludes to the act of breathing together, the gathering of agents in close quarters to hatch a plot. Rational people know that this is not how most things, even most very bad things, actually happen. However comforting, conspiracy thinking is a cultural temptation worth avoiding; there simply is no worldwide They. What we notice, though, is that there doesn't have to be, for things like world wars and extreme poverty and human rights abuses to happen. It is probably not the case that the presidents of the Fortune 500 get together and just *decide* to tax the middle class into the dust. If this happens, we say to ourselves, it is merely an effect of their each pursuing, on their own, the "rational" (that is, profit-maximizing) interests of business and capital.

Or is it? Reducing all conspiracy theory to fusion paranoia tars every charge of complicity with the same broad psychologizing brush. And when *every* claim about government inaction or cruelty is dismissed as raging paranoia, we lose something important: critical purchase on the world. This then leaves us with no way to separate possibly valid claims from the madness of implanted surveillance chips, international Masonic conspiracies, and cattle-stealing marauder aliens. Noam Chomsky argues, for example, that the major media unwittingly support the defence industry under cover of a mission to gather only facts. They don't do it consciously, but as the result of institutional forces beyond any individual's control. Now that may be true or false, but dismissing by simple reflex means we will never know.

We must hold on to reality; it's all we've got. There is an important difference, a difference well worth preserving, between an analysis that suggests common elite interests, or the internal logic of complex systems, on the one hand, and a genuine conspiracy theory on the other. One is susceptible to proof and the other is not; it is the difference between science fact and science fiction. In these troubled days, it helps nobody to confuse the two, especially for ostensible motives of "understanding" or "sympathy." Bryan is guilty of this confusion with regard to the alien abductees, giving their reports too much prima facie credence. But Kelly is likewise guilty when he exhibits his own kind of journalistic fusion paranoia in lumping all so-called "conspiracy" claims together under the single dismissive label.

That's a difficult thought to keep in our grasp when the world seems simultaneously so blithely interconnected and so completely out of control. But in the end, we can only do what rational people have always done when faced with flurries of apparently nutty claims: try to separate the truth from the falsity, the sense from the nonsense, the signal from the noise.

Not all the deleterious effects of conspiracy thinking are psychological. There are political dangers, too. In democratic societies, widespread feelings of being controlled by external agencies can work to undermine the possibility of good government by exploding political trust. Disgruntled citizens move quickly from genuine questioning of political authority to a position of blanket distrust. Trust is the first casualty of difficult cultural times, because finding the complicated truth is always hard and paranoia is always easy. That's why fusion paranoia remains a strong temptation not only for the credulous but for the merely disenfranchised as well.

Where does the intellectual fusion evident in the alien-abduction-meets-JFK-assassin-torches-Waco line of thought really come from? Sociologists have been telling us for decades that today's massive state bureaucracies, coupled with nightmare Orwellian or Kafkaesque visions of faceless power that have become a fixture of our imaginations, greatly increase feelings of personal helplessness in novel ways. Anxiety about being controlled is, they conclude, a distinctly twentieth-century phenomenon. Consider the fear of an ubiquitous state found equally in the Big Brother "monitors" of *Nineteen Eighty-Four* and in the orbiting government satellites. According to contemporary conspiracy thinkers, these satellites can read your morning newspaper over your shoulder, track the amount of money in your wallet using the metal security strips in paper currency, and monitor your brainwaves via supermarket bar codes. (Of course, according to *The Weekly World News*, the bar codes are actually the Sign of the Beast of the Apocalypse.)

The fear of surveillance is thus a standard anxiety of the modern era, where the technological mastery of earthly forces becomes enmeshed with the social mastery of individuals. Jeremy Bentham's nineteenth-century utilitarian idea of the "panopticon," discussed with such inventive nuance by Michel Foucault in his book *Surveiller et Punir* (1975), has become an intellectual touchstone here. The panopticon is a device by which every prisoner in a circular prison block can be viewed from a single surveillance point. It not only reduces the number of guards necessary to watch prisoners, but, in a nice twist, actually renders observation unnecessary because the individual prisoner never knows when he is being watched, and must therefore assume always. The panopticon becomes, in Foucault's subtle discussion, a vivid metaphor for the many invisible, ubiquitous, and powerful means of observation contained within the modern state: observation that is painless, punishment that is not experienced as such, oppression that is therefore not resisted.

Arthur Kroker and Michael Weinstein suggest that a modern version of the panopticon is contained in one of the many "technotopian" ideals of the Xerox Corporation. It is the so-called "fully interactive office." In this kind of

ompletely wired environment, office workers will wear tabs
nat send a constant stream of telemetry to the computer
nd, like "Star Trek" communicator badges, allow workers
o be located at any time. Combined with the equally
rekkie ideas of "ubiquitous computing" (you can interface
vith the computer from anywhere) and "relational process-
ng" (all users are handled simultaneously by a massive
Central Processing Unit)—the office as computer station,
n short—these technologies have the effect of rendering
he idea of constant computer presence not just palatable
but seductive. "In contrast to the old panoptic ideology of
Orwell's *Nineteen Eighty-Four* with its visible surveillance
mechanisms," Kroker and Weinstein write in *Data Trash*,
'the seduction of the relational self is ingested to such a
degree of intensity that the body delivers itself up for electronic execution. That is the Xerox of the future: an electronic execution machine for harvesting all the bodily
functions. The laboring body of the office worker is electronically liquidated, not in the name of punishment, but of
a therapeutic version of freedom: the full cybernetic promise
of actually being 'networked.'"

The surveillance theme continues to be a cornerstone of
conspiracy narratives, and it offers a spurious kind of intellectual integrity: the pleasure of tying off all the loose ends.
"The grisly age of the post-Christians appears as faded
images of the Book of Revelation on the one hand," Kroker
and Weinstein continue, "and a desire for conspiracy theory,
as the only possibility of narrative closure, on the other."
With new forms of high-speed communication like the virtually instantaneous Internet, such closure can be effected
more quickly than ever before. Van Wynsberghe reports
that the conspiracy community reacted with admirable
alacrity to the Oklahoma City bombing, apparently unwilling to let any event of such significance lie unexplained for
even a few days. The "explanations" ranged from the old

Jewish banking bunch, the so-called Bilderbergers, to the Japanese, who you would have thought were busy with their own apocalyptic attacks in the subway. A few theorists blamed the United Nations, crediting that agency with a degree of tactical success not evident in its other theatres of operation. The anti-government extremists—so-called "freemen" or "patriots" of Montana and Idaho—think the U.N. is also behind the banking conspiracy.

Hence, too, the worries about security strips in paper money. "It's a chip," Larry Blackburn of Darby, Montana, insisted to Timothy Appleby of *The Globe and Mail* in August 1995. "It receives a signal and it radiates a signal back. They can drive down the highway—They can also do it by satellite—and They can tell how much money you've got. That's for when They make the money switch—They've got the other money in the bank right now. It's going to be United Nations notes." Of course, security strips in money can't do any of this unless one is already being tracked in great detail by some other means, with instruments so detailed that they can follow one's exact position at all times. (It's no good Their knowing that a certain amount of money is in a given place unless They also know that *you* are there, holding it.) And if this is so—I'm willing to bet Larry, for one, believes in it—then the added surveillance of the money strips is really nothing to get worked up about.

Such "explanations" return again and again to the issue of surveillance, from the microchip Oklahoma City bomber Timothy McVeigh believed had been implanted in his buttocks to the unidentified, elusive black helicopters that militia members claim to have sighted prior to the bombing—which the raving anti-government crowd thinks was carried out on Bill Clinton's orders, purposely to discredit the libertarian far Right. Others claimed that the helicopters, which have been a feature of conspiracy reports since about

1984, were engaged in biological warfare or carried around aliens who were mutilating cattle in the Midwest. No, no, a certain UFO expert countered. *Satanists* were responsible for the cattle mutilations; the black helicopters were in fact some kind of extra-dimensional phenomenon.

The features of this paranoia do indeed seem peculiar to us when we consider the size and extent of government and technology, the sheer number of agencies that now regulate the ephemera of our lives, from driver's licences and zip codes to annual income taxes. But perhaps the judgment is a little hasty, another example of end-time myopia. Conspiracy fears were alive and well throughout the millennial outbursts of the Middle Ages, when ordinary people had very good reason to think the nobles and bishops were ganging up on them, and when, with less reason, they believed with every appearance of fervour that European Jews were involved in a massive secret plot to overturn the Christian faith—a line of thought that shows no sign of diminishing.

In fact, the roots of conspiracy theory are really as old as millenarian thought itself. One might say that the Book of Daniel, which predicts the rise of well-organized enemies of the chosen, is the original conspiracy theory. Certainly the old labels of evil agents banding together to encompass our destruction—the Antichrist, the Whore of Babylon—are still in wide circulation among people who believe, like renegade medieval prophets, that the Pope or the U.S. president or somebody else is trying to control the world by means of a sophisticated network of agents or microwaves beamed from on high. John's Revelation, which predicts the rise of the Antichrist as the gradual acclaim of a charismatic ruler only later exposed as evil, is a standard source of conspiracy-theory imagery that displays endless inventiveness. ("If most people [in the Middle Ages] believed that Antichrist was to be born a Jew," Norman Cohn writes, "there were many who believed he would be the son of a bishop and a nun.")

Even apparently natural events like the fierce outbreaks of plague in Europe in 1348 were fuel for the fire of conspiracy thinking. People speculated about which secret group had infected the water supplies with frogs, spiders, and lizards—all signs of earth, dirt, and the devil. In standard fashion, anxiety led almost immediately to violent, even terminal, scapegoating. "As the plague continued," Cohn tells us, "and people grew more and more bewildered and desperate, suspicion swung now here, now there, lighting successively on the lepers, the poor, the rich, the clergy, before it came finally to rest on the Jews, who thereupon were almost exterminated." The conspiracy mavens in our own time have not yet, so far as I know, blamed AIDS or the Ebola virus on the Jews, but I wouldn't put it past them.

Popular delusions aside, we do well, finally, to remember that medieval believers faced a situation really not very different from ours in that their paranoia was at least partly justified by events in the world. As so often happens, the kernel of truth at the heart of conspiracy theory is more than enough to generate the full-blown fusion of the deathless Them. And what was this kernel of truth in the past? That the western world was, throughout the Middle Ages and even into the Renaissance, dominated by one of the most extensive, centralized, powerful, and vindictive bureaucracies in the history of the world. Its existence, together with the corruption, cynicism, and hunger for power evident among its exalted leaders, prompted an apocalyptic Martin Luther, among others, to speculate that its "divinely selected" leader was none other than the Antichrist himself. This central bureaucracy was called the Roman Catholic Church.

Conspiracy thinking is, in common with all forms of collective madness, impressively creative in its own self-defence. Like some forms of madness or ideological indoctrination, it has the peculiar ability to interpret anything in the world as positive evidence of its truth. When, for example, a shard of metal from the Roswell incident was proved to be part of a weather balloon and not, as the conspiracy theorists had long argued, made of a material unknown to earthly metallurgy, they reacted by agreeing (as they had to) about the weather balloon—only to suggest that it was actually the balloon that caused the alien ship to crash.

In this way, conspiracy theory shows itself to be ultimately, like the alien abduction experience, a close relative of the more traditional religious fervour that gripped febrile imaginations in moments of millennial fear. Conspiracy thinking seems to offer its initiates the same all-enveloping comfort and security expressed in religious belief, even while playing on many of the same vague fears and anxieties. The theme of space aliens abducting unsuspecting humans, even standing in for them, has been a science-fiction and newspaper tabloid constant for decades. (One has only to think once more of *Invasion of the Body Snatchers*, with its weird McCarthy-era anti-communist subtext: creeping invasion by aliens *who look just like us*.) But draped over the claims of government betrayal and the conspiracy theorizing of the mental fringe, abduction tales begin to take on a practically medieval note of panic—the great credulous fear of the unknown that grips brink cultures, the fear which is in fact a perverse form of religious faith.

More than this, the concern for individual psychological well-being that now dominates the lives of so many people, with their desperate attempts to be healed, to find peace, to grasp meaning, is here also on display. It is no coincidence that the booksellers who set up their hoardings at psychics' fairs stock everything from Tarot tomes and books on

benign witchcraft, through the collected works of Susan
Powter and M. Scott Peck, to the intricate dissertations on
the great cover-up and government power plays.

Why do we find these theories so compelling? Why are
the otherworldly horrors of "The X-Files" and its various
television and film simulacra so popular now? I think it is
because, poised on the brink, we are inclined to dwell on
coming horrors, to seek out fear, even as we look to these
same horrors for a perverse form of reassurance. It seems
that, like Fox Mulder, we all really want to believe. We all
suspect—or at least hope—that the truth, whatever it may
be, is out there. Yet even as some of us tentatively prepare
to greet the coming visitors, we find that we can trust no
one. That the world is not what it appears. That dark agencies and malign forces are at work.

Here belief and suspicion arise conjoined, two sides of
the same coin. The result of this conjunction is a powerful
thought that runs through our late anxiety: We don't know
what the truth is, but it must be something significant or
the forces of darkness would not be so keen to keep it from
us. As the believers like to say of the alien crash at Roswell:
it only had to happen once, *and that changes everything.*

But into what?

SEVEN

The Best Lack All Conviction

They be blind leaders of the blind. And if the blind lead
the blind, both shall fall into the ditch.

Matthew 15:14

IN THE LATTER
decades of the eleventh century, an extraordinary man, who
was neither king nor bishop, emerged from obscurity to
become arguably the most influential person in Christian
Europe. Peter the Hermit, born near Amiens, was in his
middle age when he suddenly became famous. He was a
small, thin man with a long grey beard who had lived an
unremarkable life of religious devotion, first as an ascetic
monk, partaking of neither meat nor wine, and then as a
hermit, shunning human contact altogether.

Around 1080, Peter forsook the solitary prayer of the
hermitage and emerged from his isolation to preach to
select audiences. Soon he was moving through the small
towns of west-central Europe, holding crowds in thrall with
his message of God's hand in his life and the task of action
that lay incumbent on every Christian: to reclaim the Holy
Land by repopulating the City on the Hill with believers—
and by exterminating the infidels who crawled through
Jerusalem like parasites. Peter massed an enthusiastic, even
fanatical, following. According to contemporary accounts,
he possessed unusual charisma and eloquence, lending his
merest utterance an aura of presumptive divinity. His phys-
iognomy of emaciated devotion was often considered the

very picture of godliness.

Peter seemed to exert an almost mesmeric fascination over his audiences, sending people into frenzies of devotion and self-abasement. They rushed to pluck a hair from his humble mount, an ass, competed to drink his carefully preserved bath water, and constructed elaborate myths around his obscure life. When Pope Urban II decided to mass the First Crusade in the 1090s, it was Peter who stood at the head of a fervent horde ready to sell their possessions, purchase as many crude weapons as they could carry, and begin the long trek to Jerusalem.

Peter, it was said, had been to the Holy City once before. Entering the Church of the Holy Sepulchre on a sacred pilgrimage, he had been touched by Christ, who appeared to the monk in a shining vision and charged him with a mission to summon the Crusade. Peter carried back to central Europe a Heavenly Letter, earthly evidence of his charge from the Messiah. Its message was one of salvation for the desperately poor, the disaffected and disenfranchised of France and Germany. According to the many popular prophecies that circulated among contemporary European Christians, the end-times would begin in the approaching year of 1100. Jerusalem—the centre of the Christian world, Heaven's ground zero on earth—drew the millennial imagination like a magnet. God's messenger was now among them, wielding evidence for all eyes to see, and enjoining the holiest of all possible missions, an act of sacrifice that would guarantee safe entry into Heaven.

Few needed further encouragement. With little prosperity or comfort to keep them in their homes, the poor of Europe flocked behind Peter; their numbers, merging with Pope Urban's ambition and sense of destiny, created the groundswell of prejudice, militancy and religious devotion we know as the Crusades. Peter's fanatical followers died in their thousands, starving to death on the way to Jerusalem or in battle once there, but they died assured of their souls' salvation.

In the summer of 1983 another man visited Jerusalem on a pilgrimage, a personal journey of faith. He too had a vision in the Church of the Holy Sepulchre and was seized by an unshakable conviction of his own divinely ordained mission. He was convinced not only that he was God's chosen messenger, but also that he was the Messiah himself, returned to this earth to judge the living and the dead. Like Peter the Hermit, he too was described in first-hand accounts as intensely compelling, even semi-divine. He quickly gathered a small but devoted following who flocked to his side and jostled for the opportunity to cast themselves at his feet. His preaching combined rhetorical skill and selective biblical quotation with an intensity of belief that compelled respect, even zeal, in auditors. The women of his congregation offered him their bodies, desperate for the chance to be close to him, perhaps to bear the Messiah's child.

His followers, many of whom were poor and had little to lose, saw in him their only possible route to salvation. Though the way was difficult, though they would be scorned and even attacked by the forces of unbelief, they knew that the infidels would in the end be defeated and the Messiah would lead them to the Holy City. They sold their few belongings and purchased as many weapons as they could carry. They did not carry them, this time, to Jerusalem. They went instead to a small town called Waco, Texas. Here for a time they attempted, in the great New World tradition, to create a New Jerusalem, a City on the Hill, in a complex of wooden buildings surrounded by a barbed-wire fence. Their leader, David Koresh, urged them to greater and greater acts of selflessness. They sacrificed their money, their spouses, their children.

And, eventually, their lives. In the fiery conclusion to the now infamous 1994 siege, the Branch Davidians died in their dozens, first defending their New Jerusalem from the forces of evil, later burning it to the ground when they realized they could no longer control its destiny. They died, like the Crusaders almost a millennium before them, entirely assured of their souls' salvation.

━ ▄ ━

Most psychiatrists interested in the case now agree that David Koresh probably suffered from an extreme version of a surprisingly common psychological ailment. It is a form of paranoid delusion known colloquially as Jerusalem Syndrome, a mild affliction in which visitors to the Holy City, especially those who are moved by the cool, numinous atmosphere of the ancient Holy Sepulchre, begin to believe that they are in fact reincarnations of divine or biblical personages: Christ himself, King David, Mary, Samson, even God or Satan. There is apparently something so powerful about the charged religious atmosphere of Jerusalem—a sense that divinity wells up through the very cobbles and seeps from the walls of the ancient Via Dolorosa—that a number of otherwise unremarkable tourists fall down every year and declare themselves the reincarnation of God.

There are few hard numbers on the incidence of the syndrome because the files of committed psychiatric patients are confidential. Mental health experts say that most sufferers—about 80 percent—have some previous history of psychological or behavioural problems; it is also possible that some mild cases do not reach the stage of formal treatment. In any case, it is the otherwise normal visitors to Jerusalem—those with no previous signs of mental unbalance, who suddenly collapse into extreme delusion, claiming to be Samson or Mary or Jesus—who are the most fascinating. Where does this belief, so unshakable at the time, come from?

According to psychiatrists who study and treat Jerusalem

Syndrome, most of these sufferers have only a very mild version of the delusion: they are gripped by their mad belief for as little as five to seven days, and they return to their North American or European homes without any lasting ill effects, the belief having subsided. Many of them, back at their jobs in Maine or Ohio or Nova Scotia, speak with some diffidence and embarrassment about the conviction that held them in thrall while they were within Jerusalem's magic geography. Many, even in the throes of the syndrome, confess themselves more anxious than fervent about the unexpected belief in their own divinity. It seems they do not so much rant about their condition as *worry* about it. They often confess themselves confused about what to do. It's easy to sympathize. What, after all, would be your first move were you to suddenly realize, in the midst of an all-inclusive tour of the Holy Land, that you had been hand-picked by God to spread around the divine retribution? Who would you tell?

"The first symptom is falling behind the tour," psychiatrist Yair Bar El told Rebecca Lee of *The Atlantic*. "The second is irritation with one's travelling companions." Soon the sufferer may begin preaching or singing. This is then followed by the symptom that usually convinces tour guides to make a phone call: undressing and wrapping oneself in bed sheets. Thus attired, the newly anointed messiahs, often found wandering in the desert outside of Jerusalem where Jesus is supposed to have spent his ordeal of forty days and forty nights, are picked up by members of the Israeli Army and delivered to psychiatric care. Confronted with these manifestations of worldly power, the new messiahs do not rave and gnash; they are not uncontrollable; they do not denounce Caesar's soldiers. On the contrary, according to the soldiers, they are unfailingly polite.

Bar El, now director of the Kfar Shaul psychiatric hospital in Jerusalem, is an Argentine-born doctor who was responsible for naming Jerusalem Syndrome in 1982. Since then he has treated hundreds of messiahs and Marys at the Kfar Shaul facility. Most of them have exhibited remarkably similar psychological profiles, including early childhood religious belief often followed by mild apostasy or rebellion in adolescence. Bar El and other experts speculate that this pattern contributes to the syndrome because the sufferer's religious thoughts remain immature, as if drawn in Bible cartoons, and therefore easily influenced. Among Christians, it also seems that Catholic and Orthodox believers are less susceptible than Protestants, who make up about 95 percent of the syndrome's documented sufferers. "For Protestants the religious hierarchy has been broken," Bar El told *The Jerusalem Post*. "They have a direct connection to God, which enables them to go through a strong personal emotional experience."

His point is consistent with European church history. People have claimed to be the Messiah ever since the death of Christ, of course, and the Middle Ages were particularly chock-a-block with self-appointed saviours, not all of whom needed a visit to Jerusalem to secure their own faith. They gathered armies, killed unbelievers, whipped themselves bloody, and even engaged in wild orgies. Church authorities deplored this activity but were unwilling to meet it with the same single-mindedness they showed in, for example, rooting out heresy during the Inquisition. So when, following a visit to Rome, an appalled Martin Luther challenged the authority of the corrupt Church in 1517, nailing his ninety-five theses to the door of the church at Wittenberg, he might well have thought that one effect of Reformation would be a lessening of this sort of enthusiastic madness. Indeed, Luther was troubled by zealotry and the popular influence of charismatics, who sold indulgences as assiduously as any contemporary televangelist. Salvation, he thought, should not be bought and sold like fish in the marketplace.

Unfortunately, the effect of Luther's new doctrine of salvation by faith alone was not what he would have wished. As Norman Cohn writes of the new personal-relationship strain of European Christianity initiated by the Reformers: "Once the layman began to feel that he himself stood face to face with God and to rely for guidance on his individual conscience, it was inevitable that some laymen should claim divine promptings." Messianic ravings did not diminish after Luther; they proliferated.

According to Rebecca Lee, treatment of Jerusalem Syndrome is usually in the form of psychotherapy. Today's messiahs generally do not run amok, gathering followers and proclaiming the advent of the apocalypse. They are instead sedated and given mild doses of haloperidol, an antipsychotic drug that inhibits the neuronal uptake of the neurotransmitter dopamine. With some of the brain's dopamine receptors thus blocked, patients are less likely to find themselves experiencing the intense emotional states in which psychotic projection and certain forms of fantasy are facilitated. Pharmacologists think that elevated levels of dopamine—associated, in the neurological literature, with schizophrenia—are what accounts for the inclination of psychotics to translate possible into actual, to make the invisible suddenly appear. It is, from a certain point of view, the foundation of the bizarre leap of faith that characterizes the many new messiahs.

Other forms of treatment are more contextual. Though Bar El does not encourage group therapy, he has tried putting two self-appointed messiahs in the same room together. After thirty minutes they each claimed the other was an impostor. But such confrontations, while presumably amusing to the observing psychiatrists, are rarely helpful in shattering the messianic or divine delusion, for it is in the nature of delusion to take all challenges as further evidence of chosenness: the charge of impostor is rational for each sufferer from within the altered mental framework of his deluded belief. "It is not effective to tell somebody she is not the Virgin," Eliezer Witztum, professor of psychiatry at Jerusalem's Beersheva Mental Health Center, told Lee. That kind of challenge cannot reach into what Witztum calls "a problem of inner geography."

Witztum thinks that Jerusalem Syndrome is really "a reaction to a place, not a true psychosis" and that it arises directly from the "unique atmosphere" of Jerusalem. Certainly nothing appears so immediately helpful in the treatment of the syndrome as a simple change of venue: moving from the heady religious atmosphere of the Holy City and back to the pedestrian realities of Des Moines, Portland, or Sudbury. "The most important thing, finally," Bar El said, "is to get them away from the stimulus. Once away from the city, they are usually fine."

Jerusalem Syndrome is remarkably similar to another recently diagnosed borderline psychiatric disorder. In this form of delusion, sufferers believe they have been bitten by vampires or occupied by a demonic presence. Psychiatrists call the condition "cinematic neurosis" because the reported delusional beliefs are apparently inspired by horror films. Sufferers experience feelings of invasion or fear culled from horror-film imagery, sometimes even experiencing flash-backs to scenes in the film. They believe they are possessed by the devil, as in *The Exorcist*, or are pregnant with the Antichrist, as in *Rosemary's Baby*. They might even believe, in the *Invasion of the Body Snatchers* mode, that other people are invading aliens cleverly disguised as humans. Sufferers typically have an uncertain sense of identity and high cultural ideals which they have difficulty maintaining. In many cases the onset of neurosis follows the loss of a family member about whom the sufferer had ambivalent feelings. "Cinematic neurosis is a form of borderline crisis shaped by a film narrative, which filters into the individual because it reflects current life issues and is culturally significant to him or her," says Bruce Ballon, a psychiatrist at the Clarke Institute of Psychiatry in Toronto.

In a sense, cinematic neurosis is simply the flip side of Jerusalem Syndrome: transformation into a demonic, rather than a divine, presence. Indeed, even as they seek messiahs and saintly messengers, end-of-century cultures have demonstrated an equal fascination with invading monsters like vampires and demons. For example, 1594 saw the first production of Christopher Marlowe's unnerving pact-with-the-devil play *Doctor Faustus*. Nearly three centuries later, in 1886, Robert Louis Stevenson's *The Strange Case of Dr. Jekyll and Mr. Hyde*, macabre resurrection myth and model for so many cheesy horror stories of The Beast Within, appeared. Bram Stoker's *Dracula* was published soon after, in the thoroughly fin-de-siècle year of 1897.

Today, the sexy but doomed vampires of Anne Rice's popular novels mark the same interest. The vampire Lestat and his cronies have quickly become a model for thousands of white-powdered, crimson-lipped young people the continent over. This particular late-century vogue for gothic fashion actually dates back to lugubrious early-1980s rock bands like The Cure, The Cult, and The Cramps, who spawned a primarily British fashion trend for basic black clothing, fright-wig hair, and general gloominess of demeanour. The stimuli for the 1990s outbreak were primarily cinematic, though: Francis Ford Coppola's 1992 version of Bram Stoker's *Dracula*, in which babes-of-the-moment Keanu Reeves and Winona Ryder ran around trying to avoid a bevy of wispy female vampires in lacy bodices and push-up bras; and, two years later, the controversial film adaptation of Rice's *Interview with the Vampire*. (The author first denounced it and star Tom Cruise, then came on board with a massive, privately funded ad campaign.) In the wake of the film release, a Toronto department store sold out of a supply of fashionable dark blood-red lipstick in a matter of hours.

Other manifestations of vampire chic are less benign. CNN reported during the lunch-time news on October 31, 1995, that a number of black urban teenagers in the United States had begun sporting gold or silver fangs on their teeth, a new kind of fashion accessory that played on a vogue in the black community for decorative tooth caps, made of gold, that sport precious gems and even logos. Retailing at anything from $100 to $250, the fangs are formed from plastic molds taken of the wearer's teeth and fit over the teeth like a sort of metal mouthguard. First noticed by trend-spotters in 1995 music videos by singer Mariah Carey and black rapper Method Man, the fangs anticipated by some months the release of an Eddie Murphy film called *Vampire in Brooklyn*. Like many of the trappings of rap culture, fangs are meant to send a message of black defiance, and wearers have been beaten up by thugs, either eager to pocket the gold or just annoyed by the trend. Some New York jewellery stores now display signs saying they do not sell them, and one Brooklyn high school principal actually had to ban the wearing of fangs in his school because of the unrest they were causing. "They're a symbol of something," said one boy, his hair in cornrows, to the CNN camera. But he wasn't telling what it was, exactly, they symbolized. "That's my secret," he said, walking away.

The vampire is a millennial standard-bearer because it combines gory mortal threat with profound, even insistent, erotic appeal. Vampires traditionally cannot die but nevertheless desperately crave the sustenance of blood; they signal a deep uncertainty about the body, with its combination of vulnerability, paralysing thanatic desire, and dark sexual secrets. These predatory monsters represent a kind of inner invasion just as the tales of gathering alien hordes signal an outer one. Sometimes the two kinds of invasion are mixed in the sub-genre of science-fiction B movies that produced such forgettable efforts as *Planet of the Vampires* (1965), *Planet of Blood* (1966), and *Vampire Men of the Lost Planet* (1970), to name just three. In all of these, the threatening cinematic aliens are also bloodsuckers—a concatenation of threats some might consider excessive.

White faces and even fangs are probably some distance short of paranoid delusion, but like cinematic neurosis they are powerful evidence of how film, television and music video imagery now pervade individual experience. In a sense, cinematic neurosis also constitutes extreme proof of Arthur Kroker's thesis about recombinant culture. Here, mental disturbance is cast in terms of the best available imagery of anxiety and invasion. In segments of the culture dominated by films—rather than, say, by the Bible—it is unsurprising that this form of anxiety should take on a cinematic form.

— — —

As with Jerusalem Syndrome, cinematic neurosis can be treated successfully with short-term psychotherapy and mild antipsychotic drugs, both of which help reestablish the patient's sense of real-world identity. Matters are slightly more complicated in another contemporary form of supernatural visitation, in which the signs are physical, not mental.

In 1950, Georgette Faniel of Montreal found distinctive circular wounds on the palms of her hands; they had no obvious cause. Three years later similar wounds appeared on her forehead—again without a clear physical cause. The signs continued to appear on Faniel's hands, feet and forehead over the course of several decades.

In 1972, Cloretta Robinson, a ten-year-old black girl living in West Oakland, California, bled from the palm of her left hand; later she found marks on her right hand, her feet, her forehead. She bled for nineteen days, until Good Friday, when the bleeding suddenly stopped.

Early on Easter morning, 1974, a fifty-three-year-old

woman called Ethel Chapman, a patient at the Birkenhead General Hospital in Merseyside, England, had a dream in which she experienced her own crucifixion. When she woke up, the nurses who came to bathe her noticed small bleeding wounds in her palms.

Just after Christmas in 1991, a Washington, D.C., priest called Jim Bruse experienced spontaneous bleeding from his wrists. Soon his feet began to hurt and bleed as well, and a small wound opened up in his right side. In May 1992, Heather Woods, a forty-three-year-old Lincolnshire widow, found small itching blisters on her hands. They later grew in size and seeped blood. Similar blisters appeared on her feet, while a red crescent mark appeared on her side. Twice, a red, cross-shaped mark was noticeable on her forehead.

I found these contemporary examples of "stigmata"—the appearance of Jesus' crucifixion wounds—in Ted Harrison's 1994 book *Stigmata: A Medieval Phenomenon in a Modern Age.* The first celebrated stigmatic, Harrison notes, was St. Francis of Assisi. In September 1224, while he was wandering alone in the Swiss mountains, engaged in an ascetic mystical retreat, St. Francis was seized with a vision of a flaming seraph, and bleeding wounds opened in his palms, feet, and torso. He returned to society to display these marks of God's favour. First-hand reports say the blood flowed freely from his wounds for weeks, the gash in his side in particular bleeding so much that the monk's coarse trousers were said to be continually soaked with it.

There have been hundreds of cases of reported stigmata since the time of St. Francis—over three hundred collected by a certain Dr. Imbert-Gourbeyre in 1908, a further seventy reported by the *British Medical Journal* in 1989—all with close similarities to Francis's story. Circular wounds open in the hands and feet; a slash appears in the side; marks or thorn-wounds are visible on the forehead. Most of the cases have come from Europe, predominantly from Roman

Catholic countries. Female stigmatics outnumber males by about seven to one.

Medical doctors have coined the term "psychogenic purpura" to describe wounds that appear on the skin without obvious physical cause, and most doctors believe that reported stigmata lie in this category. The description is a little unsatisfying: it names the mystery without solving it, only adding to the conviction of believers. There is, however, an earthly explanation for the appearance of stigmata: the wounds might be self-inflicted during periods of unconscious mutilation. They can even be induced hypnotically. And a person need not be deeply disturbed for such self-mutilation to occur. Unlike the apparently aimless self-mutilation of the extreme schizophrenic, stigmata serve the all-important function of marking the recipient as chosen by God, particularly empathetic with the suffering Jesus, or otherwise in close personal contact with the divine. That is, they are extremely desirable wounds within certain contexts of religious belief. A person might not seek this sort of attention consciously, but under hypnosis or in other states of diminished awareness the unconscious mind can create unusual effects.

In 1993 the writer Jim Schnabel noted, in the London-based *Fortean Times*, that reports of stigmata were often linked to other close-contact phenomena, including UFO abductions and spiritual possession. Stigmatics reported being taken over by evil spirits or whisked away by off-worlders. Schnabel noted the many commonalities among these forms of peak experience—the feelings of chosenness and the sense of mission—and suggested that they might be a late-century variation on the disturbing psychological disorder known as Munchausen's Syndrome. In Munchausen's—named for the celebrated eighteenth-century fabulist whose wildly exaggerated tales were first published in English in 1785 and quickly became popular juvenile reading—a combination of false symptoms, exaggeration, self-mutilation and self-induced illness is used by insecure or unbalanced people as a means of getting attention, especially from family members and medical professionals. Munchausen's sufferers are typically hypochondriacal, in and out of hospital all the time with a variety of minor ailments. In order to secure medical admission and the care and attention they desire, they will starve themselves, induce vomiting to dehydrate their bodies, and even ingest poison. (In a related disorder called Munchausen's by Proxy, individuals inflict the same physical damage on a child or spouse.)

Like the UFO researchers, Schnabel argued that many of the divine and/or alien visitations reported in recent years appeared to "target" people with similar personalities and with similar backgrounds of social and economic disadvantage: poor women or young girls, for example, often those already in hospital for the treatment of some other ailment. In such cases, there is often an apparently indiscriminate combination of paranormal experiences going on at once. Most stigmatics report hearing the voice of God in their heads; many report other forms of contact with other kinds of super-human agencies. Georgette Faniel, for example, has, in addition to reporting her stigmata, penned hundreds of pages of automatic writing culled from her "communications" with God; she also reported being pregnant at the age of sixty-two and encouraged speculation that her pregnancy was the result of a divine visitation.

None of this, of course, diminishes conviction among some Christians. "We can look at possibilities, hysteria of an egotist, the welling up of the unconscious, divine intervention at a time of ecstatic experience," the Reverend David Lockyer, a friend of stigmatic Ethel Chapman, told Ted Harrison. "Does it matter where the explanation lies?" Well, yes, it probably does. The sincerity test should not be the only assessment ever levelled on the authenticity of extreme beliefs: it is not enough that the believers really believe. Harrison himself is nicely balanced on the issue of cause— just as he was in his previous book about odd popular belief, *Elvis People*—and he offers no final solutions. Yet, after describing an Irish stigmatic called Christina Gallagher, Harrison does make a significant prediction. Gallagher, an Irish housewife, has talked since 1993 of a coming "chastisement" of the world in 2000; her stigmatic marks are, she says, a sign from God that we must turn from our sinful ways. "In all probability," Harrison comments at the close of his book, "throughout the world over the coming year there will be an increase in stigmatists. Indeed the last ten years of this century could see a peak of activity."

David Koresh was not diagnosed with Jerusalem Syndrome, but psychiatrists now speculate that he suffered from it. Evidently, his return to the United States did not shake him in his conviction that he was Christ reborn. The existence of the syndrome, and of stigmata, too, raises some interesting questions about religious faith and the prospect of a Second Coming in these last days of the millennium.

How, for instance, will believers separate the genuine Messiah from the mass of crazies merely claiming to be him? Religious scholars who attempted to intervene in the Waco stand-off repeatedly complained that FBI and ATF agents were not interested in taking Koresh's claims to divinity at face value, contributing, in the experts' view, to the hostility and violence that marked the end of that confrontation between God and Caesar. Their evidence was read into the record at the congressional hearings held following the Branch Davidian immolation, and it contributed to the emerging condemnation of the government's role in that event. But from the perspective of the government agencies, a claim to messianic status was simply further evidence of the problem, not something that they should take into account in Koresh's favour. Rebecca Lee is surely right when she remarks that, were Jesus to arrive today in Jerusalem, he too would be taken without further ado to Kfar Shaul, diagnosed with a rather persistent case of Jerusalem Syndrome, and given a small dose of haloperidol.

Some people take that as a sign of a thoroughly psychologized culture's hostility to religious belief, but it could equally be interpreted as a retroactive diagnosis of the mild psychotic condition of the original Messiah. At the time of Jesus' celebrated sojourn in the desert, when he secured his own conviction that he was the son of God, the city of Jerusalem was already steeped in the aura of another man taken for the Messiah: John the Baptist. The countryside surrounding Jerusalem was a powerful nexus of religious fervour. Was Jesus simply the most celebrated early sufferer of a fairly common form of mental illness, then? Did he merely have an excess of dopamine coursing through his brain? From a thoroughly sceptical point of view, as Albert Schweitzer noted in his book *The Psychiatric Study of Jesus*, the long ordeal in the desert, during which Jesus fed on locusts and wild honey and conceived his holy mission, simply marks the transition from "the latent to the active stage of [his] paranoia."

To be sure, Jesus never retreated into an armed compound, nor did he enjoin his followers to resist secular forces with violence. On the contrary. Yet the basic problem remains: we have no way of testing claims to messianic status that go beyond the unacceptable blanket policy of taking all claims at face value. And that, surely, is a lingering difficulty for latter-day millenarians. How can there be a Second Coming when we cannot even be certain there was a First? And even assuming we are confident that Jesus was the real thing, how can we choose among the several Messiahs that now stumble out of the Holy Sepulchre each year?

A little unexpectedly, traditional religious denominations are preparing for the millennium without much fuss or bother. There will be planned announcements from Pope John Paul II, who, according to a disapproving Conor Cruise O'Brien, is desperate to live out his term at least to 2000 so that he can go down in history as the pontiff of transition. Other denominations will offer their members whatever wisdom they can. Yet it is unlikely you will hear Anglican ministers or Episcopalian deacons announcing from their pulpits that the end is nigh. That caution is, for a growing number of people, a strike against mainstream Christian denominations. Many believers, now gripped by a fervour amounting almost to mania, are turning to more extreme forms of religious devotion. Hence the recent rise of so-called "post-denominational" churches, the Charismatics and Pentecostals, with their wailing and speaking in tongues and belief in direct divine intervention.

Alexis de Tocqueville said in the 1830s that "religious insanity is very common in the United States," and there is no evidence to suggest he would be forced to revise the judgment today. North America has declined to a lowest-common-denominator belief in the supernatural, elbowing aside not only atheistic scepticism—that goes without saying—but even the more traditional and socially conscious religious observances like attending established churches and engaging in time-honoured ritual. The supernatural force is often called God, but the fact that this New Religiosity sits so comfortably alongside astrological beliefs, New Age music, holistic massage, and amateur psychotherapy should tip us off to what is really going on. We are facing one more desperate face of the end-time search for meaning and direction. Unfettered by such "externally imposed" constraints as consistency or tradition, our seekers give pride of place to more and more tractable supernatural beings: not gods but angels, not divinities but personal guardians. Indeed, for the post-denominational or New Age dissenter, the unsatisfying thing about traditional religions is that they don't offer hard evidence of the supernatural and they don't provide an interventionist program in which prayer gets answered directly, in healing or recovery.

In 1994, Dan Wakefield, a Presbyterian turned Unitarian, published *Expect a Miracle*, a book on the upsurge in reported miracles in the United States, and he makes a strong case that miracles are not confined to what he calls "kooks." "People like to dismiss it as the fringe," Wakefield says, "but there is a real, mainstream thing." According to a 1995 poll by *Time* magazine, for example, 69 percent of Americans believe in miracles. And yet there is an obvious fallacy in Wakefield's position, just as there was in the claims at the UFO and alien symposium that rising incidence of abduction reports is proof of their truth: the fact that more and more people believe a thing does not make it true. If believing in miracles or extra-terrestrials is lunacy when five people do so, it is still lunacy when five thousand—or even five hundred thousand—do.

Still, try and tell that to the growing number of people who gather in their hundreds, even thousands, near where I live, a place distant from the fundamentalist excesses of the Sun Belt and not previously known for religious extremism. Since early 1994, people have been coming from across Canada, the United States, and even further afield to visit a charismatic church, situated in a strip mall near the Toronto International Airport, where people have reported numerous incidents of divine visitation. At the aptly named Toronto Airport Vineyard Christian Fellowship, these people can roll in, scramble through the arrival gate, feel God's presence, experience the fits of giggling or twitching that mark the so-called "Toronto Blessing," and be back on their return flights without even springing for a downtown cab fare.

What I find notable about recent tales of miraculous intervention is how many of them are medical in nature. These are not miracles of human hope over circumstance: the real miracles of human resilience that emerge so vividly from the concentration camps, say, or the deadening poverty of the inner cities. No, these miracles concern God the Great Physician: people with fatal illnesses are "miraculously" cured, guys who have been electrocuted "miraculously" confound negative prognosis, kidney stones "miraculously" disappear when prayer circles are organized, brain tumours, certain to be fatal, "miraculously" dissolve.

Like the Ultimate Conspiracy Theory, this system of belief has the twin benefits of being both deeply satisfying and entirely unfalsifiable. In his treatise on *Ethics*—a work so hostile to Church authority that it was prudent to publish it only after his death in 1677—the philosopher Benedict de Spinoza described the will of God as "the asylum of ignorance," a place to which credulous people retreat when no explanations can be offered for events in the world. "And hence it comes about," Spinoza added, "that someone who wishes to seek out the true causes of miracles, and to understand the things of nature like a man of learning, and not stare at them in amazement like a fool, is widely deemed heretical and impious, and proclaimed such by those whom the mob adore." There is, in the end, no possible counter-evidence to the "thesis" of God's will, because everything that happens, good or bad, is His will. The miracle theory also has another benefit: people who could never hope to understand the complexities of brain surgery, for example, and who may indeed harbour a deep distrust of medicine, get to say, in triumphant Gumpism, "Those damn doctors, who think they're so smart, were wrong!"

Because miracles are so satisfying in this superficial way,

more traditional church authorities are chary of giving them too much credence. "Miracles can be like crack," says the Reverend Clarence Hardy, a West Harlem Baptist minister, "you never quite get enough of them." Certainly it seems that the believers of our own day, from fairly mainstream Christians through to the "sense of wonder" fringes of the New Age and harmonic convergence crowd, are growing in their appetite for the miraculous. "People are hungry for signs," says Roger Pilon, head of the International Medical Committee for the shrine at Lourdes, the most important miracle-validating agency other than the Vatican. Pilon notes that the Vatican seems to be going miracle crazy in the last days of the millennium. His agency has not approved a miracle since 1989; the Vatican recommended twelve in 1994 alone.

Nor is the millennial echo lost on supporters of the new miracles. "We live in an exceptional time," says Peter Wagner, a professor of church growth (whatever that may be) at Fuller Theological Seminary. "In the Middle Ages in Europe, perhaps, there may have been something comparable. But certainly in the history of the U.S. we have never seen such a frequency of signs and wonders." Wagner seems unaware of the possible cultural causes of this frequency, but he is certainly definite in his views on challenges from groups like the Jesus Seminar, an annual gathering of biblical scholars who meet to dispute the factual accuracy of the Scriptures. These scholars overturn biblical literalism with plausible explanations of events described in the Bible: Jesus' resurrection was, they suggest, the result of a temporary coma induced by crucifixion. The Star of Bethlehem was really a comet or a conjunction of stars in the sky. Jesus' famous healing of the halt and lame was really, they speculate, a matter of psychosomatic or even psychotherapeutic suggestion—He commanded them to take control of their illnesses, to believe in the power of positive thought,

ınd lo, they walked. Still other biblical scholars offer, in the
manner of the late Northrop Frye, literary or metaphorical
ınalyses of the Scriptures as influential but literally untrue
myths, "words with power."

These disputes do not reach those whose belief is deeply
pound up with miracles, of course. "I don't pay any attention whatsoever to the challenges, no matter how scholarly
they are," Wagner told Nancy Gibbs of *Time*. "Why should
I, when I see healing happening all the time?"

The intricacies of the debates among biblical scholars
can begin to make Wagner's just-say-no attitude look tempting. And indeed, for most believers, the academic disputes
are of no possible interest, because even if decisive scientific
or historical evidence of the Scriptures' falsity were secured,
it would provide no real disproof. So long as faith is defined
as a matter of the heart alone, it remains entirely immune
from any kind of rational challenge. As Pascal famously
said, "*Le coeur a ses raisons que la raison ne connaît point.*"
Indeed, for those inclined to believe, for whatever complex
of historical, cultural, or psychological reasons, this immunity is a point in faith's favour: belief is held *despite* the arguments of reason. For those of opposite inclination, the
immunity of faith from debate is the first and most important clue that it is ideology, not knowledge: it cannot ever
be rationally punctured.

The trouble with miracles, as some thoughtful theologians realize, is that they place the believer in an uncomfortable middle position. Jesus used his miracles—the
healing and loaves and fishes and so on—to prove that he
was not yet another deluded paranoiac but in fact the Son
of God. And that appeared to work, at least among that
group of men who wrote the accounts of his life and death
we know as the Synoptic Gospels. Yet Jesus was not happy
about the apparently endless appetite of his followers for
these outward signs. "Why does this generation ask for a

sign?" he angrily demanded of the faithless.

Perhaps he knew, as Rev. Hardy of West Harlem knows, that a taste for miracles can be addictive and, what is worse, undermining of faith as it is usually understood. After all, once you start looking for signs to confirm your faith, you might just find yourself put off your faith when the signs fail to come.

— — —

If personal guardians are on offer—angels or spirits or whatever—that will help protect me from the rising tide of violence and uncertainty, I decide I must seek mine out. After all, you never know. It was Pascal himself, in his famous wager about God's existence, who made it clear that taking out spiritual insurance policies is rational. Putting your money on God costs little and promises unlimited bliss; putting your money on *no* God pays off here and now, maybe, but the potential costs are daunting. (There is a way of hedging your bets, by the way. Given God's penchant for unconditional forgiveness, a confirmed sinner can always change sides when things start to look bad. Hence the popularity of death-bed conversions.)

I am invited to a lecture called "Man and the Universe" given by some devotees of a group known as the Inner Peace Movement (IPM), a Washington, D.C.-based organization founded in 1964 by a Puerto Rican man named Francisco Coll. The brochure for the lecture promises that it will "give you a bigger picture of yourself and the world around you," which sounds appealing. It also promises to clarify "the different states of consciousness on planet earth and explore the seven year cycles of life." There is some talk of auras and energy fields and so on. But what I'm really interested in is the angels. "You have angels," the promotional poster says. "We all have angels. Find out how to communicate with them to get your own answers to life."

Like everyone else, I can no longer avoid angels. They have stormed through the popular culture since about 1990. They are now visible virtually everywhere, especially in those cinnamon-scented gift shops, wellness centres, and Christmas stores that are a year-round fixture in some shopping malls. Their images, ruthlessly excised from earlier works of devotional art, appear in picture-books and desk calendars, on posters and cards, as statues and pendants. They sport personalizing nicknames and descriptions; special powers of healing and companionship are ascribed to them.

According to the IPM people, much of this recent popularity is actually giving angels a bad name. Like flash-in-the-pan pop stars, they are in danger of becoming overexposed. In fact, according to IPM authorities, the angels do not have personal names. They do not, as the images suggest, literally have wings and flowing robes. They are instead, according to the lecturer, "graduates of the school of planet Earth," supernatural beings charged with the personal care of those who remain below. Angels are, in other words, a group of what might be called super-souls, elevated individuals who hang around in cosmic space to give guidance to the rest of us.

During the opening lecture, Susan, a relentlessly cheerful middle-aged woman, who is dressed in celestial blue and wears a ceramic cherub around her neck, mentions the imaginary friend she had as a child and notes that this was her first brush with the angels. Now, when she feels an involuntary shiver sometimes, she knows that they are near. She also talks to them a lot; they are like voices in her head. Susan has a lot of angels and that indicates, she says, that she was meant to work with people: she needs lots of company to help her. She travels the world, living with amazing frugality on a diet consisting mostly of brown rice, and spreads the good news about inner peace. She got involved with IPM after her eldest son died of cancer at a young age and, in search of answers, she found her way to an IPM lecture just like this one in a Vancouver hotel.

Now it happens that I am subject to involuntary shivers quite a lot. I'll be sitting reading or watching television and my whole body will ripple from top to bottom like a garden hose being shaken out. So this is how my angels let me know they are around! I can't yet talk to my angels, of course, because I lack the ability to hear them speak. Also, I haven't paid the sixty-five-dollar fee for a personal consultation with a "sensitive" like Susan or the other IPM types at the lecture, during which I could establish direct contact with my angels. I can, however, hear what my angels have to say by working in tandem with one of the sensitives at the meeting.

Here's how it works. I give some personal object to a sensitive and, because he's a sensitive and he's holding something that has me all over it, my angels swing in close to his angels. Because he can talk to his angels, and his angels can (of course) talk to other angels hovering nearby, we can close the link by having him tell me what my angels are thinking. As a system of communication this is not terribly efficient, but considering the difficulties of translation from two wholly different realms of existence, not to mention two different forms of being, it is not entirely inelegant. I give my wedding ring to a "sensitive" called John, who, for some reason I cannot fathom, sports a little flashlight in a leather holster attached to his belt. John is young, in his twenties, and he is slightly lumpy and badly dressed in a mild computer-nerd manner. But he is very friendly and he takes my wedding ring with evident enthusiasm. I must say, I am looking forward to this. Who wouldn't? I really want to hear what the super-beings devoted to my spiritual well-being have to say to me. I mean, am I doing all right? Is my life all it could be, spiritually speaking? Is there other work I should be doing? Could I be happier? Have I chosen the right path to personal development and wholeness and so on?

The results are a bit disappointing. John closes his eyes in a show of concentration and then says: "I see you working with your hands, maybe with glass." I am a little nonplussed. The only work I do with my hands is typing, and the only important glass in my life is the screen on my computer monitor and the tumbler I drink whisky from. But what the hell; John is about to tell me more. "I see a car, a small car." Pause. "It's a convertible."

I am thinking: Excellent! I don't even own a car, let alone a sporty convertible, but I have always wanted a Mazda Miata or, failing that, one of those little Saturns with the detachable hard roof—you know, the ones with the... well, never mind. But are the angels telling me to buy one? Or are they saying that one is coming? It makes kind of a big difference, but I figure either way this is *very good news.*

What about spiritual well-being, though? Life direction? Don't the angels want to tell me about the course my life is taking, the possibly disastrous choices I have made? Don't they want to tell me I have strayed from the true path? No, nothing. John adds a few more details about the car, says that I am probably a clear thinker, a sentiment I find only mildly flattering, and opens his eyes, returning the wedding ring to my hand. This is a keen disappointment. John has told me the little stuff, and I want to hear some big stuff.

I decide to try another sensitive, an older woman called Elise who was involved in the IPM presentations that led off the meeting. She is blond and rather girlish in her manner, and she speaks in a way that prompts me to say, though only to myself, "It's okay to use your grown-up voice now." During the lecture part of the evening Elise also lost her way several times, confused the IPM slogans that I had already memorized, and then, apparently apropos of nothing, quoted the tag from St. Paul that the seventeenth-century English Ranters were given to uttering: "All things are pure to the pure." What did she mean? How does that sentiment relate to the IPM angels stuff? Was she maybe calling us to engage in some kind of Ranter-style free love session? I had no idea. I looked around for guidance, but nobody else seemed to know either.

Elise doesn't need to hold anything to get into contact with my angels. She waves off my suggestion that I give her a glove to hold. She just gives me a hard look, closes her eyes and says, "I see you pursuing a course of study." Okay, this is in some sense true. "I also see cars," she adds immediately. "I don't know why. Cars."

The cars again. Now I'm really starting to feel a little put upon. Are the angels suggesting a car is on its way, a gift from an unknown force? Or are they telling me I ought to get out there to the strip malls and just buy a damn car? Well, they're not saying, and neither, as a result, is Elise. She just shrugs. "Your angels cannot interfere with your free will," Susan tells us. "They are there to advise and guide, not to make decisions for you." I don't see how this car business is helping me get my own answers to life, but there you are. I am probably in spiritual conflict somewhere.

Now the evening has given way to a kind of group participation stunt in which we all, sensitives and regulars alike, read each other's auras: the halo of spiritual energy that surrounds us all and tells those who can see how we are faring. You can get your aura photographed at a psychics' fair, but I've never done it, and I am fairly eager to have mine read. I didn't, however, count on having to read anybody else's. What do I know about auras? It occurs to me, rather cynically, that all this participatory stuff—reading auras, holding our hands close together to feel the energy that leaps from person to person, and so on—has the desirable effect of forestalling rational detachment. It is hard to remain critical when you are standing a few feet away from someone, your eyes closed, telling them what their aura says to you.

At first I am at a loss for things to say. The done thing, I soon realize, is to devolve into banal but flattering generalities of the sort found in Hallmark greeting cards and newspaper horoscopes ("You are kind, warm-hearted, and generous"). Should you want to get specific, you can always read the clothes. What people choose to wear says a lot more about their character than any aura. But it is all a bit embarrassing, this aura reading, and embarrassment takes the critical faculties off-line. In the midst of our round of aura-reading musical chairs, switching from partner to partner, I still manage to wonder why this sort of easily digested message of inner peace is so popular in our time. Why did the angels storm across the continent in the 1990s?

Well, for one thing, they clearly satisfy a common human desire for personal protection, for a sense of accommodation. The angels' message of spiritual okayness is vastly more popular, and more attractive, than the stern directives of traditional religious belief. They tell you, as that nauseating text "Desiderata" did during its 1970s heyday, that you are a child of the universe, that you have a right to be here. And they do it in the nicest imaginable way. The angels are chummy, watchful, and uncritical. They don't push and prod; they are basically cut down to our size. God, after all, is often too much to deal with, and even Jesus can be a handful sometimes. He is demanding, and he expects an awful lot of us.

Like the cult around the Virgin Mary, the angels cult—which is no longer always or even usually Christian—allows people to feel that the spiritual link they crave is welcoming and warm, not cold and judgmental. The New Age angels found in the glossy *Angel Times Magazine*, for example, or the best-selling "Angels" wall poster, sweet to the point of nausea ("Angels love you for who you are…"), are not at all like the Christian archangels, many of whom, as we know, were hard-nosed warriors like St. Michael or terrifying messengers like St. Gabriel. The New Age angels are more like Susan's ceramic pendant, cherubic and friendly. They are non-threatening avatars for the confused inhabitants of a threatened age. We like them. More important, they like us.

In the summer of 1224, just a few months before St. Francis of Assisi would find himself bearing Christ's wounds during his Swiss retreat, an aged hermit was found wandering in a forest between the towns of Tournai and Valenciennes. Like Peter the Hermit a century and a half before him, this man had the traditional appearance of the God-appointed seer: long hair, flowing beard, the emaciated limbs of the ascetic. According to contemporary observers, he was recognized as Baldwin IX, Count of Flanders and Emperor of Constantinople, a legendary leader who had dominated central Europe during the transition from the twelfth to the thirteenth century, leading the Fourth Crusade in 1202. Baldwin had in fact been killed while campaigning in the east in 1205, but his legend lived on, aided by a general longing for the super-human leader he might have been. In retrospect, his memory grew beyond all reasonable proportion. He was spoken of as almost divine, half-demon and half-angel. On being taken for this celebrated ruler, the Valenciennes hermit was immediately hailed as the messiah-king, returned to save Christendom from the forces of darkness and unbelief.

It is not clear whether this was his idea or simply something he went along with, but the hermit—now known to scholars as Pseudo-Baldwin—was quickly crowned Emperor of Constantinople and Thessalonica. The sumptuous ceremony, held at Valenciennes in May of 1225, combined all the splendours of western and eastern ritual. "Clad in imperial purple," Norman Cohn writes,

> borne in a litter or mounted on a noble palfrey, surrounded by the banners of his domains in the East and West and preceded by the cross which traditionally preceded the successors of Constantine—yet still wearing the long beard of a holy hermit and carrying the white wand of benevolence instead of a metal sceptre—he must indeed have seemed the messianic Emperor, come at last to fulfill the old Sibylline prophecies.

Contemporary accounts of the coronation give evidence of the enthusiasm. "If God had come down to earth he could not have been better received," one observer wrote. Large crowds followed him as he went to Lille, Ghent, and Bruges to accept money and tributes. People dropped to their knees as he passed by in imperial procession. He was especially popular among the poor, who were recovering from yet another famine. "The poor folk, weavers and fullers, were his intimates," the same observer said, "and the better off and rich people got a bad deal everywhere. The poor folk said they would have gold and silver…and they called him Emperor."

Soon, despite their misgivings, the rich and powerful followed suit. Princes in neighbouring dominions sent their messengers to his court and Henry III of England offered to forge an alliance. Louis VIII of France did likewise, prompting the new Emperor to travel in full regalia to the French court at Péronne. But this, as Cohn remarks, was "a fatal blunder." In Louis's presence, the reincarnated Baldwin showed himself unable to recall things the real Baldwin would certainly have known, and he was soon unmasked as an impostor. He was in fact a serf called Bertrand of Ray, from a small town in Burgundy. He had gone on the Fourth Crusade—as a minstrel—and in his home town had, it turned out, a reputation as a charlatan and impersonator. Bertrand was allowed to flee from the French court, but he made yet another mistake: he returned to Valenciennes, pitching the town into chaos. The rich burghers tried to arrest him but were prevented by crowds of the still-loyal poor, who instead threw some of the wealthy into jail. The local government was dissolved and most of the town declined into drunken revelry, while a few of the townspeople began fortifying the walls for the anticipated retaliation by French forces.

It never came. Bertrand, utterly unnerved now, fled from Valenciennes with a large sum of money stolen from the town's treasury. He was soon captured and paraded in disgrace through the towns he had so lately conquered, now jeered and mocked by the crowds who had called him their saviour. In October of 1225, just seven months after his triumphant coronation as Emperor, he was hanged in the marketplace at Lille.

The hapless Bertrand had the misfortune, or perhaps the lack of wit, to allow his personal ambitions to be caught up in a powerful imaginative force in Christian eschatology: the idea of the warrior-messiah, first set out in the Book of Revelation and later embroidered by the Sibylline prophecies. The messiah who comes in John's story is arrayed for battle, and he slays Satan's armies through force of arms. Added to a long-standing tendency among martial peoples to deify their kings, many of whom held the post by virtue of military success, and bolstered by the popular expectation of the Second Coming, the idea of an Emperor of the Last Days exerted immense imaginative power. He was to come, defeat the forces of darkness, and inaugurate the long reign of peace that was predicted before the final confrontation between the forces of Heaven and Hell.

This messiah-king was fervently sought for more than a thousand years of Christian history, and various kings and emperors were hailed as the first earthly sign of the Final Judgment. This happened to legendary early warrior-kings, like Constantine and Charlemagne and their various heirs, who consolidated the Christian world during the first millennium after Christ; it also happened to later monarchs, especially those associated with the Crusades, like Frederick I, known as Frederick Barbarossa for his red beard, and his grandson Frederick II.

Indeed, the periodic re-appearance of this divine leader was often taken as evidence that a single Emperor existed and merely slumbered between manifestations, waiting until the time was ripe to be reborn. Frederick II, who went on a crusade in 1229 and captured the city of Jerusalem, was a brilliant and versatile leader, highly intelligent yet given to cruelty and licentiousness, and he exerted a strong imaginative pull on fellow soldiers and regular subjects alike. When he died in 1250 it was a heavy blow to his followers, who had predicted an apocalyptic confrontation with the forces of evil—this time identified with the corrupt Roman church led by Pope Innocent IV, who was anything but—in the prophesied year of 1260.

It was immediately rumoured that Frederick was not dead but only hiding, or asleep, and through the latter part of the century various impostors, pseudo-Fredericks, announced themselves. These appearances only contributed to the mythic status of the deceased emperor and the intense longing for his return. When one of the impostors was burned at the stake in the 1280s, it was reported that no bones were to be found among his ashes, only a small bean—evidence, they said, that the divine Frederick had been lifted to Heaven in order, one day, to return. He was expected by many well into the fourteenth century.

A parallel story in Christian prophecy at this time told of a powerful *false* leader who would arise in the time before the Last Days. In appearance almost divine, the Antichrist would oppose the Emperor and deceive the people with miracles and a convincing show of good will. But he would be Satan's servant, and his armies, the people of Gog and Magog, might attack at any time. Thus, for example, were invading Turks and Saracens demonized by Christian princes to stir the fervour of their people. Yet the dialectic of good and evil created in the popular imagination by these prophecies made it easy for claims and counter-claims to be made on behalf of earthly leaders. "It frequently occurred," writes Cohn, "that a pope would solemnly declare his opponent—some turbulent emperor or maybe an anti-pope—to be Antichrist himself; whereupon the same epithet would be flung back at him."

One central feature of millennial panic, then, is that great leaders should be somehow *missing*, even as the people are beset by pretenders and false prophets. The people wait in anticipation of the great leader, harbinger of the true Saviour's triumphant return. At the same time, they fear that the time is already past, that no leader will save them, and that the earth will flow with fire. The theme is double-edged; it embraces both hope and despair. There is also the further doubleness of doubt: for every person who hails a given pretender to leadership as the true king, there is another who sees him indisputably as the evil Antichrist.

The historical parallels lay bare a strong desire for political leadership that has nowhere diminished in our own day, even if its form has altered. In our own form of leadership crisis, we do not typically expect a quasi-divine leader to roust himself from his slumber and assume the mantle of the Emperor of Last Days. Yet our deep misgivings about actual political leaders suggest an unresolved longing for something more transforming: the gifted and trustworthy leader as a kind of earthly saviour, what Thucydides called, in an even older expression of this longing, "the best man." Pericles, said Thucydides, was such a man, who, because "clearly above corruption, was enabled, by the respect others had for him and his own wise policy, to hold the multitude in voluntary restraint. He led them; not they him."

We have not found the modern version of Pericles or Frederick. On the contrary, misgivings about political leadership are expressed everywhere. This is perhaps most evident in apathy and anger about the political process. During the 1992 American presidential elections, for example, the populist demagogue Ross Perot, who offered little in the way of platform except an expression of resentment at "how things are done," captured 19 million votes, terrifying leaders from the Republican and Democratic parties to such an extent that in early 1995 they all began courting the "Perot vote" in expectation of a hard-fought 1996 campaign. Yet the actions of the voters tell less than half the story. In 1995, only 62 percent of the American population was even registered to vote—compared to 88 percent in Mexico and over 90 percent in Canada. And during mid-term elections in 1994, only 39 percent of Americans bothered to cast their ballots; of these politically active citizens, only 24 percent knew the names of their senators or representatives.

There is, further, a sense that routine distrust of governments, the sort of thing that any of us might feel now and then, can easily lead, in extreme cases, to a debilitating belief in the all-encompassing power of the "They." The popularity of anti-Washington sentiment is growing, expressed in unnerving incivility by talk-radio rabble-rousers like Rush Limbaugh and reaching, in some cases, the extremes of quasi-anarchist militias and self-declared "freedom zones" in Montana, Idaho, and Michigan. Not every harsh critic of government is about to start laying in the AK-47s and freeze-dried food, of course, but it is a fairly short step, these days, from "I think Bill Clinton is a bad president" to "Bill Clinton ordered the Branch Davidian genocide." If you doubt this, just watch CNN for a few days.

We can probably date the convergence of these two broad themes—loss of faith in political action and belief in high-level conspiracy—from the traumatic event of the keynote year of 1963: the Kennedy assassination. What happened in Dallas remains the ground zero of conspiracy thinking, even if the field has spun off into all manner of extra-dimensional lunacy. The event also marks the destruction of a leader who, albeit undeservedly, represented the brighter hopes of a nation in transition. It is received wisdom to date America's loss of faith from the Watergate scandal, and that indeed remains a powerful series of events in the formation of the political cynicism now so apparently widespread; but the foundations were actually laid by the elimination of Nixon's prime-time debating foe, his nemesis John Kennedy. American political culture lost its leader on November 22, 1963. It also, apparently, lost its belief in leaders.

It is true that the highly visible and deeply shocking public assassinations of three decades ago have ceased to be a frequent feature of North American public life, but the odd wacko still fires an automatic-weapon at the façade of the White House, prompting more and more siege-like security measures to cut off that public building from its country's citizens. (New York's *Spy* magazine recently published, in their now regular "Millennium Approaches" feature, an illustration of the twenty-first-century White House, completely covered by a protective bubble of bullet-proof glass.) And even if the events recede in time, the legacy of those assassinations is not diminished. They are still a blot on American cultural memory. The Warren Commission laid nothing to rest.

The literal assassination of The Leader has been replaced

by more or less genteel bureaucratic and journalistic character assassination, the relentless attacking of public figures
under the banner of the "character issue." These virtual
attacks frequently extend past the boundaries of justifiable
accountability, of course. It is as though the senators and
news anchors firmly believe that only a saint could justly
aspire to be president or a Supreme Court judge. The
method of attack is no longer criminal, in other words, but
the effect of undermining confidence in the chosen leader is
identical. The prospective leaders are scrutinized and belit-
tled in lengthy confirmation hearings. Their merest utterance is dissected during nationally televised debates. Not
surprisingly, they are found wanting. In the midst of all this
scrutiny, which has not yet managed to create better leaders,
we have become a culture without heroes, without illusions.

At the same time, and not coincidentally, never has
there been more emphasis on the rosy ideal of leadership.
We seem to long for some mythically wise leader, a King
Arthur figure to rescue us from our iniquity.

Lacking religious faith, we seek our leader now not in myths
of the slumbering emperor but in the social-scientific baffle-
gab of the lecture hall and in the profit-driven air of the
corporate boardroom. "Leadership studies" programs have
sprung up at more than six hundred universities across
North America, where earnest graduate students now pore
over the collected wisdom of Machiavelli, Aristotle, and
Ayn Rand looking for clues. At the same time, a whole
leadership industry has developed in the tense world of big
money, spawning training programs and self-help manuals
like toadstools and generating millions of dollars of revenue
for seminar-givers, database-crunchers, and pamphlet-writ-
ers of dubious insight.

"In some respects the leadership cult resembles a real

culture," critic Benjamin DeMott writes. "It possesses a distinct language. It honors heroes and texts comparatively unknown to the general public. It consistently defines past and present reality on its own terms. And it displays a strong determination to enlarge the spheres of its influence." DeMott reported his exposure to leadership studies in bitter retrospect, after spending a weekend evaluating grant proposals made to a U.S. government pork barrel called the Dwight D. Eisenhower Leadership Development Fund.

Cult or not, leadership now dominates the discourse of North American business. A 1988 *Fortune* magazine article titled "What Makes for Magic Leadership?" was an early part of the canon (now "accorded reverence befitting Paul's second letter to the Corinthians," says DeMott), followed a year later by Max DePree's *Leadership Is an Art* and, the big kahuna of biz-whiz books, Stephen R. Covey's *The Seven Habits of Highly Effective People*. The callow soon noticed how Covey's sales figures were mounting, and the boom was on; there are now too many leadership books to mention. Soon came the university programs, the anthologies, and the juicy federal grant programs—DeMott reports that the average award from the Eisenhower fund is $175,000 (U.S.). There are even a few crossover efforts, including a 1995 bestseller called *Jesus, CEO*, that make no bones about the religious undertone of the leadership cult.

Companies and universities are now lining up to take your money in exchange for leadership training. The idea behind this is simple, if troubling: whereas people used to think that leadership was something that could not be taught, the leadership industry now tells us that good leaders are made, not born. There is a millennial echo in the boardrooms of the nation, or at least in the advertising of seminars and training programs—lots of talk of "Leadership Styles for the New Millennium" and "Forging Into 2000!" and "Negotiating a Brave New Century."

The programs on offer, which range from the routinely corporate to the borderline wacko, are listed in continuing-education newspapers or posted on-line by services like the Skillslink Report, a sort of electronic clearing house for the training industry. You might pay as little as $200 for a half-day Dale Carnegie seminar in a suburban industrial park, where you would learn how to win friends and influence people, or as much as $1,800 a day for a week-long role-playing retreat in tony enclaves like Niagara-on-the-Lake or Colorado Springs.

At the daft end of the spectrum lie companies like Eidetics Integrated 3-D Management Systems, a group of "eidetic psychologists" devoted to the development of organizations as "wholeness systems." The Eidetics people have produced an expensive full-colour brochure to sell their stuff, chock-full of weirdly complicated diagrams, references to unpublished "research," and punch-out cardboard models that can be assembled into little octahedrons (I guess that's the 3-D part). It is as if Doug Henning's Natural Law Party had decided to go corporate. "Eidetics" apparently means vivid mental imagery, and the approach seems to hinge on "creative visualization." According to the Eidetics literature, the octahedrons are key learning tools because they illustrate the various facets of human motivation and the essentials of leadership. Each side of the figures has a word or phrase printed on it—intuition, anxiety, volition, manifestation, and so on—with one side reserved for the goal of "integration" or "wholeness."

Other offerings are not quite so bizarre. In search of the new leadership wisdom and mindful of the crisis in leadership, I make my way to the offices of MICA Management Resources Inc., one of the many slick companies cashing in on the leadership crisis. At MICA's plush downtown Toronto offices I enter tentatively into the new leadership nexus. I am not allowed simply to observe, however, since interactivity is the order of the day. I have to undergo a complex "leadership effectiveness analysis." And I'm glad I do, really, because I learn some interesting things about myself.

For instance, when it comes to personal leadership qualities, I am apparently no Captain Picard. The "Star Trek" hero's avuncular tough-love style has recently become a model for boardroom behavior—right down to the infamous "Picard manoeuvre," in which the Captain tugs his tunic down after making a tough decision. Unlike him, however, I do not value input from my subordinates. Nor, it seems, am I a sensitive, caring listener. In fact, when it comes to leadership style, it seems I am in "Star Trek" terms not so much Picard as Borg—that is, the relentless collective entity bent on the domination of all carbon-based life-forms. That's right: tests show that, as a leader of people, I am big to the point of mania on technical and strategic thinking, but so dismissive of consensus-building and co-operation that I make Cesare Borgia look like a softy.

My fellow leadership analysands at the MICA seminar are a pretty normal cross-section of the business world. There is Peggy, a personnel manager from a large pharmaceutical company in need of some new managerial thinking; Rick, a retired bank exec now involved in running a volunteer board; Tucker, a handsome man who calls himself an "outplacement consultant," which I happen to know is a euphemism for the guy hired to hold your hand after you've been fired; and the Stomachman.

The Stomachman is actually Richard Zinck. He is a tall, ordinary-looking guy with a nice smile and a good line of self-deprecating humour. Zinck is the owner of a Guelph, Ontario, catering-truck company called Stomachman Ltd. He gave himself and his company the Stomachman name as an advertising ploy, hitting on something people would remember, and on the day we meet he sports a bright

Stomachman necktie, which shows a cape-wearing, hot-dog-wielding superhero who apparently flies around town delivering coffee and nosh to hungry on-site workers the city over. (The same figure, complete with red cape and purple jumpsuit, appears on Zinck's business card.) Stomachman tells me he had 800 of the garish ties custom-made to boost his business profile. He doesn't tell me what happened to the 799 he is not wearing.

The five of us spend a morning thinking and talking about leadership in our different walks of life, a discussion that is "facilitated" by two staffers from MICA. The Mican tag-team is keen to sell us their "technology" and its various "instruments" (that is, tests and manuals) so that we can analyse leadership effectiveness back in our own "corporate cultures" (that is, companies). Our leader that day is Wanda Parker, an attractive, fortyish woman who is almost unbearably perky. Parker is the director of client services at MICA, and a partner in the company. She is also a master of the techno-speak that resounds through today's strangely psychologized corporate world. At various points during the morning she speaks of "leveraging a behaviour," "tasting a direction," and "top-lining an issue." She uses the words "norm," "trial," "benchmark" and "outsource" as verbs. She seems entirely at ease with the adjectives "impactful" and "360"—as in 360-analysis, otherwise known as "the whole picture." I am not entirely sure, but I think "360" is also used as a verb. I think we "360" ourselves; or possibly we are "360'd" by some outside force.

DeMott, too, noticed this strange mixture of pop psychology, Pentagonese, and watered-down philosophy of science coursing through the leadership-training world. "Keywords and phrases include 'megaskill,' 'capstone experience,' 'futures-creative,' 'program design matrices,' and 'diversity training,'" he wrote. "Key proverbs and sayings are pretentiously gnomic. ('Your self is your paradigm.' 'Your paradigm is that part of you which your enemy wants to know.')"

The strange thing about the leadership industry's jargony morass is how easily everyone else seems to pick their way through it. At times during the MICA seminar I feel my brain veering off in sheer perplexity at the words flying past me. It feels as though Parker is uttering sentences that, like Noam Chomsky's celebrated "Colourless green ideas sleep furiously," follow the rules of syntax without making semantic sense. This does not seem to be a widely shared response, however. Peggy, Rick, and Tucker lap it up. Even Stomachman, your basic ordinary guy, a guy you could imagine having a beer with, takes it all in without demur.

The linguistic and theoretical shoddiness is par for the course in the booming training industry. "Spelling was relaxed," DeMott noted of the proposals he read during his weekend-long initiation into leadership speak. "Grammar sucked." ("There is a major difference in today's world than in the world of yesterday's great leaders," noted one proposal, from the University of Arizona.) DeMott also offered a frightening sampling of what happens when leadership-training academics get together and, in the usual academic fashion, read scholarly papers to one another. "Robert Browning's 'My Last Duchess': A Contrast in Management Styles," one title read. "Lessons for Leadership in T.S. Eliot's *Murder in the Cathedral*," offered another. "Group Dynamics and Crisis Management in *For Whom the Bell Tolls*." "Christopher Marlowe and the Crash of 1987: Literary Lessons for the Contemporary 'Overachiever.'"

MICA doesn't go in for that kind of literary or philosophical analysis, but it is typical of the business side of the genre, running various New-Agey "people development" programs, from Edward de Bono's "Six Thinking Hats" to something called "In Praise of Hierarchy." These are designed to help companies meet the challenges of what is invariably described by training gurus as "the downsized economy" of the 1990s—what Parker herself likes to call "the white-knuckle decade." The Micans also have access to a "leadership database"; based in Portland, Maine, it consists of more than 200,000 detailed responses to a massive standardized questionnaire. It is my responses to the questionnaire, fed into the computer, that spit out the numbers casting me in the role of Master of the Universe.

In addition to scraping the ceiling in strategic and technical skills (both 95th percentile against the database population), I manage the unusual feat of being both highly conservative and very innovative (85th and 70th percentile respectively)—probably some kind of verdict on life as an academic. I am cruelly low on empathy (25th percentile) and apparently indifferent to persuading others of the merits of my ideas (30th percentile). But my lowest scores are reserved for the part of the survey called "Team Playing." My brutal 5th percentile showing in consensus-building is matched only by one that measures respect for authority. Apparently, MICA-person Anne Grieve says as she looks over my test results, I am "unusual in my scepticism about authority figures." Scepticism? On this evidence I must be one small step away from sociopathic violence.

Still, given the right context—warring street gangs, maybe, or feuding Italian city-states—I might be one hell of a leader. As Parker says, "There is no *one* way to lead."

That seems true—true enough, in fact, to be a matter of common sense. Like most ideas designed to be ingested quickly, the facilitation approach to leadership is long on the obvious, short on the profound. The new guru of leadership studies in the 1990s, Warren Bennis, has outdistanced the competition by giving advice like this with an air of scientific authority. And he has succeeded brilliantly. Like Thomas Homer-Dixon, Bennis has been called in to consult with U.S. vice-president Al Gore, and Parker praises him to the skies. Yet, on examination, his best-selling 1989 book *On Becoming a Leader* reveals a mind mostly at rest. His lessons are hoary with age yet presented with an air of breathless discovery. Leaders must respond to changes in context. Vision must be clear. Communication is key.

What is disturbing about the current run of leadership studies is not the idea of training per se. That is nothing other than a reasonable response to the desire for better leaders, and it is the same response offered by virtually anybody who writes about leadership. The disturbing thing is rather the relentless *technicality* of the approach. Leadership training is not sold on the wisdom of its lessons, for that wisdom could be had much more cheaply in your local bookstore—or simply by pausing to think a while. It is sold instead on the air of "technological" sharpness contained in the surveys, overheads, and feedback tools. This is technotopian leadership, to use a Krokerism. It is virtual leadership.

People in the corporate world pay for this air of technicality because technical solutions to tractable problems are exactly what they understand. One of Parker's selling points for the MICA "technology" was that company execs could see the data staring them in the face: can you move your 30th percentile in communication closer to your subordinates' expectation of 70th percentile? Never mind that quantifying complex behaviour is a mug's game, or that hoping to find out how you can become, say, "more communicative" is, even in a three-day seminar, ridiculous.

The irony in all this talk of new ways of thinking and developing leadership is that it eventually boils down to the one and only way of thinking really welcome in the corporate world: the logic of manipulating the world for higher profit. In the end, no amount of linguistic creativity and punch-out 3-D figures will change the fact that the world of business is one ruled by numbers and dollar signs. In this context, leadership studies are just the latest version of the royal road to a higher number, the only one that really matters: the bottom line is always...the bottom line.

DeMott, charged with doling out taxpayers' money to the new leadership gurus, is willing to go even further in his denunciation of the leadership cult. In his eyes, leadership studies is actually a dangerously anti-democratic form of elitism, creating a version of the problem leadership training allegedly set out to solve. "[F]ear of the mob lies deep in the American grain," he wrote, "and the leadership culture reflects its continuing pervasiveness." Two "political fantasies" shaping the technocratic form of leadership, then, are that "(1) there are no major differences of interest in American society demanding fair settlement; (2) ways of evading the responsibilities and entailments of a democratic political system can always be found." Here elitism meets populism—DeMott calls them the "twin killers of democratic hope"—and ploughs genuine political challenges under. From this gloomy perspective, leadership studies is worse than self-defeating; it is dangerous: "another sign of Establishment enthusiasm for replacing politics with social science, open argument with manipulated consent."

The soul-searching prompted by the crisis in leadership should be welcome. Yet the approaches that dominate here, the corporate and academic technicality, ultimately render the leadership crisis deeper than before. We will not find effective leaders by studying shallow advice manuals or attending "facilitated" weekend workshops. If there was hope, in the mind of Al Gore or elsewhere, that the new corporate and academic focus on leadership would help solve the democratic disgust with elected leaders, or would generate a new third-millennium vision for our troubled social and economic times, it is fated for disappointment. When it comes to meeting the needs of a deeply divided and pluralistic political culture, not just those of a business or an academic program, leaders are not so easy to create.

Most crucially we lack the necessary condition of effective leadership identified in Garry Wills's thoughtful 1994 book *Certain Trumpets: The Call of Leaders*: agreement on the preferred destiny of the country. (This statement holds on both sides of the 49th parallel.) Without such agreement, we are destined to repeat the bitter denunciations of actual leaders even as we continue to hope for a new political messiah to arrive.

Though there will be pretenders both heralded and self-proclaimed, the truth is that no slumbering Frederick or Baldwin will awake to save us. That is simply the reality of our earthly status: leaders, even great ones, are still human, not divine. Our tragedy is not, however, that the saviour will not come; it is rather that we have apparently given in to the opposite millennial temptation. Every leader who rises to prominence is really just a new Antichrist.

■ ＿ ■

Such negativity, the evident loss of cultural and political faith, remains a vivid temptation for many people today, especially those young enough to view the uncertainty of the third millennium with more alarm than acceptance. A profound lack of belief, a cynicism approaching nihilism, now lies alongside the fervent desire to believe that is evident among devotees of angels and miracles.

Consider, as an example of this, the immensely popular films of Quentin Tarantino. Here comedy is provided, as in *Pulp Fiction* (gross returns by the middle of 1995: $107 million U.S.), by accidentally blowing off someone's head as a car goes over a bump in the road. Character is illustrated by using the words "nigger" and "fucking" as often, and as inventively, as possible. Tarantino's visual style has been much copied since the release of his first film, *Reservoir Dogs*, in 1992, but his attitude is the thing most imitators strive to realize: the fuck-you coolness, the bitter humour and cheerful amorality. Do these cultural signifiers suggest a generation of North Americans who find no possible meaning in meaning? I think they do. To believe in something deeper than, say, the twisted "professionalism" of the vicious jewel thief Mr. Pink in *Reservoir Dogs* is, from this now powerful point of view, strong evidence of a lack of irony, that crucial cultural commodity.

This phenomenon is by no means restricted to the shadow-play of the Cineplexes. Veneration of Mr. Pink and other ruthless celluloid killers—Mr. Pink T-shirts are sold on the sidewalks of my neighbourhood in Toronto, alongside shirts sporting Dr. Seuss characters and Hergé's Tintin—is simply a cinematic version of what has been called "serial killer chic." (The identification is admittedly a little unfair to Mr. Pink, who is a serious thief and only incidentally a killer.) The fanatic devotion to sociopathic mass murderers like Charles Manson, Ted Bundy, John Wayne Gacy, or Jeffrey Dahmer is a fascinating stress sign in the culture. Their much-reproduced faces become charismatic magnets for erotic or amatory fantasies. Within six months of his capture and imprisonment, the Oklahoma City bomber Timothy McVeigh had received four marriage proposals.

Serial-killer trading cards and T-shirts probably lie toward the benign end of a spectrum of devotion that declines into declarations of love and even violent imitation, but the whole spectrum of responses is disturbing. The glamourization of senseless violence is now all but complete. Several recent serial-killer films—*Kalifornia, Natural Born Killers, The Doom Generation*—exhibit the new confluence of murder, fandom, and the counter-cultural aura of the road movie, while another, *True Romance*, makes extreme violence a twisted form of youthful courtship. Murder is arguably the hippest possible mid-1990s undertaking; it is, as the character Mallory says in *Natural Born Killers*, "so cool" to kill.

In a twisted way, the impulse of killer-worship is actually aesthetic. Fans of serial murderers in effect render the killer's destructive act into a creative one, a kind of acted-out cultural criticism. But in this way fans manage to avoid the real impulses behind killing, and, moreover, the reality of violence. "The reformatory hardened and violent [killers] and the frail violence-aesthetes would, in spite of their physical resemblance, find each other repellent, and for good reason," says Toronto poet Lynn Crosbie, herself a semi-reformed serial-killer devotee. "Most sensitive artists spent a lot of time in high school dodging the blows of someone like Manson, and Manson and his early associates (such as the convicted murderer Alvin 'Creepy' Karpis) were hardly plastering their cells with Brian Eno posters." In this view, Quentin Tarantino is simply a violence aesthete who happens to be paid handsomely to act out his geeky fantasies. Acting in his own films, he gets to carry weapons, shoot people in the face, say "fuck" all the time, and call large black men "nigger" without fear of reprisal. Some would call this the ultimate white-boy dream.

Have we become truly unshockable, then? Are contemporary filmmakers and their fans, who dote on violence, the twentieth-century manifestation of a medieval millenarian sect that Norman Cohn calls "an elite of amoral supermen"? These people, late followers of the Free Spirit heresy, took their belief well beyond accepted cultural boundaries, preaching self-deification through sex and murder and forming anarchistic communes that attacked Church authority with fervour and inventiveness. Sometimes it seems as though the cultivation of a cool surface of knowingness, an etiolated moral condition in which no amount of torture or violence makes us sick, is the real point of contemporary movie-going. Fans of ultra-violent films defend them by arguing that the violence they show is unreal, cartoonish. It is true that the violence is unreal—it happens on the screen, not in real life—but this argument should worry us more than it does. The kind of "ironic" detachment in which nothing ruffles the cool surface is not a state worth pursuing, despite what the slick cleverness of a director like Tarantino would encourage us to think.

In fact, the surprising popularity of this thoroughgoing irony—really a form of nihilism—proves that Arthur Kroker really was right: for some of us, anyway, cultural anxiety *is* virtual. We cannot actually feel the cultural pessimism of the Symbolists, those scions of the last *fin de siècle*, or find the liberating nihilism of Nietzsche, which combines despair over "the last man" with hope for the coming "Overman." In a virtual culture, even feelings of fear or revulsion come to us already encrusted with thick layers of undermining hyper-awareness. We deflect the emotions we long to feel by comparing them to something else, or by mocking ourselves for feeling them. In this kind of self-consciousness, we make ourselves into the joke: here we are laughing at ourselves laughing.

Some of the jokes are delicately poised on this crux. Take, for instance, the elaborate parody cult known as The Church of the SubGenius, a Texas-based group of ironic conspiracy theorists that offers "fraudulent but profound explanations for inexplicable manifestations" and urges its followers to "pull the wool over your own eyes" and "relax in the safety of your own delusions." The Church, with a far-flung community of several thousand "ordained ministers," most of whom joined by mail or via the Internet, takes as its motto "You'll PAY to know what you REALLY think." It is overseen by a fictional entity called J. R. "Bob" Dobbs, whose image is a 1950s advertising-style clean-cut man clenching a pipe in his teeth. The Church urges followers to pursue "slack," a state of culture-subverting grace in which they reject all the "pinks": people who have been duped by the messages of advertising, government, and popular culture. In the Church's official magazine, *The Stark Fist of Removal* (a sort of synonym for death), Bob and his minions outline The Conspiracy of Them, the descendants of an evil alien known as Jehovah One—that is, all other religions, governments, multinational corporations—to eliminate Us, who descend from a group of benign space aliens called Xists. "They're Out To Get YOU!!" one issue reads. "Global conspiracy to keep those who are 'different' silent. WEIRDMEN ARISE!! The Future Revealed by startling means. Find out who 'They' are and how to overcome them for big \$\$\$."

The Church has attracted devotees in most urban centres across North America, including a few prominent weirdos: the band Devo, the underground cartoonist Robert Crumb, Pee Wee Herman. And it has a strong following among microserfs, the twentysomethings who populate Silicon Valley as wage-slaves for large corporations. The Church appeals to the disaffected, incredulous, and annoyed. "IF you suspect that things are much worse than you ever suspected," a downloaded Net version of the SubGenius newsletter says:

> IF the only thing you've been able to laugh at for the last 5 years is that fact that NOTHING is funny any more—
> IF you sometimes want to collar people on the street and scream that you're more different than they could possibly *imagine*—
> IF you see the whole universe as one vast morbid sense of sick humour—
> IF the current "Age of Progress" seems more like the Dark Ages to you—
> —Your secret wishes can now be granted in full—*once you know what they are!*

So far, over thirty thousand copies have been sold of The Church's own "horror bible," *The Book of the SubGenius: Lunatic Prophecies for the Coming Weird Times*. Appropriately, *The Book* predicts a coming apocalyptic battle between Them and Us, attempts at covert removal, and the intervention of the good aliens. It will all blow out for good, with all pinks punished and all subgenii rewarded, when the world finds ultimate slack at 7:00 a.m. on July 5, 1998.

The delight of the SubGenius cult is that its parody is so bang-on, such a deliciously accurate send-up of the kind of thing one can see presented in all seriousness at psychics' conventions, UFO symposia, or angel seminars. It incorporates so many elements of current millennial craziness, in fact, that it is, at first glance, almost indistinguishable from the real thing. And that seems to be the point. The cultural criticism contained within the Church of the SubGenius is actually quite muted. That is surely part of its appeal to a generation as disaffected with political rhetoric as with religious nuttiness.

Yet that leaves the Church hovering oddly near the real thing. By being too clever, the elaborate imitative critique of cults and religions risks becoming *in fact* a cult and religion, its irony evolving into something so self-enveloping that its satirical potential is nullified. This has not yet happened, perhaps mostly because the Church remains a little-known preserve of the smart and disaffected. If it ever grew beyond its marginal status, its would be struck down by its own popularity. Or, perhaps, by The Stark Fist of Removal.

Matt Groening's "The Simpsons" illustrates a similar point. The long-running TV series, about the trials of a quintessentially going-nowhere American family, was once poignant as well as funny. Homer Simpson, a nuclear-power technician who once complained "I'm going to lose my job just because I'm dangerously unqualified," illustrates the routine materialism and stupidity of his culture even while suggesting the essential appeal of averageness that lies beneath his beer belly and pointless rages. Recently, however, "The Simpsons" has become a pared-down and often vicious denunciation of lower-middle-class life, letting pass no opportunity to mock the ignorance, greed, thoughtless chauvinism, and lack of initiative shown by Homer and his son, Bart. (Wife Marge and daughter Lisa, who offer voices of standard good behaviour, function within the show as a Greek chorus of disapproval on the two males.)

This is often howlingly funny, but in the end the joke is really on us because the moral centre has dropped out of this satire. The superficial knowingness that makes so many of the incidental jokes of "The Simpsons" funny seems to fold us back upon ourselves in a way that renders meaning impossible. "The Simpsons" is structured as a parody, a satirical comment on the poverty of America's television-dominated culture, but its participation in the object parodied begins to hollow out that attempt at criticism. There is a deliberate confusion of laughing at and laughing with—so much so that I once heard a lumpy guy sitting next to me on a plane, and displaying all the Homeric characteristics of a thoughtless beer-loving lout, say that "The Simpsons" was his favourite television show. At the same time, this double-edged quality of the satirical attempt is just what makes the show such a pleasure to watch. "The Simpsons" is seductive. Some of the show's funniest jokes, for example, play on Homer's desperate and almost constant ingestion of inane TV, along with his doughnuts and beer, or make sly reference to the show itself and its distributor, the cheesy Fox Network.

"The Simpsons" is therefore, if you like, virtual satire. It is an example of what happens when clever people like the show's Harvard-educated writers do not have the courage of their moral convictions. Instead of genuine satire—real social commentary that also happens to be funny—they offer a slyness that stands for nothing. At the same time, it is no coincidence that one of the hottest young filmmakers working today, Tarantino, is a purveyor of what might be called, by extension, virtual film noir—a genre in which there isn't even the depth of cynicism, the sense of underlying moral outrage, found in classic pulp fiction. We no longer sense the ethical confusion of Philip Marlowe or Sam Spade as they struggle with human evil; the ethical substance of film noir is now gone, leaving only the surface of corruption. Tarantino makes much of the fact that he was "educated" not through life experience but through years spent as a video-store clerk, greedily ingesting the celluloid world of violence and emptiness. This probably accounts for his technical brilliance and feel for dialogue; but it also accounts for the emptiness of his films. When Tarantino makes a movie, he doesn't express an attitude or a view; he merely quotes it.

And you know what? All the family values rhetoric in the world is not going to change the cultural parameters that make virtual satire and virtual noir so popular today. In fact, the vehemence of recent conservative rhetoric about the "decline of values" in film and on television is merely evidence that the challenge to the Ozzie-and-Harriet view of the world is deep and irrevocable. Recent attacks on "Hollywood's value system" are entirely beside the point here because Hollywood's value system, as everybody knows, is exactly the same as Wall Street's. It is: make as much money as you can. Hollywood's power-brokers have no more stake in the "values" of Oliver Stone's *Natural Born Killers* or Tarantino's *Pulp Fiction* than they do in *Forrest Gump* or *Free Willy*. Rather, they have exactly the same stake in all of them, namely, that they should max out at the box office and make a lot of dough for everybody involved.

The dual appeal of our cinematic dreams—vicious yet entertaining nihilistic violence on the one hand; lachrymose, empty-headed drivel on the other—is somehow entirely appropriate to the Janus-faced millennial times. Here ironic despair lies next to false hope, each rubbing into the other, energizing them and fuelling the distracting controversies of the so-called culture wars. But the real cultural conflicts are not between factions like these, and still less between often meaningless groups like "the Left" and "the Right." The real conflicts are within us, in the warring desires and fears we all feel.

Why do we find the nihilism of *Pulp Fiction* or "The Simpsons" so very entertaining? Is this Kroker's "will to virtualization"? A deep loss of faith in our better selves? Some grand cultural suicide bid? I don't know. I do know that the precise diagnosis will remain elusive so long as we hide our eyes from the deep contradictions that afflict us here, on the brink.

EIGHT

Faith No More

What does it mean to be romantic in the last decade
of the twentieth century? This was the question Fay
put to her brother Clyde. "To believe anything can
happen to us," he said, and gave her a look.

Carol Shields, *The Republic of Love*

I AM STANDING
in the shopping concourse of yet another airport, worrying
in a more or less idle way about three things: The green-
house effect. My recent birthday. And the fact that I don't
own a single thing worth more than a thousand dollars.

I see from the magazine covers at the airport newsstand
that the experts are still bickering, as experts will, about
global warming: yes it's happening, no it's not. I must say,
global warming seems real enough to me, especially if you
consider the weird knock-on effects of climatic turmoil. The
globe's rising temperature can actually create colder winters,
it seems. Global cooling, it should be. Our furnace was
knocked out twice during one brutal winter when the temperatures plunged and the winds rose, once for three frigid
days, while we huddled around the fireplace burning imitation logs because somebody had stolen all the real logs out
of the garage.

It's not our garage. It's not our fireplace, or our furnace.
We don't own the house. No, we simply help pay down part
of the landlord's mortgage every month in the form of a
large cheque. Rent. It's just money out the window, like
warm air in winter.

A few days before this trip, on my birthday, I found

myself thinking about the future. As usual, it was pretty murky. I couldn't see even a year ahead with any clarity. (Would my contract be renewed? Who knew?) I found no shortage of things to worry about, however: Pension funds ringing empty by the time I retire. Big debts I had no hope of paying off. Continuing constitutional crisis in Canada. I felt depressed rather than panicky at these prospects, which is what happens when I worry. I'm a natural brooder. My horoscope that day suggested that instead of indulging in typical Piscean gloom and paranoia, I should try instead to cultivate feelings of *pronoia*: that is, a belief that the universe is conspiring to do good things for me. It said the pronoiac's attitude is actually infectious; the more I believed it, the truer it would be.

I was quite taken with this idea—for about thirty seconds. Then it occurred to me that pronoia, while dear to millennial visionaries like California's Extropian Fellowship, is probably, from the point of view of psychological diagnosis, just as delusional as paranoia. The hard truth is that the universe isn't conspiring for good *or* ill. The universe is entirely indifferent to my hopes and fears. Yours too. It doesn't care.

Gloomy again, I gaze at the rows of glossy best-sellers and chunky paperbacks, with their lurid embossed covers, that dominate the airport's bookstore. Jostling for position on the shelves, among the romances and political thrillers, the alarmist non-fiction and the books on tape, are the spiritual self-help manuals and guides to post-denominational faith. Faith is all the rage here. Faith is in, hip, hot.

The angels are here, and near them, in among the inspirational audiotapes, is the New Age "hot-tub music" of composer Richard Souther. Souther has transformed the poetry of the celebrated twelfth-century Catholic nun and scholar Hildegard von Bingen into best-selling ambient synth-pap. St. Hildegard, I see, now comforts rather than challenges. There is nothing left in Souther's music of her tough idiosyncratic theology, nor any glimmer of her frightening vision of the Antichrist, whom she saw as "a beast with monstrous, coal-black head, flaming eyes, ass's ears and gaping, iron-fanged maw." The palliating poultices for the ravaged twentieth-century soul are all here, and they are, as the clerks will tell you, *moving well.*

Nearby is a book that promises an evolution of human consciousness post-2000. This one is called *Starseed: The Third Millennium* and it is by Ken Carey, billed as the author of a previous book called *The Starseed Transmissions.* Or rather, on closer inspection, it turns out that these books are not exactly *by* Carey at all. Like Rael, Carey has been communicating with extra-terrestrials. His brother-in-law, a garbage collector in Connecticut, found an old Royale portable typewriter, still perfectly serviceable, by the side of the road. It seemed a propitious discard. Carey took the typewriter to his office and soon, in an ecstatic delirium, he found himself typing out six hundred double-spaced pages of messages from entities who communicate by telepathic awareness.

By means of this appropriately modified twentieth-century version of the automatic writing popular with amateur mystics a century ago, the extra-terrestrials told Carey a lot of things, things that he somehow convinced a reputable publisher to pass on to the wider world. For example, they said that the period 1987 to 1989 marked a change in human consciousness, suggesting that we were on the verge of an important breakthrough in our spiritual evolution. "The coming millennium is to be a time of access to the infinite informational systems of Eternal Being," they tell Carey on page 149 of *Starseed.* "By the year 2011, humankind will have reached its due date for the cohesion of its collective consciousness," the entities say a few pages later. "The awakening itself will signal the millennium of

Christian prophecy." A warning to the sceptical follows: "Do not wait for signs and wonders to believe," the Starseed aliens command. "There are already portents before you that would have turned many ancient races back to God." The book goes on at some length to describe these signs, and it ends in a weird flurry of elliptical phrases that are intended to suggest, one imagines, the new consciousness of the global awakening, but are somehow more reminiscent to my ear of bad undergraduate poetry: "...streaming starbows' stellar rains...cascading, tumbling...glowing colors falling, freely flowing...swirling round and white-hole-vortex round, spilling deep...into these fields...eternal fields... fields of stars..."

Despite my instinctive disapproval of this sort of thing, I have begun to see its attractions. We are not yet indulging in the kind of vicious and self-denying end-time religious fervour that was common in Savonarola's Florence—though those days may soon be upon us. For the moment we are more inclined to take refuge in what Nietzsche called "metaphysical comfort": the reassuring thought that there is an extra-human agency whose purpose is to look after me. Those who reject that reassurance often react too far in the opposite direction, elevating their nihilism—the inability to believe in anything, especially themselves—to the level of conscious choice, even a positive character trait. Uncertain and anxious, we find the dominant forms of pre-millennial belief are thus either dark and brutal, like the desperate visions of divided societies called up by filmmakers and political theorists, or fuzzy and cosy, like the sort of spiritual mish-mash on offer in the bookstore. Both responses demonstrate a worrying loss of faith *in ourselves*.

The only way to begin countering this loss of conviction is to remind ourselves that the song of the false prophet always remains the same, whatever form it takes. Whether in nihilistic or in New Age, pop-psychology language, the message of the end-time charlatan is everywhere identical. *These are the end-times. Destruction is nigh. But you need not worry, for salvation can be had—at a price to be negotiated.*

We must have something to put in place of the mendacious faith of the charlatans, the dream-merchants of the millennium. But what? Poised on the cusp, what kind of genuine faith—if any—is left to us?

—_—

I was convinced I knew what faith was when I was a teenager. At the time I was living in Winnipeg, Manitoba—a place I've come to think of, with some affection, as Plague City. Winnipeg makes an effective backdrop for a personal struggle to understand how a benevolent God could have created such a hostile universe. It seems to me the most afflicted city in North America, maybe the world.

Most people know about the brutally cold Manitoba winters. Each year, Nature makes a serious attempt to kill its inhabitants with routine minus-40 temperatures, blizzards, snow drifts higher than tall men, cracked engine blocks, frostbite. (I actually got mild frostbite once, waiting for a bus without a toque on a windswept street corner. The tops of my ears went dry and hard, like the freezer-burnt corners of a cut of beef, and then peeled clean away.)

Not many people are aware, however, of the *other* God-sent dangers of life in Plague City. There are annual spring floods, when the accumulated snow of that mother-of-all-winters suddenly melts. The water runs onto the lawns and into the basements of people who, like residents of San Francisco, never seem to learn that Nature neither forgives nor forgets. In the spring of my high school years, we were often called out to be volunteer sandbaggers. We'd drive out to the southeast corner of the city and spend long, weary days filling bags with sand and stacking them into walls against the encroaching flood. Despite the freedom sand-bagging granted from my regimented Jesuit school, I grew to hate it. The sand was wet and heavy, the rough burlap rubbed our damp hands raw, and the people we helped were, to my judgmental adolescent eyes, curmudgeonly and bitter. They spent most of their time watching the water level as it spread across the horizon. You could feel the hopelessness in those gazes. Would the water recede before it smashed against the little wall of sand? Would the wall hold?

The spring floods also meant the advent of the brief Manitoba summer, and the annual tent caterpillar invasion. Each year, a blanket of voracious insects devoured the big elm trees along the street where I lived near the Assiniboine River. Heavy clumps of them used to drop out of the branches and land on our heads. Spraying a garden hose into a tree would bring down a canopy of them, descending on spider-thin filaments like an invasion force of abseiling commandos. The trip to my junior high school became a gingerly dance among the sidewalk deposits, punctuated by the awful feeling when a clump of six or ten of the little bastards landed on my shoulder or head. Some of my friends used to run to school in a barely controlled panic at that time of year, but that meant crushing dozens of them underfoot.

By the time the caterpillars were gone it was time for the mosquitoes, who came in waves during the summer, some bearing the deadly encephalitis virus but most just vampirically hungry. The summer also brought spectacular prairie thunderstorms, when the heat of the long day built into towering, mile-high cumulo-nimbus clouds on the western horizon. Thunder and lightning rolled out of the western prairie like God's personal wrath, drenching the scorched earth of the surrounding farmland. Sometimes the up-drafts of hot air created hailstorms of amazing ferocity: I routinely saw hail the size of marbles, even of squash balls. The hailstorms brought flash floods as the clouds split and dumped their accumulated moisture in sudden, helpless payloads.

It was almost a relief when the weather started turning cooler in September. Almost. Because the thing about a Plague City summer is that it's never quite long enough to let you forget that winter.

— _ —

I head back to Plague City one spring to give some lectures on political theory at the University of Winnipeg. But the lecture trip is not exactly the triumphant return I once imagined.

To make the scheduled morning gig in Winnipeg, I have to leave Toronto in the bleak pre-dawn hours. Not a big breakfast-eater at the best of times, I find that the microwaved meal served up by the flight attendant as we belt over Lake Superior has all the appeal of a sharp blow to the head. The watery quiche, the pink-grey sausage, the bloodshot eye of cherry tomato—these things, appearing on my fold-down tray, suddenly fill me with a queasy early-morning conviction that food is inherently disgusting. That, somehow, it is humiliating to be a bodily creature at all, an ugly bag of mostly water. I opt for coffee.

When the plane descends on Plague City at 6:00 a.m., the sun is no more than a strip of burnished copper along the dead-straight horizon. From the air, Winnipeg is in the middle of a flat checkerboard of farm lots and plumb-true roads. It looks small and crappy, the rivers muddy and the houses humble, indistinct lumps of grey. At ground level the impression is not much better. There are boarded-up buildings, run-down clapboard houses, bleak and dirty streets. When the snow melts in Winnipeg in the spring, it leaves behind a thick layer of _street scree_—the accumulated grit, sand, and dog shit of the long winter's snow. This stuff is everywhere, swirled across the pavements like geological striations, and an early thaw this year means I am right in the middle of it, constantly shaking scaled-down chunks of rubble out of my shoes and the cuffs of my trousers. My host, a handsome middle-aged professor of political science, is unfailingly friendly in the midst of the downbeat environment. Winnipeggers are like that. It is some form of defence mechanism, I think, or maybe a sign of winter madness.

My lectures go pretty well, with just the usual number of people nodding off, snickering quietly to their neighbours, or asking questions that convey no glimmer of understanding. It's all over by about lunchtime. I end up with lots of time to kill. So I go walking, setting off from my hotel and striking out in the direction of the old neighbourhood.

It is a fitfully sunny March day. Dodging the major street-scree deposits, I soon pass the junior high I attended, J. B. Mitchell. It is a tough school in a tough neighbourhood, and when I was there in the mid 1970s, a fight broke out almost every day in the schoolyard or along the streets on my way home. These scraps were occasionally vicious, though they usually stopped well short of grievous bodily harm and involved no weapons beyond rocks or broken glass. It goes without saying that, in the midst of this schoolyard violence, my friends and I all imagined ourselves complete tough guys. We fought and swore like storm troopers. We also drank and smoked drugs with what strikes me now as shocking casualness. In the group of kids I hung out with, there were a couple who regularly smoked a joint before the bell rang for classes in the morning. This seemed incredibly cool to me at the time, though I now realize they were eleven or possibly twelve years old, and it unsettles me.

I didn't fight much myself, but, being a fat kid who was also good at school, I was an obvious target for the hulking neanderthals who effectively ran the school. I was harassed regularly, mocked for my weight, and once beaten soundly—my face smashed against a locker until blood flowed freely from my nose and mouth—when for some reason (deep, unreasoning respect for private property?) I refused to surrender a Yale lock to a reigning bully called Mike Walls.

Walking along past the junior high, I cross the train-yard where we used to put pennies on the tracks so that the passing trains would crush them into smooth copper ovals, and where one of my schoolmates lost half his right foot when he caught it in a railway switch as he walked over the rails on his way home for lunch. I walk past the field—mostly a rectangle of black gumbo mud—where we used to splatter our jeans with lighter fluid and then set them on fire as we ran out to the street and past shocked pedestrians. I walk past the bus loop where we picked up rides in a choice Winnipeg pastime called bumper-shining. You run behind the bus, grab onto the bumper, and then slide along the frozen road on your boots. It's great. (New Yorkers on rollerblades now apparently do the same thing with passing cabs.) In fact, bumper-shining is probably a paleolithic forerunner of the extreme sports now televised on ESPN, up there with BMX cycling and snowboarding. Unfortunately, we failed to invent the peculiar slang needed for an exclusive bumper-shining youth subculture; and, for obvious reasons, bumper-shining can't thrive in southern California.

I walk past the old place at 219 Kenaston, a government-issue house (my father was in the air force) where for the first time I was given my own room. It was here that I had some of my most meaningful adolescent experiences, like falling asleep as I listened to Queen's "Bohemian Rhapsody" on my space-age-white clock radio, and deciding I was in love with Marilena Grande, the hazel-eyed beauty who sat across from me in home room. Kenaston is a wide street, a truck route from the south side of Winnipeg, and big eighteen-wheelers used to rumble past our front door. The house itself is identical to all the others in a depressing row along the street, one of possibly four or five prefab designs that account for the housing on every military base across Canada. I am prepared for the leaden uniformity of the row, but as I walk by, the pokiness of the old house takes me by surprise. Was it always that pukey green colour? Was it always that boxy and small?

I walk farther, past the air force base and toward my high school, St. Paul's. It was in many ways a typical Catholic high school for boys. The Jesuits who ran it were big to the point of mania on two things: learning and football. Not always in that order. The school motto was the Latin tag *Sicut miles Christi*, which we were quickly taught in Latin class to translate as "Like soldiers of Christ." The school sports teams were called the Crusaders, the school newspaper was *The Crusader*, and the school emblem was a heavily caparisoned medieval nobleman, mounted securely on an armoured horse, apparently just off to the Holy Land to kill a few Jews and Muslims.

Even as a teenager, the school's note of militant zealotry struck me as a bit incongruous, especially given the character of the school's patron saint, that vigorous but peaceful proselytizer. After all, Paul was famous for being knocked *off* his mount, and his humility and good sense would probably have made him balk at the millennial wackiness and outright bigotry typical of the Crusades. But no matter. It was a terrific relief after the trials of J. B. Mitchell Junior High to arrive at St. Paul's in 1976. I had to wear a jacket and tie, it's true, but I also got to hang out with people who knew who wrote "The Waste Land" and when the First World War ended. And the only blood I shed during my four years there was the result of honourable injuries sustained on the football field. There was little high school violence in general, certainly nothing like the gangland attacks that, by 1995, were common enough in Winnipeg schools, as elsewhere in North America, to force authorities to such drastic measures as security cameras and weapons checks. Of course, St. Paul's being a boys' school, there was lots of viciously expressed homophobia, but that seemed to me, even then, simply a perverse form of homoeroticism.

I arrived at the school on my first day, in September of 1976, thirteen years old, wearing a very happening mid-1970s disco outfit of wide-lapel maroon polyester blazer, grey flannel bell-bottoms, and a maroon-and-white shirt in a loud paisley pattern more suited to a pair of pyjamas. My ensemble was completed by a maroon velvet clip-on butter-fly bowtie that might easily have flown me to the moon if its massive wings had been twirled fast enough. I was the dude of the freshman class.

I was also terrified. I knew nobody at the school. All my J.B. Mitchell friends had gone to co-ed public high schools in other parts of the city. At St. Paul's there were kids from all over Winnipeg, some even hailing from the distant east-ern European enclaves of the North End. And they were all Catholic. I was not a very serious Catholic in those days, and I stayed cautious about that part of school life.

I never made the varsity football team, who appeared to most of us as elevated über-beings, with necks outside their ears, who patrolled the hallways with the God-given arro-gance of comic-strip superheroes. They were the most basic of elites, the one based on genetic fluke. Still, many of the routinely sub-heroic students like myself were caught up in the school's football ethos. Eight teams of us played full-contact intramural football every year, complete with uni-forms and pads—if nothing else, a remarkable financial outlay for a school of four hundred.

Ballooning to 205 pounds in grade eleven, I made an effective plug in the middle of the offensive line. I modelled myself on Bubba Baker, a now largely forgotten lineman for the Detroit Lions of the late 1970s, whose number, 60, I always wore. Football at St. Paul's had about it vestiges of old-fashioned muscular Christianity, combined with the sort of mindlessly hearty *mens sana in corpore sano* rhetoric of an English public school. In this milieu, cheerfully pounding the blocking sled or smashing some other adolescent in the mouth, I found myself actually starting to take that soldier of Christ stuff seriously. I never scored a touchdown for Jesus, being a lineman, but I did once miraculously intercept a pass, and during each play I reverently offered up my pain, which was considerable, to Our Lord. The dark purple bruises that blossomed down the length of my forearms and thighs after every game were my own kind of stigmata—outward signs of an inner state of gridiron grace.

This may sound unusually pious, if not slightly insane, but it was really just par for the course at St. Paul's. The school somehow just made it seem *de rigueur* to have this cheerful and aggressive faith—and for a time, like almost all of my classmates, I did. And anyway I did not become actually *fervent* in my belief, like the pimply God Squadders who hung out with the Jesuits after class and fought with each other over who got to light the candles in the school chapel.

Meanwhile, back in the classroom, the Jesuits were teaching us how to think critically, how to uncover bad arguments and reason logically from premise to conclusion. The logic-chopping we learned was not, however, Jesuitical casuistry, the sly ability to make rational arguments for any position, however disagreeable. (I had to wait until graduate school to learn that skill.) I just got a good, if very traditional, education. The famous boast of old-time Jesuits—that a child in their hands at seven was theirs forever—was far from true in my school. At St. Paul's nobody tried to recruit me to the Vatican secret service or convert me into an intelligence officer for Christ. Mind you, the Jesuits did not get their hands on most of us until we were already teenagers. Maybe it was a case of lost opportunities.

The peculiar thing, I now think, was how keen the Jesuits were on critical thinking, given that it sat so uneasily with the Christian faith of the school's culture. No doubt they saw faith and reason as intertwined, but it troubled me.

I had discovered, as so many believers have, that the most accessible comfort of Christian faith is the permission it gives you *not* to think—to believe even (or especially) when there is no evidence available. Yet in teaching us how to argue and in giving us a sharp fallacy-alert, the Jesuits were almost acting to undermine the foundation of their own order. I found this paradox intoxicating and, for a while, debilitating.

Like many Catholic schoolboys, certainly like a majority of my classmates, I entertained thoughts of becoming a priest myself one day. The Jesuits seemed to us to have a pretty cushy life. They were smart and well-educated; most of them had travelled extensively. The common room of the Jesuits' private residence, attached to the school, resembled to our eyes an exclusive gentlemen's club, with plush leather armchairs, a lovely big billiard table, and racks of sophisticated intellectual magazines. True, the Jesuits weren't allowed sexual intercourse, but, as teenagers at a boys' school, we already knew that sexual pleasure doesn't necessarily have to involve other people.

In fact, the only time most of us got to see the nicely appointed Jesuit residence was when one of the lay teachers (a phrase we predictably found hilarious) took us down to the common room for a notorious St. Paul's event, the annual Self-Abuse Lecture that was delivered to the members of the grade eleven class. Looking back, I like to imagine the teachers in the common room, drawing straws for this unpleasant duty, the Jesuits pale with anxiety and the others trying to suppress subversive giggles. In my grade-eleven year it was Johnston Smith who shepherded us down to the common room, and we sat there in the leather armchairs, afraid to meet each other's eyes, as he, with admirable gravity and thoroughness, went through the reasons why masturbation was wrong. I still remember the central argument: You know masturbation is wrong, Smith said, because you *would not do it in the living room on Sunday afternoon.*

He paused for emphasis. We continued to look anywhere but at each other. It sounded convincing, but was it really? There are lots of things you would not do in the living room on a Sunday afternoon, and not all of them are wrong. I snorted, though only mentally.

I have often wondered, since that moment in 1979, whether this awakening of critical intelligence during the self-abuse lecture was a turning point in what a Christian would call "my faith life." Who knows? I can only say it struck me then, as it does now, as a silly argument. In fact, at around this time a lot of the arguments offered by the Catholics began to appear flawed to me.

In my final year at the school my parents moved, leaving the dreary Kenaston Street place for a condominium at Plague City's western edge. During the winter this new location meant a long bus ride to school, but that fall, and in the following spring, I took to riding my bike. It was a fairly long way, probably seven or eight miles, and the rubber tire of adolescent fat that had circled my middle finally melted away as I became proficient, then fanatic, at cycling. I dropped from 200-plus pounds down to about 155, and meanwhile grew a few inches. My graduation picture from that summer of 1980 shows me as an undeniably skinny boy in a three-piece suit with one of those circa-1970s David Cassidy shag haircuts.

My Catholic faith, too, began to melt away during those long solitary bike rides through Assiniboine Park on frosty Plague City mornings. Cycling is a meditative form of exercise, if you are on the road before heavy traffic clogs the streets. Belting along at my steady twelve miles an hour, I found myself turning over in my mind the age-old questions of faith, in particular the so-called problem of evil. Does a benevolent God exist? If so, why is there so much evil, pain, and suffering in the world? What kind of God could create a world like this? What do our lives mean in the midst of all this?

When I went to university the next fall, I spent an inordinate amount of time looking for convincing proofs of God's existence, and I encountered some novel ones. I found lots of people who had answers to offer, and sometimes I thought I had found an answer that was good enough for me, but none of them held up for very long. None of them seemed as real to me as those internal monologues tracked by the sound of my bicycle wheels.

My favourite proof of God's existence is still the "ontological argument" offered by St. Anselm. A twelfth-century Benedictine monk who was Archbishop of Canterbury for a time, Anselm was no stranger to millennial fever, as it happens, or to what passed for celebrity in medieval Britain. When he returned from Rome to the cliffs of Dover on September 23, 1100—a heavily weighted year for the medieval Christians, stronger even than 1000—the historian Eadmer wrote, in his *History of Recent Events in England*, that "we found the whole country exultant with great joy at Anselm's arrival. For a hope, as it were, of resurrection to new life, was springing up in everyone's mind."

In his *Proslogion*, Anselm wrote that God must exist because God is by definition the supreme being. Anselm's reasoning is a model of intellectual sleight-of-hand. We *know* that God is the supreme being, the being "than which none greater can be imagined"—or, to use Anselm's words, *aliquid quo nihil maius cogitari possi*. This idea is simply what the very concept of God carries within it; it is what we understand by the idea of God. Assume, then, that God does not exist. What we immediately find is that a God that does not exist is not the greatest imaginable being. We can imagine a greater entity, namely one just the same but with the added supremacy of actually existing. Therefore it follows that God exists.

Anselm had the good grace to say in the *Proslogion* that, despite this being a valid proof of God's existence—indeed, an argument only a fool would deny—he for one believed in God as a matter of faith, not argument. Argument, he said, was only a means of clarifying what we know already by faith. Anselm's personal motto, *credo ut intelligam* ("I believe in order that I may understand"), is a little ambiguous on the precise relationship between reason and faith, but in the end, faith is clearly in the driver's seat for him.

What I eventually realized was that the search for a proof of God's existence is doomed to either of two unattractive results: trivial failure or empty success. Either the proofs fail, which leaves the question unresolved and faith triumphant over reason, or the proofs succeed, but only at the cost of an intellectual parlour trick that offends a sense of logical integrity. I realized that, in Anselm's terms, I was a fool. I did not really believe in God, and I approached the arguments without faith.

I gave up the search.

＊＿＊

Rejecting Christian faith can create a troubling vacuum at one's spiritual centre, as I soon discovered, and into this vacuum can rush all kinds of ideas, both soothing and terrifying. When traditional answers no longer aid us, the new, sometimes twisted forms of religiosity characteristic of our day find fertile ground. So, too, does a misplaced faith in the power of human reason we call scientism—reaching at a peak the sort of arrogant techno-spirituality espoused by the gurus of *Wired* magazine. Neither of these is an adequate response to the challenges of the approaching millennium. The future is not entirely in God's hands, but it is not entirely in our own hands, either.

Despite all our efforts at control, life on this planet is in many ways getting obviously worse: we have seen that real-world analogues of the disasters foretold in scripture, both holy and unholy, are not hard to find. There is more crowding, more poverty, more conflict, more disease. There is less fuel, less space, less water, less understanding. Such things can indeed be strongly suggestive of a coming apocalypse—despite the fact (and it is a fact) that Christian scripture has no genuine predictive power. "*Revelation* gives us no reason to believe that the religious millennium will coincide with the calendar millennium," humorist Roy Blount, Jr., wrote recently in *New Choices* magazine. "The arithmetic of inspiration is not that simple." No, it isn't. Despite all signs of collapse, I do not believe the world is slated for fiery destruction in a few years' time. Though computers may crash in the new confusion of 20-prefix dates, there will be no decisive battle between the forces of good and evil. Judgment Day is not hard upon us.

There are nevertheless some reasonable grounds for the anxiety we feel. More than this, the anxiety is, wittingly or not, compounded in countless ways by the intricate feedback loops of popular culture. In fact, the idea of apocalypse has its momentary attractions even for the sceptical, for there is a perverse part of us all that longs to see the final spectacular act in the tired human drama, to share the big-bang ending, to feel the deep satisfaction of ultimate narrative closure. On the eve of the millennium, we can expect to see this strange desire acted out in violence and social upheaval. We can anticipate scenes of mass hysteria and terror, familiar to us as much from the speculative fiction of Kathryn Bigelow's 1995 film *Strange Days* as from the medieval apocalyptics. Only a minority will feel the deep pull of the millennial deadline, perhaps, but it is a minority that (like the technophobe minority) includes some of us all of the time and all of us some of the time.

Even failing that—let us say, plausibly enough, that media overexposure of the idea of social apocalypse renders it so tiresome by 2000 that no one wants to think about it any more—some of us will nevertheless be tempted to forge a personal narrative closure, an individual gesture of finality. What will happen to those who, on December 31, 1999, find themselves too disappointed, too afraid, or simply unwilling to stagger on into the third millennium? Some psychiatrists I have spoken to already confess, off the record, their fears of mass suicides and other forms of violent temporary insanity that will greet the emptiness of a Second Coming that does not come.

Because millennial anxiety is in part generated, and reinforced, by the arbitrariness of the calendar, it is tempting for clear thinkers to dismiss it entirely, to wave it off as the ravings of street-corner prophets and self-styled messiahs. But that is a mistake. If the temptation to give in to millennial anxiety must be resisted—and it must—so must the temptation to dismiss that anxiety out of hand. "I could pretend that this turning over of the eon's odometer is no big thing to me personally," Blount continued in his article. "[B]ut I have to be realistic. The turn of the millennium, I am afraid, will make me feel older than time…. Will this put a spring in my step? I doubt it." Nor in anyone else's, either. The turn of the millennium is an intimation of mortality for all of us. Its precise cultural shape is still negotiable. But in waving off millennial anxiety, we succeed only in surrendering to it. The coming millennium becomes an apocalypse after all: human-made, yes, but devastating nonetheless.

The true threat of millennial anxiety, the true apocalypse, is not the fire and brimstone promised in Revelation, the wailing and gnashing of teeth of Judgment Day. It is instead the destruction of hope, of faith in ourselves. The armageddon we face is the elimination of the idea that there is anything we can do to make this world one in which we feel at home.

If, however, we consider it correctly—with the right mixture of scepticism and sensitivity—millennial anxiety can prove, contrary to expectation, liberating. It can help us see ourselves more clearly, both our bright surfaces and our dark hollows. And the kind of faith that such reflection helps to foster, a faith in ourselves that is neither unreasoning nor hyper-rational, may be the only kind of salvation we need—or can expect—in these confused end-times. In fact, this kind of reasoned faith in our possibilities is closely related to another great virtue celebrated by St. Paul, namesake of the high school where I found, and then lost, my naive form of Christian faith. That virtue is hope.

The great Jewish philosopher Emil Fackenheim once said that the truly evil genius of the Nazi Holocaust was that it set out not only to murder the Jews in unimaginable numbers, but also to murder their hope. Like the torturer O'Brien in George Orwell's *Nineteen Eighty-Four*, the brilliant cruelty of the Nazis lay in the destruction of not just the flesh and blood in the body but also the very sense of self in the spirit. In times of crisis or affliction, as we know, this kernel of personal identity retreats away from the vulnerable body. When pain and hunger are daily realities, we shrink inside our bodies to distance ourselves, that part of us that is most real, from the body's pain. In this, we are once more the mind-body dualists that Descartes sketched: uneasy amalgamations of the material and the spiritual. The terrible lesson of our century, of this late- or perhaps post-modern time, is that the personal centre, too, proves all too vulnerable.

This centre, the soul, is destroyed not through pain of the primitive, physical sort, but by a form of torture that actually shreds the fabric of one's being. Winston Smith, the doomed rebel of Orwell's novel, is tortured in many physical ways, but the ultimate torture is reserved for what happens in the notorious Room 101. Here a cage of starving rats is fitted over Winston's head—not so much, we realize, to inflict the pain of the rat bites as to inflict the *dread* of them. Room 101, O'Brien tells Winston, is the place where everyone's greatest fear comes true. Faced with the thing he fears most, the rats that terrified him in the slum tenement of his childhood, Winston can resist O'Brien no longer.

That much, perhaps, we expected. The real shock is that the betrayal of Winston's ideals, when it finally comes, is not political but personal. He screams to O'Brien that the rat cage should be used on Julia, the young party member with whom he has carried on his secret, forbidden affair. It is Winston's sincere and irrevocable desire that the rat-cage torture should be done to the one he loves, which leaves him, his very self, in tatters. Now we see that the unmaking of Winston's world, not information or routine political betrayal, is what O'Brien has been after all along. O'Brien— like the Nazis, like all nuanced practitioners of pain—uses the fine-edged and subtle tools *of reason* to etch his horrible destiny on Winston. O'Brien does not care about physical pain; he does not even care about Winston's politics. His own commitment to Big Brother's party is in large measure ironical. What he really cares about—*all* he really cares about—is the high-level game of finding the single threat that will reduce Winston to nothingness, the mere shell of a man who cannot even bear the sight of his former love because she reminds him of his shame.

O'Brien is, according to the American philosopher Richard Rorty, a precise and luminous illustration of what the intellectual becomes when a fascination with "lesser" things like progress and justice wanes. In the figure of O'Brien we see instrumental reason—which creates the world of technology's dreams, the bright future of bubble cities and personal levitation devices—curling back on itself. It swallows its own tail in a grand and terrifying pro-ject of "rationalized" self-destruction. The *Amazing Stories* dream becomes the nightmare of *The Terminator*.

It is somehow appropriate to find ourselves now, near the end of this report, confronting the actual Holocaust, the historical centrepiece of our own miserable century. Nazism, with its vision of racial purity and a "thousand-year Reich," is itself a horrible kind of millennial dream. That it ends in darkness, a darkness so complete it provides what is perhaps the central image of horror in our cultural imagination— the concentration camp—is eloquent testimony to the volatility of human ambition when unfettered by compassion. For here we see the terror that lies at the heart of the ideas of progress and control. Instrumental reason creates and maintains the modern world: the world of mass production and mass comfort, but also the world of mass surveillance and mass destruction. The connection between rationality and the gas chambers is real. The Holocaust, as any visitor to the memorial at Dachau must know, was a thoroughly rational affair. It was systematic murder, carried out with the dispassionate bureaucratic efficiency of a cost-reduction program. The Jews, like any unwanted deficit, were rationalized.

The Holocaust also marks, for many people, the real death of God. It is the traditional argument from evil in its most apocalyptic form. "There's no way there can be an all-powerful and a just God," Yehuda Bauer, Professor of Holocaust Studies at the Hebrew University, said in a recent *New Yorker* article on the troubling legacy of Adolf Hitler. If an all-powerful God allowed the evil of the Holocaust to happen, he is evil himself, Bauer argued. If he is just and simply couldn't prevent the evil, he is "a nebbish." "I don't need a God like that," Bauer said. The fork is a stark one, and Jewish intellectuals in the years following the Second World War have wrestled mightily with its insistent logic. Some have even put God on trial, in their art and fiction, and found him guilty of war crimes—a kind of Nuremberg for the armies of Heaven, not the Reich.

Nevertheless, as always, with the darkness there may come some glimmer of light. Emil Fackenheim, too, has grappled with the problems posed by the Holocaust, and found in it a surprising reaffirmation of faith—a faith much chastened and battered by the century's terrible events, to be sure, but the more powerful for being thus redefined. Having identified the true nature of the Nazi Holocaust, its attempted murder of hope, Fackenheim has gone on to argue that the Nazis' murder of hope has an unexpected positive effect. From the ashes of despair, indeed from the very real ashes of the Auschwitz gas ovens, he suggests, rises a new kind of hope, a hope revitalized precisely by the stiff challenges of hope's murder.

—■—

On the other side of hopelessness lies a new sense of possibility. On the other side of the millennium lies a new century, and a new thousand years. What might they bring?

At least since Thomas More wrote his famous *Utopia* (subtitled, in some editions, Millennium), the utopian vision has been used to raise hopes, to encourage change, and to restore a sense of possibility. Utopias, whether in literature or in the individual imagination, are not prophecies. They cannot and should not be assessed for factual accuracy. They can also be extremely dangerous if we take them too literally. Utopias are really ways of imagining what is not but what might be. They are, if you like, dreams. They begin with the great liberating conditional: *What if...?* And so far from undermining them, this conditional quality is what gives utopias their peculiar power. The German philosopher Ernst Bloch, whose massive work *The Principle of Hope* surveys utopian writing with magisterial scholarly panache, knew that hope literally springs eternal in the human breast. It is a basic condition of our existence, Bloch argued, even in our apparently darkest hours, to sketch out a better future. Without that possibility, we cease to be—we cease to have any reason for being. Bloch knew this from experience: a Jewish intellectual, he experienced first-hand the shadow of Nazi persecution, the fear of hope's murder at any moment.

Where, in these late-millennium days, to begin the project of hope? Some ambitions are small in scale but important for all that. The writer Judith Martin, better known as the syndicated columnist Miss Manners, published in 1983 a *Guide for the Turn-of-the-Millennium*, telling us, among other things, how to deal with the etiquette of fax communications and automated bank tellers. Her hope is that we will all be "perfectly behaved" by the turn of the millennium. By late 1995, though, the dissemination of new-era etiquette seemed to have reached something of a brick wall. I found Martin's *Guide*, reissued on audiotape, on the remainder table of my local bookstore, marked down to a third of the suggested list price. It seems that cut-rate manners are now the order of the day.

At the other end of the spectrum lie the bigger hopes— the worthy but often vapid wishes for peace and harmony— that used to characterize high school valedictory addresses. Of course, these high-flown hopes nowadays serve more to prop up cynical political agendas than to further the real interests of citizens frightened of a world they do not understand. If the important day-to-day hopes of Miss Manners are being dashed by the realities of increasingly uncivil big-city life, the hypocritical high-falutin hopes of speechmakers and spin doctors are on the rise.

Underneath these different kinds of hope, the prosaic as well as the high-minded, there flows a strong current of dread. We must accept this as part of our condition: the visions of the world's fiery end, the prospect of mass hysteria and suicides, the panic and terror of previous apocalyptic outbreaks, are always with us. The influence of such visions can only grow as we edge toward the brink, for the dismissals of anxiety by the allegedly strong-minded are no more helpful than the whippings-up of any millenarian doomsayer. What most of us really feel, I think, is the need to occupy some middle ground, to recognize the reasonable grounds of anxiety without letting that anxiety get the better of us.

I was pleased to notice in the summer of 1995 that *The Journal of Philosophy*, the venerable flagship of North American academic philosophy—a journal published without fail since its founding at Columbia University in 1904—had apparently printed its first contribution to millennial anxiety. A six-page article by someone called Martin H. Krieger, of the University of Southern California, appeared with this arresting title: "Could the Probability of Doom Be Zero or One?"

Krieger argues in the article that the world can be divided into three groups when it comes to assessing the probability of doom—defined by him as "a state of non-events" or "the end of the future." There are "apocalypticists," he says, who hold that doom will surely happen (probability one). There are also "marginalists," who believe that doom will surely be forestalled (probability zero). And then there are "modest sceptics," who believe—consistent with something called "the Kolgomorov zero-or-one theorem"—that doom will either happen or not happen. Because doom will happen as the last in a very large number of events, Krieger says, it has no calculable intermediate likelihood between zero and one. For "modest sceptics," the probability is not zero or one, but rather zero-or-one. It will happen; or it won't.

Sensing the dissatisfaction such a result might arouse in the average reader, Krieger concludes his essay with a disclaimer of sorts. The notion of doom-probability may well be oxymoronic, he says, "for doom is a transcendent and unique event, and probability concerns the mundane."

Well, yes. After all, how reassuring is it to be told that doom is either going to happen or not going to happen? On the other hand, it is surely something—hats off to Krieger, and to Kolgomorov, too—to have it proven beyond a shadow of a philosophical doubt.

—_—

I will end, perhaps appropriately, with a confession. I confess that I have no concrete suggestions for the shape the third millennium should take. Nor do I have any detailed party directions for how best to celebrate the most momentous New Year any of us will live through. I wish I did, sometimes, because I suspect that without some big event to mark the occasion we may all find the experience dangerously anticlimactic. The year 2000 will not be written on the skies, as the *Spectator* editorialist hoped in 1892, and for most of us the last New Year's Eve of the millennium will probably pass just like so many others, with us searching for that mythical perfect party that nobody but 1930s film characters ever seems to get to.

There will be, I nevertheless dare to hope, momentous events afoot within each one of us. For somewhere in the distance between manners and rhetoric, somewhere in the wide expanse between probability zero and probability one, lies hope's true country: the individual imagination. Here, and only here, can we hold ourselves truly responsible, in the one court of appeal that really matters—the one in which we sit in judgment on ourselves. Only here, finally, can we modest sceptics form the wishes and desires that will take us bravely into the next thousand years.

I hope to see you there.

Acknowledgments

THIS BOOK CLEARLY owes a great deal to the writers, thinkers, and artists whose work I have discussed. My thanks to all of them, especially those who took the time to speak to me personally.

I had valuable assistance and advice from other important sources. Mathew Ingram, by day an investment reporter for *The Globe and Mail* but at other moments a dedicated purveyor of the bizarre, kept me stocked with detailed information on the fringes of the culture, culled from his vast files. Chris Kutz and Peter Levine, fellow survivors of New Haven, kept me up to date on some important American developments, as did Jody and Bruce Davie. Matthew Parfitt added nice historical detail on the nineteenth-century *fin de siècle*. Greg Sinclair shared some of his encyclopedic knowledge of science-fiction films of the 1950s and '60s. Charlie Foran read a draft of the entire manuscript and helped me improve its clarity, as well as noting the places where less was probably more. And Todd Ducharme, who has been predicting the end of the world for about as long as I have known him, offered legal advice at a price I could handle.

Some of the material in this book first appeared, in a very different or early form, in two Toronto-based publications. I thank the following editors for their interest in my work and help in making it better: Katherine Ashenburg, Warren Clements, Cheryl Cohen, Phil Jackman, and Liz Renzetti, all of *The Globe and Mail*; and Bruce Headlam, Mark Stevenson, and Ken Whyte of *Saturday Night*. Thanks also to everyone at Penguin, especially my friend and editor, Jackie Kaiser, who had faith in the idea of this book from the beginning.

Thanks finally, and most of all, to Gail Donaldson, who along the way took time out of her own research to read, clip, underline, discuss, and encourage. At the end of the day, she sustains me—and gives me hope.

Notes

Let the End Begin

3   Isaac Asimov's Three Laws of Robotics are outlined in several novels, including *The Caves of Steel* (Greenwich, Conn.: Fawcett Books, 1954), a science-fiction murder mystery that pits a human and android police tandem against a clever criminal.

6   Peter Lorie, *The Millennium Planner: Your Personal Guide to the Year 2000* (New York: Viking, 1995). Details of the Atlantean prophecies can be found in Graham Hancock, *Fingerprints of the Gods: A Quest for the Beginning and the End* (London: Heinemann, 1995), and Rand and Rose Flem-Ath, *When the Sky Fell: In Search of Atlantis* (Toronto: Stoddart, 1995). Writer Michael Posner discussed the millennial resonance of the Atlantean fixation in his article "At the Twilight of the Millennium," *The Globe and Mail* (July 29, 1995), p. D5.

7   The 1993 increase in the *Fortean Times* annual "Strangeness Index" was reported in the February/March, 1994, issue of the London-based magazine. The Japanese parody cults and "Armageddon" rice dish were reported in *The Globe and Mail* (May 2, 1995), p. A18. *Time*'s cover story (Richard Corliss, "The Invasion Has Begun") and *Newsweek*'s (Rick Martin, "Alien Invasion") both appeared on July 8, 1996.

8   Dr. Mark Farine is quoted in Peter Steel, "December 31, 1999: Judgment Day?" in *Weekly World News* (May 23, 1995), pp. 8–9. Details about New Year's Eve plans for 1999 are taken from the Introduction to Hillel Schwartz, *Century's End: A Cultural History of the Fin de Siècle* (New York: Doubleday, 1990).

9   New York City's party plans were reported by Bruce Weber in "As

the Millennium Nears, A City's Wheels Turn," *The New York Times* (July 22, 1996), pp. B1-2. The quotation by Norman Cohn is from his *The Pursuit of the Millennium: Revolutionary Millenarians and Mystical Anarchists in the Middle Ages* (New York: Oxford University Press, 1970), from the Introduction. Cohn's book is far and away the best source in English on medieval millenarianism. "Like everyone else I'm finding it harder and harder to pick up a book," says the narrator of Martin Amis's *London Fields*, "but I can still manage brief engagements with Cohn, with his fascinated, his fully gripped intelligence."

10 Robert Kaplan, "The Coming Anarchy" (February 1994), pp. 44–76; Matthew Connelly and Paul Kennedy, "Must It Be the Rest Against the West?" (December 1994), pp. 61–84; Adam Walinsky, "The Crisis of Public Order" (July 1995), pp. 39–54. *The Atlantic's* penchant for mid-decade doomsaying arguably began even earlier: see, for example, Charles C. Mann, "How Many Is Too Many?" (February 1993), pp. 47–67 (on population disasters) and Peter F. Drucker, "The Age of Social Transformation" (November 1994), pp. 53–80 (on accelerated social change).

11 Daniel Bell and *The New Yorker*, as quoted in Schwartz, *Century's End*. Irving Kristol's essay "Countercultures" (1994) appeared originally in *Commentary* and is reprinted in his collection *Neo-Conservatism: The Autobiography of an Idea* (New York: The Free Press, 1995), pp. 136–47.

12 The comment is made in a letter from Arendt to McCarthy, quoted in a review of *Between Friends: The Correspondence of Hannah Arendt and Mary McCarthy, 1949–1975* (New York: Harcourt Brace, 1995) in *The New Yorker* (March 20, 1995), pp. 97–102. See also *Eichmann in Jerusalem: A Report on the Banality of Evil* (New York: Viking, 1964).

14 Adam Phillips, "First Hates: Phobias in Theory," in his *On Kissing, Tickling, and Being Bored: Psychoanalytic Essays on the Unexamined Life* (Cambridge, Mass.: Harvard University Press, 1993), p. 24.

ONE: *Shards of Apocalypse*

17 "Killer Virus" and "Disease Strikes Back" were the cover stories for *Newsweek* and *The Economist*, respectively, in their issues of May 15, 1995.

18 Richard Preston's essay "Back in the Hot Zone" appeared in *The*

New Yorker (May 22, 1995), pp. 43–45. It was an update to his book *The Hot Zone* (New York: Random House, 1994). See also Laurie Garrett, *The Coming Plague: Newly Emerging Diseases in a World Out of Balance* (New York: Farrar, Straus & Giroux, 1994).

19 Terence Rafferty's review of *Outbreak* appeared in *The New Yorker* (March 20, 1995), pp. 105–7.

20 The Iris Murdoch novel in question is *A Severed Head* (London: Chatto and Windus, 1961), p. 246.

22 H. G. Wells, *The War of the Worlds*, as quoted in Schwartz, *Century's End.*

24 Marianne Macdonald's article on the Millennium Commission appeared in *The Independent on Sunday* on September 18, 1994. Conor Cruise O'Brien's highly negative assessment of the commission is found in the chapter "The Millennium Commission" in his *On the Eve of the Millennium* (Toronto: Anansi, 1994).

27 The quotation from George Fox is from Norman Cohn, *The Pursuit of the Millennium*, the appendix on the Ranters, pp. 287 ff. Many of the historical details in this chapter are from Cohn, passim, but especially Chs. 1 and 3.

32–33 William Robertson and Charles Mackay as quoted in Schwartz, *Century's End.* The quotation from Michelet, from the article "The Year 1000" in his monumental *History of France*, is found in the first chapter of O'Brien's *On the Eve of the Millennium*, together with a discussion of the Enlightenment legacy.

34 Schwartz, *Century's End*, from the Preface.

38–52 The quotations in this section (Luther, Columbus, Botticelli, Savonarola, Suzette Labrousse, and various magazine editors) are drawn from Schwartz, *Century's End*, passim.

56 Wendy Kaminer, *It's All the Rage: Crime and Culture* (Reading, Mass.: Addison-Wesley, 1995), p. 9.

Two: *The Prophet Zone*

68–71 Details of the account of Elizabeth Clare Prophet's doomsday cult are from a story by Timothy Egan, "Thousands Plan Life Below, After Doomsday," in *The New York Times*, March 15, 1990, pp. A1 and B6; and from Egan's *Times* follow-up, "Guru's Bomb Shelter Hits Legal Snag," April 24, 1990, p. A16.

70–72 Predictions made by the Baha'is Under the Provision of the Covenant were written by Neal Chase and released to the press

between August 1993 and October 1994; they appeared in
Harper's (February 1995), pp. 22–24.

78 The Rapture bumper sticker was the inspiration for David
Clewell's poem "In Case of Rapture," published in *The Missouri
Review* (Spring 1993). The poem was reprinted in *Harper's*
(January 1994), pp. 30–31. The Aum Shinri Kyo cult attacks were
widely reported. I have relied mainly on Associated Press wire
stories that appeared in *The Globe and Mail* (April 2, April 22, and
May 20, 1995); Susan Byrne's article "Land of the Rising Cults,"
in *The Irish Times* (April 1, 1995); and a *Time* cover story, "Prophet
of Poison," by David Van Biema (April 3, 1995), pp. 18–25.

81-85 Thomas Homer-Dixon's articles are "On the Threshold:
Environmental Changes as Causes of Acute Conflict,"
International Security (Fall 1991), pp. 76–116; "Environmental
Scarcities and Violent Conflict: Evidence from Cases,"
International Security (Summer 1994), pp. 5–40; and "The
Ingenuity Gap: Can Poor Countries Adapt to Resource Scarcity?"
(unpublished at time of this writing). Also, with Jeffrey Boutwell
and George Rathjens, "Environmental Change and Violent
Conflict," *Scientific American* (February 1993), pp. 38–45.

85 Robert Kaplan, "The Coming Anarchy," *The Atlantic Monthly*
(May 1994), p. 44. All subsequent quotations are taken from this
article. Used by permission.

87 Marcus Gee, "Apocalypse Deferred: The End Isn't Nigh," *The
Globe and Mail* (April 9, 1994), pp. D1 and D3; the reply by
Homer-Dixon, "Is Anarchy Coming? A Response to the
Optimists," appeared on the op-ed page of *The Globe and Mail*
(May 10, 1994).

90 Ismail Serageldin was quoted by John Vidal in "Next, Wars Over
Water?" *The Guardian* (August 20, 1995); Vidal's article was
reprinted in *World Press Review* (November 1995), pp. 8–10.

92 Wayne's Koestenbaum's resonant phrase appeared in his review of
a book by poet Henri Cole in *The New Yorker* (May 1, 1995),
p. 86.

THREE: *To Have and Have Not*

95 These statistics are from the following sources: LH Research Co.;
Washington, D.C. police department; the British Consulate-
General of the United States; Corrections Compendium of
Lincoln, Nebraska; and the Alcohol, Tobacco and Firearms
Bureau.

98   Bob Herbert's comment appeared in his *New York Times* column on October 5, 1995; it was reprinted in a compendium of commentary on the O. J. Simpson verdict in *The Globe and Mail* (October 7, 1995), p. D5.

99   Quotations are from Kaplan, "The Coming Anarchy."

101   James Dale Davidson and William Rees-Mogg, *The Great Reckoning: How the World Will Change in the Depression of the 1990s* (Toronto: Summit Books, 1991). The statistics on population and debt are, unless otherwise noted, taken from Peter Lorie, *The Millennium Planner: Your Personal Guide to the Year 2000* (New York: Viking, 1995), passim.

102   I have drawn these details from an account of the Christian Prince murder, "Teen Acquitted in Yale Slaying," *The Washington Post* (March 11, 1993), p. B4, by Dale Leonhardt.

104   C. B. Macpherson, *The Political Theory of Possessive Individualism: Hobbes to Locke* (Oxford: Clarendon Press, 1962); see also his *The Life and Times of Liberal Democracy* (Oxford: Oxford University Press, 1977).

106   A diverting account of Jefferson's Pell Mell Etiquette can be found in Judith Martin, *Common Courtesy: In Which Miss Manners Solves the Problem that Baffled Mr. Jefferson* (New York: Atheneum, 1985).

107   This and all subsequent quotations by Fussell are from Paul Fussell, *Class: A Guide Through the American Status System* (New York: Summit Books, 1983), passim. Fussell also discusses L. P. Hartley, *Facial Justice* (London: Hamish Hamilton, 1960) and Roger Price, *The Great Roob Revolution* (n.p., 1970).

108   William Henry III, *In Defense of Elitism* (New York: Basic Books, 1994).

111   Richard J. Herrnstein and Charles Murray, *The Bell Curve: Intelligence and Class Structure in American Life* (New York: Free Press, 1994). The various reviews and reactions to the book are collected in Steven Fraser, ed., *The Bell Curve Wars: Race, Intelligence, and the Future of America* (New York: Basic Books, 1995) and Russell Jacoby and Naomi Glauberman, eds., *The Bell Curve Debate: History Documents Opinions* (New York: Random House, 1995).

113   The global decline of human sperm counts was reported by B. Seshadri in the London-based *Contemporary Review* (April 1995) and reprinted in *World Press Review* (June 1995), p. 47.

113–114   Dinesh D'Souza, *Illiberal Education: The Politics of Race and*

Sex on Campus (New York: Free Press, 1991); *The End of Racism: Principles for a Multiracial Society* (New York: Free Press, 1995).

115 Benjamin DeMott, *The Trouble with Friendship: Why Americans Can't Think Straight About Race* (New York: HarperCollins, 1995). DeMott's condensed the argument of this book in an essay, "Put on a Happy Face: Masking the Differences Between Blacks and Whites," *Harper's* (September 1995), pp. 31–38.

116 Charles Murray, *Losing Ground: American Social Policy 1950–1980* (New York: Basic Books, 1984).

119 For the quotations from Christopher Lasch, I have relied on his essay "The Revolt of the Elites: Have They Canceled Their Allegiance to America?" *Harper's* (November 1994), pp. 39–49; excerpted from *The Revolt of the Elites: and the Betrayal of Democracy* (New York: Norton, 1995). Used by permission.

120–121 This and following quotations by Michael Lind—as well as the statistics on campaign spending and tax cuts—are taken from his essay "To Have and Have Not: Notes on the Progress of the American Class War," *Harper's* (June 1995), pp. 35–47; excerpted from his *The Next American Nation: The New Nationalism and the Fourth American Revolution* (New York: Free Press, 1995), passim.

125 Ted C. Fishman, "The Bull Market in Fear: Stock Speculation Becomes the Rule of Prudence," *Harper's* (October 1995), pp. 55–62. Used by permission.

126 John Kenneth Galbraith, *The Culture of Contentment* (Boston: Houghton Mifflin, 1992).

127 Christopher Lasch, *The Culture of Narcissism: American Life in an Age of Diminishing Expectations* (New York: Norton, 1979).

129–30 John Rawls, *A Theory of Justice* (Cambridge, Mass.: Belknap Press, 1971). I have summarized the argument of the section entitled "The Original Position."

133 Source for statistics on voting patterns is the U.S. Census Bureau.

134 Patrick Kennon, *The Twilight of Democracy* (New York: Doubelday, 1995).

134 Michael Lewis, as quoted by Michael Lind in "To Have and Have Not."

FOUR: *The Virtual Future*

137 Sections of the Unabomber Manifesto were published in *The Globe and Mail* on August 2, 1995; I have relied on that excerpt for all subsequent quotations in this chapter. The full text of the manifesto was published a day earlier by *The Washington Post* and *The New York Times*.

138 The quotations from Kevin Kelly's book *Out of Control: The Rise of Neo-Biological Civilization* (Reading, Mass.: Addison-Wesley, 1994) that appear here and later in this chapter were drawn from an excerpt of that book, "The Electronic Hive: Embrace It," *Harper's* (May 1994), pp. 20–25. Used by permission. The quotations from John Perry Barlow, here and later in the chapter, are from a letter to the editor, *Harper's* (August 1994), p. 5.

140 The quotation from George Steiner appeared in Robert Everett-Green's essay "Resurrecting the Media Messiah," *The Globe and Mail* (July 22, 1995), pp. C1 and C8. Italo Calvino, *Six Memos for the Next Millennium* (Cambridge, Mass.: Harvard University Press, 1988), from the Preface.

141 Nicholas Negroponte, *Being Digital* (New York: Knopf, 1995). Clifford Stoll, *Silicon Snake Oil: Second Thoughts on the Information Highway* (New York: Doubleday, 1995). For some quotations I have relied on an excerpt published in *Report on Business Magazine* (June 1995), pp. 71–76. See also J.C. Herz, *Surfing on the Internet: A Nethead's Adventures On-Line* (Boston: Little Brown, 1995). Dale Sproule's interview with William Gibson, "Nostalgia for the Future," appeared in *Books in Canada* (March 1995), pp. 6–10.

143–44 James Gleick reviewed Stoll and Herz in an essay called "Net Losses," *The New Yorker* (May 22, 1995), pp. 87–89. Used by permission.

146 Julie Chao, "Net Loss: The Pioneers Move On," *The Wall Street Journal* (June 18, 1995); reprinted in *The Globe and Mail* (June 20, 1995), p. A10.

147–48 Gary Chapman's *New Republic* essay was reprinted in *The Globe and Mail* (May 13, 1995), p. D8, with the headline "Jaded Cyber Elite Disdains a Teeming Mass of Rubes."

148 Mark Dery, ed., *Flames Wars: The Discourse of Cyberculture* (Durham, N.C.: Duke University Press, 1995), from the Introduction. Quotations from Gleick are from his review, cited earlier.

154 Stoll's rosier view of computer technology, quoted by Gleick in the review cited above, is defended in an earlier book, *The Cuckoo's Egg: Tracking a Spy Through the Maze of Computer Espionage* (New York: Doubleday, 1989).

155 Arthur Kroker, *The Postmodern Scene: Excremental Culture and*

Notes

Hyper-Aesthetics (Montreal: New World Perspectives, 1980); *Spasm: Virtual Reality, Android Music, and Electric Flesh* (Montreal: New World Perspectives, 1993).

156 Arthur Kroker and Michael Weinstein, *Data Trash: The Theory of the Virtual Class* (Montreal: New World Perspectives, 1994), p. 18; all quotations here are taken from Chs. 1 and 2. Used by permission.

157 The quotations by John Oughton are taken from his review essay "Net Profits," *Books in Canada* (March 1995), pp. 23–25.

164–65 Bill Gates was identified as the Antichrist in an anonymous letter posted on the Internet in 1993. The column by Scott Adams was downloaded from the Internet and sent to me by Bruce Davie, then of Bellcore.

167 Martin Heidegger, "The Question Concerning Technology," in *The Question Concerning Technology and Other Essays* (New York: Garland, 1977).

169 Some details of the Doomsday Clock and *The Bulletin of the Atomic Scientists* have been drawn from an excellent article by Marcus Gee, "Fifty Years on the Nuclear Cliff," *The Globe and Mail* (August 5, 1995), pp. D1 and D5.

173 Kirkpatrick Sale, *Rebels Against the Future: The Luddites and their War on the Industrial Revolution* (Reading, Mass.: Addison-Wesley, 1995), as quoted in Daniel J. Kevles, "E Pluribus Unabomber," *The New Yorker* (August 14, 1995), pp. 2–3.

176–77 The interview with Arthur Kroker was published as "Wired Flesh: Arthur Kroker's Virtual Hell," in *Adbusters* (Summer 1995), pp. 35–40. The mock television ad "The Product Is You" appears in the same issue, p. 41.

177 For the basics of the meme theory, see Richard Dawkins, *The Selfish Gene* (New York: Oxford University Press, 1989 [revised edition]) and Daniel Dennett, *The Intentional Stance* (Cambridge, Mass.: MIT Press, 1987).

FIVE: *Our Bodies, Our Selves*

181–83 The quotations from David Bowie, Trent Reznor, and Nelson Thall, as well as details of the music videos in question, are taken from Peter Howell's perceptive essay "Videos Go Gruesome," *The Toronto Star* (September 17, 1995), pp. F1 and F9.

186 John Updike's "The Disposable Rocket" appeared in *Michigan*

Quarterly Review (Fall 1993) and was excerpted as "Men's Bodies, Men's Selves" in *Harper's* (November 1993), pp. 17–19.

190–91   The ground zero of Cartesian dualism is Descartes's *Meditations on First Philosophy* (1641). Gilbert Ryle's denigration appears in his discussion of dualism in *The Concept of Mind* (London: Hutchinson, 1949). The philosopher Colin McGinn described his conversion to "mysterianism" in "Out of Body, Out of Mind: Philosophy's Limit Experience," *Lingua Franca* (December 1994), pp. 66–71.

192–93   Richard Sennett, *Flesh and Stone: The Body and the City in Western Civilization* (New York: Norton, 1994). Details of Sennett's argument are taken from Robert Everett-Green's essay "Imagining the Body," *The Globe and Mail* (March 25, 1995), pp. C1 and C12.

193   Oliver Sacks's entertaining accounts of neurological disorder are found in *The Man Who Mistook His Wife for a Hat* (London: Duckworth, 1985) and *An Anthropologist on Mars: Seven Paradoxical Tales* (New York: Knopf, 1995).

196   William A. Ewing, as quoted in Robert Everett-Green, "Imagining the Body."

198   Barbara Gowdy, *We So Seldom Look on Love* (Toronto: Somerville House, 1992).

199   Elaine Scarry, *The Body in Pain: The Making and Unmaking of the World* (New York: Oxford University Press, 1985). Scarry has addressed the topic of millennial consciousness in a more recent work, *Les Fins de Siècle: English Poetry in 1590, 1690, 1790, 1890, 1990* (Baltimore: Johns Hopkins University Press, 1995). Patti Smith's defence of Mapplethorpe was detailed in "Their Friendship, Their Masterpiece," *The New Yorker* (June 19, 1995), pp. 29–30.

202   Tom Singman's account of his daughter's navel-piercing appeared in *The New York Times Magazine* in December, 1995. It was reprinted under the title "Navel Manoeuvres" in *The Globe and Mail* (January 28, 1995), p. D1.

204   Details of piercing techniques and quotations have been taken from *Re/Search: Modern Primitives* (San Francisco: Re/Search Publications, 1989). Quotations later in this chapter by Chris Schilling and Dick Hebdige are from the source material included at the end of *Re/Search*.

218   Eurydice's article appeared as part of a series on the shape of the future in *Spin* (November 1995). Used by permission.

219 Marjorie Garber, *Vice Versa: Bisexuality and the Eroticism of Everyday Life* (New York: Simon and Schuster, 1995).

219–20 Martine Rothblatt, *The Apartheid of Sex: A Manifesto on the Freedom of Gender* (New York: Crown, 1995). Used by permission. Newt Gingrich, *To Renew America* (New York: HarperCollins, 1995).

223 Kate Bornstein, *Gender Outlaw: On Men, Women, and the Rest of Us* (New York: Routledge, 1994).

Six: *The Truth Is Out There*

233–34 *The Guardian*'s report on the alien autopsy video was reprinted in *World Press Review* (October 1995), from which these quotations are taken.

241 C.D.B. Bryan, *Close Encounters of the Fourth Kind: Alien Abductions, UFOs, and the Conference at M.I.T.* (New York: Knopf, 1995). James Wolcott's quotations, see also p. 251, are taken from his review of Bryan, which appeared in *The New Yorker* (July 31, 1995), pp. 75–77.

241–42 John E. Mack, *Abduction: Human Encounters With Aliens* (New York: Scribner's, 1994). The "invisible college" of UFO researchers was described in Yvonne Abraham, "The Alienation Effect," *Lingua Franca* (December 1994), pp. 9–11.

260–61 Details of the life of Lord Clancarty are from "Lord of the UFOs and Alien Landings Dies at 83," *The Guardian* (May 23, 1995), p. 3.

261–63 Scott Van Wynsberghe's witty articles on the attractions of conspiracy theory are "True Believers: Memoirs of a Former Conspiracy Theorist," *The Globe and Mail* (January 21, 1995), p. D2; and "Whodunit? The Jews, the UN, the Japanese or the evil Clinton?" *The Globe and Mail* (July 8, 1995), p. D2.

264 Michael Kelly, "The Road to Paranoia," *The New Yorker* (June 19, 1995), pp. 60–70. I have also relied on two articles by Garry Wills, "The New Revolutionaries," *The New York Review of Books* (August 10, 1995), pp. 50–55; and "To Keep and Bear Arms," *The New York Review of Books* (September 21, 1995), pp. 62–73.

268 Foucault's *Surveiller et Punir* was published in English as *Discipline and Punish: The Birth of the Prison*, Alan Sheridan, trans. (New York: Vintage, 1979). "Discipline" doesn't really capture the sense of carceral observation conveyed in Foucault's original title.

268–69 The discussion of Xerox's "relational processing" is pp. 52–54

of Arthur Kroker and Michael Weinstein, *Data Trash*; quotation
is from p. 58.

270 Timothy Appleby, "Frontier Justice," *The Globe and Mail* (August
3, 1995), p. A1.

SEVEN: *The Best Lack All Conviction*

275–76 Details of the life of Peter the Hermit are from Norman
Cohn, *The Pursuit of the Millennium*, pp. 62, 67, 94, 129.

278–82 The details of Jerusalem Syndrome were reported by Rebecca
Lee in *The Atlantic Monthly* (May 1995), pp. 24–38. Used by
permission.

282 Cinematic neurosis came to my attention by way of a research
memo distributed throughout the University of Toronto in
September 1995.

286–89 Ted Harrison, *Stigmata: A Medieval Phenomenon in a Modern
Age* (New York: St. Martin's Press, 1994), Conclusion. Opinion is
divided on the blame the FBI bears for the Waco disaster. But see,
for an analysis of the agency's "action-imperative" tactics and
their role in precipitating the disaster, Alan A. Stone, "How the
FBI Helped Fuel the Waco Fire," *Harper's* (February 1994), pp.
15–18. (The article is adapted from Stone's report to the U.S.
Department of Justice.) James Tabor and Eugene Gallagher's book
Why Waco? Cults and the Battle for Religious Freedom in America
(Berkeley: University of California Press, 1995) places the
incident in a larger context of state hostility to religion.

290 Albert Schweitzer, *The Psychiatric Study of Jesus Christ: Exposition
and Criticism* (Boston: Beacon Press, 1958).

291–95 Details of the new prominence of miracles—and the
quotations in this section—are drawn from a cover story by
Nancy Gibbs, "The Message of Miracles," *Time* (April 10, 1995),
pp. 38–45.

295 Northrop Frye's works on the Bible and literature include *The
Great Code* (Toronto: Academic Press, 1982) and *Words With
Power* (Toronto: Viking, 1990). The predations of the Jesus
Seminar, which assesses scripture for its literal truth, were
discussed in a fine article by Charlotte Allen, "Away With The
Manger: Tampering with the Gospel Truth," *Lingua Franca*
(February 1995), pp. 22–30.

303 ff. All quotations from Norman Cohn in this section are from
The Pursuit of the Millennium, Ch. 5. For the details of Pseudo-

Baldwin, see pp. 90-93; the legacy of Frederick II is discussed in Ch. 6, especially pp. 112-14 and 116–18.

309–10 Benjamin DeMott's brush with the leadership gurus was reported in "Choice Academic Pork: Inside the Leadership Studies Racket," *Harper's* (December 1993), pp. 61–77. DeMott's quotations in this section are taken from the article.

318 Garry Wills, *Certain Trumpets: The Call of Leaders* (New York: Simon and Schuster, 1994); an essay drawn from this book, "What Makes a Good Leader?" appeared in *The Atlantic Monthly* (April 1994), pp. 63–80.

319 Serial killer chic is effectively analyzed by poet Lynn Crosbie in "Loving the Killer: Where Art and Life Don't Meet," *This Magazine* (March/April 1995), pp. 12–15.

321–23 Most of the information on the Church of the SubGenius, including the quotations in this section, has been drawn from the Church's freely distributed "Online Pamphlet," available through their main Web homepage, http://sunsite.unc.edu/subgenius. Some additional detail has been drawn from the following articles: Tom Hawthorn, "The Mysterious Bob Cult Hones Its Devilish Wit on Society's Sacred Cows," *The Globe and Mail* (January 31, 1987), p. E5; Robert Everett-Green, "A Cyber-punk's Guide to the New Eden," *The Globe and Mail* (February 7, 1991), p. C1, and "Things Get Ugly in the World of Underground Art," *The Globe and Mail* (March 30, 1990), p. C3.

Eight: *Faith No More*

327 Recent articles on global warming have, even while arguing about the evidence, made it clear that overall upward changes in temperature may create localized drops, resulting in Arctic conditions in hitherto temperate regions. See, for example, Ross Gelbspan, "The Heat Is On: The Warming of the World's Climate Sparks a Blaze of Denial," *Harper's* (December 1995), pp. 31–39; and a series of newspaper articles collected under the title "As the World Burns," *World Press Review* (July 1995), pp. 6–11.

328 The recent cult of St. Hildegard—and the New Age appropriation of her music—was discussed in Tamara Bernstein, "Holy Hildegard: A Medieval Nun with '90s Sex Appeal," *The Globe and Mail* (May 6, 1995), p. C13.

329 All quotations are from Ken Carey, *Starseed: The Third*

Millennium (New York: HarperCollins, 1991); this book has
recently been reissued under its subtitle only.

343 All quotations are from Roy Blount, Jr., "Q: Looking Forward to
the Year 2000? A: Yeah. Right. My Young Grandson Will Have
More Teeth Than I Do," *New Choices* (June 1995), pp. 64–65.
Details of the computer programming glitch were reported by
James Gleick in "Oh-Oh," a Fast Forward column that appeared
in *The New York Times Magazine* on June 2, 1996, p. 19.

346 Richard Rorty's analysis of *Nineteen Eighty-Four* is found in his
essay "The Last Intellectual in Europe: Orwell on Cruelty," in
Contingency, Irony, and Solidarity (Cambridge: Cambridge
University Press, 1989), pp. 169–88.

347 An effective discussion of the challenge Hitler poses to faith, the
problem of evil in human form, is Ron Rosenbaum, "Explaining
Hitler," *The New Yorker* (May 1, 1995), pp. 50–69. The quotation
from Yehuda Bauer is taken from this article.

348 Ernst Bloch, *Das Prinzip Hoffnung* (Frankfurt: Suhrkamp, 1959);
in English, *The Principle of Hope*, translated by Melville Plaice,
Stephen Plaice, and Paul Knight (Oxford: Basil Blackwell, 1986).
Judith Martin, *Miss Manners' Guide for the Turn-of-the-Millennium*
(New York: Simon and Schuster, 1990); audio version by Audio
Renaissance Tapes (1990), distributed by St. Martin's Press.

350 Martin H. Krieger, "Can the Probability of Doom Be Zero or
One?" *Journal of Philosophy* (July 1995), pp. 382–87.

Index

Adams, Scott, 164-65
AIDS, 18, 19, 64, 92, 200, 225-26, 272
aliens, 13-14, 22-23, 56, 147, 227, 230-61, 264, 266, 267, 268, 271, 273, 284-85, 287, 288, 292, 329-30
Amis, Martin, 17, 134-135
Anderson, Laurie, 156
angels, 67, 296-302
Anselm, St., 341-42
anti-Semitism, 22, 35, 37, 73, 147, 262, 270, 271-72, 347, 348
Appleby, Timothy, 270
Arendt, Hannah, 11, 97
Aristotle, 3, 309
Asimov, Isaac, 3, 157
Atlantis, 6-7
Atwood, Margaret, 113
Augustine, St., 194

Baldwin IX, 302, 318
Ballon, Bruce, 283
Bar El, Yair, 279-82
Barlow, John Perry, 138, 153
Bataille, Georges, 181
Battelle, John, 157
Baudrillard, Jean, 161
Bauer, Yehuda, 347
Bell, Daniel, 11

Bennis, Warren, 315-16
Bentham, Jeremy, 268
Bertrand of Ray (Pseudo-Baldwin), 302-4
Black Death. See plagues
Blavatsky, Helena, 50
Bloch, Ernst, 348
Bloom, Harold, 67, 68
Blount, Roy, Jr., 343-44
Blumberg, Paul, 122
Bockelson, Jan, 39-40, 72, 73,
body-building, 186-89
body decoration, extreme, 182-85, 201, 204-6, 214
body piercing, 183, 200-206, 214, 259
Boesky, Ivan, 44, 45
Boniface VIII, Pope, 34
Bornstein, Kate, 223
Botticelli, Sandro, 41
Bowie, David, 181, 183
"brink culture," 12, 274
Branch Davidians. See cults
Bruse, Jim, 286
Bryan, C.D.B., 241, 242-43, 251, 253-54
Buckley, Christopher, 264
Burke, Edmund, 118
Burnet, Thomas, 27

Calvino, Italo, 140
Carey, Ken, 329-30
Carroll, Lewis, 251
Chapman, Ethel, 286, 288
Chapman, Gary, 147, 150
Chase, Neal, 70-71
Chateaubriand, Vicomte François René de, 50
Chomsky, Noam, 264-65, 266, 314
Church of the SubGenius, 321-23
cinematic neurosis, 282-83
Clinton, Bill, 73, 109, 270, 308
Club of Rome, 87-88
Cohn, Norman, 9, 32, 36, 38, 183, 231, 271, 281, 303, 306, 320
Colombo, John Robert, 229, 243, 252
Columbus, Christopher, 40, 41
conspiracy theories, 231, 234-40, 242-74, 293, 307-8
Coupland, Douglas, 258
Covey, Stephen R., 310
Cronenberg, David, 179, 196
Crusades, 22, 33, 35-36, 41, 224, 239, 275-78, 302, 304-5, 336
cults: Aum Shinri Kyo, 7, 78-79; Baha'is Under the Provisions of the Covenant, 70-71; Branch Davidians, 72, 277-78, 289, 308; Raelians, 226-28, 232, 329; Taisokyo, 7

Daniels, Ted, 8
Davidson, James Dale, 101
Davis, Mike, 135
Dawkins, Richard, 177
de Bono, Edward, 314
de Chardin, Pierre Teilhard, 138
de l'Etoile, Eudes, 35
DeMott, Benjamin, 115, 310, 313, 314, 317
DeMotto, Richard, 234
Dennett, Daniel, 177, 178
DePree, Max, 310
Dery, Mark, 148
Descartes, René, 190, 192, 199, 345

de Tocqueville, Alexis, 67, 291
Disraeli, Benjamin, 129, 133
di Tura, Agnolo, 37
Dixon, Jeanne, 6
Dr. Strangelove, 17-71
D'Souza, Dinesh, 113-14, 116
Dürer, Albrecht, 41

Eadmer, 341
Ebola, 17-19, 22, 92, 272. *See also* killer viruses
Eco, Umberto, 262-63
Ehrlich, Paul, 87
environmental collapse, 9, 10, 22, 27-28, 52, 56, 70, 80, 81-93, 97, 99-101
"Eurydice," 218, 224
Everett-Green, Robert, 193
Ewing, William A., 196
extra-terrestrials. *See* aliens

Fackenheim, Emil, 345, 348
Fail-Safe, 170-71
Faniel, Georgette, 285, 288
Farine, Dr. Mark, 8
Fishman, Ted C., 125
Flem-Ath, Rand and Rose, 7
Forrest Gump, 44, 160, 325
Fort, Charles, 241
Foucault, Michel, 268-69
Fox, George, 27
Francis of Assisi, 44, 286, 302
freak shows, 198
Frederick I (Frederick Barbarossa), 42, 305, 307, 318
Freud, Sigmund, 14, 15, 51, 52, 60, 258
Frye, Northrop, 295
Fussell, Paul, 107, 110, 122,

Galbraith, John Kenneth, 126, 127
Gallagher, Christina, 289
Garber, Marjorie, 219
Gardner, James Finn, 110

Garrett, Laurie, 17-18
Gates, Bill, 164
Gates, Henry Louis, Jr., 111
Gee, Marcus, 87, 88
gender confusion, 215-24
Gibbs, Nancy, 295
Gibson, William, 141, 144
Gingrich, Newt, 86-87, 115, 132, 220, 224
Gleick, James, 143, 148, 243
Gore, Al, 85, 315, 317
Gould, Stephen Jay, 111
Gowdy, Barbara, 198
Gumpism, 44, 55, 110, 122, 293

Hacker, Andrew, 115
Hancock, Graham, 6
Hardy, Rev. Clarence, 294, 296
Harrison, Ted, 286, 288-89
Harvey, William, 192
Hebdige, Dick, 212
Heidegger, Martin, 167
Helmsley, Leona, 45
Henry, William III, 108-11, 119, 122
Herbert, Bob, 98
Herrnstein, Richard J., 111-12, 116, 119, 127
Herz, J. C., 141
Hitler, Adolf, 22, 48, 347
Hoban, Russell, 55
Holocaust, 10, 11, 22, 345, 347-48
Homer-Dixon, Thomas, 80-93, 120, 129, 315
Huxley, Aldous, 88, 121, 126
Hynek, J. Allen, 242

Imbert-Gourbeyre, Dr., 286
imitatio Christi, 35-37, 183
Inner Peace Movement (IPM), 296-301
Innocent IV, Pope, 305
Invasion of the Body Snatchers, 236, 273, 282

James, P. D., 113
Jefferson, Thomas, 106
Jerusalem Syndrome, 278-83, 285, 289, 290
John Paul II, Pope, 291
Jones, Jim, 67, 68

Kafka, Franz, 267
Kaminer, Wendy, 55
Kaplan, Robert, 85-87, 92, 93, 99-101, 135
Keillor, Garrison, 110
Kelly, Kevin, 138, 140, 146, 151
Kelly, Michael, 264, 267
Kennedy, John F., 10, 48, 261, 263-64, 267, 308
Kennon, Patrick, 134
Kevles, Daniel J., 173, 176
Kieninger, Richard, 8
killer viruses, 17-20, 255, 289-90
King, Rodney, 98
Koestenbaum, Wayne, 92
Koresh, David, 67, 68, 72-73, 240, 256, 277, 278
Krafft-Ebing, Richard von, 217
Krieger, Martin H., 350-51
Kristol, Irving, 11
Kroker, Arthur, 155-66, 177, 178, 196, 212, 268, 285, 316, 321, 326
Kubrick, Stanley. *See 2001: A Space Odyssey* and *Dr. Strangelove*

Labrousse, Suzette, 48
Laing, R. D., 242
Lapham, Lewis, 119
Lasch, Christopher, 119-21, 123, 124, 127, 129, 132, 134, 135
leadership studies, 309-18
Lee, Rebecca, 279, 290
Lewis, C. S., 227
Lewis, Michael, 134
Limbaugh, Rush, 307
Lind (cartoonist), 108

Lind, Michael, 120, 123, 126, 128, 132, 134, 135
Locke, John, 25, 118
Lockyer, Rev. David, 288-89
Lorenzo de Medici, 41, 56
Lovelock, James, 83
Ludd, Ned. See Luddites
Luddites, 137, 160, 166, 172-73, 175-76
Luther, Martin, 38, 272, 280-81

Macdonald, Marianne, 24
Machiavelli, Niccolò, 41, 309
Mack, John E., 241-42
Mackay, Charles, 33
Macpherson, C.B., 104
Maimonides, 47
Malthus, Thomas Robert, 87-90, 113
Mamet, David, 106
Manson, Charles, 319, 320
Mapplethorpe, Robert, 199-200
Marks, David, 24
Marlowe, Christopher, 283
Martians, 22-23. See also aliens
Martin, Judith, 349
McLean, Martin, 256
McLuhan, Marshall, 11, 140, 155, 182, 190, 214
McVeigh, Timothy, 73-74, 227, 270, 319
Meier, Eduard "Billy," 235
Melanchthon, Phillip, 39
MICA Management Resources Inc., 311-16
Michelet, Jules, 33
Mill, John Stuart, 128, 151
Millar, Robert G., 227
Millennium Commission, The, 23-24
Millennium Planner, The, 6
Millennium Society, The, 8
Miller, Walter, 55
Miller, William, 49
Millken, Michael, 44
miracles, 292-96

Montanus of Phrygia, 31
More, Thomas, 348
Morrisroe, Patricia, 199
Munch, Edvard, 161, 165
Munchausen's Syndrome, 287-88
Munda, Birsa, 50
Müntzer, Thomas, 38
Murdoch, Iris, 20
Murray, Charles, 111-12, 114, 116, 127
Mutual UFO Network (MUFON), 244, 247

Nazis, 11, 48, 166, 167-68, 257, 262, 345, 346-48
Negroponte, Nicholas, 141
Netheads, 138-41, 144
New Corporeality, 187, 196-97, 204
Nietzsche, Friedrich, 2, 160, 166, 321, 330
Nineteen Eighty-Four, 268-69, 345-47
Nostradamus (Michel de Nostredame), 6, 47, 250
nuclear war, 12, 13, 19, 22, 55, 68, 69, 70, 71, 145, 168-71, 174

O'Brien, Conor Cruise, 24, 291
Oklahoma City bombing, 72, 73-75, 173-74, 227, 248, 264, 269-70, 271
Ortega y Gassett, José, 122
O'Rourke, P.J., 89
Orwell, George, 126, 151, 267, 269, 345-46
Oughton, John, 157-58
Outbreak, 19, 149

Parker, Wanda, 313-16
Pascal, Blaise, 295, 296
Pericles, 148, 307
Peter the Hermit, 35, 275-77, 302
Phillips, Adam, 14
Pilon, Roger, 294
plagues, 9, 17-20, 22, 24, 30, 37, 38, 216, 272

Plato, 109, 118, 135, 193, 196, 199
Plimpton, George, 110
Preston, Richard, 17, 18
Price, Roger, 107
Project Bluebook, 261
Prophet, Elizabeth Clare, 68-70
Purdie, John, 234
Pynchon, Thomas, 262-63

racism, 98-99, 102, 111-18, 122
Rafferty, Terrence, 19
Rand, Ayn, 309
Ranters, 26-27, 49, 138, 300
Rasky, Harry, 65-67, 126
Rawls, John, 129-30
Rees-Mogg, William, 101
Regarding Henry, 44
Reich, Robert, 120
Rice, Anne, 283
Robertson, William, 32
Robinson, Cloretta, 285
Rorty, Richard, 346
Roswell incident, 233-35, 261, 273, 274
Rothblatt, Martine, 219-20, 222-24
Russell, Bertrand, 229
Russell, Charles, 49
Ryle, Gilbert, 190

Sacks, Oliver, 193
Sale, Kirkpatrick, 173
Savonarola, Girolamo, 40, 41, 42, 43, 45, 46, 49, 93, 184, 330
Scarry, Elaine, 199
Schiaparelli, Giovanni, 22
Schilling, Chris, 212
Schnabel, Jim, 287-88
Schwartz, Hillel, 34, 254
Schweitzer, Albert, 290
Second Coming, 29, 30, 35, 72, 139, 184, 289, 290, 304, 344
self-flagellation, 37, 38, 40, 42, 46, 184

Sennett, Richard, 192
Serageldin, Ismail, 90
"serial killer chic," 319-21, 325-26
Shakespeare, William, 14, 216
Simpson, O.J., 98, 159
Singman, Tom, 202
Slater, Michael, 149
Smith, Adam, 100
Smith, Patti, 199
Smyth-Pigot, John Hugh, 50
Socrates, 193, 194, 196
Sontag, Susan, 9
Sophocles, 217
Spinoza, Benedict de, 293
"Star Trek: The Next Generation," 179-80, 181, 194-96, 237, 255, 258, 269, 316
Steiner, George, 140
Stevenson, Robert Louis, 283
stigmata, 206, 285-89
Stoker, Bram, 283
Stoll, Clifford, 141-44, 154
Stone, Oliver, *Wall Street*, 45; *JFK*, 263; *Natural Born Killers*, 325
Strauss, Richard, *Also sprach Zarathustra*, 2, 4
Stringer, Dr. Chris, 234
Strong, Hanne, 66
Swedenborg, Emanuel, 50
Sylvester II, Pope, 32, 34

Tanchelm, 35
Tarantino, Quentin, 318-21, 325
tattooing, 202-4, 205-15, 259
Tench, Brinsley LePoer (Lord Clancarty), 260, 261
Tertullian, 31
Thales, 196
The Day the Earth Stood Still, 23, 251
The Net, 172, 265
"The Simpsons," 160, 323-24, 326
"The X-Files," 236-41, 247, 254, 255-62, 274
Thomas à Kempis, 37

Thrall, Nelson, 182
Thucydides, 307
2001: A Space Odyssey, 2-4, 167, 170
UFOs, 9, 23, 230-62, 271, 273, 287,
  288, 292
Unabomber, 137, 163, 173-76
Updike, John, 186
Urban II, Pope, 35, 276

vampires, 252, 283-85
Van Wynsberghe, Scott, 261-64, 269
Vlahos, Michael, 100
Vonnegut, Kurt, 107

Wagner, Peter, 294-95
Wakefield, Dan, 292
Washington, George, 48-49, 56, 262
Watson, James, 67
Weepers, 42, 46, 184
Weinstein, Michael, 155-59, 164, 268
Wells, H. G., 22, 240
Wilcox, Fred McLeod, *Forbidden
  Planet*, 13-14
Wilde, Oscar, 217
Wills, Garry, 318
Winstanley, Gerrard, 26
Witztum, Eliezer, 282
Wolcott, James, 240, 242, 251, 252,
  254
Wolfe, Tom, 43
Woods, Heather, 286

Yeats, W. B., 30

Zamenhof, Ludwig Lazarus, 50
Zev, Shabbetai, 47